T0145745

Pastorius.

READING AT WILLIA[MSPORT]

ly batting gave Williams[port] victory, Reading being def[eated]

William't.	AB.	R.	B.	P.	A.	E.
O'Hara, lf.	4	1	2	1	1	1
Marhe'a, ss	3	0	1	4	5	1
Cannell, cf	4	0	1	2	0	0
Conn, 2b..	4	1	1	5	2	1
Cough'n, 3b	4	0	1	1	0	0
Lister, 1b.	3	0	1	6	0	0
White, rf..	4	0	0	2	0	0
Therre, c.	3	0	0	6	4	0
Stroud, p.	2	2	1	0	0	0
Totals..	31	4	8	27	12	3

Reading 0

Williamsport 0

Two-base hit—Coughlin Conn. Left on bases—W[illiamsport] Struck out—By Stroud 5, Off Stroud 4, Odell 2. H[its] Umpire—Gochnauer. Time

YORK AT JOHNSTOW[N]

loose game Johnstown d[efeated]

MSPORT JUNE 7.—Time-
port its sixth consecutive
eated. Score:

Reading.	AB.	R.	B.	P.	A.	E
Rath, 3b..	3	0	1	1	2	0
Lynch, ss.	4	0	0	3	0	0
Lelivelt, cf.	4	0	1	2	0	0
Foster, lf..	3	0	0	0	0	0
Clay, rf...	2	2	1	5	0	0
Crooks, 1b	4	0	3	7	0	0
Barton, 2b.	4	0	1	1	1	1
Millman, c	4	0	0	5	2	0
Odell, p..	3	0	0	0	3	0
Totals..	31	2	7	24	8	1

1 0 1 0 0 0 0 0 0—2
0 0 1 2 0 1 0 x—4

Stolen bases—O'Hara,
lliamsport 6, Reading 6.
Odell 4. First on balls—
t by pitcher—By Odell 1.
—2.05.

N JUNE 7.—In a rather
d York. The game

Sac
ter, (
plays—
on b
pitche
son 2.
pitch-
Time—

JOH
pitche
and T
a run
winnir
Johnst
Domo'
Himes
John'n
Weiga
Irvine,
Follan
Thoma
Koepm
Feeney
O'Com
Scott,

TURNER PUBLISHING COMPANY
Paducah, Kentucky

TURNER PUBLISHING COMPANY
412 Broadway, P. O. Box 3101
Paducah, KY 42002-3101
270-443-0121

SABR Pictorial History Committee:
Chair: Tom Shieber

Turner Publishing Company Staff:
Publishing Consultant: Douglas W. Sikes
Project Coordinator: John Mark Jackson

Library of Congress Catalog
Card Number: 00-102471
ISBN: 978-1-63026-971-5

Additional copies may be purchased
directly from Turner Publishing Company.
Limited Edition.

TABLE OF CONTENTS

Preface 4

Publisher's Message 5

History of SABR 9

Special Stories 30

SABR Roster 48

SABR Biographies 66

Index 111

PREFACE

SABR is much like a big family, but connected by a special affection for the game of baseball rather than by bloodlines. Perusing this tome will be comparable to reading a family history and looking at the family photograph album. For members of SABR, it will recall friendships and revive pleasant memories associated with our society. Others will gain a better understanding of our organization, as the reader discovers more about who we are, what we have done in the past, and our plans for the future.

This book traces SABR's history from its inception to the present, and chronicles the progress and growth of our society from the original 16 members who met at Cooperstown, New York, in 1971 to the current membership, which is approaching 7,000 as we prepare to move into the 21st century.

The SABR history project began under the leadership of the immediate past president, Larry Gerlach, and has been three years coming to fruition. We trust that the final fruit will leave a pleasing taste with you each time you partake, and that it will continue to kindle fond memories for many years to come. This is not only SABR's story but also your story and deserves to be a valued part of your personal library.

James A. Riley, President
Society for American Baseball Research (SABR)

PUBLISHER'S MESSAGE

Dave Turner, President, Turner Publishing Company

No group in America better represents our never-ending fascination with the "National Pastime" than the Society for American Baseball Research also known as SABR. Why baseball, at all levels, has so captured the interest and passion of so many of our citizens is ample subject matter for philosophers, poets, and sports commentators alike. But it was our fascination for those most fascinated with the game that lead to the creation of this book.

The story of this book began in August 1995 when Turner Publishing Consultant Doug Sikes read an article about SABR in one of those airline magazines that one reads while taxiing to the runway. He clipped and stored it until later, while working on our first baseball book, Louisville Diamonds. Its author, Mr. Philip Von Borries, himself a devout SABR member, encouraged him to consider publishing a book about them. After a few calls, meetings, negotiations and terms, they were underway.

We are pleased to acknowledge a few of the many who labored on this project; Philip Von Borries for lighting the flame, Richard Thompson for his thorough research and writing, Tom Shieber for some hard-to-get photos, John Zajc for help all along the way, the SABR Executive Board for their proven support, and most of all former Executive Director Morris Eckhouse for his vision, diligence, and insight that helped produce a fitting legacy of this dedicated organization.

Dave Turner, President
Turner Publishing Company

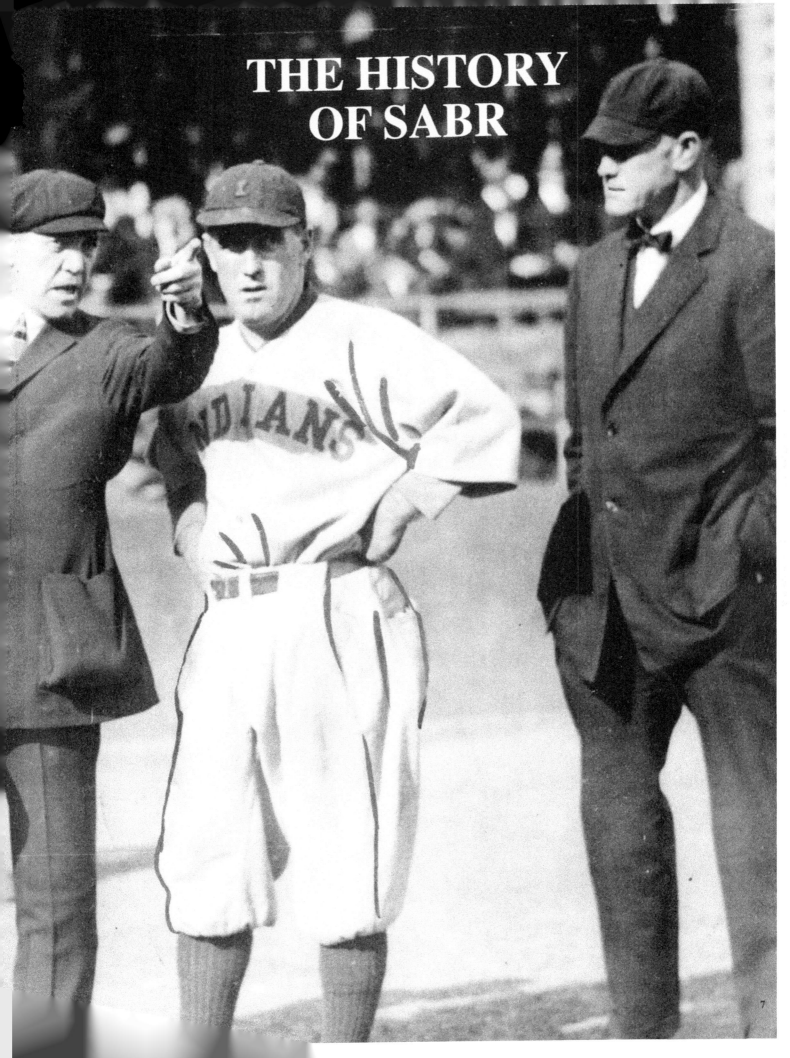

Bob Davids (left) at SABR's 20th anniversary celebration, hosted by the National Baseball Library and librarian Tom Heitz (right) in August 1991, at the National Baseball Hall of Fame and Museum in Cooperstown, NY.

A HISTORY OF SABR

by Dick Thompson

Baseball is in the fiber of America. As long as there have been baseball fans there have been baseball fanatics, those of us who search for a deeper understanding of the game. On August 10, 1971, sixteen such individuals met at the National Baseball Hall of Fame Library in Cooperstown, New York, to form the Society for American Baseball Research.

The baseball establishment ignored the Society when it was formed twenty-eight years ago. Today, as membership closes in on 7,000, the profession of baseball and the various media that report the game are well aware of the collective knowledge and expertise of our group.

The logical place to begin a history of the organization is with its founder, L. Robert "Bob" Davids. Bob's dedication and contributions to both the Society and baseball have been evident for all to see. In 1985 Bill James wrote in *The Bill James Historical Baseball Abstract*, "This book is dedicated to the man who has done more for baseball research than anyone else living—L. Robert Davids." In 1994 the National Baseball Library and Archive at the National Baseball Hall of Fame in Cooperstown named a study room in his honor.

Bob was born in Iowa in 1926. Following military service in World War II, Bob enrolled at the University of Missouri where he received a degree in journalism in 1949 and a master's degree in history in 1951. After moving to Washington, D. C., he began a thirty-year career with the United States Government, working at the Pentagon and the Atomic Energy Commission. He received a Ph.D. in international relations from Georgetown in 1961.

Bob was a freelance contributor to *The Sporting News* from 1951. His first article, on Ralph Kiner, earned him $7.50.

At the ceremony to honor the twentieth anniversary of the Society on August 10, 1991, Davids outlined the factors and steps that led to the organization of SABR:

1. The death of J.G. Taylor Spink in 1962 and the subsequent transition of *The Sporting News* to an all-sports publication which sharply reduced the baseball publishing efforts of several future SABR members.

2. My January 8, 1966 letter to Barnes Publishing Company proposing a baseball book with chapters to be written by Lee Allen, John Tattersall, Keith Sutton, Ray Nemec, Leonard Gettleson and myself—which Barnes quickly declined.

3. My parallel decisions in January 1971 to publish the *Baseball Briefs* newsletter and to send letters to Bob McConnell, Ray Nemec, Cliff Kachline, and others proposing the formation of a "Statistorian" type group and asking names and addresses of other interested researchers. Almost all responded favorably and provided other names.

4. Cliff Kachline's agreement to provide a meeting site at Cooperstown the day after Hall of Fame inductions on August 10, 1971.

5. Multiple responses from *Baseball Briefs* subscribers and new contacts providing a growing mailing list of some 40 persons who were sent invitational/instructional letters on March 19, April 16, and June 28, the final letter containing the meeting agenda. The rest is history.

The organization became an entity with Davids' March 19, 1971, letter:

This letter is being addressed to about 25-30 persons interested in baseball history and statistical research (I use the term "statistorians"). You are an addressee because I have seen your name in *The Sporting News* in past years, appended to an interesting historical or statistical article, or your name has been passed on to me by Ray Nemec, Bob McConnell, Leonard Gettleson, or Cliff Kachline.

There may be many more than 25 or 30 baseball statistorians around the country. We don't really know, but I thought some effort should be made to organize this "motley crew" into a more formal group. For that reason we plan to hold an organizational meeting at Cooperstown, New York on August 10-11, 1971. Cliff Kachline, Hall of Fame Historian, has kindly invited us to meet in the museum library. The Hall of Fame baseball game and induction ceremonies will be held on Monday, August 9. Why don't we meet then on August 7-8? Impossible, says Cliff. The place is busier than Washington on Inauguration Day. You could come on August 9, take in the induction festivities and get a motel room for the night, but not before, and then be available for meetings the next day.

What would be accomplished at the Cooperstown meeting? From general to specific, your attendance would provide an opportunity (1) to see Cooperstown and the always changing Hall of Fame Museum; (2) to meet and exchange first hand views with other statistorians; (3) to review specific areas of baseball interest to avoid duplication of effort; (4) to establish an informal group primarily for exchange of information; or (5) to establish a formal organization with officers, dues, a charter, annual meetings, etc.; (6) to consider the establishment of a publication in which our research efforts could be presented; and (7) to take up additional matters which you may suggest in response to this letter.

What do you do now? You should send me a note saying something along the lines of (1) Your idea of a get-together of the baseball statistorians sounds great, I would like to attend; (2) I am interested in your efforts to organize this group, I would like to be included but cannot get away for a meeting at Cooperstown this summer; or (3) your plans for an organization are completely impossible; take me off your mailing list, quick. I would also hope that you would include in your response the name of additional baseball "nuts" who might qualify or be interested.

The next step would then be for me to send to those of you who could make this meeting this summer the information of hotels and motels which you would need for the night(s) of August 9 and 10; August 10 only; or August 10 and 11, depending on your travel plans.

Bob mailed a second letter on April 16. The important excerpts are as follows:

Although I still haven't heard from several addressees, I thought I should not wait any longer to get out report No. 2 to those who did respond. Let me say first that my initial mailing of 32 letters brought back 20 replies and three envelopes with "ad-dress unknown" stamped on them. Of those 20, there were 17 who expressed interest in the idea of an organization and a desire to be part of it; three expressed mild indifference. Eleven said they plan to go to Cooperstown. Several of you suggested additional researchers and I sent off 10 more letters.

Most of you responding stated your interest in an organization publication wherein you could present some of your research results. This sounds feasible.

Several mentioned interest in first hand exchange to find out what others are doing. I was surprised at the range of specific interests—baseball photos, baseball parks, birthplaces, home runs, etc. Some of you said you had specific ideas of what should be taken up at the proposed meeting. Now is the time to come forward with these ideas so I can prepare a draft agenda. Be completely candid in your suggestions, for nothing is frozen in place at this point except the date—August 10.

The sixteen founding members who met in the Baseball Hall of Fame library on August 10 were Bob Davids, Dan Dischley, Paul Frisz, Dan Ginsburg, Ray Gonzalez, William Gustafson, Bill Haber, Tom Hufford, Cliff Kachline, Bob

Participants at SABR's organizational meeting on August 10, 1971 at the National Baseball Library in Cooperstown, New York. Back row (left to right): Neil Campbell, Bill Haber, Keith Sutton, Dan Dischley, Dan Ginsburg, Tom Hufford, Ray Nemec. Front row (left to right): Cliff Kachline, Ray Gonzalez, Bill Gustafson, Joe Simenic, Paul Frisz, Tom Shea, Bob McConnell, John Pardon, Bob Davids. Campbell, almost hidden behind Kachline, was a visitor at the meeting. Pat McDonough is the only founding SABR member not pictured.

McConnell, Patrick McDonough, Ray Nemec, John Pardon, Tom Shea, Joe Simenic, and Keith Sutton.

They defined the following five objectives:

1. To foster the study of baseball as a significant American social and athletic institution.

2. To establish an accurate account of baseball through the years.

3. To facilitate the dissemination of baseball research information.

4. To stimulate the best interests of baseball as our national pastime.

5. To cooperate in safeguarding the proprietary interests of individual research efforts of members of the Society.

At the organizational meeting Davids was elected President, Pardon Vice-President, and McConnell Secretary-Treasurer (Stan Grosshandler also held this dual office in 1972 and 1973 before it was split into two separate roles). Several proposals were discussed regarding a name designation with a baseball acronym before Bill Gustafson's suggestion of Society for American Baseball Research and SABR were decided on. (A draft masthead, appearing very similar to the current masthead, was presented in the October, 1977 *SABR Bulletin*. The logo, a continuing concern since 1971, was put to a vote and agreed upon at the 1978 National Convention.). Also agreed upon were annual dues of $10, plans to establish a constitution, an annual meeting, and the publication of a newsletter.

The purpose of the newsletter, known to all as the *SABR Bulletin*, was to carry pertinent information and facilitate exchange of information. Bob Davids edited the *SABR Bulletin* for the first 12 years, a total of 67 issues, and since August 1983 it has been the responsibility of the Society's Executive Director. The *SABR Bulletin* was published quarterly from 1971 through 1973, bi-monthly from 1974 through 1986, eight times a year in 1987 and 1988, and four times in 1989. In 1990 plans were made for monthly publication although several editions each year have usually been combined. Regular features of the *SABR Bulletin* have included information on recently held and upcoming regional meetings, committee reports, a bookshelf section advertising current baseball publications, a research exchange for members' research needs, "The Pres Box"—a column written by the Society's current president or his designate, and "Names in the News," which publicizes current and public relations events pertaining to Society members.

THE ELECTED OFFICIALS

Bob Davids served three terms (1971-72, 75-76, 82-84) as president of the Society. Others have been Ron Menchine, who had a speaking role in the Dustin Hoffman-Robert Redford film, *All the President's Men*, which consisted of saying "Yes" three times (1972-73), Robert Allen (1973-74), David Voigt (1974-75), Gene Murdock (1976-78), Cliff Kachline (1978-80), Kit Crissey (1980-82), Cappy Gagnon (1984-86), Gene Sunnen (1986-89), Rich Topp (1989-91), Jack Kavanagh (acting, July-December,

This table, pictured in a 1990 photo, was one of two at which 16 individuals gathered on August 10, 1971 to form the Society for American Baseball Research (SABR).

SABR Bulletin No. 1

Newsletter of the Society for American Baseball Research - August 1971

Sixteen baseball historians and statistical researchers from 11 States met at Cooperstown, N.Y. on August 10 to organize the Society for American Baseball Research (SABR). This is the first organization of its type to be established in the 100 year history of Organized Baseball. The 16 who took part, plus an observer from Ontario, Canada, were representative of some 40 "statistorians" across the country who have expressed interest in such an organization. Here is a summary of what was accomplished at the meeting.

✪ The following objectives were adopted:

1. To foster the study of baseball as a significant American social and athletic institution.

2. To stimulate interest in baseball as our National Pastime.

3. To establish an accurate historical account of baseball through the years.

4. To coordinate and facilitate the dissemination of baseball research information.

5. To cooperate in safeguarding the proprietary interests of individual research efforts.

✪ It was generally agreed that the organization should have a constitution to provide basic guidelines and procedures. The officers will work as a committee to draft a constitution for consideration by the membership. The objectives, outlined above, will be incorporated into that document.

✪ After a discussion of whether there should be two memberships -- active and associate -- it was decided that there should be at this time one full membership with annual dues of $10 (more about that later). A membership card will be provided with the hope that it will facilitate your admission to libraries and other places where you carry out your research.

✪ Discussion of a name for the organization centered around geographic coverage, a possible acronym, and a means of covering both the historical and statistical aspects of the groups without a long title. It was generally agreed that the word research accomplished the latter. In regard to geographic scope, it was stated that American was broader than national. Society was preferred over association. Efforts to come up with a name resulting in a baseball acronym like RBI or something similar proved fruitless. Consequently, we became the Society for American Baseball Research.

The first issue of The SABR Bulletin, *published in August 1971.*

Jim Riley, former Negro Leagues player Jimmy Dean, Vincent Broomes and John Pardon (left to right) at the 1996 SABR National Convention. Riley was elected SABR President in 1999. Pardon was SABR's first vice-president (1971) and also served on the SABR Executive Board from 1979-1989.

The SABR Executive Board meets at Kansas City in 1996. President David Pietrusza is at the head of the table.

(1975-79), Marge Daniels (1986-90), Bob Davids (1974-75 and 1976-80) Cappy Gagnon (1987-1991), Larry Gerlach (1991-1997), Steve Gietschier (1997-1999), Stan Grosshandler (1974-75 and 1977-81), Fred Ivor-Campbell (1992-96), Rodney Johnson (1999-), Tom Jozwik (1983-87), Cliff Kachline (1974-76 and 1980-82), Vern Luse (1985-87), Norman Macht (1999-), Bob McConnell (1974-80 and 1982-86), Lois Nicholson (1998-), John Pardo⌐ (1979-83 and 1985-89), Frank Phelps (198⌐ 85), Richard Puff (1989-93), Jim Riley (199⌐ 99), Mark Rucker (1990-94), Rick Salamon⌐ (1994-98), Tom Shieber (1997-), Eric Simonsen (1983-85), and David Vincent (1993-97).

Since the division of the secretary-treasurer position, the following members have served as secretary: Bill Shlensky (1974-75), Randy Linthurst (1975-76), Tom Hufford (1976-77), Tom Zocco (1977-78), Bob Hoie (1978-80), Vern Luse (1980-82), Bill Humber (1982-83), John Pardon (1983-85), Luke Salisbury (1985-87), Phil Lowry (1987-88), Len Levin (1988-90), Claudia Perry (1990-92), Bob Ruland (1992-1996), Norman Macht (1996-97), Dave Pietrusza (1997-98), and Dick Beverage (1998-).

THE MEMBERSHIP DIRECTORY

The first *Membership Directory*, one of SABR's most basic and vital tools, was mailed in October 1971. It was a four-page mimeographed list containing fifty-two names. Since then, the Directory has remained the communication link that weaves the Society together.

The second edition, with 105 listed members, had twenty subject categories for members' interests, and a map showing the geographical location of the membership, most of whom clustered in the eastern part of the country. Only twenty members lived west of the Mississippi River.

The 1974 *Membership Directory*, prepared by Bob McConnell, contained the names, emphasized with a "Miss," of the Society's first two female members, Evelyn Begley and Joanne Neel. Neel appeared in the 1973 *Membership Directory* as a Ph.D. who listed her interests as Connie Mack and the birth of the American League. What became of Dr. Neel is unclear, but Evelyn can still be found today in a leading role of the Society's New York City Casey Stengel Chapter.

The 1974 edition listed the average age of the Society member as 42. The oldest member was 86 and the youngest 17. It also listed members' occupations for the first time.

The 1975 *Membership Directory* printed a two-page constitution of the Society and also contained a list of deceased members. The Society's constitution and bylaws have been published in each subsequent edition, but the last listing of deceased members was printed in 1988.

By 1980 the Directory, edited by Bob McConnell, contained 1,200 members and had became a huge typing job. Plans for computerization fell through at the last minute.

The 1981 *Membership Directory*, edited by Gregg Tubbs, contained a ten-year history of the Society written by John Pardon.

In 1982 Tubbs printed a geographical list-

1991), Lloyd Johnson (1991-93), David Pietrusza (1993-97), Larry Gerlach (1997-99), and Jim Riley (1999-).

Phil Lowry won the Society's presidential election in 1991 but was unable to assume the office due to health issues. Newly elected vice-president Jack Kavanagh took over as acting-president until a new election could be held. A new ballot was sent to the membership with the September 1991 *SABR Bulletin*, listing John Holway, Lloyd Johnson, David Pietrusza, and Bill Shlensky as candidates. Holway's campaign statement alleged that the Society had lost an unexplained $40,000 in the previous four years. This drew a reply in the October *SABR Bulletin* from Society treasurer Bob Ruland denying that the Society had any current financial troubles and that the problem Holway referred to had preceded the current Executive Director by eighteen months. Holway withdrew his name from the slate and a new presidential ballot had to be sent with the October *SABR Bulletin*. The election results were announced in the January 1992 *SABR Bulletin*. Lloyd Johnson won the election with 185 votes.

Individuals who have served in the role of Society vice-president have been John Pardon (1971-72), Paul Frisz (1972-73), Joe Simenic (1973-74), Dick Cramer (1974-75), Emil Rothe (1975-76), Stan Grosshandler (1976-77), Art Schott (1977-78), Bill Gustafson (1978-80), Jerry Gregory (1980-82), Tom Evans (1982-83), Cappy Gagnon (1983-84), John McCormack (1984-85), Tal Smith (1985-87), Luke Salisbury (1987-89), Ron Gabriel (1989-91), Jack Kavanagh (1991-93), Claudia Perry (1993-95), Dick Beverage (1995-97), and Fred Ivor-Campbell (1998-).

Society treasurers have been Eric Simonsen (1974-75), Ray Gonzalez (1975-77), Dick Burtt (1977-79), Frank Phelps (1979-81), Robert Soderman (1982), Bill Hugo (1982-84), Joe McGillen (1984-86), Cappy Gagnon (1986-87), Skip McAfee (1987-90), Bob Ruland (1990-92), Norman Macht (1992-95), Paul Andresen (1995-99), and Len Levin (1999-).

At the 1974 National Convention the role of secretary-treasurer was split into two positions and, at the same time, a four-person Board of Directors was established with staggered four-year terms. Members who have served on the Board are Bill Carle (1988-92), Dick Cramer

ing of all members by ZIP code order in addition to the standard alphabetical listing.

For financial reasons, no *Membership Directory* was published in 1985, but it returned in 1986 under the direction of Society Executive Director Lloyd Johnson. That issue, thanks to the efforts of Marge Daniels, Gary Skoog, and Gillian Tingley, was the first computerized version. It also was the first to accept advertising as a revenue generator for the Society. Ads cost $250 for a full page, $150 for a half page, $100 for 1/3 page, and $50 for a 2x2 inch box. By 1989 those prices had risen to $400 for inside cover, $300 for full page, $200 for half page, $150 for 1/3 page, and $25 for a business card.

In 1987, editor Harold Dellinger, who was also in charge of the 1988 and 1990 editions, included a ten-page listing of Society members who had authored, edited, published, or compiled books and newsletters on baseball. He also included a list of members who were book dealers, ran fan clubs, or owned card/memorabilia business.

The 1990 *Membership Directory* featured a Frank Phelps article titled "Baseball Research Before SABR," a must read for members interested in early baseball research.

For budgetary reasons, the *Membership Directory* became a bi-annual publication beginning with the 1991-1992 edition.

THE SABR SALUTE

The initial SABR Salute was given to Fred Lieb in the 1976 *Membership Directory* and was designed as a manner of recognizing the contributions of some of the older members of the Society, many of whom had made great contributions to baseball historical research before the Society came into being.

Lieb, who passed away on June 3, 1980 in St. Petersburg, Florida at the age of 92, had been the baseball editor of the New York *Press*. He had also been past president of the Baseball Writers Association of America and author of several of the Putnam team histories. Lieb was initially hesitant to join the Society in fear that it might hurt his reputation if the organization failed. Instead, the Society thrived, and Lieb's presence gave it early respectability.

Subsequent SABR Salutes were given to Leonard Gettleson in 1977; Bill Schroeder in 1978; John Tattersall in 1979; Alex Haas in 1980; Bob Davids in 1981; Al Kermisch in 1982; Emil Rothe in 1983; Ellery Clark in 1984; James Bready, Joe Overfield, Tweed Webb, Ralph Lin Weber and Art Schott in 1986; Bob Lindsay and Vern Luse in 1987; Ray Gonzalez , Ray Nemec, Pat McDonough and Keith Sutton in 1988; Harry Simmons and Tom Shea in 1990; Gene Murdock in 1991; Stan Grosshandler and David Voigt in 1993; Eddie Gold, Jack Kavanagh and Joe Wayman in 1995; Ralph Horton, John Pardon and Bill Weiss in 1997; and Fred Ivor-Campbell, Norman Macht, and Frank Williams in 1999.

The members who have received the SABR Salute should long be remembered for their contributions.

Leonard Gettleson, a member since 1971, passed away on December 24, 1977. He had worked closely with Ernie Lanigan for many years on various *The Sporting News* publications

The 1972 SABR Membership Directory.

The 1982 SABR Membership Directory.

like *Daguerreotypes* and *The Sporting News Record Book*.

John Tattersall passed away in Boca Raton, Florida on May 29, 1981. At a cost of $10,000, the Society purchased his collection of research material which consisted of seven file drawers of folders that pertained to all the major league home runs hit since 1876. Tattersall had gained national recognition in 1953 when *The Sporting News* published a story about his correction of Nap Lajoie's 1901 batting average. The New York *Times* and *Time* magazine subsequently mentioned this. Fascinated by statistical research, Tattersall had years earlier set out to catalogue every home run in major league history. Upon John's death Bob McConnell took on the role of maintaining this list. In 1990 the Society's Computerization Committee assumed the task of converting the log into an online format. The Tattersall-McConnell Home Run Log would eventually evolve into the 1996 Macmillan book, *SABR Presents The Home Run Encyclopedia*, edited by Bob McConnell and David Vincent. McConnell to this day, however, states that ninety percent of the material in the Tattersall-McConnell log was due to Tattersall's efforts. Bob claims he has just updated the material and made a few corrections.

Former Society president Gene Murdock died on July 23, 1992. Professor Murdock had been the chairman of the history department at Marietta College from 1972 to 1986 and was very interested in oral histories. Among his published works were *Ban Johnson* (published in 1982), *Baseball Players and Their Times: Oral Histories of the Game, 1920-1940* (1991), and *Baseball Between the Wars: Memories of the Game by the Men Who Played It* (1992).

Keith Sutton, an original Society member, died in Honesdale, Pennsylvania, in early 1992. His material had appeared in *The Sporting News* from 1950 to 1975. In 1973 he published the 260-page *Wayne County Sports History*. Christy Mathewson had played semipro baseball in Honesdale in 1898 and 1899 and Sutton was considered the expert on that portion of Mathewson's career.

Tweed Webb passed away on April 27,

SABR Salute recipients Fred Lieb and Gene Murdock were pictured on one of SABR's early special publications, an index to Baseball Research Journal.

1995, in St. Louis at the age of 89. Webb was a pioneering authority on the Negro Leagues.

Webb's death was sandwiched between the loss of two of the Society's original members. Tom Shea died in March, 1995, in a nursing home in Cohasset, Massachusetts, at the age of 90. Bill Haber died in Brooklyn from an asthma attack in June of the same year. A very strong argument can be made that Shea and Haber were baseball's greatest biographical researchers. Sportswriter Bill Madden of the New York *Daily News* said of Haber, "In terms of sleuthing, Dick Tracy, Magnum and Jim Rockford had nothing on Haber." Shea's story can be found in the 1998 edition of *The National Pastime*.

Pat McDonough, another of the Society's original members, passed away on March 2, 1996. He was active as a newspaper writer and editor for over fifty years and his specialty was relief pitching research.

Emil Rothe died in Chicago, Illinois, on

November, 27, 1996. On November 19, 1989, Rothe became the first Society member to have a SABR regional group named in his honor.

Ralph Horton, who passed away in October, 1998, worked for the Rawlings Sporting Goods Company where he was instrumental in initiating the Gold Glove Awards. After his retirement Ralph started his own publishing company and reprinted old baseball guides and record books, a project that has and will greatly benefit present and future generations of baseball historians.

THE NATIONAL CONVENTIONS

The Society's founding meeting in 1971 is considered the first annual meeting. The second of what came to be called National Conventions was held in Washington, D.C., from June 23 to 24, 1972, with twenty-three members in attendance. Eventually, the meetings have come to be referred to by number. The 1999 National Convention, for example, was called SABR 29.

The 1973 National Convention was held at the Sheraton-Chicago Hotel in Chicago from June 22 to 24 with twenty-three or, depending on the source, twenty-six attendees. The cost was $15 for a single room and $20 for a double. Negro Leaguer Dave Malarcher was the guest speaker.

Original plans called for the 1974 National Convention to be held in Newark, New Jersey, but plans were changed and the meeting was held at the Holiday Inn in Philadelphia from June 22 to 24. Dick Cramer and Ben Weiser were the organizers, and forty members and guests attended. The speakers were former Phils and Reds announcer Gene Kelley, Negro Leaguer Ted Page, and writer Fred Lieb.

Sixty-four members attended the 1975 National Convention which was held in Boston from July 11 to 13. Society members took in a game at Fenway Park. Eric Simonsen was the convention chairman. Jumpin' Joe Dugan was the speaker.

Forty-five members attended the 1976 National Convention at the Howard Johnson Motor Lodge in Chicago from June 25 to 27. The Convention Committee was led by Emil Rothe and Bob Soderman with assistance from Eddie Gold, Bill Loughman, and Stan Grosshandler. Lew Fonseca was the banquet speaker and the Treasurer's report listed the Society's assets at $1,150 at convention time.

Gene Murdock, Merl Kleinknecht, and Bob Hunter headed the committee that produced the 1977 National Convention in Columbus, Ohio, from June 24 to 26. It was attended by seventy-four members. Kit Crissey was in charge of a midwest players reunion which, held in conjunction with the convention, drew twenty-four former players, among them Johnny Lipon, George Sisler, Jr., Jim Fridley, Dick Hoover, Roy Hughes, Danny Kravitz, George Spencer, Larry File, and Jim Waugh. Former Cards and Tigers catcher Johnny Bucha was the main speaker at the Friday night welcoming social.

Eighty-one members attended the 1978 National Convention at the Paramus, New Jersey, Paramus-Parkway Holiday Inn from July 28 to 30. Al and Barbara Wicklund were the convention organizers. The Wicklunds, and Cliff and

Founding members in attendance at SABR's 20th anniversary celebration in August 1991, included (left to right) Dan Dischley, John Pardon, Bob Davids, Cliff Kachline, Pat McDonough, Tom Hufford and Joe Simenic.

The Dodger Sym-phony provided entertainment during the banquet at the 1991 SABR National Convention in New York City.

Hall of Fame broadcaster Mel Allen (at podium) was the keynote speaker at the 1991 SABR National Convention in New York City.

Evelyn Kachline, should probably share the title of the Society's first "couple." Tony Lupien, ex-major leaguer, Harvard graduate, and longtime Dartmouth College baseball coach, gave a "scholarly discourse on player organizations, personnel management, and the pension plan." Clearly this foreshadowed his and co-author Lee Lowenfish's book, *The Imperfect Diamond.* The Society attended an old-timers game honoring the 1949-53 Yankees that preceded a Yanks-Twins game. The player panel, put together by

Kit Crissey, included Hinkey Haines, Walt Hunzinger, Charlie Hargreaves, Russ Van Atta, and the big star of the day, ninety-one-year old Jack Martin who had also appeared at the October, 29, 1977, regional meeting in Raritan, New Jersey.

Bill Borst organized the 1979 Convention which was held at the Lennox Hotel in St. Louis from June 29 to July 1. One hundred and fifteen people, seventy-eight of them members, attended. Mike Shannon was the banquet speaker,

Major League Baseball player and manager Dick Williams (left) was the keynote speaker at the 1993 SABR National Convention in San Diego. Next to Williams is Kurt Bevacqua, former big league player and MC for the convention banquet.

Hall of Famer pitcher Robin Roberts was the keynote speaker at the 1994 SABR National Convention in Arlington, TX.

Hall of Fame pitcher Jim Bunning (at podium) was the keynote speaker at the 1997 SABR National Convention in Louisville, KY. Former major league pitcher Ned Garver looks on.

and Cool Papa Bell, Andy High, and Buddy Blattner were all in attendance. Room rates were $17.50 for a single and $22.50 for a double. The Treasurer's report listed $14,000 in Society assets at convention time.

The Society numbered 1,145 when sixty-two members and about twenty guests attended the 1980 National meeting at the TraveLodge International Hotel at the Los Angeles Airport from July 11 to 13. Room rates were $36 for single and $40 for double. Roy Smalley, Sr. was the banquet speaker. Wally Berger, Jigger Statz, Quincy Trouppe, Bert Shepard, former Pirates General Manager Joe L. Brown, and American League umpire Joe Rue also spoke.

The 1981 National Convention was held in Toronto, Ontario, from July 24 to 26 at the University of Toronto's Erindale campus. This was the first time the meeting was held outside of the United States and the first time the convention was held at a college. Dormitory rooms cost $13.65 a night. One-hundred and forty-seven individuals, ninety-seven members and

fifty guests, attended. Due to the players strike the Blue Jays-Orioles game had been cancelled. Speakers were former major leaguers Goody Rosen, Phil Marchildon, Roy Hughes, and Reno Bertoia. Former Negro Leaguers Gene Benson, Buddy Burbage, Jeep McLain, and Sy Morton were also in attendance.

The 1982 National Convention was held at Towson State University near Baltimore. One-hundred and fifty-one members were included in the 227 total attendance. Sparky Anderson and Ernie Harwell were the featured speakers. The player panel consisted of Billy Hunter, Dick Hall, Roy Hughes, Al Rubeling, and Rex Barney.

There were 262 attendees at the 1983 National Convention at Marquette University in Milwaukee from July 15 to 17. Tom Jozwik was the organizer. Hal Goodenough, a boyhood teammate of Mickey Cochrane from Bridgewater, Massachusetts, and later a baseball executive, was the guest speaker. Other ex-players on hand were Ken Keltner, Andy Pafko,

Mike Hegan, Fabian Gaffke, Lester Lockett, Ted Radcliffe, and umpire Stan Landes.

The 1984 Convention was held at Brown University in Providence, Rhode Island, to mark the 100th anniversary of the 1884 World Series between the Providence Grays and the New York Metropolitans. There were 350 on hand from July 6 through July 8. Lou Gorman was the banquet speaker. Eric Simonsen was the convention organizer. The player panel consisted of Clem Labine, Dave Stenhouse, Tony Lupien, and Boston's Triple-A affiliate Pawtucket Red Sox owner Ben Mondor. One of the convention highlights was a recreated 1884 game with Society members wearing reproductions of nineteenth century uniforms. The game, originally scheduled for Saturday afternoon, was rained out and eventually played between games of the Sunday Pawtucket Red Sox doubleheader. Photos of the game and the players in their nineteenth century uniforms ran on the front pages of local papers the next day.

At the 1985 Convention at the Hyatt Regency in Oakland, California, room rates were $56.16 night. Over 300 heard A's owner Roy Eisenhardt speak at the banquet. The player panel consisted of Sam Chapman, Earl Robinson, and Bill Raimondi.

The 1986 National was held at the Loyola University Lakeshore Campus in Chicago from July 18 to 20. It was the last National Convention held at a college campus using dormitory rooms and cafeteria dining. A total of 479 members and guests attended. Bill Gleason was the banquet speaker. Marge and Jon Daniels and Rich and Barbara Topp, the Society's most active spouses, were the convention organizers. Chico Carrasquel, John Klippstein, Rich Nye, Ted "Double Duty" Radcliffe, Marv Rotblatt, and Nelson Potter made up the player panel. The Society's constitution was amended to make the offices of president, vice-president, and treasurer two-year positions rather than one.

The 1987 Convention was held at the Crystal City Marriott in Arlington, Virginia, from June 27 to 29. Six-hundred and thirty-one attended. John Steadman was the banquet speaker. Jay

Demarest was the convention organizer. Luke Appling homered at the old-timers All-Star game. Ex-players Chuck Stevens, Milt Pappas, Wilmer Fields, and former Red Sox General Manager Dick O'Connell were on hand. Eddie Frierson performed his one-man show, "Lunch with Christy Mathewson." A vote passed at the convention to increase the annual membership dues to $30.

The 1988 Convention was in Minneapolis from July 7 to 10 with 340 people in attendance. Andy MacPhail was the keynote speaker, and minor league home run legend Joe Hauser was a special guest. Bob Tholkes was the convention organizer and the Halsey Hall regional group the host Society chapter. A player panel was made up of Hauser, Julio Becquer, Howie Schultz, and Nancy Mudge Cato.

The 1989 National Convention was held in Albany, New York, from June 23 through June 26. Richard Puff was the convention chairman, and welcomed 524 members and guests. Phil Rizzuto and American League President Bobby Brown were the featured speakers. Society members took in the Eastern League All-Star Game and a group trip was made to the Hall of Fame in Cooperstown. This was SABR's most tumultuous National, for reasons that will be described below.

The 1990 Convention was held in Cleveland, Ohio. Total attendance was 481. Sam McDowell was the guest speaker.

SABR 21 was held at the Penta Hotel in New York City from June 28 to 30. A total of 405 members and guests attended. Mel Allen was the keynote speaker. The membership took in a Mets-Phillies game. Singer Terry Cashman did his rendition of "Talkin' Baseball" and the Brooklyn Dodger Sym-phoney also performed.

Four-hundred and eighty-five people attended the 1992 National Convention at the Adam's Mark Hotel in St. Louis where room rates were $91.77. Bing Devine was the banquet speaker. Players at the convention included former St. Louis Cardinals Stan Musial, Red Schoendienst, Marty Marion, Ted Savage, Joe Cunningham, and Tom Poholsky; and St. Louis Browns Ned Garver, Don Lenhardt, Jim Delsing, Ed Mickelson, and Babe Martin.

Three-hundred and fifty members and guests attended SABR 23 in San Diego from June 24 to June 28, 1993. Joe Naiman was the convention organizer and the Ted Williams regional group was the host group. Dick Williams was the keynote speaker after the Saturday night banquet. A panel of players from the 1984 National League Champion San Diego Padres included Kurt Bevacqua, Bruce Bochy, and Garry Templeton. The major league player panel consisted of Irv Noren, Joe Nuxhall, and Pete Coscarart; and a minor league panel included Earl Keller, Rod Graber, Al Olsen, and Tony Criscola. At a non-players panel we heard from former American League umpire Ed Runge, long-time Dodger executive Buzzie Bavasi, and announcer Marty Brennaman. Many of the convention-goers and their families attended a bus trip to the San Diego Zoo.

A total of 405 members and guests attended the 1994 National Convention at the Arlington

Hall of Famer Pee Wee Reese (left) speaks at the 1997 SABR National Convention in Louisville, KY. Next to Reese are Carl Erskine (center) and Tot Pressnell, all former members of the Brooklyn Dodgers. Reese was the third recipient of the SABR Hero of Baseball Award.

Marriott in Arlington, Texas. Robin Roberts was the keynote speaker and player panels consisted of Roberts, Bobby Bragan, Buck O'Neil, Frank Lucchesi, J.C. Hartman, and Charlie Pride.

SABR 25 was organized by Ed Luteran and the Society's Forbes Field regional group at the Hyatt-Regency Pittsburgh in Pittsburgh, Pennsylvania. Chuck Tanner gave the keynote address to the 451 attendees. Elroy Face, Bill Mazeroski, and Frank Thomas, among others, were in attendance.

The 1996 National at the Marriott Downtown in Kansas City attracted 431 members and guests. Steve Fehr gave the keynote address and the player panel consisted of Bob Feller, Bob Usher, and Clarence Marshall. Feller was honored by SABR and its Kansas City chapter with the initial SABR Hero of Baseball. The award, now given at the discretion of the Society's Executive Board, is to honor a baseball personality whose career has been marked by heroism on or off the field. Other winners have included Ted Williams and Pee Wee Reese in 1997, and Stan Musial in 1998.

The 1997 Convention was held in Louisville, Kentucky, at the Hyatt Regency Louisville. Convention organizer co-chairs were Harry Rothgerber and Henry Mayer. A total of 440 members and guests were in attendance. Pee Wee Reese and Jim Bunning were the featured speakers, with then Congressman Bunning giving the keynote address. There were rumors all weekend long that Ted Williams would attend but the Splendid Splinter, in poor health, was unable to make it. There were several interesting player panels. One consisted of Reese, Carl Erskine, Don Lund, Ed Stevens, and Tot Pressnell. The current Louisville Redbirds were represented by Gaylen Pitts, Kevin Koslofski, and Brian Maxcy. Among other players present were Ned Garver, Bill Cash, Connie Johnson, Butch McCord, Thomas Turner, Slick Surrett, Ernie Andres, and Mel Parnell. Branch Rickey III and Louisville Redbirds General Manager Dale Owens also spoke. The membership had a tour of the Louisville Slugger Museum and Bat Factory and also attended an American Asso-

ciation game between the Louisville Redbirds and the Iowa Cubs in which Iowa pitcher Miguel Batista tossed a neat two-hit shutout.

Four-hundred and thirty-seven people attended the 1998 convention at the San Francisco Airport Marriott in Burlingame, California, from June 25 through June 28. The convention chairman was Barry Mednick and Bill Rigney was the keynote speaker. Player panels consisted of former Giant players Orlando Cepeda, Hank Sauer, Eddie Bressoud, and Mike McCormick; and a Pacific Coast League panel of Larry Jansen, Gino Cimoli, Dino Restelli, Bud Watkins, and Ernie Broglio.

The 1999 National Convention was hosted by the Society's Arizona Flame Delhi chapter in Scottsdale, Arizona. Community and kids' programs were an imaginative part of the schedule, and convention chairman Rodney Johnson even laid on a no-hitter by the Cardinals' Jose Jimenez. Tommy Henrich was a delightful keynote speaker.

THE ORIGINAL COMMITTEES

The Society's first four active committees were established in 1971. They were Biographical Research, Publications, Minor Leagues, and Negro Leagues. The original Publications Committee was eventually dropped and replaced with the position of Publications Director, but several other publications committees and task forces have existed over the years to hire and assist different Publication Directors.

By 1997, the number of SABR Committees, which will later be discussed at length, had risen to eighteen.

The Biographical Committee was formed to encourage biographical research of players, managers, and officials. It has collected birth, death, and other vital statistics on close to 15,000 players and managers who have appeared since 1871. It has been said that the Biographical Committee is an extension of Hall of Fame Historian Lee Allen's biographical research club. Allen and late committee member Tom Shea provided much of the biographical

The first Baseball Research Journal, published annually by SABR since 1972.

data for *The Official Encyclopedia of Baseball*, first published in 1951 by Hy Turkin and S. C. Thompson. *The Sports Encyclopedia: Baseball*, originally published by Grosset and Dunlap but commonly known today as the Neft and Cohen book, paid the Society $600 in 1972 for player demographic data, and continued to pay $120 yearly through 1974 for updates. The four authors, David Neft, Richard Johnson, Roland Johnson and Jordan Deutsch, were all Society members and had worked on the Macmillan's *Baseball Encyclopedia*. The committee, which has been chaired by Cliff Kachline (1971-83), Joe Simenec (1983-84), Rich Topp (1984-88), and Bill Carle (1988-), has also provided data to *Total Baseball*.

The Negro Leagues Committee was formed in an effort to research and preserve for posterity the baseball history of African-Americans before the re-integration of major league baseball and to support efforts to give them due recognition. Chairmen have included John Holway (1972-73, 79-82), Merl Kleinknecht (1973-79), Phil Lowry (1982-85), and Dick Clark (1985-). Larry Lester is the current co-chair. The committee's work resulted in *The*

Negro Leagues Book, a 382-page book, edited by Dick Clark and Larry Lester, published by the Society in 1994. Members Holway, Clark, Lester, and Jim Riley, among many other writers and researchers, have produced authoritative works on the Negro Leagues and its players. By 1975 two former Negro League players, Dave Malarcher and Tweed Webb, had joined the committee. In August, 1999, the Society's Negro Leagues Committee and the John Henry "Pop" Lloyd Committee co-hosted a conference on Negro Leagues baseball in Atlantic City, New Jersey.

The Minor Leagues Committee studies and gathers data on the minor leagues. Chairmen have included Ray Nemec (1971-73), Vern Luse (1973-75), Bob Hoie (1975-81), John Pardon (1981-87), David Kemp (1987-1994), Jamie Selko (1994), Carlos Bauer (1994-1996), Ernest Green (1996-1999), and Bob McConnell (1999). The committee has produced three volumes of *Minor League Baseball Stars*, three volumes of the *Minor League History Journal*, two volumes of the *Minor League Baseball Research Journal*, and *The SABR Guide to Minor League Statistics*. No minor league, no matter how small or insignificant, has escaped the scrutiny of the committee.

THE BASEBALL RESEARCH JOURNAL

The first *Baseball Research Journal*, the cornerstone of SABR publications, was published in 1972. The objective, described by Bob Davids, was to publish an annual review of articles written and compiled by Society members. The articles would cover baseball research material previously unpublished or would deal with historical data from a different perspective. The 1973 *Baseball Research Journal* contained twenty attributed and three unattributed articles and two surveys. The Society, by asking a price of $3.00 by mail and $2.50 over the counter, received $375 in revenues. Five-hundred and twenty-five copies of the 1974 *Baseball Research Journal* were printed at a total cost of $630. Early sales and public relations efforts were under way and ads were placed regarding the *Baseball Research Journal* in *The Sporting News* and *Baseball Digest*. Davids was the *Journal*'s editor from its inception through 1983. Cliff Kachline edited the 1984-1986 editions, Jim Kaplan handled the job from 1987 through 1990, and John Holway in 1991. Mark Alvarez has been the editor since 1992. The standard size of *The Baseball Research Journal* was 6 by 9 inches until 1983. In 1984 it was changed to the current 8-1/2 by 11-inch magazine-style publication. In 1981 the *Historical Review*, a collection of articles from the first three *Baseball Research Journals*, was published, and in 1983 1,000 copies of the 1975-78 *Baseball Research Journals* were reprinted. Phil Bergen indexed the first nine *Baseball Research Journals* in 1981 and updated it in 1987. Joe Murphy has since undertaken a complete, ongoing index of all SABR publications. To date, twenty-eight editions of *The Baseball Research Journal* have been published.

Bill Rigney (left) and Hall of Famer Orlando Cepeda were two of the notable guests at the 1998 SABR National Convention in Burlingame, CA.

Charlie Kagan, John Zajc and Mike Hanks staff the registration table at the 1999 SABR National Convention in Scottsdale, AZ. As SABR's manager of Membership Services, Zajc has coordinated SABR convention registration since 1994.

THE NATIONAL PASTIME

In November 1974, a proposal was made for a second SABR publication to be called *The National Pastime*. This was a short-lived project that should not to be confused with the current Society publication of the same name. Edited by Ben Weiser, only four issues were printed. The first issue, twenty-four pages long, was mailed in February 1975, carrying a story on Fred Lieb, a Dick Cramer article on Batters Run Average, some Bob Davids "Baseball Briefs," and a few book reviews. The April 1975 *SABR Bulletin* ran mixed reviews about it.

John Thorn was named editor of the present *National Pastime* at the Executive Board meeting of January 9, 1983. He had proposed the concept of this new Society publication to the Executive Board the previous year. In addition to being its editor, Thorn became designer, production staff, publicity staff, and advertising staff. The premiere edition produced an all-star cast with articles authored by Bob Carroll, Art Ahrens, John Holway, Jim Bankes, David Sanders, Larry Ritter, Bob Broeg, G. H. Fleming, Don Nelson, David Voigt, Mark Rucker, Lew Lipset, Frank Williams, Fred Stein, Stuart Leeds, Harold Seymour, Bob Bluthardt, Pete Palmer, Al Kermisch, Ted DiTullio, and Gerald Tomlinson. Thorn received advice from various senior SABR members and had the outstanding help of Dean Coughenour in typesetting, printing, and distribution. The cost was $5 to non-members. It was mailed in late October and immediately met with rave reviews.

Thorn edited the first nine editions, with Mark Rucker as co-editor of the pictorials. Bob Tiemann edited the tenth edition, John Holway the eleventh, and Peter Bjarkman the twelfth before Mark Alvarez took over. *The National Pastime* has encompassed a wide variety of articles and photographs. Pictorial issues were done on the Nineteenth Century, the Deadball Era, and the Big-Bang Era of 1920-45. The eighth edition was a biography of Nap Lajoie by veteran newspaper writer Jim Murphy, a Rhode Islander and boyhood friend of Gabby Hartnett.

OTHER SOCIETY PUBLICATIONS

This Date in Baseball History, a day-by-day listing of significant baseball events from April 1 to October 31, came off the presses on April 30, 1976. This was reprinted in 1982. The American League office soon began distributing items from this work to its clubs and crediting the Society. Joe Garagiola quoted from it on NBC baseball games.

Minor League Stars was published in July 1978 and handed out to members at the 1978 National Convention. It contained the records of 170 players and had been in the development and research stage since its initial proposal at the Society's founding meeting in 1971. Delays resulted from the "unrecognized enormity of the task." Twenty-two Society members were listed as contributors with Bob Hoie and Ray Nemec credited with producing the lion's share of the load. Five-hundred copies had been sold by October and an additional 1,000 copies were quickly ordered from the printer. *Minor League*

The short-lived quarterly version of The National Pastime.

The annual version of The National Pastime, *edited by John Thorn, made its debut in 1982.*

Stars Volume II was published in 1985 and contained records of 180 players and twenty managers. *Minor League Stars Volume III* was published in 1992 and contained records of 253 players. *Baseball America* printed *The Minor League Register* in 1994. It was edited by Lloyd Johnson and combined the three original works with more original research.

The Society printed *Great Hitting Pitchers* in December of 1979. It was a "detailed historical account of the outstanding game, season and career records of pitchers as batters since 1876." Bob Davids was the editor and Bob McConnell, Cliff Kachline, Ron Liebman, Ray Gonzalez, Pete Palmer, John Tattersall, Paul Greenwell, and Al Kermisch were listed as contributors.

A hardcover anthology of the Society's *Baseball Research Journal* was published in 1983 by Scribners. It was edited by Bob Davids and contained forty-nine articles selected from the Society's past publications. Bill James wrote the foreword. It was 274 pages in length and cost $14.95.

In 1986, SABR published the twenty-six page monograph *Baseball in the Nineteenth Century: An Overview* by Jack Selzer, and *Green Cathedrals* by Phil Lowry, an in-depth look at the history of baseball parks.

Lowry's work was 157 pages long, and was printed in the same format as *The National Pastime* and *The Baseball Research Journal*. He compiled the project over a seven-year span and acknowledged forty-five Society members who helped him in his work. Lowry also mentioned that he received 2,316 letters from various sources while preparing the work.

The May 1987 *SABR Bulletin* announced that the Society had closed a deal with Warner Books to print an anthology of articles from *The National Pastime*. The deal, negotiated by John Thorn, netted the Society $10,000. Warner eventually published a rack-sized paperback and then licensed the publication rights to Bell Publishing which issued a hardcover edition of the same book.

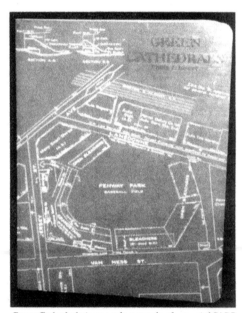

Green Cathedrals *is an early example of a special SABR publication focusing on the subject of a SABR Research Committee (Ballparks).*

In 1987 the Society published *The Baseball Research Handbook* by Gerald Tomlinson as an aid to SABR researchers.

Bill Deane's *Award Voting* was published in 1988. It is a history of the Most Valuable Player, Rookie of the Year, and Cy Young Awards.

The Society published *Nineteenth Century Stars*, edited by Bob Tiemann and Mark Rucker, in 1989. It contained short biographies on 137 pre-1900 players, written by over thirty Society members. A second volume, *Baseball's First Stars*, was published in 1996, edited by Tiemann, Rucker, and Fred Ivor-Campbell. Forty-nine Society members contributed 153 biographies.

Also in 1989, the Society published Marc Okkonen's *Federal League of 1914-1915, Baseball's Third Major League* in 1989. The sixty-four-page book included pictures, rosters, uniforms, and various diagrams and statistics as they related to the Federal League.

Cooperstown Corner, the best of Lee Allen's *Sporting News* columns from the 1960s, was published in 1990 with an introduction by Society member Steve Gietschier, Director of Historical Records at *The Sporting News*.

Run, Rabbit, Run was published in 1991. Shortly before his death in 1954, Rabbit Maranville had started work on his autobiography. It was a project he never completed. Dallas and Ralph Graber rescued the unfinished manuscript from a memorabilia dealer and Society Publication Directors Paul Adomites and John Holway, along with Publications Committee member A.D. Suehsdorf, saw it to the finish. The book was ninety-six pages long.

In 1994 the Society published *The Negro Leagues Book*. At 382 pages it became the Society's largest publishing effort to date. Aptly described as "a monumental work from the Negro Leagues Committee of the Society for American Baseball Research," it contained extensive research on Negro league rosters, standings, and biographies. It also included a comprehensive bibliography.

In 1995 the Society published *Home Runs in the Old Ballparks*, a forty-seven-page booklet by David Vincent. using material from the Tattersall-McConnell Home Run Log.

In 1998, SABR published *Addie Joss, King of the Pitchers*, by Scott Longert, and followed it in 1999 with *Uncle Robbie*, a biography of Wilbert Robinson by Jack Kavanagh and Norman Macht.

PUBLICATIONS DIRECTOR

Bob Davids had been responsible for editing almost all of the Society's publication efforts since the inception of the group. In February 1985, John Thorn was named the Society's first official Publications Director.

Page one of the 1985 April *SABR Bulletin* commented on the failure of the Society to meet its promised schedule of publications delivery. "Promises! Promises! Where's the Beef...er, Books?" ran headlines. Thorn discussed his thoughts on how the rapid growth rate of the Society was affecting his and the Society's publications goals. He promised to remedy scheduling problems and discussed long-term plans to increase the range and appeal of the Society's publications and seek a wider commercial audience. He commented on how the uneven editorial and design specifications and "seat-of-the-pants" production schedules had been addressed with the creation of his funded, part-time post of Publications Director. The projected cost of that year's publications (*SABR Bulletins*, *Membership Directory*, two editions of *The National Pastime*, *The Baseball Research Journal*, and the planned ballparks book) was $103,085.

By the middle of 1987 Thorn was ready to move to bigger projects, and the July 1987 *SABR Bulletin* informed members that the position of Publications Director had been restructured. Thorn announced his resignation, due to his overcrowded professional schedule and some unhappiness with the timeliness of publications, as of December 21, 1987. From a field of forty-two applicants, Paul Adomites was announced in October 1987 as new editor-in-chief of the Society's publications effective January 1, 1988.

Adomites held the Publications Director position until his resignation on October 15, 1990, although he agreed to stay on in the interim. Many Society members agree that the highlight of Adomites' tenure was his development and editorial direction of *The SABR Review of Books* series, a review of current baseball literature, which was published between 1986 and 1990. Richard Puff, then Publications Committee chairman, was placed in charge of finding a new Publications Director. He said of Adomites' departure, "He's done a fine job in maintaining the excellent quality of SABR publications. It's going to be difficult to find a SABR member to match Paul's editorial and production skills and his baseball knowledge."

John Holway was named Publications Director early in 1991. At the same time, Baseball Ink, Inc., a company led by John Thorn which had produced *Total Baseball*, was hired as publication production consultant. Holway held the position until his resignation and subsequent replacement by current Publications Director Mark Alvarez in April, 1992.

SABR SURVEYS

The first SABR survey, to decide which old-timers deserved to be in the Hall of Fame, appeared in the 1972 *Baseball Research Journal*. None of the forty-two ballots submitted named George Kelly, the Hall of Fame Veterans Committee choice that year. All ten of the top vote-getters; Sam Thompson, Chuck Klein, Roger Connor, Mickey Welch, Arky Vaughan, Earl Averill, Amos Rusie, Ernie Lombardi, Jim Bottomley, and Hack Wilson, are now in the Hall of Fame.

Other SABR surveys included (in 1973) Best fielders (the winners were Sisler, Collins, Brooks Robinson, Wagner, Cochrane, Speaker, Mays, DiMaggio, and Shantz); Non-players who made valuable contributions (1974); Best foreign-born players, Best players by state and Best state all-star teams (1975); Best individual games ever played (1976); Best switch-hitters (Mantle, 1978), and Best minor leaguers (1983).

The Society also conducted surveys to determine retroactive pre-1967 Cy Young Awards in 1988. A similar survey to choose retroactive pre-1949 Rookie of the Year winners appeared as an article by Lyle Spatz in the 1986 *Baseball Research Journal*.

Periodically the Society has also conducted a Centennial Celebrity Survey to elect the most famous baseball figure born 100 years ago. Mordecai Brown was the first winner in 1976 and the Society later held retroactive voting back to the year of 1871 when Iron Man Joe McGinnity came out with top honors. Winners have included the obvious players like John McGraw, Honus Wagner, Nap Lajoie, Christy Mathewson, Ty Cobb, Walter Johnson, and Tris Speaker, but also produced a few unexpected ones like Art Fletcher and Ray Schalk.

The Society's most recent survey was conducted in 1999 by Steve Nadel and Gene Sunnen. It determined SABR's choices for the greatest 100 players of the twentieth century. The choices were the subject of *Baseball Weekly*'s June 23-29 cover story.

SOCIETY SERVICES

In March 1974 the SABR Executive Board authorized the purchase of microfilm copy of *The Sporting Life* from 1883 through 1917 to start SABR's Lending Library. The purpose of the Lending Library was to facilitate baseball research. The library has grown over the years to include *The Sporting News* from 1886 through 1963, the Albert Spalding and Henry Chadwick Scrapbooks, various books, Ph.D dissertations, master's theses, guides and videos. Administrators of the lending library have included Bill Loughman, John Schwartz, Mark Rucker, Tom Heitz, Mark Alvarez, Mike Sparrow, Brad Sullivan, Jean Chapman, and Vanetta Ellis.

The passing of members Howard Lavelle and Al Peterjohn in 1974, both of whom left research material to SABR, prompted the discussion of establishing a SABR Research-Archival Library. Bob McConnell became its initial custodian. Now known as the SABR Research Papers Collection, it is maintained by Len Levin. In 1996 it contained 2,200 articles of from one to ten pages. By 1997 it had grown to 4,000 articles. Len received 496 individual requests from May of 1997 to May of 1998.

THE REGIONAL GROUPS/ CHAPTERS

The regional concept, like the overall growth of the Society, was slow to catch on but picked up speed once it got going.

On November 9, 1974, twelve people met at the Chevy Chase, Maryland, home of Ron Gabriel in what is considered the first regional meeting of the Society. This group would later become known as the Bob Davids chapter. Twenty-five years after this initial meeting the Society's web page would boast forty-seven different regional groups. Some of these chapters meet two or three times a year and draw large crowds. They have become vital parts of the Society. Other regional efforts have failed after just one or two meetings.

The Davids Chapter, the Washington-Baltimore group, has met every year since its inception. Over the last several years members have turned their meeting into a smaller version of the national convention. Former major leaguer George McQuinn was a guest at several early meetings and former major league stolen base champ George Case showed old color movies from the 1940 and 1941 seasons at their third meeting in 1976.

1976 saw Emil Rothe host the initial Chicago meeting, which was later named in his honor, on November 17 with ten members attending. On December 4 of the same year, the first West Coast/ Southern California meeting, later to become the Allan Roth Chapter, was held in Los Angeles. Sixteen members attended.

In 1977, Society member Ernest Nagy, a U.S. Embassy Diplomat in Rome, issued a standing invitation to members visiting Italy to stop in for a regional meeting. It is not known if any peripatetic members took him up on his offer.

On August 6, 1977, Kit Crissey organized a reunion of twenty-five former players in New Orleans. Crissey was a master at rounding up old ballplayers, all of whom, if asked the right questions, have great stories to tell.

The regional meeting in Philadelphia on May 6, 1978, drew forty members and nineteen players. Fifty-four people, including thirty-three members, attended the November 18, 1978, regional meeting held in Greenfield, Massachusetts. Organized by John Pardon, Tom Zocco, and the late Ed Leonard, this was the first full-scale regional held in New England.

The Philadelphia regional on April 28, 1979, drew forty-five Society members, twenty former players including Judy Johnson, and thirty other guests.

The Mid-Atlantic regional was held in Reading, Pennsylvania, on April 26 to 27, 1980. It was a two-day event that served as an alternative to easterners unable to attend the National Convention on the west coast. Fourteen former professional players and forty-six members attended.

Toronto, Ontario, was the site of Canada's first regional, where twenty members met on August 9, 1980, for a get-together organized by Bill Humber.

The New Orleans regional, now known as the Schott/Pelican Chapter, held its first meeting on January 7, 1981.

On April 11, 1981, the southern California regional was held in Pasadena with twenty-one members and eleven guests in attendance. Wally Berger, Max West, and Bill Schuster appeared as guests. A month later the initial Michigan regional, now the Fred T. Smith Chapter, took place May 2, 1981.

On August 8, 1981, nine members and two guests met outside Seattle at the first meeting of what is now the Northwest SABR Chapter. They met again in Portland, Oregon, on February 7, 1982, where twelve members and speakers Rick Wise and Gerry Staley were in attendance. The Northwest SABR Chapter covers the largest area of any SABR regional: Washington, Oregon, British Columbia, and beyond. The Chapter's newsletter goes to members in Idaho as well, and Society members have flown in from eastern Montana and northern Alberta to attend meetings, which have been held in at least eight cities (Seattle, Tacoma, Portland, Everett, Yakima, Eugene, Vancouver, and Spokane). This may be the only chapter to have met in two countries. The driving distance between the various meeting sites is about 430 miles north-south and 280 miles east-west.

The Halsey Hall Chapter, named for the longtime writer and broadcaster, met in the Twin Cities for the first time on August 15, 1981. Scott Hall was the primary organizer with assistance from Stew Thornley and Bob Tholkes. This group, which hosted the 1988 National Convention, has its own monthly cable show and maintains a nineteenth century baseball team called the Quicksteps which plays by 1858 rules.

The first "Wyoming regional" meeting occurred on November 27, 1982, when two of the Society's three Wyoming members met on a radio talk show.

A regional meeting was held in a church

Members of the Halsey Hall Chapter of SABR dress up as the "Green Monster" of Fenway Park for a "Monster Mash" ball in 1992. Chapter members pictured are Stew Thornley (left), Brenda Himrich (third from left), and Nancy Jo Leachman (fourth from left).

Jack Graney Chapter of SABR members Mike Sparrow, Morris Eckhouse, Allen Pfenninger, Mark McKinstry (left to right) and Fred Schuld (far right) commemorate the 70th anniversary of Ray Chapman's 1920 death. Pastor Thomas Schmitt (second from right) helped with the ceremony at Cleveland's Lake View Cemetery.

hall in Dorchester section of Boston on March 12, 1983, with Reverend Jim Smith as organizer. This was the second attempt at starting a Boston Chapter. A first meeting, with just a handful of members, had been organized by brothers Arnold and Harvey Soolman, and held at the Boston Public Library in 1975.

On April 3, 1983, Gene Sunnen organized the first northern California regional, now the Lefty O'Doul Chapter, at the Oakland Coliseum.

A regional meeting was held in Durham, North Carolina, on June 25, 1983. Regionals in that area were held erratically until Marshall Adesman and Francis Kinlaw put together a group that met on February 13, 1993, in Greens-

boro, North Carolina. That current group, the Carolina Chapter, now meets three or four times a year.

The first and perhaps the only Society meeting ever held in New Mexico occurred on December 12, 1983.

The initial meeting of the New York City regional group, currently known as the Casey Stengel Chapter, was held in 1984. Gary Kelleher, Bill Pechette, and Marty Appel were involved in organizing it. The group chose to honor Stengel because he had appeared in the uniform of all four New York teams. In both 1985 and 1994 the chapter meeting drew more than 200 people.

Nineteen-eighty-four was a big year for

initial regional meetings. The Madison, Wisconsin, group, the Kid Nichols Chapter, met on June 9. On June 30, a Chattanooga, Tennessee, meeting was held with thirty-seven people in attendance. A player panel included Hillis Layne, Roy Hawes, and Buck Varner.

The initial St. Louis regional, now known as the Bob Broeg Chapter, was held on July 21 with fifty-three attendees. Terry Moore, Phil Gagliano, and Bob Broeg were speakers.

On July 28, the first San Diego meeting was held at Jack Murphy Stadium. The guest panel included Kurt Bevacqua, Chet Brewer, and National League umpire Joe West. Forty-one people attended. In 1991, Ted Williams gave his approval for the chapter to be called the Ted Williams Chapter.

The inaugural meeting of the Cleveland,

Members of SABR's George Davis Chapter arranged to have an appropriate marker placed at Davis' grave site. Davis is buried in Ferwood Cemetery in Landsdowne, PA. The grave was unmarked from his death in 1941 until 1998.

Ohio, regional, now the Jack Graney Chapter, was held on August 18, with Roy Hughes and Bob Cain as featured speakers. Fifty-three people attended. This chapter, also the home chapter of the Society's current executive offices, hosted the 1990 National Convention.

The first regional meeting of the northeastern New York group, currently known as the George Davis Chapter, was held on November 1 at Union College in Schenectady. Bob Giblin was the organizer. In addition to hosting the 1989 National Convention in Albany, activities of this group have included the establishment of the Bud Fowler Memorial Fund to raise money for a monument at Fowler's grave in Frankfurt, New York, following a memorial observance held around Hall of Fame induction time in 1987. The Davis Chapter also erected a monument on George Davis' grave in Philadelphia's Fernwood Cemetery in 1998.

The initial Omaha, Nebraska, regional was held on January 12, 1985, with Jackie Brandt and Jerry Cram as guests. The southern New England Chapter, later to be named the Lajoie-Start Chapter, held its initial regional meeting on the same day. Mike Roarke and Tim McNamara were featured speakers. Credit for organizing the chapter goes to Len Levin, Gerry Beirne, Jack Kavanagh, and the rest of the gang that hosted the 1984 National Convention.

On February 9, 1985, the Pittsburgh group had its first meeting, with Steve Blass as the guest speaker. Now known as the Forbes Field Chapter after an extensive 1993 discussion about a choice of names, this chapter includes among its highlights hosting the 1995 National Convention and being the driving force behind the erection of a state historical marker on the site of Exposition Park, home of the Pirates from 1891 to 1909 and the site of the first modern World Series. Paul Adomites and Frank Boslett were the original organizers.

Tony Cavender organized the first regional meeting held in Houston on May 18, 1985, with twenty people in attendance. Claudia Perry also played a vital role in the formation of the chap-

ter which meets every January at the Houston Baseball Writers' dinner. Society members with ties to the Houston ballclub include Astros president Tal Smith, manager Larry Dierker, and pitching coach Vern Ruhle.

In March of 1988, Tony Darkin, Mark Kanter, and Walt Patterson met in a pub in London, England, for the first known meeting held outside of North America. Kanter, planning his United Kingdom trip, had called ahead looking for Society members to meet. He did the same thing on a trip to Australia in March 1990, when he visited the home of Ian McNeilly. The first official meeting in the United Kingdom, however, should be credited to the January 9, 1993, meeting of the Bobby Thomson Chapter in London. Thirty attended.

The first Phoenix, Arizona, Flame Delhi Chapter regional meeting was held December 3, 1988. The Delhi chapter played host to the 1999 National Convention.

The initial meeting of the Larry Gardner-Vermont Chapter, organized by Tom Simon, was held in October, 1993, when eight members met at the home of Wayne Turiansky to watch the first game of the 1993 World Series. This chapter's group project, *The Green Mountain Boys of Summer*, a book containing biographies of all of the Vermont-born major leaguers, was published in 2000.

Although this writer was unable to pin down the date and location of the initial Society meeting held in Japan, a second meeting on January 16 and 17, 1994, drew thirteen of the twenty-two Japanese members.

On December 3, 1994, Chris Franco organized the initial meeting of the New Brunswick, New Jersey, regional, the Goose Goslin chapter.

The initial meeting of the Jesse Burkett chapter was held at Assumption College in Worcester, Massachusetts, on September 29, 1996, with former Red Sox manager Joe Morgan the guest speaker. Ron Marshall, Worcester *Telegram* sportswriter Bill Ballou, and Assumption College Sports Information Director Steve Morris were the chapter organizers.

Organized by Rich Newhouse in order to serve Society members who did not wish to make the commute to either Detroit or Chicago, the western Michigan chapter met first in June, 1996, in Wyoming, Michigan. Currently the chapter encompasses a region south to Benton Harbor, Kalamazoo-Battle Creek, west to Lake Michigan, north to Ludington, and east as far as East Lansing. Marc Okkonen suggested the chapter be named after Wally Pipp.

The initial meeting of the Central Florida chapter, currently called the (Elden) Auker-(Andy) Seminick Chapter, was held in November, 1997. Jim Riley was the chapter organizer. In the Spring of 1998 the chapter hosted the Ted Williams-Joe Jackson Symposium, a super-regional that attracted members from England, New England and California.

The Southern Florida chapter first met in January 1998, with Society member and Florida Marlins General Manager Dave Dombrowski the guest speaker.

Cappy Gagnon organized the initial meeting of the Lou Criger Chapter, which was held in South Bend, Indiana, in April 1998.

Members of the Bobby Thomson (United Kingdom) Chapter of SABR are pictured at a chapter event. Chapter officers in the front row (left to right) are Patrick Morley, Norman Macht, Mike Ross, and Andy Parkes.

THE GROWTH OF THE SOCIETY

By the fall of 1974 the membership of the Society had risen from the original 16 members to 230. It climbed slowly but steadily through the '70s, reaching 300 in October 1975, 350 at Society's fifth birthday in August 1976, 410 in December 1976, and 634 in July 1978, before finally topping 1,000 in September 1979. By 1978 the Society had members in all mainland states except South Carolina, New Mexico, South Dakota, Wyoming, Idaho, and Montana.

On the Society's tenth anniversary in 1981 there were 1,250 members. Shortly thereafter, between 1982 and 1985, the membership skyrocketed, going from 2,800 in January 1983 to 4,100 by August of the same year. Five thousand was reached in October 1984 with 1,300 new members in 1984 alone. After peaking in 1987 with 6,393 members, the rank and file fell into the mid to high 5,000 range until climbing back over 6,000 where it has remained. On the Society's twenty-eighth anniversary on August 10, 1999, the membership was 6,600.

The December, 1988, *SABR Bulletin* broke down the 6,030 members by age. There were 77 members under 21; 682 from age 21-30; 2,111 from 31-40; 1,449 from 41-50; 734 from 51-60; 404 from 61-70; 128 from 71-80 and 19 aged 81-90. Ages of the remaining members was unkown.

The Society has been represented by members all over the world. Over the years members have resided in Australia, Belgium, Canada, China, Cuba, the Dominican Republic, Ecuador, France, French Polynesia, Germany, Hong Kong, Israel, Italy, Japan, Korea, Mexico, The Netherlands, Nicaragua, Panama, the Philippines, Poland, Scotland, Sweden, Switzerland, United Kingdom, Venezuela, Yugoslavia, and Zambia. Long-time member Dallas Adams claims the unique status of being the first member in both Switzerland and Australia. Two noted early members, Harold Seymour and Vern Luse, moved to Ireland and Yugoslavia, respectively, in the mid-1970s, no doubt bragging about the Society wherever they went. Later in 1975 the Society received a request from the Yugoslavian Embassy in Washington for assistance in locating a picture of George "Catfish" Metkovich. Lord knows what type of research Luse was conducting.

By early 1984 the Society membership included many former big league and Negro Leagues players, and other various members who were associated with the game in some official capacity. Some of those included Elden Auker, Red Borom, Gene Benson, Buddy Burbage, Bill Cash, Zip Collins, Joe Dwyer, Jim Fanning, Tom Ferrick, Joe Garagiola, Hank Greenberg, Frank Hiller, Waite Hoyt, Roy Hughes, Clarence Israel, Spook Jacobs, Ken Keltner, Larry Kimbrough, Ralph Kiner, Tony Kubek, Bert Kuczynski, Tony Lupien, Tim McCarver, Jack McKeon, Jeep McLain, Tim McNamara, Charlie Metro, Sy Morton, Joe Munson, Joe Orengo, Andy Pafko, Brooks Robinson, Oscar Roettger, Bill Sayles, Paul Schramka, Bob Scheffing, Andy Seminick, Roy Sievers, Joe Stanka, Bill Starr, Bill Steinecke, Chuck Stevens, Ed Walczak, and Ted Williams.

In August 1985 Terry Kennedy and Kurt Bevacqua became the first active major leaguers to join the Society.

Major league executives also joined the rolls of the society. Members included San Diego Padres president Ballard Smith, baseball commissioners Peter Ueberroth and Bud Selig, Detroit Tigers president Jim Campbell, Los Angeles Dodgers president Peter O'Malley, Calvin Griffith of the Minnesota Twins, Padres general manager Jack McKeon, and various other executives such as Roland Hemond, Harry Dalton, Jim Fanning, Tony Siegle, Lou Gorman, Elten Schiller, and Arthur Richman.

PUBLIC RELATIONS

Today the Society is a well-known presence in the baseball world, but early efforts to build the membership relied on a much-needed public relations plan. Stan Grosshandler and Jerry Gregory were in charge of early efforts.

Bill Madden wrote an article on the Society that appeared in the March 5, 1974, issue of *The Sporting News*. Additional articles soon appeared in the New York *Post* of July 30, and in the Wall Street *Journal* on September 13, 1974.

The Sporting News issue of April 18, 1981, ran a story on historical research into the 1910 American League batting race between Ty Cobb and Nap Lajoie. The Society and members Leonard Gettleson, Pete Palmer, Cliff Kachline, and Alex Haas were all mentioned.

The New York *Times* on February 15 and March 1, 1981, ran stories written by Society members; Richard Goldstein discussed the 1980 *Baseball Research Journal* in the February issue and John Holway discussed Happy Chandler, the color line, and the integration efforts of 1946-47 in March.

John Thorn wrote an article on the Society that appeared in *The Sporting News* the week after the 1981 convention. All of these efforts resulted in inquiries about the Society and a surge in membership growth.

In 1978 Bill James published the first *Baseball Abstract*. The sixty-eight page publication was crude by today's standards. It was offered for $4 in the June 1978 *SABR Bulletin*. Statistical analysis and sabermetrics had reached the lift-off stage.

In the fourth *Baseball Abstract*, James writes, "A year ago I wrote in this letter that what I do does not have a name and cannot be explained in a sentence or two. Well, now, I have given it a name: Sabermetrics, the first part to honor the acronym of the Society for American Baseball Research, the second part to indicate measurement. Sabermetrics is the mathematical and statistical analysis of baseball records."

ABC News was at the 1983 National Convention and Sam Donaldson did a five-minute segment about the Society on the Sunday Evening News.

The September 5, 1983, issue of *Time* magazine ran a two-page article on the new breed of baseball statisticians and mentioned Pete Palmer, Bill James, Craig Wright, and Dick Cramer.

Clearly, early public relations efforts by the Society were successful. Today the Society receives plenty of press coverage. *USA Today Baseball Weekly* covers each National Convention and references to Society members can be found in many weekly editions.

OTHER COMMITTEES

The February 1975 *SABR Bulletin* reported that Pete Palmer had a one-page analytical chart showing pitch-by-pitch results of the 1974 World Series. The announcement warned that "it may be a little complicated for the layman." This was evidently a sign of things to come, for in April 1975 the Executive Board approved two new committees. They were Statistical Analysis and Baseball Records.

Dick Cramer had begun formulating plans for the Statistical Analysis Committee the previous summer. Cramer and Pete Palmer were named co-chairman of the committee with Bill James the third and only other member. In addition to Cramer and Palmer, Eddie Epstein, Don Coffin, Rob Wood, and current co-chairs Clem Comley and Neal Traven have headed the committee over the years. Initial committee goals included coordinating statistical projects to facilitate checking of information and prevent unnecessary duplication of work. The committee newsletter, *By the Numbers*, is a forum for analysts to exchange and discuss the statistics of baseball.

Baseball statistics have come a long way from the days of Ernie Lanigan. Thorn and Palmer's *The Hidden Game of Baseball*, and James' *Baseball Abstracts* changed the way baseball statistics have traditionally been viewed.

The Records Committee job was to establish an accurate set of records for organized baseball with the focus being on information not previously collected. Bob McConnell resigned his chair seat of the Publications Committee to accept the leadership of this new committee. He has since been succeeded in order by Mil Chipp, Tom Jozwik, Ev Cope, Neil Munro, John Swartz, and Lyle Spatz.

The Records Committee has produced a Society publication, *Baseball Records Update 1993*, edited by Spatz, which documented changes to the playing records of such players as Cy Young, Walter Johnson, Tris Speaker, Eddie Collins, Babe Ruth, Lou Gehrig and Hugh Duffy.

Late in 1978 the Society's committee system was restructured. The Auditing and Nominating Committees, which had been ad hoc since their creation in 1975, were formalized. The Editorial Board took the place of the Publications Committee, and an Ethics Committee and Public Relations Committee were added.

The 1997-1998 *Membership Directory* listed the current non-research committees as (1) Nominating, (2) Auditing, (3) Tellers, (4) Regional development, and (5) Convention.

The October 1980 *SABR Bulletin* listed the then existing nine Society committees: Auditing, Baseball Records, Biographical Research, Editorial, Minor Leagues, Negro Leagues, Nominating, Public Relations, and Statistical Analysis. Seventy-nine Society members were listed as committee members.

The Ballparks Committee was formed in 1982 with Bob Bluthardt the original chairman, a seat he still holds today. Phil Lowry was also

Frank Phelps (holding trophy) was a long-time chairman of the SABR Bibliography Committee and recipient of the Bob Davids Award in 1991. Presenting the award is Bob McConnell (at podium), chairman of the SABR Minor League Committee.

John Pardon, Lloyd Johnson, Morris Eckhouse, and Maria Eckhouse staff the SABR table in Cooperstown, NY on National Baseball Hall of Fame induction weekend in 1993. Johnson was SABR's executive director from 1985-1989 and SABR president from 1991-1993.

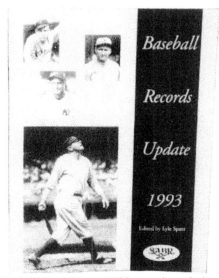

Baseball Records Update 1993 features the work of several members of the SABR Baseball Records Committee, chaired by Lyle Spatz, editor of the publication.

involved with the formation of the committee, whose mission is to "research and collect the history of past and present major, minor and Negro leagues parks." A sub-committee collects photographs of ballparks. Another committee goal is to erect plaques or memorials on the site of abandoned or demolished ballparks. Lowry's *Green Cathedrals*, mentioned earlier in the publications section of this text, was a committee project that the Society published in 1985. It was subsequently re-issued in 1993 by Addison-Wesley.

The Nineteenth Century Committee was suggested by John Thorn and Mark Rucker in the fall of 1982. Between thirty and forty members had joined by February 1983, exceeding the expectations of the organizers. In addition to Thorn and Rucker, the committee has been chaired by Bob Tiemann, Fred Ivor-Campbell, and John Husman. In addition to the two books already discussed, *Nineteenth Century Stars*, and *Baseball's First Stars*, the major accomplishment of the committee has been the Na-

tional Association Box Score Project. Based on the Michael Stagno collection of National Association boxscores, which the Society bought for $3,000, the project, thanks mostly to the efforts of Bob Tiemann and Bob Richardson, made additions and tabulations of Stagno's initial research, presenting us with a clearer statistical picture of the National Association.

The Computerization Committee was formed in 1984 to facilitate the sharing of resources and data sets related to members' baseball research. Tony Formo and Gary Skoog were co-chairs. The committee was active in the data input for the Tattersall-McConnell Home Run Log project.

The Bibliography Committee was established in 1984 to locate, identify, evaluate, classify, and describe the literature of baseball. Frank Phelps was the original chair, a position he held until stepping down in 1995. Andy McCue, who had become co-chair in 1990, assumed the full chair at that time. The committee project, suggested in 1990 by Ted Hathaway, is the *Researching Baseball Index* (RBI), a complete log (currently over 100,000 entries) of baseball literature. The committee produced the first *Current Baseball Publications*, by Joe Lawler in 1985. Published quarterly by the committee, this is a list of all baseball books published. The committee has also published *The Index to The Sporting News Registers, 1940-1995*, edited by Frank Phelps.

The Collegiate Committee was formed in 1985 to "study the relationship between college and professional baseball." Chairmen have been Al Del Rossi, Dave Anderson, John Mocek, and Cappy Gagnon. SABR president Rich Topp dissolved it when it became inactive in 1990-1992. Back in business, the committee's goal is an all-time register of major league players, umpires and executives listed by colleges attended and degrees obtained.

The Oral History Project was announced late in 1985. This would eventually turn into the Oral History Committee which was formed "to accurately record and store remembrances of baseball's past." The committee would interview subjects and then create a library of audio and video tapes. Committee chairmen have included Norman Macht and Rick Bradley.

In March 1988, the formation of two new committees was announced. Peter Bjarkman, a Ph.D. in Spanish linguistics, would chair the Latin America Committee, which would cover Cuba, the Dominican Republic, Mexico, Panama, and Venezuela. Eduardo Valero followed Bjarkman as chair.

Larry Gerlach, followed by present co-chairs Phyllis Otto and Dennis Bingham, would lead the Umpires and Rules Committee, to "study the impact of both on the development of baseball."

The Women in Baseball committee was formed in February, 1990, to study the role of women in various aspects of professional baseball. Sharon Roepke was named chair. She was succeeded by John Kovach in June of 1992. Leslie Heaphy currently holds the chair position.

The Baseball in UK/Europe Committee was formed in 1994 to "study baseball's rich but little known history in Britain and Europe." Patrick

Carroll was the first chairperson, and has been succeeded by James Combs.

The Scouts Committee was formed in 1994 to document the achievements and record the history behind scouting. The "Tom Greenwade Award" is presented at the National Convention each year to the committee member who submits the most "who signed whos" in the previous year. Jim Kreuz is the chairman.

The Executive Board meeting in Kansas City in the fall of 1994 selected Doug Pappas as the chairman of the Business of Baseball Committee. The role of the committee was to "study all aspects of baseball administration and off the field activity including economic, organizational, labor and legal issues."

Tom Shieber was named chair of the Baseball Pictorial History Committee which was formed in 1994 to "promote research into baseball's rich history as reflected through drawings, illustrations, photographs, artwork, motion pictures, videos, and in general, any form of visual representation."

In 1997 the Internet Committee formed. The September 1995 *SABR Bulletin* first mentions SABR-L, the Society's electronic listserver. Only Society members may subscribe. It is a daily hodgepodge of just about any baseball subject imaginable. It was initially moderated by Seamus Kearney who relinquished that role to F. X. Flinn in 1998. Ted Turocy took over in 1999.

The Society's newest committee, Baseball Songs and Poems, was formed in 1997 to promote research into the rich history of music and poetry related to baseball. Jeff Campbell is the chairman. Committee goals include (1) a complete index of songs related to baseball, (2) compiling a list of past and present players who were/are known for their musical pursuits, and (3) a complete index of poetry related to baseball.

EXECUTIVE DIRECTOR

On August 1, 1975, the mailing address of the Society became P.O. Box 323, Cooperstown, New York. Cliff Kachline was handling the administrative end of things with the assistance of his wife Evelyn, probably the Society's most unsung hero of its early days.

The Society, especially in the early years, has always been intertwined with the Hall of Fame. Cliff, after a twenty-year career at *The Sporting News*, had followed Ernie Lanigan and Lee Allen as Hall of Fame Historian, a position he had taken over soon after Allen's death in 1969. Society member Tom Heitz was named to the newly combined position of Librarian and Research Director in 1982. Lloyd Johnson became Senior Research Associate that year and held that post until 1985 when he became the Society's second Executive Director. Society member Bill Deane assumed Johnson's Senior Research Associate position from 1986 to 1994.

The Executive Board met in Philadelphia on January 8, 1983, to discuss the proposed Executive Director position. Cliff Kachline formally became Executive Director after a vote of the National Convention in June.

Kachline resigned as Executive Director on November 1, 1985. The Executive Board of-

SABR executive director Morris Eckhouse in SABR's first office at the Colonial Arcade in downtown Cleveland, OH. Eckhouse became SABR's executive director in 1990.

The historic Caxton Building in downtown Cleveland, OH became home of SABR's administrative office in 1993.

Seven recipients of the Bob Davids Award, SABR's highest honor, pose with the award's namesake: Cliff Kachline, Bob Davids, Ray Nemec, John Pardon, Bill Carle, Len Levin, Joe Simenic, Bob McConnell (left to right). Kachline, Davids, Nemec, Pardon, Simenic and McConnell were founding members. Kachline became SABR's first executive director after serving on SABR's Executive Board from 1974 to 1982 as director and president.

SABR President Richard Topp (left) presents the John W. Cox award to Bob Buege at the 1990 SABR National Convention in Cleveland, OH. The award, now The Baseball Weekly Award and sponsored by USA Today Baseball Weekly, *honors the best research presentation made at the annual SABR convention.*

SABR President Larry Gerlach (left) presents The Seymour Medal for 1996 to Arthur Hittner at the 1997 SABR National Convention in Louisville, KY. The Seymour Medal is SABR's award for the best book of baseball history or biography published the previous year.

fered the job to Harrington E. "Kit" Crissey, one of two finalists from a field of thirty-one Society applicants. Crissey had second thoughts and declined the job. Lloyd Johnson, who had followed Cliff at the Hall of Fame, became Executive Director on November 15, 1985. He moved to Kansas City from Cooperstown in November, 1986. The administrative address moved with him to KC.

The Society underwent its greatest political crisis at the 1989 National Convention in Albany. As Eliot Asinof, author of *Eight Men Out*, gave a talk on the Chicago Black Sox, Society presidential hopeful John Holway, a member since 1972, handed out "8 Men Out" buttons in the lobby. The eight men Holway was referring to were not baseball players, but the Society's Executive Board. At issue was the Executive Board's ousting of Johnson as SABR's Executive Director. A motion to unseat the entire Board failed to achieve a majority vote. After a wild business meeting Holway withdrew as a candidate and Rich Topp, nominated from the floor, beat out then current vice-president Luke Salisbury in a close vote for president.

The Executive Board made the following statement regarding its reasons for Johnson's dismissal.

"The growth of SABR requires that its operations become more professional and businesslike. Business meetings at the 1986 and 1987 convention were chaotic. A parliamentarian was retained for the 1988 meeting at the cost of $1,186. The Board learned of plans for members to disrupt the January and April 1989 Board meetings so a parliamentarian was hired for those meetings also.

"The audit chairman had noted excessive telephone reimbursements to the President. It turned out that these were routine but no written policy existed.

"In January 1988, the Board saw problems in operations of the SABR office. The Board did not renew the former Executive Director's contract. In January of 1988, non-Board members became involved and the Board retained legal counsel."

In March 1989 a call for applicants was made to the membership for the Executive Director position. One-hundred and six resumes were received.

After a two-month search by the Board of Directors, Norbert Kraich was hired effective May 1, 1989. Kraich lived in Garrett Park, Maryland. He had twenty years experience in public relations and marketing. The Society's address moved to Garrett Park. Society President Gene Sunnen said that Kraich "has the ideal qualifications we are looking for to help lead SABR into the 1990s." Kraich, however, tendered his resignation a few months later, effective March 21, 1990.

Morris Eckhouse was named as interim Executive Director, and the Society's mailing address changed yet again, this time to Cleveland, where it has remained.

The crisis of 1989-90 was costly in financial as well as personal terms. At the Executive Board meeting in October, 1990, Society treasurer Bob Ruland stated that the Society had seen its monetary assets reduced from

$167,000 to $91,000 during the period of March 31, 1989 to August 31, 1990. "Twenty-five thousand dollars," he continued, "was attributable to the series of Executive Director transactions."

Eckhouse was given a two-year contract as Executive Director at the Executive Board meeting in April of 1990. John Zajc was named as administrative assistant in the SABR office in June of the same year. The Executive Board voted in March, 1993, to establish permanent Society administrative offices in Cleveland. In December of that year the offices were relocated from Cleveland's Colonial Arcade Building to an office suite at the Caxton Building.

SABR AWARDS

The Bob Davids Award was established by the Board of Directors in 1985. It is given annually at the National Convention to the member "whose contributions to SABR and baseball reflect the ingenuity, integrity, and self-sacrifice of the founder and past-president of SABR, L. Robert 'Bob' Davids."

The initial 1985 winner was Bob McConnell. He has been followed by Joe Simenic (1986), Bob Hoie (1987), Vern Luse (1988), Pete Palmer (1989), John Holway (1990), Frank Phelps (1991), Bob Tiemann (1992), Bill Carle (1993), A. D. Suehsdorf (1994), Cliff Kachline (1995), Jack Kavanagh (1996), Len Levin (1997), John Pardon (1998), and David Vincent (1999).

The initial Macmillan-SABR Awards were presented at the 1988 National Convention. The award is "given to three individuals or groups of individuals whose research projects have greatly expanded our knowledge of baseball." The first winners were Rich Topp and Bob Tiemann for research regarding managerial changes; Stew Thornley for his book, *On to Nicollet*; and Melvin Adelman for *1820-1870 New York City Baseball*. Subsequent winners were: (1989) Bill Deane for *Award Voting*, Paul Dickson for the *Dickson Baseball Dictionary*, and Marc Okkonen for *The Federal League of 1914-1915: Baseball's Third Major League*; (1990) Jim Miller for *The Baseball Business*, Harold Seymour for *Baseball: The People's Game*, Dick Clark, John Holway, and Jim Riley for *Negro League Statistics*; (1991) Bruce Kuklick for *To Every Thing a Season*, Andy McCue for *Baseball By the Books*, and Rob Ruck for *The Tropic of Baseball*; (1992) Bob Gregory for *Diz: The Story of Dizzy Dean and Baseball During the Great Depression*, Herm Krabbenhoft for lead-off batters grand slam research in the *Baseball Quarterly Review*, and, Mark Stang and Linda Harkness for *Rosters*; (1993) Phil Dixon for *The Negro Baseball Leagues: A Photographic History*, Barbara Gregorich for *Women at Play: The Story of Women in Baseball*, and Bill Ryczek for *Blackguards and Red Stockings: A History of Baseball's National Association*; (1994) Mike Gershman for *Diamonds; The Evolution of the Ballpark*, Jim Riley for *The Biographical Encyclopedia of the Negro Baseball Leagues*, and Lloyd Johnson and Miles Wolff for *The Encyclopedia of Minor League Baseball*; (1995) Peter Bjarkman for *Baseball With a Latin Beat:*

Andy McCue (at podium) receives one of the Macmillan-SABR Baseball Research Awards for 1990. McCue was honored for the research published in his Baseball by the Books, *at the 1991 SABR National Convention in New York City.*

A History of the Latin American Game, Bob Burk for *Never Just a Game: Players, Owners and American Baseball to 1920*, and Jack Kavanagh for *Walter Johnson: A Life*; (1996) Jim Smith and Herm Krabbenhoft for *The Baseball Quarterly Review*'s Triple Play Project, Hank Thomas and Chuck Carey for *The California Comet*, and Michael O'Grady for *From Covehead to the Polo Grounds: The Story of Henry Havelock Oxley, Major Leaguer*; (1997) Adrian Burgos Jr. for *Jugando en el Norte, Caribbean Players in the Negro Leagues, 1910-1950*, Jim Price for *A Half Century of Pain*, and Joe Wayman for *Grandstand Baseball Annual Pitching Won-Lost Records, 1890-1899*; (1998) Clifford Blau for *The History of Major League Tie Games*, John McReynolds for *Nate Moreland, Mystery to Historians*, and Gary Smith for *Damned Yankees*; David M. Jordan, Larry Gerlach and John Rossi, for *A Baseball Myth Exploded*, Jim McConnell for *Baseball's Dark Past*, and Andrew O'Toole, for *Clemente's First Spring*, published in *Elysian Fields Quarterly*, Summer 1998.

The Sporting News–SABR Baseball Research Award is designed to honor projects that do not fit the criteria for The Seymour Medal or the Macmillan–SABR Baseball Research Award. *The Sporting News* sponsors the award, which carries a $200 cash award.

The award in 1996, went to George Hilton for *The Annotated Baseball Stories of Ring W. Lardner, 1914-1919*; Dan Gutman for *Banana Bats and Ding Dong Balls: A Century of Baseball Inventions*; and John Benson and Tony Blengino for *Baseball's Top 100: The Best Individual Seasons of All-Time*. In 1997 the award went to Dan Gutman for *The Way Baseball Works*; Richard Orodenker for *Dictionary of Literary Biography: Twentieth Century Sportswriters*; and Fred Ivor-Campbell, Bob Tiemann, and Mark Rucker for *Baseball's First Stars*. Winners in 1998 were Joe Dittmar for *Baseball Record Registry: The Best and Worst Single-Day Performances and the Stories Behind Them*; Jonathan Fraser Light for *The Cultural Encyclopedia of Baseball*; and David Nemec for *The Great Encyclopedia of 19th Century*

Len Levin receives the Bob Davids Award for 1997. Len was honored at the 1997 SABR National Convention in Louisville, KY.

Major League Baseball. In 1999 the prize was awarded Joseph Dorinson and Joram Warmund, editors, for the research done to produce the papers that were published in *Jackie Robinson: Race, Sports, and the American Dream*, the proceedings of the Jackie Robinson Conference at Long Island University; Chris Holaday for the research done to produce his book, *Professional Baseball in North Carolina: An Illustrated City-by-City History, 1901-1996*; and Marshall D. Wright for the research done to produce his book, *The International League: Year-by-Year Statistics, 1884-1953*.

The initial Cox Award, named in honor of Society member John W. Cox, who had passed away in April 1989, was made at the 1990 National Convention. The award, accompanied by a $250 honorarium, is made to the individual making the best research presentation at that year's convention. The sponsorship of the award was taken over by *USA Today Baseball Weekly* and the name was changed in 1993, to The *Baseball Weekly* Award.

The initial winner was Bob Buege for "The Milwaukee Braves: A Baseball Eulogy." He was followed in 1991 by William Chambers for "Larry Doyle's Field of Dreams," in 1992 by Jack Carlson for "Baseball Patents," in 1993 by Barry Mednick for "The Giants Stay Put (for now)," in 1994 by Tom Shieber for "The Evolution of the Pitcher's Mound," in 1995 by Dennis and Jean DeValeria for "Honus Wagner," in 1996 by John Pastier for "A Dozen New Ballparks, 1989-2000," in 1997 by Norman Macht for "Baseball's Traditional Values: What Are They?," in 1998 by Stew Thornley for "The Polo Grounds-A Tale of Four Stadiums," and in 1999 by Jean Ardell for "Left-hander Ila Borders: Crossing Baseball's Gender Line from Little League to the Northern League."

The Seymour Medal in honor of Dorothy Z. and Dr. Harold Seymour, proposed to the Board of Directors by then Hall of Fame librarian Tom Heitz, was first presented in 1996 to David Zang for *Fleet Walker's Divided Heart* (published in 1995), and subsequently to Arthur Hittner for *Honus Wagner, The Life of Baseball's Flying Dutchman* (1997), Patrick Harrigan for *The Detroit Tigers: Club and Community, 1945-1996* (1998), and Bruce Markusen for *Baseball's Last Dynasty, Charlie Finley's Oakland A's* (1999).

While not Society awards, it should be noted that long-time Society member Jack Lang, then Secretary-Treasurer of the Baseball Writers of America Association, was named recipient of the J. G. Taylor Spink Award in January of 1987. Previous members of the Society who had also won that honor included Fred Lieb in 1972, Bob Broeg in 1979, Joe Reichler and Milton Richman in 1980, and Allen Lewis in 1981.

CONCLUSION

SABR's original mission is baseball research, and the dissemination of that research through our publications. As we continue to grow, that will remain our mission.

Bibliography

1. *The SABR Bulletin*. Volumes 1-29.
2. *The SABR Membership Directory*. All 23 editions from 1971 through 1999-2000.
3. *The Bill James Historical Baseball Abstract*. Villard Books. New York. 1986.
4. *The 1980 Baseball Abstract*. Bill James. Privately published.
5. Early SABR correspondence from the files of original SABR member Thomas Shea.
6. Multiple electronic, telephone and personal interviews from various SABR members; Marshall Adesman, Mark Alvarez, Paul Andresen, Dick Beverage, Bob Boynton, Jeff Campbell, Jon and Marge Daniels, Bill Deane, Morris Eckhouse, Scott Flatow, Cappy Gagnon, Larry Gerlach, Bill Gilbert, Ernest Green, Stuart Hodesh, Fred Ivor-Campbell, Mark Kanter, Jack Kavanagh, Len Levin, Ed Luteran, Ron Marshall, Bob McConnell, Andy McCue, Barry Mednick, Pete Morris, Steve Nadel, Rich Newhouse, John Pastier, Dennis Repp, Jim Riley, Lyle Spatz, John Thorn, Rich Topp, Neal Traven, John Zajc and Tom Zocco.

"Baseball on Ice." From left: David Durgey, David Pietrusza, Joe Vellano, John Thorn and Jim McKenna.

One of the two teams participating in the "Baseball on Ice."

Frank Phelps, 1991 BDA Winner.

Seymour Medal Winner, Bruce Markusen.

SPECIAL STORIES

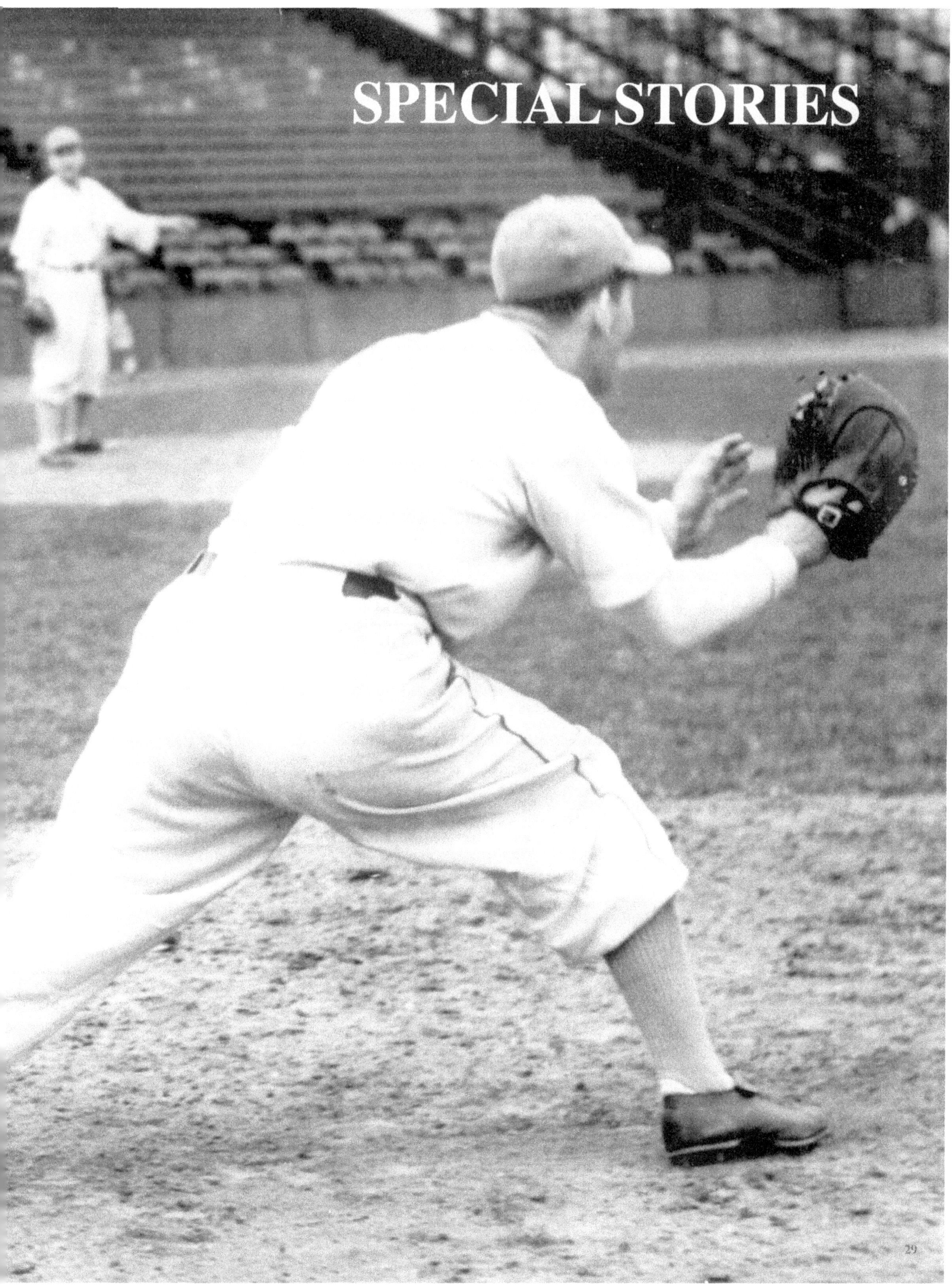

I Love The Red Sox, But Why Won't They Lose?

by Allan Wood

Snapping pencils, screaming obscenities and throwing my scorecard across the room are just a few of the reactions I've had while rooting for the Boston Red Sox. In the 20 years I've followed the team, I've seen things that defy rational analysis and had me believing in mysterious curses. My temper tantrums usually come after a bonehead play or the Sox's untimely collapse. But the 1995 season has added a new twist: I'm tearing my hair out because they're winning.

I'm writing a book about the 1918 Red Sox, the last Boston team to win the World Series. In my research, I've interviewed descendants of the 1918 players, a man who sold peanuts at Fenway Park that summer and another guy who went ice-fishing with a 22-year-old Babe Ruth. As long as the Red Sox's World Series drought continues, 1918 will retain its aura and mystery; baseball fans will be curious about the story of that distant season. If Boston wins the Series, I don't think any Red Sox fan will give a damn about 1918. I don't mean to sound selfish, but they've waited this long - can't the Red Sox wait a few more years? Is my team once again in the process of breaking my heart by winning?

We all know that their legacy of losing is what makes the Red Sox special. They are baseball's version of Ralph Kramden; the team's inability to hit the high note is what endears them to us. We witness the team's inadequacies and imperfections, and we sympathize. We curse them, but because they're human, too, we love them.

I discovered the Red Sox in October 1975, while they were losing the World Series to Cincinnati. I was 12 years old and knew nothing about the team's history of heartbreak, so I dutifully affixed a "Wait 'Til Next Year" iron-on to my blue sweatshirt. The following year, I went to Fenway for the first time. My father and I rode five hours on a bus from Burlington, Vermont, watched the Sox lose, and rode the bus back home. I did that four more times before I saw Boston win.

Last week, I spoke to Ray, a fellow Red Sox fan back in Vermont, and he's giddy with pennant fever. A true Sox fan, he's pushed aside the horrors of the past and been drawn in. We can talk about the summer of 1978 like it was last week and neither of us will ever forget staring at the TV in numb disbelief as our dreams slipped through Bill Buckner's rickety legs.

Ten weeks later, I moved to New York City. Now, living in enemy territory, my bond to the Red Sox has grown stronger. For eight years the red "B" on my cap has ignited shouts of "Bucky Dent," "Boston Sucks" and worse at Yankee Stadium. But this summer, the atmosphere in the Bronx is eerily different. I could hardly believe it when, at a recent game, not one derogatory remark was hurled my way.

This should be the time to gloat. If I wasn't writing this book, I'd be dancing around my apartment with the sports page, even though Laura, my partner, is a Yankee fan and we have

a house rule about that sort of thing. Instead, every morning I check the standings and wince. I tried to explain my predicament to Ray, but I don't think he understood. He's already talking about playoff pitching match-ups, while I find it impossible to savor any Boston victory. The Sox just won 11 straight games and all I'm getting is a knot in my stomach

I remind myself that the new wild card round of playoffs presents an added obstacle to winning the pennant. I'm even half-hoping another strike will derail the pennant race. But seriously, who really believes Cleveland isn't going to steamroll to the pennant? And if the Red Sox pull a major upset, does anyone think they can seriously contend against Atlanta or Cincinnati? In my new nightmare, it's October and I'm in front of my TV, actively rooting against the team I have lived and died with for 20 years.

All Red Sox fans are pessimists. We know that behind every silver lining, there lurks a dark cloud. Seventy-six years of history assures me the Sox will fall apart sooner or later. But what if...? Hopefully, in two months, I'll be enjoying the World Series, secure in the knowledge that the Red Sox players are home watching, too. But you never know. Baseball is a funny game.

An Ironic Oversight At SABR 19th Century Ball Game

by Rich Tourangeau 1981

Because the 1984 SABR Convention was in Providence, Rhode Island, it was perfect for a relatively new member from Boston to attend. I could drive to and from the Brown University site quite easily. It was at later conventions that I learned how important the nighttime sit-around-and-talk baseball sessions were to enjoying the national gathering.

To celebrate the 100 years since the Providence Grays beat the New York Metropolitans, SABR folks planned a recreated 1884 game, complete with authentic woolly uniforms, to be played at McCoy Stadium (home of the AAA Pawtucket Red Sox) before a regularly scheduled International League game.

A call went out and eventually two teams worth of players signed up to relive the 19th Century Championship, first by paying $200 for the uniform. Players were told the 1884 rules and practiced some fundamentals of the era. No one knew how these re-enactors would play without gloves (sneakers allowed), heavy bats and sort of what passed for an 1884 ball.

Then Mother Nature postponed the historic game with a rainstorm. The one day delay meant that some players had already left for home but those remaining were to play a few innings between games of a doubleheader. The curious PawSox crowd was a good audience for 19th century ball with its "called pitches" and basepath shenanigans. There were crazy plays to be sure, involving belt-tugging, run downs and run ins, much to the delight of the onlookers.

On a bang-bang bunt play at first base I ran into New York Met Rev. Jim Smith III (who has a true ballplayer's heart), a collision which knocked us both sprawling. Years later we met again and became good friends and one night

Rich Tourangeau as one of the 1884 Providence Grays.

at dinner at my house he retold the story and wondered aloud who smacked into him that Sunday afternoon. I think I was out, but I had already scored a run from the leadoff position (I was portraying centerfielder Paul Hines). The Mets supposedly upset us Grays in the three-inning exhibition 4-3, but I've always disputed that belief.

Ironically, no one could ever correctly recount the wild scoring plays because with all the greatest SABR minds either in the stands and on the field, not one had thought to record a boxscore of the game. To a first time conventioneer this was an unforgettable oversight.

A Patriot

by W. Kirkland Symmes

I own a baseball signed by the 1928 New York Yankees team including five Hall of Famers. It is quite a gem.

SABR is a great organization. I am pleased that Ted Williams is a member. I was a Marine pilot during the same periods that Ted was in the Marines. When you think that he lost five years of baseball time in the prime of his life, it is fun to speculate how many career records he could hold today if he had not lost those five years. In spite of one or more Boston sports writers, those who knew him well in the Marines thought of him as a very generous guy if you wanted to talk baseball. He would share his very great knowledge of the game to any interested acquaintance. When we were going through Pre-Flight School, I was so tired at the end of the day that I could sleep on a concrete floor, but Williams played on the pre-flight team with the other pros. When he didn't hit the ball through a window of the field house 400 feet away, we would boo him. He gave more as far as I am concerned than most pro ball players during WWII, and then to have to come back in Korea seven years later makes him a patriot deserving of more recognition than I have heard given to him.

How To Meet Many Great SABR Members, And Research Your First Book At The Same Time, For A Very Few Dollars

by Dave Stevens

Five years ago I became frustrated by the lack of information about Hall of Famer pitcher/shortstop/league organizer/manager/attorney/all around troublemaker John Montgomery Ward, who battled to integrate major league baseball and founded the first union for athletes. A gentle, but definitive rejection of a short article about him aggravated me, when I finally realized I hadn't the skill to capture such a colossus in an article. Though I had never written anything but that oft-shortened article, I naively stumbled off to write the first biography of Ward.

In October 1998, that book is a reality, thanks to the aid of dozens of fellow SABR members in five countries and 29 states, who contributed research, encouraged me, challenged me. This great kindness was not due to my limited charm and nonexistent book advance, but due to their dedication to research, their love of our national game and their fellowship for other members.

For the sake of a Ward bio, SABRites risked blindness by wading through faint newspaper microfilm on decrepit microfilm readers in dusty libraries and historical societies. One member scoured a graveyard to find unmarked graves of Ward's relatives, while another poured through mis-filed records in a musty basement. Morris Eckhouse and John Zajc patiently answered my many stupid questions.

I had the opportunity to meet heroes of mine, such as David Voigt. SABR members commiserated with me, when my publisher asked me to cut the biography 200 pages, which left favorites of mine, such as Deacon White, as mere mentions. My editor, SABR member Dave Biesel, guided me through that agonizing learning process.

A highpoint was going to my first SABR national and eagerly peering at everyone's nametag to see what folks who helped me actually looked like. I got very little sleep that weekend and drove my long suffering wife even battier, by raving long-distance that:

A) I just met so and so!
B) Just found out such and such about Orator O'Rourke
C) Found out about just about anything I could remotely connect with 19th century baseball, which I have come to treasure!

Established authors, such as Mark Alvarez and Lee Lowenfish, who had planned to write bios of Ward, were generous in sharing their research. Isaac Newton wrote "if I have seen further ... it is by standing on the shoulders of giants such as yourselves." The 5'9" Ward was one of the original New York Giants, and I hope that I have done some credit to such a giant of a man.

Conducting Interviews With Major League Baseball Players Past And Present At Card Shows

by Robert Obojski

The so-called "Card Show" has become a nationwide phenomenon all across the United States within the past 12 to 15 years, and while there has been criticism directed at baseball players signing for money, the positives far outweigh the negatives.

Dick Williams, who may eventually gain Hall of Fame election in the manager's category, once told this writer: "Baseball figures don't really charge for autographs, for all intents and purposes they are getting appearance fees and are giving fans what they want."

From a personal standpoint, I've attended many scores of card shows during the past decade and a half, primarily for the purpose of interviewing baseball players, both active and retired, for a number of sports hobby periodicals. Over that long stretch, we gained the opportunity to interview literally many hundreds of ballplayers, with many of those interviews coming under ideal conditions when time was not really a constraint. By contrast when you're able to get an on-field interview before a game, the time is usually limited, with the writer being able to get in only a handful of questions.

Most of the card shows we attended for reporting purposes were staged by The National Pastime (headed by Steve Hisler) and by Future Sports and Memorabilia (headed by Ron Schwartz).

It Pays To Ask The Right Questions

The bane of any reporter is asking the "dumb question," and this is a pitfall we've tried to studiously avoid in our interviews with all those storied denizens of the diamonds.

In this respect we were fortunate in our first one-on-one interview with Joe DiMaggio at a National Pastime Card Show staged at New York City's Roosevelt Hotel in the late 1980s. The first question we posed at DiMaggio was: "Do you believe that Frank "Lefty" O'Doul should eventually gain Hall of Fame selection?"

After posing the question, we noted that O'Doul averaged a fat .349 in 11 major league seasons, though he played in only 970 games. (Still, Lefty banged out 1,140 base hits in that relatively brief tenure, and led the National League in batting average in two seasons: a rousing .398 while with the Philadelphia Phillies in 1929, and .368 while with the Brooklyn Dodgers in 1932. He also slammed out 254 base hits in 1929, a National League record tied by Bill Terry of the New York Giants in 1930).

DiMaggio just loved this question because he and Lefty O'Doul were friends from way back. They were both natives of the San Francisco area and over the years they owned popular restaurants in the Bay Area.

We told DiMaggio that O'Doul did a great deal for baseball, including promoting the professional game in Japan. But Joe D. clearly indicated that Hall of Fame selection is based on only one category. That is, you can't mix player achievements with achievements in the executive area.

From that point, I got along famously with the old "Yankee Clipper," who had a reputation of not being too fond of journalists. Altogether, I was able to gain three separate interviews with Joe D, and he could be a very charming guy when it came to serious talk about baseball. In fact, I gave him tear sheets of all my stories about him, and he appreciated that.

As for O'Doul, Lefty came over to the San Francisco Seals of the Pacific Coast League as player-manager in 1935, and his star centerfielder was Joe DiMaggio who averaged a fat .398 while rapping out 270 base hits in that long 172-game PCL season. However, he lost the league batting title to Oscar "Ox" Eckhardt, who averaged .399 in 172 games with 283 base hits.

Said DiMaggio of that historic batting race, as his voice had a tinge of bitterness: "Did you ever see Eckhardt at the bat? He was a banjo hitter who only homered twice....I had power stats, but Oscar had singles stats." Still DiMag admitted that batting titles are not determined by slugging averages.

During the past two or three years we attended more than a couple of dozen card shows staged by Ron Schwartz at his Future Sports and Memorabilia establishment located on Lexington Avenue in mid-town Manhattan. Here we've found that players and ex-players, who are ordinarily tough to interview because they don't like reporters, are as friendly as pussy cats.

Dave Kingman and Keith Hernandez are two cases in point. Kingman, one of the most fearsome homerun hitters of his era, rapped out 442 homers in his career (the most by a non-Hall of Famer-a handful of sluggers have more than 442, but they're not eligible for election to the HOF at this point), didn't show any of the petulance that marked his days as a player. Said Kingman in that regard: "I was misquoted a number of times by various reporters, and I mistakenly took it out on the press as a whole. That was a mistake, but all this happened many years ago, and I believe I've grown up."

Keith Hernandez always gave the impression of being aloof when he starred for St. Louis and the New York Mets, but from my own experience he was one of the easiest of all baseball personalities to interview. If injuries didn't cut his career a bit short, he would have been a solid bet to gain HOF election. He won the Gold Glove nine times, had a lifetime fielding average of .994 at first base, and amazingly had the most assists of any initial sacker in big league history, 1,682.

A big handsome guy, he lives in New York City and is quite a man about town. He's appeared in several movies shot in New York, and appears on television regularly, including *Regis and Kathy Lee, Seinfeld*, and on several Dick Cavett interviews.

One of our most memorable interviews at Future Sports was with Jim Bouton, a standout pitcher for the New York Yankees in the 1960s, who went 21-7 and 18-13 for the Bronx Bombers in their 1963-64 pennant-winning years.

After Bouton left the Yankees following the 1968 season, he pitched for Seattle and Houston in 1969-70, and then his big league career seemed to have ended as he "lost" his fastball.

Amazingly enough, Bouton resurfaced in the major leagues when he pitched a handful of games for the Atlanta Braves in 1978 as he was nearing 40 years of age. He went 1-3 in five starts in that season, and wound up his big league career with a 62-63 record, but his overall record comes to an even 64-64 when adding his 2-1 posting in the 1963-64 World Series while with the Yankees.

Our interview with Jim "Bulldog" Bouton centered around his first invitation to the Yankees "Old-Timers Day in July '98"

Jim's son, Michael Bouton, wrote an impassioned editorial for the Sunday *New York Times* of June 21, 1998, asking George Steinbrenner, Yankees owner, to forgive past differences and formally invite his father to the annual Old-Timers event.

As everyone knows, Jim Bouton annoyed the Yankees and a good part of the baseball establishment with the publication of his best-seller *Ball Four* in 1970. In that tome, Bouton related anecdotes that were not too complimentary of his teammates including the icon Mickey Mantle.

Michael Bouton writes: "It has been nearly 30 years since my father wrote *Ball Four* and for all the hullabaloo about this book, the major detractors have all written their own tell-all books, affirming the validity of what they once called lies."

Steinbrenner read the article, and, yes, Bouton was invited to the 1998 Yankees Old-Timers Day.

Michael Bouton also emphasized that on the occasion of its 100th anniversary in 1998, the New York Public Library listed *Ball Four* as one of the most 100 most important books of the century, and that is books in any category.

Jim Bouton told us that he's working on a special edition of *Ball Four* which will be released to coincide with the year 2000, the second millennium.

We thank Steve Hisler and Ron Schwartz for giving us the opportunity to interview so many baseball celebrities at close range and under ideal conditions.

SABR XXIII

by Joe Naiman

Holding the 1993 SABR convention wasn't even my idea.

In 1989 the decision to award the 1991 convention to New York rather than Los Angeles was by a one-vote margin. With the Los Angeles organization already prepared for a future convention, I thought that the next West Coast convention would be in Los Angeles.

When I attended the 1990 national convention a couple of SABR members asked about the possibility of a future convention in San Diego. I responded that I expected Los Angeles to have the next convention.

In early fall *The SABR Bulletin* put out a call for interest in hosting the 1993 convention. This time I was asked by a local member about hosting specifically the 1993 convention, since that year was the 75th anniversary of Ted Williams' birth, and thus I was compelled to respond to the national organization that there was interest. I left a phone message by their deadline for inquiries.

The national office requested that I submit a proposal. I queried the San Diego Convention and Visitors Bureau (CONVIS), which sent me a book with various lodging facilities.

The other region that had expressed interest was West Palm Beach. The anniversary of Williams, birth, augmented by the situation that 1993 would be the 25th year of the Major League Padres, had been my planned selling point. Now I had to be somewhat competitive. Fortunately CONVIS had average humidity statistics for the summer months as well as temperature and rainfall averages.

With little guidance on writing a SABR proposal, I divided it into seven chapters. The first was an introduction noting the anniversaries, adding the 50th anniversary of Al Olsen's phantom pitching appearance with Red Sox. The second chapter covered San Diego. The third chapter covered facilities, including 1991 rates for various hotels as well as transportation, library, sports facilities around San Diego. Chapter 4 emphasized attractions within a few hours drive of San Diego. Chapter 5 talked about the convention ideas. Chapter 6 described San Diego's SABR chapter and those who I had secured as willing to help out. Chapter 7 was an acknowledgment. Ironically the proposal for SABR XXIII ended up being 23 pages.

What wasn't in the proposal was the disarray of the chapter. Our vice-president had died in January 1989, and still-unresolved issues involving his research material kept us too busy to have a regional meeting that year. The next year we wanted to have a regional meeting in Yuma, where the Padres had spring training, but the baseball strike that year scuttled that one. Fortunately I knew many local members from previous meetings, all of whom volunteered to help with the convention and gave a couple of paragraphs about themselves for the proposal, and a couple of new members were brought to my attention from the Cleveland office.

The other element of chaos surrounding the proposal was my personal life. With a marriage as well as a move to a new house and a one-week honeymoon in New Orleans, I didn't even start writing the proposal until the week I had to mail it. And with my car out I had limited time to work on the word processor. Yet I made it, not making as many copies for the local membership as I had hoped, but meeting the requirement to send something with substance to the national organization.

The Yuma meeting finally took place at March 1991, and at that meeting Bob Boynton replaced me as secretary-treasurer while my office was changed to convention coordinator. When the national board gave San Diego the nod at the 1991 national convention, the work started.

After looking at facilities and cost we narrowed the decision to seven potential hotels, all in Mission Valley. Some outside interests, concerned about the high hotel cost in New York, wanted us to consider a return to college campuses, but having obtained a rate at a couple of hotels of under $70 for four people we were now competitive with college campuses. Requests for consideration of campuses persisted until it was pointed out that alcohol-on-campus regulations keep getting stricter and SABR might have a dry convention.

When the San Diego chapter (which became the Ted Williams chapter) had a regional meeting at the stadium in September, a decision was made to form a steering committee to make future decisions for the chapter. Even after the SABR convention was wrapped up, the steering committee structure still serves the chapter well.

Additional screening narrowed the selection process to four hotels, and in Spring 1992 the Hanalei was selected. Part of my mission at the 1992 convention in St. Louis was to promote the following year's convention at the Hanalei.

Of course, nothing goes as planned. Our daughter, who wasn't due until July 22, was born the morning of June 25, twelve hours before I was supposed to leave. But with a non-refundable airline ticket and nobody leaving the hospital until after my return because of a Cesarean, I ended up making the trip.

Two weeks after the convention the Hanalei, which Atlas Hotels had put up as collateral for another property, changed ownership. An emergency meeting was held, and we changed the convention site to the Town and Country. The new ownership of the Hanalei, as well as the eventual convention, proved this to be a good decision.

The agenda was put together and speaker panels were filled. We had a special reception Thursday night with Bobby Doerr, a banquet with Dick Williams as keynote speaker, and major league, minor league, 1984 Padres, and non-player panels. Those who went to the Padres game Friday night even got to see oldtimer's night, although the Padres had traded Gary Sheffield the day before and the home team that night wasn't too exciting against the Reds.

A lot went wrong. Fortunately not many people at the convention knew what how it was supposed to go and it was well received.

Maybe someday we'll do it again.

Essay

Many baseball fans will agree that Lawrence Ritter's *The Glory of Their Times* is the greatest baseball book ever written. *Glory* is the story of baseball as told by the men who played it, and magically captures "the heart and soul of a high-spirited country a long time ago." Through SABR and my research of the life of Rube Marquard, I have formed a friendship with Mr. Ritter. In the fall of 1997, while in New York purportedly to attend a legal seminar, I had the pleasure of again meeting him for an afternoon devoted to old-time baseball. I had an important question to ask him, in the form of a favor. Could he take me into northern Harlem, to view the site where the Polo Grounds had once stood? Of course he could, he said. All I had to do was meet him in the lobby of my hotel at one o'clock.

It took an hour or more for the bus to wind its way through mid-town Manhattan, then north up Broadway alongside Central Park. Mr. Ritter pointed out the many historic places along the way, all of which fascinated his wide-eyed guest. There was Carnegie Hall and Fordham University. There was the Lincoln Center, CUNY and Columbia University. As we waited on a bus stop bench in Spanish Harlem to make our connection, he pointed out, through the trees, the top of the Ansonia Hotel, now a condominium but once

Lawrence Ritter and Larry Mansch at Mickey Mantle's Restaurant.

Lawrence Ritter at Coogan's Bluff, site of the Polo Grounds.

the home of Babe Ruth and also the infamous spot where the Black Sox first conspired to throw the 1919 World Series. We exited the bus at 155th Street and walked a block or two to Coogan's Bluff, the site of so many great moments in baseball history.

We stood at the top of the rocky hill, now covered with mangled trees and shrubs, and looked down into the vast area where the old "bathtub-shaped ballpark" had stood for so many years. Although a set of high-rise apartment units now occupies the spot, it was not hard to visualize thousands of New York Giant fans gathered here, catching a glimpse of at least part of the action below, cheering on heroes of days gone by. Here John McGraw had ranted, raved, and bullied umpires and players alike. Here Christy Mathewson had reigned as undisputed idol to a generation. Here Fred Merkle forgot to touch second base in a key 1908 game against Chicago. Here the battery combination of Rube Marquard and Chief Myers teamed up for 19 straight wins in 1912, still the record. It was here at the Polo Grounds where Carl Hubbell struck out five sluggers in succession in the '34 All-Star game, and where Willie Mays made the most famous catch in baseball history 20 years later. It was here where Bobby Thomson blasted "the shot heard 'round the world." And from here one can look east across the Harlem River and see Yankee Stadium, the Polo Grounds (or what remains of it) is baseball history.

The time went quickly by, and as daylight faded we caught the bus back to mid-town. This time we took a different route along Riverside Drive. It was nearly six o'clock when we arrived at our next destination: Mickey Mantle's Restaurant. Here we enjoyed some refreshment before our dinner and talked baseball. Or rather, I asked Mr. Ritter questions and he answered.

He told me about his childhood, his education, his military service and his family. The idea for *Glory*, he said, came in the early 1960s after Ty Cobb died, nearly coinciding with the passing of his own father. He realized that the stories of these baseball pioneers needed to be collected, and preserved, because those stories had, in a very real way, helped to shape and

define our nation in the years just past the turn of the century. And so Ritter traveled the country in search of old-time ballplayers and their stories. He told me about meeting and interviewing Sam Crawford, Smoky Joe Wood, Fred Snodgrass, Harry Hooper, and so many more. We discussed the reception these men gave him, their willingness to open up their baseball lives with him, and the pure joy with which they shared their recollections.

"Of all these men," I asked him, "who was your favorite?"

"Larry," he replied. "let me ask you - of your four children, which is your favorite?"

I got the point, of course. Mr. Ritter loved them all, a fact clearly reflected in his famous book.

As we prepared to leave, I had one more favor to ask, this time of the waitress. I needed a picture to commemorate the evening. This was quickly done and my perfect baseball stroll down memory lane was complete.

My membership in SABR has provided many benefits in just a few short years. But none compares to the friendship I have made with that greatest of all baseball historians, the incomparable Lawrence Ritter.

Larry D. Mansch
December 1998

SABR and Nolan Ryan's 300th Career Victory

by Herm Krabbenhoft

SABR meetings are always a treat. Similarly, it's always a thrill to go to a baseball game. Fortunately, SABR National Conventions usually provide a convenient mechanism to attend baseball games. For example, attending SABR Nationals has allowed me to take in games at ballparks in cities I might not get to otherwise - the Metrodome (Minnesota), Busch Stadium (St. Louis), the Ballpark at Arlington (Texas), Kauffman Stadium (Kansas City), Three Rivers Stadium (Pittsburgh) and Cleveland Stadium. The 1990 National, held July 27-29 in Cleveland, was extra special because it afforded me a veritable baseball extravaganza.

Since my wife, Patti, has family in Milwaukee, we decided to combine my attendance at the SABR Convention with our vacation. So, Patti, I and our two daughters, Mary and Jean, started on Saturday, July 21, to drive from our home in Schenectady, NY, to Milwaukee. While in Milwaukee, we took in a Brewers-Red Sox game (on the 23rd). And, because 1990 was the final year of "old" Comiskey Park, we made a day-trip (July 25) to Chicago, capped off with a game between the White Sox and Indians at that venerable stadium.

On Thursday morning (July 25), as I was getting ready to drive to Detroit to connect with my friend, Ron, "on the way" to Cleveland, I saw on the news that Nolan Ryan had failed to win *his* 300th game Wednesday night - and that his next start would be in Milwaukee on Monday night. Well, that was the day we were scheduled to begin our drive back home to New York. However, I said to Patti, "If you can get tickets for Monday's game, let's stay the extra day and leave on Tuesday." Naturally, she agreed.

On Thursday evening Ron and I took in the Detroit-Boston game at Tiger Stadium. When we got back to his house, I called my wife to find out about the Ryan game. She had good news and bad news - she did get tickets for the Monday game; but it was later announced that Ryan would start the Tuesday game instead. She said she'd try to get tickets for Tuesday's game. On Friday evening I checked with Patti - YES! She had succeeded in getting us tickets for the potentially historic game.

Sunday evening, after attending the SABR Indians-Yankees double header, I drove back to Milwaukee to rejoin my family and take in the Brewers-Rangers games. The Express came through for us and he struck out eight in an 11-3 triumph - the 300th win of his amazing career.

Finally, on Wednesday (August 1) we began our drive back home. We spent the night in Cleveland. And, you guessed it, we took in the "Family-Night" game between the Indians and Royals. What a SABR Convention-vacation - eight baseball games in four different ballparks, highlighted by Nolan Ryan's 300th career victory.

The Old Glove

by J. Thomas Hetrick

Thanks to old age and exposure to the elements, my baseball glove could be mistaken for an ancient relic. I purchased the "Bob Friend" signature model 493 on Easter Sunday 29 years ago. Up until last summer, it served as a workable, tangible link to my passion for baseball.

After one particularly hard toss from a sinewy young man half my age, the friendly leather caught (or didn't catch) its final ball. The sphere entered the glove's webbing and exited straight through, as if the ball were possessed by fire.

No wonder. The mitt looks as rustic and weather-beaten as a fan who remembers Mickey Mantle in his prime. Numerous grass and dirt stains gathered there as an earthy badge of honor. Cracks abound in the brown leather, producing an intricate design not unlike swarming networks of capillaries. The glove is so worn with shedding flakes of leather that the name of the manufacturer cannot be read. The original stitching, loosened through overuse, has been re-knotted a hundred times. When the stitching started to disintegrate, I bound the glove together with shoestring and an occasional piece of coat hanger.

Today, even the ink markings scratched into the leather read like barely visible ancient hieroglyphs. These markings contained the uniform numbers of my three favorite players; #21 Roberto Clemente, right fielder for the Pittsburgh Pirates; #9 Ted Williams, Boston Red Sox slugger of two generations past; and #33 Frank Howard, gargantuan homerun hitter of the Washington Senators.

My new glove's debut in organized baseball was less than auspicious. Planted firmly on my left hand, I'd imagined that it would inspire me to legendary feats on the ball field. With all the might my 11-year-old body could summon, on my very first pitch in Little League, I recoiled and threw. Intended for the heart of the plate, the ball veered slightly off course. I cringed as it sailed wide, right between the shoulder blades of the waiting batter. A dull thud reverberated through the ball yard. Parents and kids jumped up and screamed in the ensuing pandemonium. Two coaches raced toward the scene, joining the umpire, the catcher, and the crumpled body of the injured boy. On the safety of the mound, my face turned as white as a sheet.

I could hear them all saying, "Are you OK? Does it hurt?" I prayed for the safety of the boy and hoped all of our lives could return to normalcy. Meanwhile, a series of freakish thoughts entered my head. Suddenly, the warm summer day turned into an inferno. I was sweating like a condemned man. The ball that had been nervously returned to me by my catcher, seemed cursed. So did my glove. I stared down at the instruments of my torment, hoping that the last few seconds had never happened. Sooner or later, the police would arrive, and they'd whisk me off the jail. I was convinced my fate had been sealed by a single errant pitch.

Eventually, the sore-backed youngster did manage to return to life. He was helped down to first base by a horde of concerned coaches and parents. The game resumed and I was somehow given a reprieve. The police never came. The

very next hitter dribbled a slow roller back to the mound. I crouched down on one knee to field the grounder. Textbook form, just as I'd been taught by the coach. Unfortunately, the ball skipped off my glove for an error. I'd nearly killed my first batter and muffed my first chance. About the only saving grace was that I could not be demoted. Then, as if by divine intervention, my once-shaky arm transformed itself into a powerful cannon. The glove became an extension of my hand. Instead of approaching each pitch with trepidation, I simply blew balls of smoke past the unsuspecting batters. Nearly everyone struck out from that point forward. My team provided run support and I had won my first game.

As I matured into manhood, "Bob Friend" served me well, surviving nearly three decades of ball playing. I remember the crisp games of catch with friends, my father's herky-jerky delivery and sandlot softball. For a time, I stored the glove, some baseballs and a bat in the trunk of my cars, despite only the remotest possibility of actually playing baseball on any given day. Like an athlete hanging on to the last vestiges of his career, I fiercely protected my glove. The mere thought of using another was sacrilege.

Unfortunately, the glove had lost its functionality. No longer could it be trusted to catch thrown or batted baseballs. The aforementioned young man's throw was hardly the first ball that had passed through the webbing, hence the heroic measures employed to prolong its life. Retirement was the only answer. I carefully placed the relic on top of a bookshelf and said thank you for the tens of thousands of balls securely trapped over the years. Good-bye old friend.

The next day, I finally broke down. I went to a mega-athletic wear store to purchase a new glove. High on a bookshelf, the new kid on the block resides next to my care-worn friend. He's a smallish black leather "Brett Butler" model. Maybe Butler and Friend could learn from each other. Old reliable Bob Friend anchored the Pittsburgh pitching staff for more than a decade in the 1950s and 1960s. The courageous Brett Butler, a veteran of baseball wars in the 1980s and 1990s, missed much of last season with throat cancer. One week after I forced the new and old leathers to "share lockers," I took Butler's namesake outside.

The sun beat brightly off the bill of my black Pirates cap. I gripped the shiny white baseball tightly, admiring the perfection of its tight, intricate stitching. After an overwrought windup, I whipped it forward with all the intensity my 38-year old body could muster. Waiting for the toss was the young man that had burned my old leather. Emery Conrad bordered at our house that summer. For an instant, I imagined him as my former self; bright, eager, athletic. The sphere sailed about 25 yards before the leather cracked with that familiar, vibrant sound. Then, Conrad reared back and blistered his best fastball in the direction of my new black mitt. Just for a moment, I fantasized the life of my old glove; my brief foray into Little League, fabulous diving catches playing softball, and the never-heard roars of the crowd. I stuck out the "kid" belt high and heard that unmistakable pop. Just as I'd been coached. Mr. Butler would do just fine.

I Remember

by John J. Eisenhardt

I was born August 30, 1917 in Bristol, PA and joined SABR in September 1981, as soon as I knew about it. I followed baseball since I can remember, as a kid I kept scoresheets of World Series games and first All-Star game that I heard on the radio.

The first baseball game I can remember watching was in 1928 and Ty Cobb, his last year in baseball, was with the Philadelphia Athletics in Shibe Park, Philadelphia. I was in the stands near 3B and remember him in right field and Joe Hauser at first base for the A's. I don't remember the score or who won the game. The only other player I remember was Babe Ruth, he hit two homeruns in the game. They were the three baseball players the men talked about the most, the reason for remembering them then.

I wondered why I remembered Joe Hauser, and years later I looked up his record. He came to the A's in 1922, and in 1923 tied for 5th in homeruns. The next year, in 1924, he was 2nd in homeruns to Babe Ruth with 27 homeruns, .288 batting average and 115 runs batted in with the 2nd Division Team. In 1925 he broke his leg and was never the same in the Majors. But he was the talk of the minors with 63 homeruns in 1930 and 69 in 1922. He was the only minor league player to hit more than 60 homeruns a year twice.

We were taken to the game by my next door neighbor, a baseball fan who owned a touring car. He owned the only car on the street (maybe the only one in the neighborhood) and it had to be cranked up. Saw them in the winter, the colder it was, the harder it was to start. It had isinglas curtains you could roll right down, in case there was a change in the weather. Once a year, from 1929-1931, I saw the champion Philadelphia A's in Shibe Park with busloads of kids from Bristol, near Philadelphia. Saw Jimmie Foxx hit a homerun and yelled to "Doc" and "Flit" Cramer center field (not regular Mule Haas), he put his hand behind his back and waved his fingers at us.

Us kids got big laughs at the fans sitting on the rooftops, watching the game from across the street. Years later I found out it was a big business. Seats were built on the roof and fans were charged a slight admission by the tenants - until Connie Mack built a big fence in right field.

From left: Joseph and John Eisenhardt, Sr. at Cedar Beach, April 1969.

Next, I saw the Phillies and Dizzy Dean of the St. Louis Cardinals at Baker Bowl with the knot-hole gang. In 1921 my uncle bought a crystal radio set. I was 4 years old and remember him turning knobs all the time trying to get a baseball game. He was listening to the World Series of 1921 with earphones (or whatever they called them then). He said I kept pestering him and finally, he handed them to me. One time I heard Babe Ruth hit a homerun and ran out and yelled to my next door neighbor, "Babe Ruth hit a homerun!" several times to him. Another time, Frank Frisch got a hit. I probably would never remember saying it, except the man next door kept reminding me of it, making fun of how I said Babe Ruth and Frank Frisch, especially every World Series time.

About the crystal set: years later my uncle was retired and living in Maryland and I wrote to him about it. He wrote back and told the story. He was 14 and got a woman to act as his mother and signed for him to pay $1.00 a month. When his mother found out, angry, she asked, "how are you going to pay for it?" So he got a job stocking groceries on shelves.

I moved to Long Island in 1934 and by 1937 earned enough money to pay and watch Major League baseball games at 25 and 50 cents. I saw a lot of opening day games at Yankee Stadium and Yankee World Series games in 1937, 1938 and 1939.

In 1938 I saw Carl Hubbell pitch and beat the Phillies in the first game of a doubleheader at the Polo Grounds. The only game I saw in Ebbets Field in 1938 was when Johnny Vander Meer pitched his second consecutive no-hitter. A note about that game: it was the first night game in Ebbets Field and before the season started, two carloads of us planned to go to that game. We had no idea who would be pitching and that we would see history being made!

In 1939, I saw the first televised major league baseball game, between the Brooklyn Dodgers and the Cincinnati Reds. The antenna was on the Empire State Building - good for 50 miles they say. I saw the game from the street and the television was in the window of a sporting goods store!

In 1941 I saw at least five games of Joe DiMaggio hitting in his record 56 straight games. I had scorecards for most of the games I saw before WWII. I was drafted in August of 1941 in peacetime, before Pearl Harbor, and put the scorecards etc. in a rail road YMCA locker. Those days if you passed your physical, you were drafted immediately. When I got back to my locker, I was told of a fire, and everything in it destroyed, there was no locker left.

In the army I was transferred to the 3rd Division, amphibious, in September 1942 and in October I was with the largest convoy at the time in the Atlantic Ocean. We were told we were going to invade Africa (2nd front it was called then) on November 8, 1942. I was in the first wave on the beach and wounded in the leg seriously enough to go back on the next boat to the States.

Back to baseball! I saw the New York Mets opening game at the Polo Grounds in 1962, the Mets opening game at Shea Stadium in 1964 and the All-Star game at Shea Stadium in 1964.

I was the scorekeeper for the local base-ball team, Port Jefferson AC, before WWII and after the war, scorekeeper for the Local Order of the Moose baseball team. I wrote stories for both teams and sports for the local weekly newspaper.

In 1980 the *Sporting News* polled its readers in March for pennant choices and World Series winner. Of 1300 readers and over 200 sportswriters, I was the only one to pick all four division winners and world series winner.

Heard some games of every World Series, either on the radio or TV from 1929 to the present time.

In 1948 I married Anna Vecchio. A son was born in 1949, twin daughters in 1950 and another son in 1956.

I have been retired since 1976 from the Long Island Rail Road. I am a member of the American Legion, The Loyal Order of the Moose and an Historian for the local VFW.

1946-1948

by John W. Burgeson

"Robert William Andrew Feller, magnificent and incredible, today celebrated a date with destiny."

More than 40 years have passed since those words appeared on the front page of the Youngstown (Ohio) *Vindicator*. The date was May 1, 1946; on April 30th the mighty Bob Feller had pitched the second no-hitter of his brilliant career. I was a sprout of 15; my pesky little brother, Paul, was an uncomprehending child of 8, whose throwing arm was giving new meaning to the term "wildness." 1946 was the year I explained to Paul the game of baseball, pointing out to him the game's importance in God's eternal plan. And how the Indians would soon, surely very soon, win the pennant, and be the World Champions of the only sport that mattered. Over the years, I explained a lot of things to my little brother; in this case there was success!

I had seen Feller pitch before, in the late 1930s, in Cleveland's old League Park. After the Tribe's 2nd place finish in 1940, the team had fallen on tough times. But the boys were home from the war now, Feller, Hegan, Keltner, Lemon, Robinson, Edwards, Conway and Mack, and everyone knew that Cleveland's day was imminent! It was to take two more years. In 1946 they would finish a dismal 6th, in 1947 a more respectable 4th. Owner Bill Veeck brought up the first Cleveland Black player, Larry Doby, that year, and the fans of Cleveland responded by setting new attendance records. Player/manager Lou Boudreau, unique in the major leagues, was drawing a mighty team together.

For northeastern Ohio, 1948 was the zenith of the 20th century. The cold war was still just name calling, the USA was without world equal. And now, oh joy! This was to be the Indians' year. The Yankees, the hated, feared, detested, despised New York Yankees, would finally be vanquished!

Yankee-hating was an art form in those days in northeastern Ohio. Paul and I were burying the hostilities of boyhood in Indian "rooting" and Yankee "bashing.' We admired the New York players immensely as individuals; loathed them collectively; never asked ourselves "Why?" Still don't. Tradition.

A year earlier, Veeck had moved the Tribe permanently from League Park into the gargantuan caverns of Cleveland's Municipal Stadium. He had made a vow to fill that enormous memorial to 1928 pre-crash-optimism by bringing home an American League pennant. Now there were cynics in those days, as there are today, who jeered. But most of us, particularly those who read the sports pages of the *Vindicator* and the *Cleveland Plain Dealer*, had no doubt of ultimate success. Attendance peaked in 1947; in 1948 it peaked again, as 2,260,627 fans spun the turnstiles, not a few of them being our long suffering father and his two boys. It was the year of Joe Earley (remember him?), pitcher Don Black's cerebral hemorrhage at the plate, manager Boudreau's .355 MVP season, and the entry into big league ball of "rookie" Satchel Paige, then a youthful 41! It was the year the Tribe traded their power hitter, Pat Seerey, along with pitcher Al Gettel, to Chicago for Bob Kennedy. Bob hit .301 for us that year, while "big Pat" claimed only the league strikeout title and Gettel finished 8 and 10 on an 8th place club.

1948 was the year of war hero Gene Bearden, 20 and 7, and the year Bob Lemon completed his development from a fair outfielder to a great pitcher, 20 and 14. It was the year Bob Feller lost an incredible number of one-run ball games, yet finished 19 and 15. The rest of the pitching staff, Zoldak, Muncrief, Black as secondary starters, Klieman and Christopher as ace relievers, would have been mainstays on any other team. A new guy, Mike Garcia, not yet "ready for prime time," was showing promise for the future. And Paige of course, called up late in the season after Black's injury. Dad took Paul and me to see him pitch in a night game on August 20. It was there that "Ole Satch," with his dazzlingly brilliant "hesitation pitch," set down Bill Wight and the White Sox with three hits, 1-0, on his way to a season 6-1 record. Attendance that night, 78,382, set records for the stadium and for any night game anywhere. It took hours (it seemed) to exit the park, and it was cock-crow by the time we reached home the next morning!

Well, the season ended with Boston eliminating the Yankees on the final day to tie the Tribe for first place. The next day, we trounced the Red Sox, 8-3, in a single game playoff on Bearden's five-hitter and Boudreau's batting heroics. The Indians went on to take the Series from Spahn, Sain (and no two days of rain) and the rest of the Boston Braves in six games. In our high school, we even listened to one of the games during algebra class - unheard of! Oh yes - do you remember Joe Earley? You don't? No, he was not the same as Tom Earley, who pitched from 1938 to 1945 for the Braves. Nor Jake Early, a catcher of the same era for Washington! Yet, Joe was a very important person to the Cleveland ball club in 1948! You might even say the most important person!

It was mid-summer in Cleveland, and Bill Veeck (bless his soul) was promoting baseball like no one had ever had before! Fireworks, free nylons, baby-sitting services during the game; Bill had a great imagination! Among his promotions, he conceived "Fan appreciation night." Joe Earley was the lucky (random) selectee from the stands. Joe stood there, at home plate, representing all of us. We were fans of the best team in the world. The 1948 Cleveland Indians. The champions. Bravo, Joe!

A Personal Story
by Chuck Brodsky

I went to Cooperstown in September of 1997 to give a concert of baseball songs in the Bullpen Theater at the National Baseball Hall of Fame. Most likely it was the first concert ever held there, according to the Hall's Research Department director, Tim Wiles. Tim in the past had helped me find information for a couple of song topics and he's an avid folk music fan. I play about 150 concerts a year, primarily folk music clubs, church basement coffeehouses, and festivals, but how could I ever, in my wildest dreams, imagine that I'd be invited to sing at the Hall of Fame? As I entered the Hall, the very first thing that caught my eye, even before the statue of The Babe, was the beautiful poster announcing my concert. It was made by the Hall's in-house art department and which, of course, now hangs at home on my wall.

As I carried my guitar through the great chamber filled with the plaques of all who've been inducted, I stopped briefly for a silent tribute to Whitey, Lefty and Schmidtty.

It was all just too good to be true I kept thinking, throughout my 30-minute concert, and when it was over, things quickly moved into the surreal. Turns out the subject of one of my songs, Dick Allen, was in Cooperstown representing the Phillies organization at the Eastern League's annual awards festivities. The song and the album it appears on are both titled *Letters in the Dirt* a reference to this childhood hero of mine getting booed at old Connie Mack Stadium, and his writing "Boo" in the dirt around first base in response. I once sent him a homemade cassette with a live version of the song, but ever since the CD came out I had not yet sent him a copy. So I figured I'd head over to the Otesaga Hotel where Mr. Allen was staying, and leave one for him at the front desk. Who should be standing in the lobby when I walked in but Dick Allen himself! So I went over and introduced myself as the guy who'd written the song about him. I showed him the album and how I titled it after him, and then I opened up the CD booklet to show him a photo I'd taken of the word "Boo" in the dirt. Well, next thing I know he's pinching my cheek, tears in his eyes. My childhood hero, and I had moved him. And then it was me who was signing my autograph for him.

Chuck Brodsky

So You Think You Know Baseball
by Thomas J. Adams

So you think you know the Grand Old Game
With its myriad facts and figures you're a pro,
But before you enter the Fanatic Hall of Fame
Here are a few things that you must know.

What are bleeders, taters, ribbies and Ks
What are ducks on the pond and a tall can of corn,
Who was famous for his fadaways
What route is known as around the horn?

What are switch and Punch and Judy hitters
Who was known as the Big Train,
What are sinkers, sliders and spitters
Why did Braves fans pray for rain?

When does the leadoff batter hit
What spot does the cleanup occupy,
What's a player doing when he's 'dogging it'
How are pitchers hung out to dry?

Who's 'sitting in the catbird seat'
And who was the coiner of that phrase,
What is meant by throwing heat
And batters going the other way?

What's a rope, a Texas Leaguer, a dying quail
Where's the keystone and hot corners at,
Where do celler dwellers dwell
What is meant by the pitch being fat?

When is a batter in the hole
How are pitchers knocked out of the box,
What happens when bats go cold
What city housed the Black and Go-Go Sox?

Where do players go when they are sent down
What does it mean to be called up,
How do hitters take pitchers downtown
What's baseball's proverbial coffee cup?

What leagues are Cactus and Grapefruit
What are side-arm, submarine and over the top,
Who's the man in the monkey suit
Who's given the green light or signaled to stop?

What does a batter do for his wrists to break
What calls for a pow wow on the mound,
What are phenoms, hotdogs and flakes
What happens when a runner is gunned down?

Who were the Gashouse Gang and Murderers Row
Who are firemen, pilots and battery mates,
What are pepper games, pitchers' duels and fungos
What do runners score when they cross the plate?

What are clubhouse lawyers and jockeys on the bench
What are Annie Oakleys and the suicide squeeze,
Who are runners and hitters that pinch
What does it mean to speak Stengeleze?

What does the crowd do in the 7th inning
How does a pitcher doctor the ball,
What player gets a "W" for winning
What park has its famous Green Monster wall?

Where does the ball go when hit in the alley
How does a baserunner go for two,
What does it mean that he killed a rally
When should the cutoff let the throw go through?

What are fielder's choices, force and double plays
Who hit the "Miracle of Coogans Bluff,"
What are promotional bat and Ladies Days
Why is a batter said to be 'handcuffed?'

Where does one go when given the thumb
Why do pitchers often waste a pitch,
What's the Hotstove League and bleacher bums
What does a batter have when he develops a hitch?

Who labors from out of the bull pen
Who's motions are herky-jerky, windup and stretch,
Who are bench warmers, scrubbies and utility men
What's a circus, a basket and a shoestring catch?

What are pick off plays, hit and run and double steals
Where do we find the Hall of Fame,
What stadium did the Bambino build
Who's Bucketfoot Al and how did he acquire that name?

What are the Sr. and Jr. circuits and the circle called "on deck"
What is meant by hugging the lines,
Why was Boom-Boom a nickname given to Walter Beck
What do coaches do when they give and steal signs?

What advice did Ueck give for catching a knuckle ball
Who are aces, starters, long-men and relievers,
When the team gets into trouble who gets the call
What tools are worn by all receivers?

What are options, free-agents, trades and the gate
Dusters, brush-backs, chin music and sticking it in your ear,
Why do batters skip rope at homeplate
Who gave us the hopeful cry, "Wait 'til next year"?

If you can answer these questions and more
On baseball academic test,
You're bound to make an excellent score
And rank among your class' best.

The Voice Of The Braves

by Mort Bloomberg

Forty years have elapsed since Jim Britt broadcast a Braves baseball game. To this day I can't tell whether his call of the game turned me into a devoted fan of the Boston Braves or whether my affection for the team is the reason I feel he belongs in Cooperstown alongside such fabled broadcasters as Red Barber, Mel Allen and Vin Scully.

Without doubt, however, Jim Britt was Braves baseball to me during the late 40s and early 50s. I have vivid memories of hiding my portable radio underneath the covers at night listening to him describe yet another comeback victory that the Braves made during their successful pennant chase of 1948. The losses piled up progressively from 1949-52, but the drama in his voice always gave me new hope that the outcome of tomorrow's contest would be better.

Jim died in 1980, a largely forgotten figure. A book he had wanted to publish was never completed, and there is no known record of his own view of himself as a broadcaster. Critics have described him as pompous or neurotically meticulous. Arguably, he was quite fond of alcohol and suffered through a messy divorce. Were these accounts true? I neither know nor care. He was my link to the Braves. A very articulate announcer, he was able to convey much with few words. You always knew where his allegiance lay. So much so that when a choice arose in the late fall of 1950 between covering the Braves or that other so-called ball team in Boston, he chose the Braves. The subsequent decline in his career when the Braves went to Milwaukee two and one-half years later has been traced to this fateful decision. His obituary in the *Boston-Globe* ended by saying that "in truth life had turned its back on him a long time ago."

Not a corn ball "homer" like Phil Rizzuto, Bob Prince or Harry Caray, he reported what he saw on the playing field in an objective way (Spartan even, by today's standards). But one could sense from the sound of his voice that he had unshakable faith in the Braves despite that arid summer of 1952 when they won 64 out of 155 games and drew but 281,278 paid admissions to the Wigwam for the entire season. That's why I was so angry and sad when Lou Perini suddenly pulled up stakes in the middle of spring training in 1953. After all, they already had assembled on their roster in Bradenton Warren Spahn, Eddie Mathews, Johnny Logan, Del Crandall, Lew Burdette, Bob Buhl, Sid Gordon, Billy Bruton, Joe Adcock and Andy Pafko. Their fortunes were on the rise, and of equal significance to me, the Red Sox were floundering. Right to the very end, the Boston Braves exhibited bad timing.

Talk about grasping at straws in the face of shattered dreams: here is my letter to the *Boston Traveler* as it appeared in that paper as a follow-up to a comment by an irate reader that "the Braves belong in Milwaukee like beans belong in beer."

I agree that something should be done to have the Milwaukee games brought to Boston by radio. The Braves are still first in the minds of many New Englanders and should have a fine

Thomson At The Bat

by Tom and Doris Adams

The outlook wasn't hopeful, for the New York Giants that day
Losing by three runs, with one inning left to play.
They'd trailed the mighty Bums, in August by 13 games
But when the season ended, their records read the same.

They'd played like Supermen, in the stretch run for the pennant
Now the playoff games, would determine who would win it.
No love was lost between the two, arch rivals for many years
Wherever they were playing, the air was filled with boos and cheers.

The first game was at Ebbets Field, before a partisan crowd
And when they emerged as winners, the Giants were feeling proud.
Now it was on to the Polo Grounds, where they were their fans' heroes
But when nine innings were over, Labine had beaten them 10-0.

Again it was back at the Polo Grounds, for the entire ball of wax
With both teams poised and ready, to perform up to their max.
Each knew it wouldn't be easy, as they battled to the wire
With Yanks waiting in the wings, like from pan into the fire.

Dressen chose Newcombe for the task, of winning it once and all
While Durocher countered with Maglie, by handing him the ball.
The game broke badly for the Giants, when Reese and Snider walked
And when Pee Wee scored on Jackie's hit, the stands were abuzz with talk.

The score stayed one and zero, until seventh inning
When Irvin scored on Thomson's fly, they had a chance of winning.
Then the roof fell in, as Maglie lost control
And when the Dodgers eighth was over, they were in a four-one hole.

Now its down to final frame, as Durocher encouraged his men
"We've come from behind before, and we can do it once again."
Now Dark led off the ninth, and reached first on a hit
And when Mueller followed suit, around to third he lit.

All throughout the stands, fans stood and craned their necks
Could this be another finish, the kind they'd come to expect?
With Irvin coming up, Dressen approached the mound
To embolden his big twirler and get him settled down.

When Irvin fouled out to Hodges, Dodgers' feelings began to rise
Only two more outs to go and they'd claim the NL prize.
But Lockman hit a fastball, into left field for a double
Now the Dodgers knew, that this could mean big trouble.

Lockman reached second easily, but Mueller sliding at third base
Badly twisted his ankle, and had to be replaced.
Hartung came in off the bench, to run for his teammate
Then Dressen called for Branca, thus tempting the Gods of Fate.

Now up steps our hero, Bobby Thomson, The Flying Scot
If he couldn't win the game, perhaps he'd tie the knot.
While Chuck was instructing Branca, saying, "Get this fellow out"
Leo was counseling Bobby, "Look for one that you can clout."

Now Thomson steps up to the plate, to face his cross town foe
The first pitch is down the middle, but Bobby lets it go.
Now Branca looks in for the sign, then heaves a mighty hurl
The collision it makes with Bobby's bat, is heard around the world.

The ball flew on a line, heading for the left field stands
As all held bated breaths, it fell among the fans.
The runners circled the bases, at homeplate they were mobbed
The Dodgers walked off dejected, feeling that they'd been robbed.

Sometimes the game is easy, sometimes the game is rough
Especially when your opponent, works miracles near Coogan's Bluff.
All over this fair land, when baseball tales are told
Fans will always remember, when Durocher's men struck gold.

There was no joy in Mudville, when Casey blew the game
And for all Dodgers rooters, feelings were the same.
For everywhere in Brooklyn, hearts were sad and low
But Giantsville's sun was shining, when Thomson struck his blow.

team this year. Let's do something about it now and not wait, like a year ago, when we were a little late in deciding to promote the Braves.

Since my prospects for becoming the next Spahn, Earl Torgeson, Willard Marshall or Bobby Hogue were remote, to put it mildly, I had decided that my best option was to become Jim Britt's successor or at least his sidekick. I definitely could do a better job than Bump Hadley ("Heads up and keep pitching" was his tag-line on the air years after fracturing Mickey Cochrane's skull in three places with an errant pitch"). Bump was that era's answer to Ralph Kiner with malapropisms and miscues like "that ball is going, going... and it is dropped by Sam Jethroe in short center field." And I had to be an improvement on Les Smith who was just plain boring.

I saw Jim twice. On the first occasion he and a few ball players from the team came to the Winthrop (MA) Jewish Community Center as feature speakers at a Hot Stove League banquet. They arrived late in various states of intoxication turning the event into a total disaster. As for the second time, I caught up with him in the reserved grandstand at Braves Field while he was en route to the broadcast booth with just enough time to autograph my scorecard before a Phillies game in 1950.

Not knowing what steps to pursue for career in baseball broadcasting, I wrote him at The Yankee Network for advice. To my surprise, this reply arrived from him in January 1952:

Thank you very much for your nice letter. I'm not at all certain that my suggestions will be of help, but here they are:

I took an AB in college, University of Detroit. I majored in English and philosophy, minored in speech and history and studied law following my graduation from college. I was always interested in speaking, singing and sports. I taught public speech and debating in Detroit high schools, finally got into radio more or less by accident, not in one of the many ways open to those interested today.

Most important, for either a sports broadcasting or sports writing career-get a good, well-rounded education Go to college, if you can. There's no possible substitute. Then make the rounds of the various small radio stations and/or newspapers to attempt to get a job. It may be hard to break in. But the job is interesting and well worth all the time and trouble it takes to get started. Good luck in whatever you do, wherever you go.

In trying to pull my thoughts together now after so many years, I really can't say with certainty what means the most to me. Perhaps its the brief encounters in person and by mail with my childhood idol who signed-off his nightly Sports Round-up Show "If you can't take part in a sport, be one anyway, will ya." Maybe it's the games themselves on WHDH and WNAC. Possibly it was being at what Al Hirshberg called "antiquated and barny" Braves Field. It could have been the players on the diamond during the postwar era: Sibby Sisti, Tommy Holmes, Johnny Logan, Bob Chipman, Paul Burris and even Walter Lanfranconi - names I will forever cherish. Then again it could be simply their colorful uniforms. One thing I do know for sure is my quest will continue for play-by-play tapes of games that involved the Tribe prior to 1953, especially at Braves Field.

One of the founders of the Boston Braves Historical Association, Mort Bloomberg was born and reared in the Boston area and now lives and teaches in Connecticut.

Braves Reunion
by Bob Salsberg

BOSTON (AP) - Mort Bloomberg was 12 and a diehard Boston Braves fan when his team lost to the Brooklyn Dodgers at Braves Field on September 21, 1952.

Little did he know that it would be the last time his beloved team would take the field in Boston. As spring training was about to begin the following season, the Braves announced they were moving to Milwaukee, ending a 76 year tradition of National League baseball in Boston.

"When the Braves moved in 1953, it was like a death in the family," said Bloomberg, who grew up in the Boston area and now resides in Brookfield, CT.

Forty years after the Braves played their final home game in what is now Boston University's Nickerson Field, Bloomberg and other members of the Boston Braves Historical Association were gathering at the Boston University campus Sunday to share memories and memorabilia.

"It was the club nobody ever had a chance to say good-bye to," said Dick Johnson, curator of the New England Sports Museum. In 1988, the museum hosted a 40th reunion of the 1948 National League Champion Braves' team. The museum helped the association organize and plan this weekend's event.

Most younger Bostonians are only vaguely aware that Boston was a two team baseball town for almost half a century.

Boston had one of the original National League franchises when the senior circuit was formed in 1876. The team went by various names including the Red Stockings and the Bean Eaters before becoming the Braves in the early part of this century. The team's name was briefly changed to the Bees in the late 1930s but was changed back to the Braves by overwhelming public demand a few years later.

Although they never played during the regular season, the Braves and the Boston Red Sox developed a fierce fan rivalry that some baseball historians believe was based on class distinctions more than anything else.

Saul Wisnia, a freelance sportswriter, is researching a book he plans to call *From Yawkey to Milwaukee*. The book will look at the demise of Boston as a two team city.

"It was a fight they pretty much lost from the beginning," said Wisnia of the Braves effort to compete with their more popular crosstown rivals.

The Braves had many great moments and big names. Babe Ruth finished his career with the Braves in 1935 and once hit three homeruns in one game.

But, according to Wisnia, the Red Sox became the choice of the city's elite, while the Braves struggled to keep their audience. "The Red Sox were the aristocratic, star-laden team and the Braves were the working class team."

Wisnia said while attendance waned and the team's financial problems grew, Braves management struggled to compensate. Fenway Park and Braves Field were only a few short trolley stops from each other, but at times they seemed worlds apart.

To entice fans, Braves Field became the first major league ball park in the country to install an electronic scoreboard and served such relative delicacies as fried clams at concession stands.

For about a dollar, kids could buy a season pass to sit in the leftfield grandstands during Saturday home games and this group became known as "the knothole gang."

But for all its efforts, the team could not seem to erase its image as the other team in town. And when they left, they left royal fans like Mort Bloomberg bitter.

For 10 years, Bloomberg said he was so upset he didn't even follow baseball. Moreover, he blamed the Red Sox for his team's departure. Although he is more good-natured about it today, his animosity toward the Sox remains, to the point of his refusal to mention the team or its ball park by name.

"To this day, 'many Braves fans will not want to be associated with the F-park (Fenway) or any member of that organization.'"

Bloomberg is taking a special delight in the fact that the Red Sox are finishing this season in last place and notes the irony that the Braves, who have long since left Milwaukee for Atlanta, are the defending National League champions and back in the playoffs for a second year in a row.

Bloomberg said the Boston Braves Historical Association was formed last winter and now claims about 150 members from New England and beyond. Sunday's meeting is the first for the group.

Several players from the 1952 team plan to attend, including Sibby Sisti, Sam Jethroe and Johnny Logan. The event is open to the public for a $12 fee and the agenda will include speakers, a slide show, a movie of the 1948 World Series and, in what Bloomberg says will be a highlight for him, a tour of what remains of the old Braves Field, where dirty smoke from coal trains at the nearby rail yards used to blow into the faces of players and fans, perhaps symbolizing the team's working class reputation.

"Braves Field has been referred to as an ugly old barn, but to me its like a shrine," he said.

A Farewell Interview With Merl DeMoll

For the last two decades the voice you would hear on the line when you called the *Acipco News* office was that of Merl L. DeMoll. He retired April 1, 1990 after 38 years service, 20 years as editor of the award winning employee publication which will complete its 75th year in print this September. For 240 issues of the *News,* his name appeared on the masthead as editor, and for 106 issues, nine years as associate editor.

Mr. DeMoll is fourth in a succession of editors who have carefully preserved the same functional informative editorial approach over the decades. This tradition was established by the publication's first editor, Ralph R. Silver (1915-27), who was a staff reporter for the *Birmingham Age-Herald* (now *Post Herald*) prior to his *Acipco* employment.

Mr. Silver observed all the proprieties of newswriting characteristic of his day. This "gentleman's journalism" has been remarkably preserved to the present day under the pens of editors, Cecil A. Carlisle (1927-53). Roland L. Paulin (1953-69) and Mr. DeMoll (1970-90).

"Gentleman" is a word often used to describe Mr. DeMoll. In addition, he is reputed to have a photographic memory (which he denies) and has been described as a walking, talking encyclopedia of *Acipco* history. In a recent interview we asked him to recollect a bit of his own history with the company.

"I was attending Birmingham Business College in 1951 when a teacher advised me to seek employment at *Acipco,*" he said. "I was hired by Buell B. Warren, assistant works manager in charge of personnel and public relations, as a secretary for Mr. Frank Coupland, who was works manager. That was when very few women were in the work force."

J.C. King was employment manager at the time and J.T. Vann was assistant works manager in charge of operations. In this capacity Mr. DeMoll, along with Harry Allen, helped to handle the company safety program and performed other clerical tasks. During these years he learned the people, the supervisors and the workings of *Acipco.*

"In 1954 I became scorekeeper and reporter for the company baseball team, an association I thoroughly enjoyed since I loved sports and which helped to bond me to the *Acipco* family," he recalled. "I considered it an honor and privilege to be affiliated with the baseball team then because it had such a successful tradition."

By January 1955, Mr. DeMoll had become well acquainted with the Eagan Plan and enamored with its Christian ideals. In that month he was transferred to the Time office as one of two payroll clerk/timekeepers. While making rounds documenting time and attendance, he gained a further understanding of *Acipco* and its people that laid the foundation for knowledge gained over the years.

His "beat" was the Foundry Department, the Bolt Department (then a unit of the Melting Department near the present day site of the Brass Foundry), and the support departments such as the machine shop, construction, maintenance, electrical, research and inspection. During one-time checking round Mr. DeMoll experienced what he described as a fitting for a "greenhorn."

"I was in the old 2-1/2" and 3" pipe foundry, 'M' Foundry it was called, and walked right across a dust-covered tar tank," he said. Like Bre'er Rabbit, he found himself ankle deep in warm tar. "The foreman saw me and I got a lot of guffaws. I was not allowed to forget that (incident) for quite awhile," he recalled. "Things were a bit more primitive then."

From the beginning Mr. DeMoll's "bird-dogging" talents were put to use. He had been writing safety articles and human interest features along with sports reports since his days in the works manager's office, the time office and the Mono-Cast Department. Meanwhile, Roland L. Paulin had been named *Acipco News* editor in 1953 and publicity department manager in 1957. The responsibilities of his two-person department were increasing and too many irons were in the fire.

One fall Saturday in 1958, during the Alabama-Georgia Tech game, Mr. Paulin called Mr. DeMoll to ask if he would be interested in helping out in the Publicity Department. Alabama won and Mr. DeMoll said yes. He stayed in the Publicity Department for two years, being named associate editor of the *Acipco News* in March 1961 and editor in January 1970. In January 1986 the publication was placed under the Manufacturing Division and assigned to the Personnel Department and later to the Employee Relations Department when the Human Resources Division was organized.

Over the years, Mr. DeMoll has been a conscientious steward of the Eagan Plan, careful to keep fresh its ideas within the pages of the news in October 1981 he started a series, "Memories of John J. Eagan," highlighting the Golden Rule inspired principles on which the company was based. He went to the Atlanta museum where the founder's original papers are deposited and brought back some historical material for use in the series, which was suggested by the Board of Operatives after an inspiring talk given by Ann Eagan Goodhue to the Acipco National Management Association Chapter, May 19, 1981. The series featured excerpts from Mr. Eagan's writings and memories of people who knew him.

"In this series we tried to reinvigorate the Eagan Plan concepts and link them with the present day," Mr. DeMoll explained. "Some of the most rewarding articles I've done were from interviews of pensioners who related personal experiences with Mr. Eagan."

During Mr. DeMoll's tenure as editor, the *Acipco Bulletin* was conceived as a supplement to information reported in the *News.* The weekly newsletter was developed in 1986 under the guidance of vice president and works manager, E.E. (Gene) Langner, in an effort to communicate practical information to employees on a timely basis.

Also during his tenure, the *News* received honors for two consecutive years (1974 and 1975) from the Freedoms Foundation, Valley Forge, PA, in the category of corporate publications. The Valley Forge Honor Certificates cited the publication for "helping to achieve a better understanding of the American way of life."

That citation could easily be rewritten and presented to Mr. DeMoll personally "for helping to achieve a better appreciation for the *Acipco* way of life." Merl DeMoll will be greatly missed, but the quality of his work is preserved in the *Acipco News* archives and his positive influence on employee morale will long be remembered.

Triumph At Christie's Auction Memorabilia
by Steve Cummings

Playing With The Heavy Hitters: The Auction At Christies

It was last fall in the dismal city of Tacoma that I first heard it was going on the auction block. I knew it existed, since I'd owned a reproduction of this grand piece of baseball memorabilia for years, but I never thought I'd see an original. In the ensuing year, it seemed like every conversation with collectors and dealers focused on wild card speculation about the ultimate auction value of this piece, who would bid on it and whether it was worth entering the race for it when I finally would be hammered down in New York City on September 20, 1997 at Christie's East.

Sometime in the spring, I made plans to take my younger daughter, Tasha Alexandra (13), to Gotham so she could see a real city and I could revisit the horns, subways, delis and art deco skyscrapers unseen since 1972. So the item provided an impetus to use those frequent flyer miles and go on a road trip across the nation in only 4:45 from Seattle to JFK. The Christie's catalog had arrived about two weeks prior to the seven day series of road games. First glances at such catalogues usually generate intense ambivalence, since there are so many beautiful pieces of memorabilia that are so expensive and therefore so unattainable. Kind of like an all-star squad of 450 players, fingering the catalog's tempting pages brings forth anxiety about possible acquisition, extended obsessiveness about which items to bid on, and further anxiety about a diminishing bank account. So, there it was, for real, lot #417, with a rather low estimate, I thought. It ought to go for at least double, shouldn't it. Only six others were known to exist in the baseball world and this was the first one ever publicly sold.

Four days prior to the auction, Don Flannagan of Christie's East (the main Christie's is an elegant museum with far more expensive antiques just around the corner from this converted garage!) let me fondle this piece. No one stood guard over my shoulder or warned me to be careful. Flannagan chatted with me briefly, then wandered off to deal with more important matters. It was in nice shape except for a few water stains and clipped corners. It was not a baseball card. I had a fleeting fantasy of stuffing it in my pocket and running out onto 54th Avenue. Trouble is, I can't run very far or very fast and I'm too claustrophobic for jail. Besides, you can't act on every impulse you have, can you?

So I talked all week in New York City with other interested parties about the piece. I made sure the hotel woke us up in plenty of time that Saturday morning and we took one of the city's finest yellow taxis to the auction house. I begged for Paddle #406 because of Ted, finally settling for #667 for good luck. I figured there were two other lots I was sure to "win," but never did I think for a moment that Lot #417 would come my way, hence batting .667 (two out of three ain't bad). The paddle was plastic and I used it to swat Tasha on her butt whenever she got out of line, which was less often than me, actually. She's much more socialized than I am. The paddle hurt, she said.

With about 100 people present, the auction began promptly at 10:00 a.m. with a lady auctioneer at the mahogany podium. She turned out to be the president of Christie's East and sold about 80 lots briskly per hour. Funny thing is that all they were serving were tiny cups of water and square-foiled packets of chocolate. No booze, coffee or plush seating, but not Spartan either. The stuff was hanging on the walls, neatly displayed in glass cases, but never was presented directly by the auctioneer at the podium. Instead, a color slide of each piece was flashed, along with an electronic scoreboard which showed the instantaneous current bid, translated in six foreign currencies, just like at the ballpark.

For the most part, each piece was presented in the same tone of voice as its predecessor, except for a few pricey items that brought extended extra-inning bidding wars. The grand salamis that I recall through the blur of at bats were two signed baseballs and a Lou Gerhig contract. One ball consisted of all but Matty's signature amongst the initial HOF inductees; the other had the AL squad on the ball from the first (1933) All Star Game. Some guy behind me bid $55,000 for the first ball. He seemed like the kind of guy who could write a check for $55.00 just as casually as an amount one thousand times larger.

It was like a doubleheader as the first part of the auction ended after 2:20, with a break between games, and my item came up finally at 3:17 in the afternoon. I had "won" my two other pieces easily and sat through hundreds of scrawled baseballs, mesh uniforms and hockey sticks until my piece came up. As Lot #417 approached, I became fidgety and prepared my camera to flash on the electronic scoreboard to record the winning bid for Diamond Angle posterity. Then the lot magically appeared at the precise time as its number. Hmm! In the afternoon, there was a congenial gent who served as the beggar at the podium. Yeah, I began palpitating, but not sweating, camera and paddle ready. Bidding began at $3,000, and I decided to place an early bid up rapidly to 10 grand and then mysteriously began to trickle. What the hell was going on? Many expected the piece to "go through the roof." There was a spread-out series of agonizing bumps of a thousand bucks apiece that came from some unseen moneyed folk. We sat in the front row. I was in a zone much like Carlton throwing to McCarver's mitt. Once the bidding got past five figures. I started thinking about whether this piece would ever be publicly available again. The bidding seem to stretch out for teasing minutes, as the gavel almost hammered the piece down for good several times. Finally, the guy in the blue suit high above pleaded in a jocular way with me, knowing I wanted the thing, for just one more bid! My paddle levitated beyond conscious control. Disbelievingly, the piece was hammered down at just about the right price. I muttered to Tasha, "I won the damned thing" and promptly shot the scoreboard for archival purposes. Cheers went up in the stands as if I had won the

ballgame. I was numb. It is still sinking in. A lady from *The Maine Antiques Quarterly* took photos of us. My Brooklyn friend congratulated me and introduced me to several of his colleagues. I had won the item and batted 1.000.

I had won Sol White's *History Of Colored Base Ball*, published in 1906, accompanied by a previously unknown 1907 supplement. A modest pamphlet with red covers, surprisingly glossy paper innards, tightly bound with great photos, it is the rarest baseball book in the world. The max.

Area Man Takes Uniform Look Into Baseball

by Mart Tardani, Chronicle staff writer

"No one in the world knows more about baseball uniforms than Marc Okkonen."

Sports writer Sarah Ballard made that observation in *Sports Illustrated's* special baseball issue this past spring in a feature entitled *The Fabric of the Game.*

High praise indeed for the work of a Muskegon man who has devoted the better part of the last five years researching major league baseball uniforms worn from 1900 to the present.

"I've been stuck on baseball even before I graduated from Muskegon High in 1951," says Okkonen who has been self-employed for the past nine years as a graphic artist-writer.

He spent hundreds of hours researching Reach and Spalding baseball guides at a sports library in Los Angeles, an area in which he had lived for 13 years. When it became obvious to him that new sources were needed, he moved to the Albany, NY area.

From there he was able to make the short trip to baseball's Hall of Fame in Cooperstown to pore over photographs contained in *Sporting Life,* a magazine which was regarded as baseball's "Bible" until 1915.

But the most important source for confirmation and location of facts was newspaper microfilm and files he studied at the national baseball library of the Library of Congress in Washington, DC, Okkonen said.

And so now he has completed a book in camera-ready condition. It consists of 270 pages of print and photographs in color of every uniform worn by every major league team since the turn of the century.

Okkonen says he has already invested "a considerable amount" in his research and other costs incurred over the years.

You take a number of 8 1/2 x 11 color illustrations of baseball uniforms to a commercial photographer and you'll soon learn it's very expensive to convert them to color prints and to have them reduced in quantity to the size you need," he said.

So far though, he has found no buyer for the book he has authored.

"Publishers are reluctant to do anything about the book because of the costs involved. My guess is that it would cost from $50,000 to $100,000, much of that to pay for the time I've spent to prepare the pictures for the camera-ready condition that they are in," Okkonen will tell you.

The 56-year-old native of Muskegon is heartened, though by the encouragement he has received from other sources.

"I've gotten a lot of support from the people at the Cooperstown library and the (baseball) commissioner's office. They'd like to see the results of my research published," the noted baseball historian stated.

All of his painstaking work has not been in vain, though.

In fact, over a dozen major league teams have published the history of uniforms their teams have worn over the years, either directly or indirectly, as a result of Okkonen's tireless work.

"The Los Angeles Dodgers have already paid me for an article on the history of their uniforms dating back to when they were the Brooklyn Dodgers to the present. They are going to publish it in their 1990 yearbook. It will be the Dodgers' 100th anniversary, you know."

Count one more prospective sale for Okkonen since the Braves will be observing their 25th season in Atlanta and are considering using one of his stories in their upcoming yearbook.

A member of SABR (Society for American Baseball Research), Okkonen found his fellow members to be a valuable source of information. He wrote the history of the now defunct Federal League. That outlaw baseball operation existed for three years, including two as a major league in 1914 and 1915, before disbanding.

"It was interesting to learn that the league included teams from Indianapolis, Chicago, Kansas City, Brooklyn, Newark, Buffalo, Baltimore and Pittsburgh. Writing that publication was very fascinating," Okkonen said.

There are times, though, that make him wonder why more teams aren't truly interested in their tradition.

"I've always been interested in baseball history," he admits. But I'm not sure all the major league owners really care that much about the history of their team. I tried to use my skills as an artist to develop the art work, my general knowledge of baseball and the perseverance to do the research."

His work on the history of baseball uniforms has left him with one conclusion.

"When you consider how long baseball has been in existence, its amazing to realize uniforms haven't changed all that much. I mean, players still wear kickers and a cap," Okkonen said with a knowing smile.

He is currently working on yet another project. Okkonen has, in fact, done considerable research on major league baseball parks as they were in the early 1900s to 1915.

"I wonder how many people know Baltimore was a charter member of the American League in 1901 and 1902 before moving on New York to be known as the Highlanders and then the Yankees."

Another little known fact: The Milwaukee Brewers were also a charter member of the junior circuit prior to packing their bags and performing as the original St. Louis Browns.

"How many people know the Cubs have actually played at six different locations in the Windy City during their long history?" he asked.

The Detroit Tigers are unique, Okkonen research has disclosed.

"No other club in baseball has been at the same location as long a period as the Tigers. They've been at Michigan and Trumbull since 1896, the fields being known over the years as Bennett Park, Navin Field, Briggs Stadium and the current Tiger Stadium."

Okkonen has in his possession minute drawings of the Detroit baseball park as it grew from year to year.

Okkonen smiles over enterprising home owners of that era who constructed rickety "wildcat" stands outside the ball park and made a killing by selling seats. The Tiger organization, however, put a stop to the competition by installing a canvas across the fence to block the view of those fans.

To this day, Okkonen has a dream of obtaining a complete broadcast of a Tiger game as done by Hall of Famer Harry Heilmann, who had a large audience when he worked games in the 1940s and earlier.

Incidentally, Okkonen, who obtained his college degree later in life (1970) from University of Michigan-Dearborn, wrote an article which appeared in the July 9th issue of the *Detroit Free Press* on the anniversary of Heilmann's death. Heilmann died on that date in 1951.

"(Tiger broadcaster) Ernie Harwell read the story and was kind enough to call me on the phone. I told him of my obsession for finding a tape of a Heilmann broadcast. Darned if he didn't locate a highlight tape of my hero which featured parts of his best broadcasts.

Dentist Active Through Interest In Sports, History

by Sue Kurth, Horizons editor

Although he's been a dentist in Beloit since getting out of the military in 1964, he may be best known for the programs he gives on various topics.

Dr. Dan Green has presented programs dressed as Teddy Roosevelt, shown his slide collection of churches from around the world, slides of the island of Aruba off Venezuela's coast and talked on sports topics like the first team to beat the Packers and baseball humor.

And he doesn't charge for any of the programs. If someone insists on handing him a check, it goes directly to United Way, said Green.

But those involvements are just the tip of the iceberg for this busy volunteer. He also is a member of the Noon Lions, is on the Beloit Sports Hall of Fame Committee, is an ambassador, serves with the Beloit Snappers and has been very involved with Crime Stoppers.

Green has been chosen the *Beloit Daily News* Volunteer of the month for March.

He has worked with the Noon Lions for 34 years, the past 10 calling Bingo for the visually handicapped during monthly Pioneer Club meetings sponsored by the Lions.

"They love for me to do it and I love doing it," said Green, adding club members play Bingo a few times each year.

Of the Lions Green said "Lions do a lot for the visually handicapped. They have a great spirit and is a great organization."

He has also joined other Lions in ringing bells for the Salvation Army, recalling years when they stood on street corners downtown exposed to the elements. In 1974 or 1975 Green served as president of the Noon Lions. He has also joined other Lions in supporting a chili fund raiser for Special Olympics, coordinated annually by Bob Champion who Green calls "my hero."

The Lions also play softball against Special Olympians before a Snapper's game once each season.

"We always let them beat us," said Green.

As a 14-year member of the Beloit Sports Hall of Fame, Green has helped arrange for plenty of speakers for the annual banquet and usually gives the invocation. He also does some of the research for information to be printed on plaques. Jerry Elliott chairs the committee.

"My interest is in history and in recognizing sports men and women who have achieved," he said, adding he also served a couple of terms on the Beloit Historical Society Board in the past.

Green himself lettered in basketball, track and cross country in high school, and track and cross country in college. He also wanted to play football, but after two concussions gave it up.

Since 1974 he has been a member of the Ambassadors group of the Beloit Chamber of Commerce, having taken his turn at being in charge of coordinating groups to attend ribbon cuttings. He served as chamber president in 1976 and was a board member even before that.

"We're supposed to be an image group for the city," he said.

He has served on the Blackhawk Technical College Dental Advisory Board, and taken students into his office for learning experience.

It has been 55 years since Green joined Boy Scouts and he has never given up his membership, even after earning the Eagle Rank (the highest rank available to boys). But he's more than a member. He has served since 1968 as chair of the Eagle Scout Board of Review for Arrowhead District.

"We've passed about 300 Eagles," he said, adding that only two percent (of scouts) ever get there."

He is especially proud to be carrying on a heritage in scouting which crosses marriage lines.

"My father-in-law (Mr. James C. Ellis) was active in scouts in Rockton," said Green, adding that Steven Spielberg, Gerald Ford, Neal Armstrong and many other famous Americans were Boy Scouts.

Green also worked with troops when his own son, Scott, was young.

He has served with the Beloit Snappers since 1982 and was supportive of men like Everett Haskell, Joe Moen and George Spelius who brought the team to Beloit. Green, along with 19 others, was one of the original investors. He has also served as vice president, president and chairman of the board.

While he remains a member of the First United Methodist Church, he is much less active than he was for many years. He has been on the Pastor-Parish Relations Committee, chaired the administrative board, been past chair of the Council of Ministries, and is a former

Sunday schoolteacher and a former 20 year choir member.

He served two terms on Crime Stoppers, chairing it from 1995-96.

"It's really an outstanding board," he said, proud that the Quick 50 program was begun in the high schools during the years he served on the board.

He has helped with the actual pay-outs to anonymous tipsters.

It's a tremendous thing and a real asset to the community," he said.

Green was also part of a 100-person committee which recommended to the school board that Beloit Memorial High School be renovated several years ago. He was president of the Wisconsin Dental Society from 1979-80, chaired the Wisconsin Council of Professionals, which includes pharmacists, dentists, doctors, architects, hospital administrators, veterinarians and nurses.

Green has chaired United Way divisions at campaign time, been on the YMCA Board of Directors, was on the Salvation Army Advisory Board and was a Beloit College Trustee and is past president of the Alumni Association. He still participates in career fairs and other events at the college. He was on a committee during bicentennial planning which got bike-ways started around the city, and had helped out at Rotary Grand Prix events, though he isn't a Rotarian.

It was drama instructor, Betty Reinholz, who encouraged Green as a senior to go out for the play "Our Town." He claims that event helped him to gain self-confidence, and called Reinholz "a legend in her own time."

Green moved to Beloit with his family from Pennsylvania when he was just three. He graduated from Beloit High School, Beloit College and then did his dentistry work at Northwestern University. He served three years with the military, stationed in Germany, returning here to open a dental practice in the same office he still uses today. The biggest change? Today he can "sit down while doing dentistry." The office, he claims, offers "the best view of the city."

Green and wife Cornelia have two children, Scott and Mary Ann.

An admittedly active person, Green likes to bike, play golf and read.

As retirement nears Green is already eyeing extra activities he'll have time for.

"Maybe I'll volunteer with Stateline Literacy Council. I want to get into something that can really help people," he said. "I like helping people. A lot of people have helped me over the years. This is giving back to Beloit what Beloit gave me. I got a great education here."

Our high school had no baseball, I played summer legion and semi-pro baseball at Beloit College.

Notre Dame Boasts Rich Baseball History

by Cappy Gagnon

Thanks to the Gipp, Rockne and Rudy, all the world knows about Fighting Irish football. How many people know of the baseball contributions of the sons of Notre Dame? A few hundred words is way too little to express these accomplishments, but let's take a quick overview.

Cap Anson was one of the first players in the National Association, the first Major League, in 1871. Cap was arguably the most prominent baseball figure in the 19th century as player, manager and colorful character. Cap played on the Juanita's at Notre Dame, the campus of champions in the mid-1860s. He was the playing manager of the Cubs back when that was a good thing.

Bert Inks was Notre Dame's top player in 1888, the first year Notre Dame played games off campus. Bert had an undistinguished career in the majors, but the Ligonier, IN native was the favorite player of Ford Frick, who became baseball commissioner. Frick mentioned Bert in his autobiography.

Willie McGill had an interesting pro career. He pitched for the Irish in the very first varsity baseball game in April 1892. Thanks to McGill's pitching, the Irish whipped Michigan. Willie should have been up to the challenge, since he made his Minor League debut in 1889 at the age of 15! He pitched a no-hitter that year, the youngest man to ever do so. He made his Major League debut in 1890, winning 20. While working his arm into shape for his third Major League season, Willie stopped off to get the Irish varsity program off to a good start. The sore spots from Michigan were not pleased to see the famous McGill in the box.

Lou Sockalexis came along to Notre Dame five years later. He had been expelled from Holy Cross for problems with alcohol. The same fate befell him at Notre Dame after a month on campus. Notre Dame loaned Sockalexis train and cab fare to Cleveland so he could sign with the Cleveland Spiders. Firewater again brought down the Abnaki Adoni, but not before he achieved such fame that when the Cleveland team needed a new nickname, they chose "Indians" in honor of the first Native American to play in the majors. Cleveland needed the new nickname in 1915 because their manager, Dode Birmingham from Notre Dame, had benched the player, Nap Lajoie, for whom they were then named the "Naps."

In the first decade of this century, several men from Notre Dame played significant Major League roles. Ed Reulbach was one of greatest pitchers, the only man to pitch a doubleheader shutout, the first man to pitch a one-hitter in the World Series and the first man to win three consecutive winning percentage titles.

Red Murray was a great fielder, slugger and base runner, finishing second in stolen bases three times. Two of the times Red finished second, the leader was Notre Dame's Bob Bescher, who led four times and held the National League record for five decades. Bert Daniels, though not quite as accomplished as the others, had a unique talent, he was struck by pitches at a rate surpassed by only one batter in baseball history. Cy Williams won four home run titles in the majors. A dead-pull hitter, the first "Williams Shift" was created because of Cy.

John Mohardt came to Notre Dame shortly after WWI. Mohardt had dropped out of high school in the 10th grade. The Irish accepted him, in consideration of his intellectual abilities and athletic talents. By the time his athletic career ended eight years later, he had earned All-American recognition while blocking for George Gipp, played with Red Grange on the Bears, played with Ty Cobb on the Tigers, earned his MD from Northwestern and completed surgical residency at the Mayo Clinic. Gipp played three baseball games for Notre Dame, even though it was reputed to be his best sport.

Ed Walsh Jr. was not nearly as good a pitcher as his Hall of Fame dad, who came to Notre Dame to help coach him, but he did hold an accomplishment. While in the minors, young Walsh stopped Joe DiMaggio's hitting streak at 61 games! Young Walsh once pitched a big league game with Billy Sullivan Jr., also from Notre Dame, as his catcher. This remains the only game in Major League history where sons of a Major League battery comprised a Major League battery.

There were two men from Wisconsin named Red Smith in the class of 1927 at Notre Dame. One became the first Pulitzer Prize winning sports writer, the other played Major League baseball and professional football. Two other Notre Dame men from the 1920s had significant baseball creations. Bert Dunne had a one-year Minor League career after a fine Notre Dame performance. He is better known as the inventor of the batting tee and the writer of baseball instructionals and hitting films. Arch Ward displayed no athletic talent here, but became a great sportswriter and created the All-Star Game.

The same year Ward created the All-Star Game, 1933, Notre Dame's Frank Shaughnessy saved the minor leagues by creating the "Shaughnessy Plan." This post-season playoff, modeled after hockey, added spice to late season games, keeping fan enthusiasm at a high level during the depths of the Depression.

Rubert Mills drowned in 1929 while saving his best friend in a boating accident. At that time, Mills was about to win election as Sheriff of Essex County, NJ. Fourteen years earlier, Mills was the only New Jersey native on the New Feds, the Federal League team from Newark.

Mills put his Notre Dame law degree to work in 1916. The Federal League had folded after two costly years competing with the American and National Leagues. Mills insisted that the team pay for the remaining year of his contract. The team refused, claiming that Mills would not be paid because he was not playing. Mills complied by going to the ball park every day and participating in his own workouts. After a few weeks, the franchise relented and paid off Mills. While at Notre Dame, Mills once earned four athletic monograms in the same season. The first man to do this, Dutch Bergman, also played for the (guess what?) Cleveland Sockalexi.

John McHale played for the 1945 World Series Champion Detroit Tigers. He was later named Major League Executive of the Year during a 40-year career as scouting director, general manager, team president and league vice president while serving the Tigers, Braves and Expos.

Notre Dame had a few 1950s "bonus babies," including Diamond Jim Brady. Brady picked up three economics degrees here and became the president of Jacksonville University. He was followed to Notre Dame and the Majors by a high school teammate. Jim Hannan, who would later be the founding president of the Major League Baseball Players Alumni Association, wrote his master's thesis on the Major League Baseball Pension Plan.

Carl Yastrzemski came to Notre Dame in 1957, playing only one year of freshman baseball before signing with the Boston Red Sox. His MVP year of 1967 led the Bosox in their Impossible Dream year.

Ron Reed had a long career as a Major League pitcher. He was a much better hoopster at Notre Dame, winning the All-American mention in 1965. He could dunk like Michael (Jordan), when dunking was uncommon. He was one of two men from Notre Dame named Reed (Billy was the other) who played Major League baseball and professional basketball.

In the 1960s, Dan McGinn, a 1966 classmate of mine, achieved three large Major League accomplishments with the Montreal Expos. He hit the first homerun for the expansion Expos, won the first game pitched on foreign soil and pitched a three-hit shutout to stop a Tom Seaver winning streak at 16. Dan punted for the Irish football team and earned the nickname "Dangerous Dan."

Dan's catcher at Notre Dame, Rich "Moose" Sauget, had a long Minor League career but never got into a Major League game, despite being with the Atlanta Braves for one week. Rich wrote his master's thesis on the economic impact to St. Louis of the 1967 World Series.

In October 1997, Craig Counsell knocked in the tying run and scored the winning run for the Florida Marlins. In 1998 left-handed pitcher Chris Michalek became the 70th Major Leaguer from Notre Dame when he pitched two games for the Arizona Diamondbacks. The general manager of the Diamondbacks is Joe Garagiola Jr., who graduated from, well, you get the idea.

Notre Dame-a baseball factory.

Cappy Gagnon ND '66 is writing a book, Anson to Yaz, *about the history of baseball at Notre Dame, Cappy is the Coordinator of Stadium Personnel for Notre Dame and supervises student employees in the Notre Dame Security Police Department.*

The views expressed in this column are those of the author and not necessarily those of The Observer.

Mr. Baseball
A Day At The Diamond
With Bill Humber

by Bruce Meyer

It is early afternoon and the fans are restless and noisy. The St. Catharines Stompers, a Blue Jay Class A farm team, are battling the Auburn (New York) Astros. The field is alive with young men who are giving the best summers of their youths in pursuit of professional baseball careers. A few serious ball fans have driven all the way from Toronto to check out the future of the franchise and to ease their anxieties during a prolonged Jays losing streak. There are some loyal locals who have come to cheer the home team, but the crowd is composed mainly of school children on field trips, witnessing professional baseball at its lowest level and getting anti-drug messages from the police and the fire department.

As the game progresses, the kids are climbing all over the stands; many have drifted to the playground beside the concession booths. The message appears to be lost on most of them, i.e., that baseball equals good clean fun. For them, the game is just too slow. The real fans, however, remain glued to their seats. Some are even keeping line scores. For those devoted few, the St. Catharines Community Stadium is a little piece of heaven.

"Pretty prosaic name for a ball park, eh?" remarks Bill Humber (Vic 7T2) as he crosses his arms and squints at the diamond. "They should have called it The Vineyard or the Stomping Grounds. 'Stadium' sounds so unpoetic, so un-baseball."

By day, Humber is chair in the Faculty of Continuing Education at Seneca College, but baseball is his delight. The desktop computer in his office at Seneca contains the program Total Baseball, and on the shelves, the usual array of textbooks is interspersed with copies of his own volumes, *Cheering for the Home Team: The Story of Baseball in Canada (1983)*, *Let's Play Ball: Inside the Perfect Game* (1989) and *Diamonds of the North: A Concise History of Baseball in Canada* (1995).

Since 1979, each February he has taught a course named "Baseball Spring Training for Fans" to a handful of enthusiasts who cannot wait for the Grapefruit Circuit (spring training games in Florida) to begin. As a one time gesture at the end of the first course, Humber organized a weekend pilgrimage to the Baseball Hall of Fame in Cooperstown, NY. Seventeen years later, the trip is still an annual affair, fanatics from all walks of life gather for a weekend of baseball trivia and hero worship. The rallying cry, the parting and greeting phrase, says Humber, is "Next year in Cooperstown."

Humber was the key figure behind the Royal Ontario Museum's 1989 exhibit "Let's Play Ball: Inside the Perfect Game," and is currently on the Board of Governors for the soon-to-be reborn Canadian Baseball Hall of Fame in St. Mary's, Ontario.

In his spare time, he also coaches a team of 14 and 15 year olds in his home town, Bowmanville, Ontario, (a team named Bowmanville Glass and Mirror; their motto "We bend but we never break"). He believes in the public nature of games and their role in community life. For Humber, the game is a living tradition that spans more than 160 years of Canadian history.

As Canada's foremost baseball historian, in his recent book, *Diamonds of the North*, Humber chronicles with scholarly accuracy the story of the game as it has been played, and played with passion, north of the border. In a period that stretches from Dr. Adam Ford's account of the first recorded North American baseball game in Beachville (near Woodstock, Ontario) on June 4, 1838, to Joe Carter's homerun blast on Oct. 23, 1993, he has attempted to capture the detail, the thrill and the beauty of the way Canadians play the game. He has haunted not only the archives and the small town libraries, but the parks like this one in St.

Catharines where, he believes, the real game lies rooted in the consciousness of the fans.

It is not in the office, but on the diamonds of Bowmanville, or in Toronto's Sky Dome, or at little, minor league parks where Humber follows his avocation. For him, baseball is not only the ideal game, it is a Canadian game, as Canadian as hockey. And what is more, the first baseball game was likely played in Canada, not, as tradition would have it, in Cooperstown, NY.

"Cricket was the game of gentlemen and Tories. Upper-class stuff for the British minded, the traditionalists. Only ruffians and democrats played baseball. It was the game of farm boys. A game for men with dirty hands. And when you think of it, baseball is a very democratic sport. Almost like parliamentary democracy. One man standing there trying his best against the majority, and the majority trying to throw him out."

As he speaks, Humber keeps his eyes fixed on the game. A pitch crosses the plate, and the batter is punched out.

In *Diamonds of the North*, Humber points out that the first game of baseball in Canada took place in the midst of the Rebellion of Upper Canada in 1837-1838; on Military Muster Day, the annual holiday in honour of George III's birthday. The date, according to the Ford letter to the *Sporting Life* magazine, is almost a full year before the day Abner Doubleday is said to have played the famous first game at Cooperstown. Doubleday, of course, never claimed that he invented baseball. Even the Museum at Cooperstown (on a wall behind a door, safely tucked away from the major halls of the American shrine) admits that Doubleday did not invent the game at Cooperstown. Humber takes special delight in that.

Although on a smaller scale, Canadians have been quick to seize upon the opportunity of raising a lucrative shrine to the games' origins.

"In 1981, after I discovered Dr. Ford's document in a collection at Western, I went to Beachville, I spoke with people at the county museum, and they knew nothing of it. Now they make a big industry of the whole thing."

Humber chuckles. "When I went to Beachville in 1985 to film a documentary for the CBC, the producer asked me where the field was, exactly, and I said it was probably somewhere around, but let's just go out to a grassy place and take the shots there. These local kids were watching. They asked what we were doing. We said, 'We're filming a documentary about the first baseball game.' They said, 'Oh, its not here, its down there in that farm field.' There were these rolling fields and farm fences to crawl over and huge muddy patches. I said, 'Let's forget about that and do it here.' And the camera crew were happy to oblige. But the site is well documented now. What they should do is turn it into a Canadian field of dreams."

When it is suggested that there was poetic irony at the root of the Blue Jays' World Series win over the Atlanta Braves in 1992, (the International Olympic Committee having recently chosen Atlanta over Toronto among others as the host city for the 1996 Olympic Games), Humber stretches the point further with some fascinating facts.

Canadians won the first international professional attempt at a world series. The team was the London Tecumsehs of 1877, one of the premier teams of that era, with Albert Spalding's Chicago White Stockings and Boston's Red Stockings. The Tecumsehs beat a Chicago team to claim their crown.

"That London team may have been one of the finest Canadian squads ever put together. I went in search of the site of the original homeplate for Tecumseh Park. There was this old janitor there, and he started saying 'Yep, I remember back in the 20s at the time of the great flood here.' I had to interrupt him and say I was looking for something from the 1870s, not the 1920s. I felt awful for one upping the old guy. His memory wasn't antediluvian, after all."

Asked to explain how the University of Toronto fits into this picture, Humber is quick with his array of information. Professional baseball was played at U of T as early as the 1850s, on the cricket oval of King's College Circle. Teams such as the Canadian Pioneers were the toast of the sport during the fledgling days of the professional game.

On a personal level, however, Humber's passionate attachment to baseball came after his time at Victoria College. "I wasn't really interested in baseball while I was at Vic." Soccer, he says proudly, was what I played." Vic didn't really have a baseball team at that time.

"My interest in baseball does go back to the 1950s when my dad would take my brother and me down to Maple Leaf Stadium. One of the most vivid memories of my youth is a game we went to in 1957. Toronto won the pennant on the last day of the season, and as the game ended, a tremendous storm came up as Toronto got the final out. Quite a dramatic moment."

There was a period after the 1960s when baseball declined in North American. It was related to the fact that games became very uninteresting pitching matches, decided by a solo homerun or a stolen base. "I drifted away at that point. As a student, the only time I watched baseball all year was when I went over to Hart House to watch the World Series, almost more as a matter of ritual than a matter of interest. I remember watching the 1969 World Series when the Mets won. A Canadian, a U of T grad, Ron Taylor, was pitching."

In St. Catharines, the sun is growing hotter and reflects off the aluminum benches. Humber looks at his watch. The game is going slowly, we are in the horse latitudes of the fifth inning. There is a conference going on at the mound. No one seems to be in a hurry.

"I hope they get the game in before sundown. At this rate! This is just like in the early days of baseball, when morning games were common practice. Its one o'clock, and we're only in the fifth inning."

A large, purple plush grape, mascot of The Stompers, prances rudely in front of us and blocks our view of the plate. Not even at this level can baseball escape the pressures of kitsch and salemanship that have haunted the game in recent memory.

Humber laments, "When I was at the Babe Ruth Centennial Conference at Hofstra University in New York a few months ago, there were signs up: Please remember: do not ask the players for autographs! This is an academic conference! You just can't escape all the souvenir trappings of the game."

His trip to the conference was a mission in support of his "baseball is Canadian" thesis. He went to tell those assembled that Babe Ruth was a closet Canadian.

"Here are the facts. Babe Ruth hit his first professional homerun in Toronto, at the Hanlan's Point Park on the Island. His first wife was a Canadian. Joe Lannin, the Boston Red Sox owner who signed Ruth to his first major league contract, was born in Quebec. But the fact that really excited me was that I was co-discoverer (with St. Mary's University professor, Colin Howell) of the fact that Babe Ruth was taught to play baseball by a Canadian."

Brother Mathias, a priest at St. Mary's Industrial School for Boys in Baltimore (where Ruth spent his youth for being "incorrigible") was actually a French speaking Cape Bretonner named Martin Boutlier, born in 1872 in Lingan. That area of Nova Scotia has always been a hotbed of amateur ball, right back into the middle of the last century, with the first Canadian newspaper reference to the game in Joseph Howe's, *Novascotian,* in 1841. "Just think, if the scouts had paid more attention to Canadian baseball, we could have produced a whole army of Babe Ruths."

Humber recalls what brought him back to baseball: the contemporary literature of the sport, in particular Roger Kahn's, *The Boys of Summer,* published in 1972. His reading on the subject became voracious. He paraphrases author Thomas Boswell: The great thing about baseball is that it is like a Victorian novel. It has so many chapters, so many ebbs and flows, loves and hates, wars and peaces, climaxes and anti-climaxes. That's the same rhythm there is to a baseball season.

"Good baseball literature," Humber notes, "both fiction and non-fiction, has that quality too. It follows the ups and downs to some kind of logical conclusion. That, for me, has always been the joy of baseball. Taking away the pennant race and introducing wild card teams under the new playoff system was a sad thing to happen to baseball."

It is through the literature of baseball that the games continue long after final out of October. Humber likes to laugh about his contribution to the works of one of baseball's more notable pens, W.P. Kinsella.

"When the short story "Shoeless Joe Jackson Comes to Iowa' first appeared in the literary magazine *Descant,* I wrote a fan letter to Kinsella. I said, 'Your short story was like the last inning of a perfectly executed ball when you prayed for extra innings so you would never have to go home.' I kept a copy of the letter. He wrote back a very nice response."

In 1983, Kinsella enlarged the story into the novel *Shoeless Joe,* which became the basis for the movie "Field of Dreams." On page 231 of the book, Humber found Ray Kinsella (the protagonist) talking to someone and asking what it will be like when he meets his father. The response is "Once you meet him it will be like the last inning of a perfectly played ball game, you'll pray for extra innings so you'll never have to go home." He thought, wait a minute, that sounds awfully familiar! "Some-

one I told that to said, that's plagiarism, and I said no, that's the highest form of flattery."

The fifth inning has just ended. The homeside is down 2-0. Some of the teachers are shepherding their weary charges onto buses. In a bleacher seat down near the left field foul pole, away from the crowd, sits a lonely figure in a baseball cap sporting the crest of the visiting team. The man was keeping a line score but gave that up to concentrate on the game. Humber strikes up a conversation with him. The man is from Port Hope, Ontario and is the father of Jason Green, a player on the Auburn team, who pitched the previous night's contest. Jason was called up from the Florida Instructional League for a good look by the Jays, and his father decided to follow his progress whenever possible. The boy has a good arm. Perhaps Jason Green from Port Hope will be the one in a hundred thousand whose dream of being a big league star really comes true.

In the end, the St. Catharines Stompers lose 3-0. "But hey," says Humber as we walk back to his van, "there's a whole new ball game tomorrow."

An Opening Day Memory
by Frank "Bud" Kane

Sportman's Park, Wednesday afternoon, April 16, 1941, Opening Day. The American League Champion Detroit Tigers were in town to play the Browns.

Some schools in St. Louis let classes off on opening day afternoon, but not St. Luke's. It was a beautiful spring day and my friend George Gaffney and I has agreed at recess that morning, we had to get to this game. The problem was to come up with a believable excuse for Sister Bernard to let us off for the afternoon so she wouldn't call and check with our mothers. Sister Bernard was known as the strictest nun at St. Luke's; one classmate described her "a Prussian general in drag." We decided on our stories: my aunt died and I had to go to the wake, and George had to go to the dentist. We both received skeptical looks and she made George open wide and show her the cavity, but we were free!

By pooling our financial resources we each had enough for streetcar fare (10 cents), a scorecard (five cents), a hot dog 15 cents and a coke (10 cents). Of course, we got in free with our "Brown Brigade" cards (the Browns version of the Cardinals Knothole Gang).

We took the Forest Park streetcar, transferred to the Grand Avenue line and got to Grand and Dodier about an hour before game time. The field looked beautiful and a big crowd of almost 25,000 was gathering, including a whole section of newly drafted GIs from Jefferson Barracks; also a big contingent of Browns Brigade kids in our left grandstand section. George and I bought our scoreboards, hot dogs, cokes and settled in.

Eldon Auker and Buck Newsom treated us to a pitching duel for seven and a half innings. Rudy York homered to the left field bleachers in the seventh for the Tigers only run. Rookie Johnny Lucadello had four hits, Johnny Berardino made several great plays at shortstop, Harlond Clift made a diving stop on Hank

Greenberg's grounder over third and threw him out, and Chet Laabs grabbed Barney McCosky's drive off the right field screen and cut him down at second on a fine throw to Berardino as he tried to stretch it into a double.

Then in the bottom of the eighth the Browns sent the crowd into a frenzy with a barrage of seven hits good for seven runs. Auker set the Tigers down in the ninth and the Browns had an 8-1 victory. Next morning's *Globe Democrat* reported: "TIGER MEAT WELL BROWNED, an eighth inning rally in which 11 men batted and seven of them hit safely to score seven runs, blasted big Buck Newsom right out of the ball park and gave the Browns an 8-1 victory over A.L. Champion Tigers in the opening game of the season yesterday before a jubilant throng of 24,667."

The jubilant throng let out another big cheer when the big scoreboard in left field showed that the Cardinals scored two runs in the ninth off Vander Meer and Mort Cooper had won over the Reds in Cincinnati 4-2. The *Globe Democrat* story concluded: "Berardino turned in a job of shortstopping that was sensational and Judnich, Laabs and Radcliff dragged down some well-hit drives as their contribution to a perfect day."

It really was a perfect day and we had a happy streetcar ride home. But I don't think Sister Bernard believed us for a minute.

How Mel Lehan Found His Own Field Of Dreams
by Pete McMartin

There he was, wearing a major leaguer's glove and taking a throw from Cal Ripken, the man who had surpassed Lou Gehrig.

On Sept. 25, 1997, Mel Lehan, 53, was diagnosed with esophageal cancer. Actually, it was a misdiagnosis. It was cancer of the esophagus and the stomach. Two weeks later, surgeons did their work.

When he came out of chemotherapy in mid-December, Lehan could barely walk. His immune system had reached ebb tide. For two months, he quarantined himself in his Kitsilano home and by the time he emerged in February, he had resolved to do things he had always wanted to do but never had.

One of the things he wanted to do was spend more time with his daughters, whom he loves fiercely. He has three daughters; Shaina, 18, Kathleen, 15 and Mira, 10. Right now he is in California with Mira, doing Disneyland. In June, Mel, a baseball fanatic, will take his daughters on a tour of the old major league baseball parks. Mel could think of no better shared experience for them than visiting Wrigley Field, Yankee Stadium, Tiger Stadium and Fenway Park.

The other thing he wanted to do was attend spring training in Fort Lauderdale, where Mel's beloved Baltimore Orioles train. Mel has been an Orioles fan since the old Vancouver Mounties were the Orioles' farm team.

At any rate, Mel, who isn't a rich man, thought the hell with the cost, he would go to spring training. A man never knows how many springs he has left in him.

Mel Lehan (left), and Cal Ripken chatting on the bench, March 24, 1998 in Fort Lauderdale, Florida.

"I am trying," Mel said, "to enjoy every minute."

The only other time he'd acted on such impulse was the time he flew to Baltimore to catch Oriole superstar Cal Ripken play his 2,131st game in a row, breaking Lou Gehrig's record for consecutive games played. Ripken, Mel says, is the greatest ballplayer of his time.

So in March, Mel went to Fort Lauderdale.

But before I describe what happened there, I should tell you a few things about Mel.

He has lived his entire life in Kitsilano. When development in the 1980s threatened to change Kitsilano, Mel threw himself into community activism, trying to preserve the neighborhood's character.

He ran four times for council, helped form a network of city-wide neighborhood associations, chaired the Kitsilano Residents' Association. Mainly, he was just a good citizen.

Earlier this month, friends organized an appreciation night for him at Kitsilano's St. James Community Square, a neighborhood center. Over 300 people showed up. It was standing room only. They raised money to help pay for a trip to Europe for the Lehans this summer.

But there was another, more singular, act of kindness. Before Mel departed for spring training, a friend, who wishes to remain anonymous, phoned Ripken's press agent in Baltimore, explained Mel's situation and asked if Mel could meet Ripken and get an autograph. Ripken's agent phoned back: Okay.

Mel knew nothing about this. When his wife, Barbara, told him three days before the event, he was ecstatic.

"I had three days to be excited," Mel said.

On the big day, Mel wore a commemorative Oriole baseball cap he bought at Ripken's 2,131st game. When he got to the ballpark, he was led to the Orioles' dugout and told to do whatever he wanted, Cal would be along in a moment. Mel picked up a bat and swung it.

A few minutes later, Ripken appeared. He was bigger than Mel expected and even more handsome and sculpted than he appeared on TV. And very, very nice.

"He had me at my ease in five seconds," Mel said. "He wasn't condescending, just real natural and we talked about baseball. He gave me long, intelligent answers, not the kind of stock cliches that baseball players have when they answer questions. He was fabulous."

Mel doesn't remember how long they talked, he was too engrossed in the moment, but Ripken's handler came over to the dugout and told Ripken it was time to go. At this, Mel's face dissolved. It was as if someone had deflated him.

Ripken, seeing this, waved his handler away. He shouted to Oriole star outfielder Brady Anderson, out on the field: "Hey Brady, give me your glove!" And Anderson threw Ripken his glove and Ripken handed Mel the glove and the two men walked out on to the diamond.

And Mel remembers the sky being a sky blue and the grass being grass green and the world arranged in all its elemental beauty. It was warm. Ball players lolled on the grass, laughing. And Mel stood on the grass with his beloved Orioles around him and Ripken, standing as far away as a man would when playing catch, set himself, raised his arm and threw the ball. It came at Mel with that audible hiss major league throws have when they bite through the air and Mel, who played organized baseball until he was 22, when he pitched a 1-0 shutout and hit in the winning run in the last game he ever played, raised the glove and caught the ball cleanly. "It was Heaven on Earth," Mel said. "I was suspended in time for a few minutes, playing catch with my buddy Cal. It was wonderful."

"In Appreciation of Moments with 26 Pre-WWII Baseball Men"

by James D. Smith III

Whether visiting them "at home" (penthouses to convalescent centers), corresponding by phone or mail, or meeting at gatherings along the way, what a privilege it has been to share moments with bearers of The National Pastime such as these.

Joe Wood ('08, Red Sox), who was a living expression of "the glory of their times," remembered Cy Young, rookie Babe Ruth as Adonis, and praised rifle-armed catcher Forest Cady "because he made up for my slow delivery."

Chet Hoff ('11, Highlanders), who lived to 107 and remembered the era of wooden ballparks, volunteering that he'd gladly take the mound today to be paid 10 million dollars and pitch complete games. Amazing!

Paul Otis ('12, Highlanders), whose sole major league hit was off of Walter Johnson, and who relished being invited to eat oysters with Hal Chase before a broken leg retired him into insurance sales.

'Shag' Thompson ('14, Athletics), who remembered the 1914 World Series with regret (he never played), and didn't like Mr. Mack because, even when the team deteriorated, he was given no chance to be a regular.

Bob Wright ('15, Cubs), who pitched to his baseball hero, Roger Bresnahan, and seven decades later made the first pitch at Wrigley's 75th anniversary game. He saw Matty and the Honus in the twilight...

Jimmie Reese ('17, Angels), who began as a PCL bat boy under Frank Chance, roomed with The Babe, and in his 90s remained an Angels conditioning coach and impish, picture-framing gentleman. On his wall: "How rapidly doth fame fleeeth."

Al Conkwright ('20, Tigers), who rode boxcars to make games in the West and, given his major league chance, enjoyed pitching for Ty Cobb who he said was a great competitor but treated him well.

Joe Hauser ('22, Athletics), who hit 60 plus home runs twice, loved Milwaukee and his Irene, and still remembered his friend Hap Felsch weeping when the 1919 Series was mentioned. "Unser Choe."

Johnny Kerr ('23, Tigers), who was a scrappy archive of West Coast baseball, but loved his American League years, especially being in a Senators uniform at the 1933 World Series.

Lou Dials ('25, American Giants), who took the field with many of the early Negro Leaguers and, while never a great player, was a great promoter and representative of an era past.

Dick Bartell ('27, Pirates), who respected the '27 Yankees but really loved the National League brand of baseball, and told stories illustrating how he got the nickname "Rowdy." And, yes, Pie Traynor was that good!

Woody English ('27, Cubs), who was the last of the '33 All Stars, with a sense of joy at being a Cubs shortstop and of responsibility as a gentleman while managing in the AAGPBL. Always thanked me for calling.

Edgar Munzel ('29, Herald Examiner), who "saw 'em all" covering Chicago baseball, and made a pact with John C. Carmichael never to write a book. His recollections of McCarthy, Hornsby, Appling, et al? Priceless!

Rick Ferrell ('29, Browns), who was the last of the '33 AL All Stars, and could not understand why the "Commissioners Office" stopped sending him invitations (or even greetings) marking the Annual Classic.

Luke Appling ('30, White Sox), who spoke highly of Woody, often of Ted Lyons and with

In 1984, SABR recreated an 1884 game when the Providence Grays beat the New York Metropolitans. (Courtesy of James D. Smith III)

a scientist's precision when addressing the subject of hitting (and strategy of the foul ball).

Smead Jolley ('30, White Sox), who loved the San Francisco Bay Area, building its bridges and starring on its PCL ball fields, and spoke of Fenway Park with a slow, infectious, unforgettable smile.

Ben Chapman ('30, Yankees), who communicated the thrill of using superb athletic skills aggressively, and the wisdom that came from commitment to The One whose December 25 birthday he shared.

George Detore ('30, Indians), who was a model of flexibility: third baseman turned catcher, New Yorker in the PCL, wartime manager who effectively had his infield drafted.

Tony Freitas ('32, Athletics), who savored his Portuguese heritage and fishing, and spoke candidly about the triumphs (and limitations) of finesse pitching to batters like The Babe, The Beast and Smudgie.

Frank Crosetti ('32, Yankees), who personified "Yankee class" when the hand that shook the Babe's, the Clipper's, the Mick's graciously wrote a thank you note for my get-well card (heart surgery).

Buck Leonard (33, Baltimore Stars), whose voice brought to life the 'Golden Age' of the Negro Leagues (Josh!), whose off-field morality matched his on-field excellence, and whose HOF induction speech declared "the greatest praise comes from our Lord and Savior, Jesus Christ."

Red Barber ('34, WSAI), who was a master of language (vivid, crisp, gracious), in the broadcast booth, on the phone and in print and could illumine "Dem Bums" and Episcopal liturgy discussions alike.

Bill Starr ('35, Senators), who grew up watching games at Comiskey and Wrigley, grew from bullpen catcher to minor league magnate and grew into his role as an apologist for vintage baseball.

Bill Conroy ('35, Athletics), who never forgot the joy of being 18 and accepting Connie Mack's invitation to be an American League batting practice catcher at the '33 All Star Game.

Bobby Doerr ('37 Red Sox), who managed to open his PCL career at 16, play hard while making no enemies, inspire many with his devotion to his wife and family and thank the Lord for it all!

1984, the recreated 1884 Metropolitans. (Courtesy of James D. Smith III)

Ted Williams ('39, Red Sox), who was the greatest hitter ever, and whose San Diego, Minneapolis, Boston path was followed decades later by our family's as well. What a grand moment when he seemed interested!

A Pilgrimage To Yankee Stadium
July 4, 1998
by Scott Pitoniak

I once sneaked out to center field by myself as a youth to see how things looked from Mickey Mantle's point of view and felt the same tingle some people get from Civil War battlefields. - Wilfred Sheed, Baseball and Lesser Sports

The #4 train we had boarded at Grand Central Station 20 minutes earlier emerged from the dark, clammy subway tunnel beneath the Harlem River and rumbled like an old-fashioned rollercoaster up the rusty, elevated tracks. Before screeching to a halt high above the corner of River Avenue and 161st Street in the South Bronx, I caught a glimpse of the mountainous, white concrete edifice.

"There it is! There it is," I said, pointing

with the wide-eyed wonderment of a young boy. "Yankee Stadium! The house that Ruth built! The most famous ballpark in the world!"

My wife and kids looked at me as if I were crazy.

"Dad, be quiet," 11-year-old Amy implored, poking me in the ribs. "You're embarassing us."

"Yeah, Dad," chimed in 8-year-old Christopher, grinning mischievously. "Settle down before you have a heart attack."

There was no danger of that, though the palpitations were similar to ones I felt 32 years ago when my father and I made this same baseball pilgrimage for the first time.

"It's just a big building, Dad," said Amy, her logical assessment sounding sacrilegious to a 40-something guy who once hung on Mel Allen's every word.

"Amy, you don't understand," I protested mildly as we walked off the train. "It's more than a building. Much more."

The old stadium had a biblical look. I assumed it had been standing on 161st Street since before Christ. Years later when I saw the actual Roman Coliseum, I couldn't suppress an inner gasp of recognition. Ahh! It's like Yankee Stadium. - Laura Cunningham, Sleeping Arrangements

As we pushed through the turnstiles beyond the left-center field fence two hours before the Yankees' Fourth of July game against the Baltimore Orioles, I clutched my son's hand the way my dad had clutched mine so many summers ago. Within moments, we were engulfed by the cavernous sight of 50,000 blue seats and several million blades of green grass.

While soaking it all in, I was reminded that this was not my father's ball park any more. Massive, multi-million dollar renovations two decades ago had modernized the 75-year-old stadium, taking away some of its architectural charm. Gone was the roof that had covered the entire third deck, and, with it, the ornate copper facade overhang that Mantle had smashed baseballs against. The outfield walls had been moved considerably closer to homeplate. Death Valley, a place where 450-foot fly balls once went to die in the gloves of speedy outfielders, had been reduced to a memory.

Still, despite the downsizing, the romance remained. If you let your imagination run wild, you could visualize the Babe and the Iron Horse, Joe D. and Yogi. You could still hear Allen, the Voice of the Yankees, exclaim into his microphone, "How about that?"

As we waited in line to view the monuments, Yankees third baseman Scott Brosius deposited a batting practice home run 10 feet from us. An usher named Tony picked it up, walked over to Amy, and said, "Honey, this one has your name on it." My incredulous daughter couldn't believe her good fortune. The radiance of her smile was exceeded only by the afternoon sun.

Some ball yard, huh? - Babe Ruth

With time to kill before the first pitch, I took my son up the ramp to the third deck in right field. He started to run, and I told him to slow down before he fell. It occurred to me that my dad had once issued the same warning to me at the very same spot.

The upper deck at the Stadium is not a place for those fearful of heights. The steps are so steep, that upon descension, you get the impression that your next step will be a 120-foot free-fall to the field. Christopher and I went halfway up the stands, and I pointed to the back row and told him about home runs the Mick used to launch up here. Christopher looked uneasily down at the field and toward homeplate, a good 500-plus feet away. "Dad, that's impossible," he said. "'Even Mark McGwire couldn't hit them this far." I just smiled.

The game that day was closely contested, with the Yankees eking out a 4-3 win on a blown ninth-inning call that went against the O's, My son was disappointed he didn't witness any home runs, but he was thrilled to see Yankee shortstop, Derek Jeter, make an acrobatic play and drive in three runs with two base hits.

My kids seemed to enjoy the game, but they weren't riveted the way I once was. They appeared more interested in trips to the concession stands and souvenir shops. They enjoyed imitating the vendor who kept bellowing in thick, New Yawkese: "Git your cold beah, heah. Git your cold beah." At one point, my soccer-playing daughter asked me where first base was. She also wondered if we were sitting anywhere near where that half-ton concrete support beam that had crashed down in April. My wife looked at the finely manicured grass and wondered why I couldn't get our yard to look like that.

Midway through the game, I closed my eyes briefly, and tried to imagine my dad and the facade and the Mick muscling baseballs into the clouds. I wished Andrew Pitoniak could have shared this moment with his son and grandchildren. I wished he could have sat there among us. I would have told him how much I appreciated all the times he had made those eight-hour roundtrips from Rome, NY, to the Bronx for Sunday afternoon doubleheaders. I would have told him how much I loved him.

It had been almost 28 years to the day since we had made our last trip to this baseball cathedral. It was Oldtimers' Day at the stadium that afternoon. Six months later Dad's heart beat a final time.

There are ghosts in this building. - Joe Torre, Yankees manager

Sinatra's "New York, New York" blared over the speakers as we filed out of the park,

and as I held my daughter's hand, I felt quite contented. I was thankful that my children had indulged my nostalgic feelings; that they had not been too embarrassed by their old man. Perhaps one day they'll realize this isn't just a big building; that no ballpark in the world can hold a Louisville Slugger to this place. Perhaps they'll make a pilgrimage with their children, too, providing the place hasn't been razed by then. Maybe they'll even ask me to join them. That would be so sweet.

Better Late Then Never
by Keith Olbermann

I should have been SABR's youngest member, number 30-something on the seniority list, and have passed my 25th anniversary by now. But I was a little too shy.

As a 14-year-old, I spent my part of our family vacation in Cooperstown walking each morning through the picturesque streets of the village, directly into the library at the Hall of Fame. As a baseball historian in the larvae stage, I had become annoyed that no one had kept a comprehensive record of team coaches, so I decided to compile my own. The library was a well-staffed and immaculately kept-up facility then, but surprisingly empty, and the staff graciously helped me through stacks of baseball registers and Heilbroner's books. I dutifully compiled, by hand no less, lists dating back to 1921 (and thumbed in amazement through the old blue books that actually listed Babe Ruth's home address every year). The list was later "published" by my friend Mike Aronstein, who basically founded the more respectable parts of what is now known as the sports memorabilia industry. I'm certain we gave away more copies than we sold.

In any event, the visit to the library brought me face-to-face with my first copy of the SABR Research Journal. Membership was still in double-digits then, and Bob Davids was as encouraging of new applicants as we are today. But I thought, what the hell, I was just a kid, and how was I going to get to the next meeting in Maryland anyway? By bike?

So I didn't join. And as SABR mushroomed through the 1970s and 1980s I kept buying the journals and making my own forays into research. Finally in 1984, Syd Cohen and a batch of the New Englanders decided to commemorate the first World's Series by re-playing a game, in full garb and complete accordance with the ancient rules, at McCoy Stadium in Pawtucket. By this time, I was a sportscaster at a Boston television station, and connived a camera crew to join me to cover this foray into virtual time travel.

Seeing Joe Lawler, Syd and all the rest, groaning and sweating under the sweaty multi-pound flannel uniforms finally induced me to join. Syd even procured me an extra New York Metropolitans' uniform (perhaps, it occurs to me now, this was the birth of the Turn-Back-The-Clock Uniform craze), which I still have; as I still have my SABR membership. Not number 50 closer to number 1400, but proudly retained these 15 years and intended to be for as many more as I have.

SABR Boston Regional, 1985. Top: Peter Gammons, Pete Palmer, Ellery Clark, Cliff Kachline. Bottom: Rich "Dixie" Tourangeau, Jim Smith, Bob Wood.

Larry Aaronson
Franklin A Aasen
Craig W Abbott
Brett Abbott
Ken D Abramson
David C Accardi
Michael A Accardo
Ernie Accorsi
Stephen Acee
Edward Achorn
Jody Ackerman
Alan J Ackerman
Mike Ackerman
Dick Acton
Richard D Adair
Robert K Adair
Edward Adamczyk
Tom Adams
Bruce Adams
Richard D Adams
Robert H Adams
Bruce Adams
Donald L Adams
Stephen C Adamson
Ross Adell
Bruce Adelson
Marshall Adesman
Barry Adico
Richard Adler
Martin Adler
John Agius
Michael Agnello
Mark J Agnello
David Agostinelli
Gustavo N Agrait
Tim Ahlgrim
Arthur R Ahrens
Chuck Ailsworth
Russell Aiuto
William E Akin
Thomas N Akins
Gary M Akizuki
Barry Alan
William J Albach
Edwin L Albrecht
David L Alexander
Charles C Alexander
Paul J Alfano
Charles E Allen
Raymond D Allen
John Allen
John B Allen
Tom Allen
Douglas Allen
David M Allen
Bob Allen
David L Allen

Don Allen
David E Allred
James Alt
George Altemose
Andrew Althaus
Thomas L Altherr
Mark Altschuler
David W Alvarez
Mark Alvarez
George Amadio
Delphin Ambrose
Robert Amdur
Peter Amero
Larry Amman
Nick G Anagnost
Donald Andersen
Richard H Anderson
Scott Anderson
Robert C Anderson
Roy Anderson
Eddie M Anderson
Edwin J Anderson
Robert H Anderson
Michael Anderson
David W Anderson
David K Anderson
Raymond Louis
    Andreotti
Paul Andresen
Don Andrews
Peter G Andrijeski
John Antonucci
Drew Apoldite
Martin Appel
James Apple
Terry Appleby
Sheldon Appleton
Peter P Aprato
Bill Arata
Steven D Archer
David Arcidiacono
James Arciold
Jean Ardell
Frank Ardolino
Paul Arganbright
Arizona State University
Angel M Armada
Ronald D Armagast
Michael C Armijo
Mark Armour
Jonathan Arnold
Ralph A Arnold
William Arnold
Kirk Arnott
Michael P Aronstein
Richard W Arpi
Guy Arrigoni

Norman Arrington
John P Asiello
Priscilla Astifan
David Atkatz
Tom Atkins
William R Atkison
Richard Attiyeh
Auraria Library
Douglas Averitt
Michael Avery
William B Aylward
John A Ayoub
Scott D Azie
Lawrence S Azrin
Frank J Azzarello
Orville E Babcock
Rory Babich
Bert C Bach
P. Bryon Backenson
Charlie Bacon
Ralph Badenhop
Jan Bagin
David Bailey
Gary A Bailey
James Bailey
Michael Bailey
Rand E Bailey
Bob Bailey
Mel Bailey
Bob Baillargeon
Bradley Bain
Jeff Baird
Len Baird
R. Alan Baker
Will Baker
Phil Baker
Steven N Baker
Stuart L Baker
Robert W Baker
Richard H Baker
Jim Baker
M. Charles Bakst
Lawrence Baldassaro
Joseph A Baldassarre
William P Baldauf
Don W Baldwin
Jeffrey E Ball
David Ball
James A Ball
Bill Ballew
David Ballheimer
Bill Ballou
Heidi Bamford
Stephen M Bannen
Tom Banocy
David Barash
Guy Nickolas Barbieri

Alan Bard
Jim Bard
David Barish
Steven Barkan
Davis O Barker
Harry Barker
Alan S Barkin
Jon K Barlow
Edward L Barmakian
Russ Barmmer
Robert C Barnett
John E Barnett
Theodore M Barnett
Robert K Barney
Adam Barnhart
Robert Barrett
Ronald M Barrett
Daniel J Barrett
David W Barrett
Peter Barrows
David R Barstow
Ted Bart
Jeff Barto
Tye Basham
Michael N Bass
Roland L Bassett
Carl Bassi
Jim Bastian
Walter L Bates
John Bates
David M Bates
Gil V Batman
Leon J Battista
Carlos Bauer
Paul Bauer
James L Baughman
Joe Baum
Lawrence Baum
James Baum
E.J. Bavasi
Terry A Baxter
Frederick Bazemore
Peter S Beagle
Dick Beahrs
Harold W Bean
Gordon Beard
Sarah M Beardslee
Wm Michael Beasley
Larry Beatty
Michael Beck
Eric W Beck
James M Beck
Peter Becker
Bob Becker
Michael Beckerich
Jim Beckett
Robert Beckoff

Larry Beebe
J. Harland Beery
Timothy J Beever
Evelyn Begley
Damian Begley
Jay D Behrens
Jeffrey R Beichel
Rev. Gerald Beirne
Lewis J Belfont
Mark Belgya
Geoff Belinfante
Douglas S Bell
Paul A Bell
Rob Bellamy
Joseph F Belle Isle
Gerard J Belliveau
Stanley S Belostock
Frederick M Benario
Robert Bencks
Michael Bender
William E Bender
Joe Benedetti
Chuck Benedict
John Benesch
Barry Bengtsson
Merton Benikoff
Craig Bennett
John Bennett
Jay Bennett
Paul M Bennett
Steve Bennett
Jim Bennie
James Benoit
Henry J Benoit
Alexander Bensky
John C Benson
Robert C Benson
Russell K Benton
Bruce Berard
David Berenson
Joey Beretta
Philip S Bergen
Morey Berger
Daniel Berger
Sy Berger
John Bergez
Robert A Berghoff
Irwin B Bergman
Charles Bergoffen
Dean H Bergy
Carroll Beringer
Samuel Berkowitz
Peter Berkowsky
Gai I Berlage
David Berland
Robert C Berlo
Brian Berman

Henry S Berman
Jay Berman
Richard J Bernal
Thomas Bernard
John Bernauer
Robert S Bernhardt
Max G Bernhardt
R Elfren Bernier
Herb Bernstein
Mark F Bernstein
Robert D Berwick
Alan Bescan
Mark Beskeen
Philip Bess
James Peter Bessolo
Gregory Beston
Dell Bethel
David J Betman
Frank Bettencourt
Henry N Betzer
Michael Betzold
Robert Beukelaer
Richard Beverage
Lynn E Bevill
Charlie W Bevis
Ron Bianchi
Thomas Biblewski
Eric Bickel
William Bickers
Wilhelm Bier
David B Biesel
Marky Billson
Joseph J Bilota
Dennis Bingham
Robert Bionaz
Steve Birch
William Birely
Kenneth Birkemeier
Phil Birnbaum
Ronald W Bischoff
Furman Bisher
Jeff Bishop
John Bisiccia
Walter Biskupski
Harm Bisschop
Marvin Bittinger
Donald F Bittner
Richard J Biunno
Peter C Bjarkman
Barry Lee Bjork
Jay Black
John L Black
John Thomas
Blackburn
Thomas R Blaha
Charles P Blahous
John F Blair
Lowell L Blaisdell
Mike Blake
John C Blake
Mark Blanchette
Clarence Blasco
Willard H Blaskopf
John S Blau
Clifford Blau

Kenneth E Blazek
Richard B Bleiberg
Anthony P Blengino
Steve Block
A.G. Block
Alan J Bloem
Stephen Blomberg
Charles H Blomquist
Burt L Bloom
William P Bloom
Mort Bloomberg
Alan Blumkin
Robert F Bluthardt
Robert F Bobrowski
Robert K Bodenstein
Gib Bodet
Richard N Boe
Robert W Boehm
Richard H Bogard
Robert S Bogart
Terry Bohn
Charles Boisclair
Michael Bojanowski
Andrew A Bokser
Phillip J Bolda
Tom Boles
Jim Bollinger
Norman P Bolotin
Todd P Bolton
Chip Bomyea
Michael Bonanno
James D Bonebrake
Charles Bonfanti
Daniel L Bonk
Carl A Bonk
Al Bonowitz
Larry S Bonura
Timothy W Booker
Leslie J Boone
Edward Booth
William J Bordonaro
Stephen D Boren
Bob Borgen
Thomas J Borkowski
Jess S Boronico
Ray Borowicz
William A Borst
Francis J Boslett
Bruce R Bosley
James C Bostain
Talmage Boston
Charles S Boswell
Abbey M Botkin
Kevin Boucher
Frederick Henry
Boughter
Grant Boulden
John P Bourg
Thomas A Bourke
William C Bousquette
Kim B Boutelier
John M Bowden
Robert M Bowen
Jack Bowers
William T Bowler

Frank P Bowles
James R Bowman
John S Bowman
Bruce Boxdorfer
Burton A Boxerman
Jim Boyd
Jonathan A.T. Boyd
Alex Boyd
Lou Boyd
Thomas J Boyd
David L Boyd
Jim H Boylan
Daniel Boyle
Francis P Boyle
Bob M Boynton
Richard H Bozzone
George E Brace
R.W. Bradford
Richard W Bradley
Leo H Bradley
Rex L Bradley
David J Bradley
James Gregory
Bradsher
Robert M Brady
Michael Brady
Patrick D Brahney
Ray Brandes
Mark Brandsgard
John F Brandt
James Brannan
Michael Brannan
Jack C Braun
Patty Braunstein
Arnie Braunstein
Terry D Brazeal
John Brazil
James H Bready
Robin Brecker
Steve Breen
Gregory Brehm
George-o Breitbeck
James F Brennan
James F A Brennan
Francis Brennan
Charles Brereton
Dick Bresciani
Michael J Bresciani
Sean Bresnahan
Chuck Brewster
John Briar
Dennis Bricault
Edward D Brickley
Scott Brickwood
Ron Briley
J Fred Brillhart
Dale Brinkley
Darryl Brock
Steve Brockett
Arthur F Brod
Norman P Brodesser
Bob Broeg
Stephen B Bromley
Matthew B Bronski
David A Bronstein

Elisabeth Brooke
Charles A Brooks
Isaac C Brooks
Harold E Brooks
Edward Brooks
John K Brooks
Vincent Broomes
Randy Brough
James A Brown
James A Brown
Gordon W Brown
Karen Brown
Darrel M Brown
Charles C Brown
Robert M Brown
Robert S Brown
Jeff Brown
David A Brown
Paul D Brown
Robert J Brown
Garry P Brown
Borden Brown
B.G. Brown
Edward Brown
Patrick Brown
William E Brown
Joe L Brown
Geoffrey Brown
Robert W Brown
Robert Browning
Reed Browning
Richard M Brozman
Robert Bruce
Kenneth J Bruck
Robert M Brunell
Ernie N Brunetto
Leo Brunner
Harry P Brunt
Henry C Bryan
Jay Buckley
Stephen Buckner
Steven G Budnik
Frank J Budreck
Bob Buege
Alan J Buehler
John M Bukovinsky
William W Bulger
George D Bullock
Robert Bulster
Laurence H Bump
David Buonanno
John J Burbridge
Kenneth E Burchfield
Paul R Burden
Robert Burdette
John W Burgeson
Bill Burgess
Basil Burgess
John W Burgoon
Robert F Burk
John G Burk
James D Burke
Charles Burkhardt
Douglas Burks
Fred Burley

Phillip Burnette
J. Randolph Burnham
Steven Burns
Tom Burns
William Burns
Jane I Burns
Robert J Burns
Brian Burns
Robert R Burns
Bill Burns
Peter Burnside
James H Burster
Thomas S Busch
Leonard Busch
Howard Bushman
Scott Bushnell
David R Bussan
Joel Bussert
Joseph G Butash
Michael Butler
Frank E Butler
Richard Butler
C. Baylor Butler
William Byam
Thomas Byker
Michael Byrd
Rod Caborn
Lewis C Cady
Darlene Cahill
Jean Calaway
Stanley J Calderon
Jay Caldwell
Robert A Caldwell
Leon H Califf
William J Callahan
Kevin Callahan
James R Callis
Rick Cambere
David B Camburn
Daniel Cameron
Paul Cammarata
Helen Hannah
Campbell
Bernie Campbell
Mark Camps
Nancy Canada
Terry Cannon
Larry S Canoff
Agustin Cantens
Ray C Cantor
Arthur Cantu
Ralph J Caola
Robert Capone
Joseph M Caporale
Richard J Capp
Charles W Carey
Paul Carey
Eufemio Cariaga
Peter Carino
Bill Carle
Richard Carletti
Peter Carlson
John W Carlson
Kip Carlson
Michael Carlson

Michael R Carlson
Keith M Carlson
Michael D Carminati
Thomas A Carnes
Gene Carney
Skip Carpentier
Patrick Carpentier
Katharine K Carr
James T Carr
Bill Carr
Ken Carrano
Bruce H Carrier
Patrick Carroll
Bob Carroll
Winfield B Carson
Joe F Carter
Greg Carter
Bo Carter
Robert Carter
Craig Carter
John B Carter
M. D. Carter
Al Cartwright
Michael J Caruso
Gary Caruso
William Carvalho
William A Carvell
Thomas L Carwile
Nelson S Case
Dick Case
Gary Casey
Larry Casey
Jim Casey
William Cash
Frank K Cashell
Timothy Cashion
James Cashman
Chris Casserly
Joe Castiglione
Angel Castillo
Jerry Casway
Bill Catalanello
David K Catanzaro
Richard Catanzaro
Terry Catapano
John C Catau
Daniel Cattau
Louis E Cauz
Pete Cava
Anthony V Cavallaro
B. Benjamin Cavallo
Anthony Cavender
Ed Caylor
Bob Cebelak
Frank Ceresi
John Cernocky
Glen Cerny
Edward A Cesarone
Gregory Chaberski
Wayne Chambers
Tom C Chandler
Bob Chandler
Randall H Chandler
Gary P Chanko
Steve A Chapin

Jackson Chapman
Stephen Charak
James M Charlton
Warren W Chase
Frank J Chase
Tom Chase
Chester Chatham
Norton Chellgren
Nancy G Cheney
Lane Chenoweth
Stephen Cherrington
Steven Cheskin
Isao Chiba
Michael Childers
Dick Chillemi
Richard L Chilton
Frank M Chimkin
Michael Chobanian
Jeff Christensen
Jeff Christensen
Ralph J Christian
John H Christman
Thomas Chuey
Carl Chun
Irwin Chusid
Robert D Ciandella
John F Cicatiello
Frank Nick Cilfone
Public Library of
Cincinnati & Hamilton Cty
Charles Citrin
James Civilla
Lynn Clanton
Matthew Clark
Mark Clark
Donald M Clark
William M Clark
John S Clark
Marion A Clark
Robert Clark
Richard C Clark
Charles T Clark
Joe Clary
Dick Clement
John A Cleveland
Cleveland Indians BB Co.
Robert J Clifford
Richard Clifton
Merritt Clifton
Scott Cline
Tom Cline
Rodger L Coauette
Brent Cobb
Rich Coberly
James J Cochran
Richard M Cochrane
Ed D Coen
Mark E Coen
David Coennen
Phil Coffin
Donald A Coffin
William T Coffman
Bruce Cohen
Mark Cohen
Jerry Cohen

Ronald B Cohen
Neil B Cohen
Marc Cohen
Paul L Cohen
Richard S Cohen
Syd Cohen
David A Cohen
Dave Cohen
Stanley A Cohen
Stanley Cohen
William Cohn
Steven Cohn
William Cohon
Gary Cokins
Anthony C Colao
Dan Colavito
Eric Colby
Bob Coldeen
Phil Cole
David Cole
Robert C Cole
Terrence Cole
Norman Coleman
Gary L Coleman
Kenneth Coleman
Gehrig Coleman
Tom Collelo
Ritter Collett
Dale R Collett
Michael Colley
Fred Collignon
Lenore N Collins
Richard L Collins
David A Collins
John P Collins
Barry Collward
Joseph Colucci
Craig C Combs
Clem Comly
Vincent A Comparato
Robert Composto
Doug Compton
Michael Conlon
Thomas Conlon
John Connelly
Troy Conner
Scott Conrad
Steve Constantelos
John H Contois
Timothy K Conway
Gary Conwell
Gary E Cook
Waide J Cook
Jack A Cook
Ernest V Cooke
Dan R Cooley
Kenneth Cooper
Mark W Cooper
Jeffrey Cooper
Edward Cooper
Everett L Cope
Warren P Corbett
Bernard M Corbett
Ross Corbett
Bill Corcoran

Jerry J Corcoran
Charles E Corcoran
Ray Corio
Gregg A Corliss
Brian Cornforth
Don J Cornish
Frederick S Corns
Stephen J Corrado
Gabriel B Costa
Rory Costello
Joseph P Costello
William Cothrum
Robert Cotter
Dean Coughenour
KC Coulter
Richard J Courtens
Barbara Couture
Bruce W Cowgill
Patrick J Coyne
M. Dennis Coyne
David Craft
Arthur J Craig
Stephen T Craig
J. Alexander Craig
Peter H Craig
Richard D Cramer
Jerome J Crane
Dan Crawford
Charles Craze
Chuck C Creger
Richard C Crepeau
Robert Crestohl
Keith Crider
Thomas P Crilley
Michael Crimbly
Clyde E Cripe
Harrington E Crissey
Joseph A Cronin
Mark X Cronin
John J Cronin
James R Cropper
Bill Cross
Jerome Crosson
Greg Crouse
Lawrence Crowe
William Crowell
Richard D Crowley
Bernard J Crowley
Doug Croy
Ed P Crump
Charles Crupi
Michael Crusco
Stefan Csik
Joseph M Cuddy
Richard A Cuicchi
Michael H Cullers
Peter B Culter
Lee A Cummings
Stephen J Cummings
Bruce Cummings
E. Stephen Cunerd
Frank H Cunliffe
Kevin Cunningham
John W Cunningham
John T Cunningham

Wallace J Curley
William Curran
Robert E Curtin
Bradley L Curtis
John D Curtis
Ralph C Curtis
Elliot Curwin
Edward Czapran
Richard J Czarnec
John Czarnota
Larry D'Agostino
Dennis D'Agostino
Frank D'Amico
David D'Antonio
Debbi Dagavarian-Bonar
Don L Daglow
Jeffrey R Dahl
Brian Daly
John F Daly
Craig A Damon
W. Harrison Daniel
Frank L Daniel
Marge Daniels
Stephen M Daniels
Jon A Daniels
Michael N Danielson
Keith E Danish
Douglas Dannay
James Danner
David Dannov
Eric Danoff
Cecil A Darby
Anthony Darkin
Rabindranath Darling
Jennifer Darnell
Robert L Darwin
Rick Dasch
Charles S Dautel
David A Dauyotas
John Clay Davenport
L. Robert Davids
Dan L Davidson
Rick Davies
David Davis
William J Davis
Harry A Davis
Christopher Davis
Scott P Davis
James Davis
Michael J Davis
Stephen J Davis
Raymond Davis
Tom R Davis
O.K. Davis
Thomas Day
Daniel DeBartolo
Leon DeHaven
Jesse C DeLee
Mark DeLodovico
Joseph C DeLuca
Don DeMuth
Christopher DeRosa
Frank R DeSantis
Karel DeVeer
Jack DeVries

Ted D DeVries
Paul DeWitt
Robert Deal
Charles E Dean
Robert H Dean
Bill Deane
Paul Debono
Vic Debs
Thomas R Dedrick
F. Timothy Deeth
Eddie Deezen
Gerald Degerstedt
Rocco A Del Sesto
Justin DelVecchio
Jim Delaney
Gene Delisio
Louis A Dell'Orco
Harold L Dellinger
David G Delpino
Jeff Demetrescu
Richard Dempsey
Michael E Dempsey
Keith W Denebeim
Joseph Denehy
Robert Deneroff
Chris Denison
Alan J Denman
Andrew Dennis
David A Denny
Richard E Derby
Carl F Desens
George Desko
George Desorcy
Mike Detering
David A Detwiler
Thomas Paul Deveikis
Jeff Devine
Sean Devlin
Tom Devlin
Richard C Devlin
Dave Devouton
John Dewan
Francis E DiBacco
Bob DiBiasio
Matthew DiFilippo
Angelo DiFrancisco
John E DiMeglio
Len DiSalvo
Ted DiTullio
Ken DiVincenzo
Chris Dial
Ron Diamond
William Diamond
John Dibbern
Mitchell Dickerman
Wayne E Dickman
Paul Dickson
Thomas A Diedrich
Robert George Diehl
Larry Dierker
Russell E Diethrick
John Dietrich
Joseph A Digles
John P Dillon
A. John Dimond

Daniel J Dinardo
Richard & Debbie Dinda
Joel Dinda
Dan E Dischley
Dave Distel
Jim Distelhorst
Joe Dittmar
Larry Dix
Philip H Dixon
Mark C Dobson
John W Docke
Martin Dodd
Earl E Dodge
  Dodgertown
Bernard W Doescher
Tim Doherty
Andrew Dole
William P Dolney
David Dombrowski
Russ Domski
Michael Donaghue
Michael T Donlin
William A Donnelly
John Donovan
John J Doorley
Michael D Doran
George Dorer
Bob Dorrill
Bruce Dorskind
Charles S Doskow
Jack Dougherty
Sean H Douglas
Michael Douglas
John R Dowling
David I Downey
James L Dowsey
Thomas C Doxsee
David Doyle
Patric J Doyle
John C Draeger
Thomas D Drake
Alan L Drake
Edward Dramin
Donald Dregalla
Bob Dreher
Peter Dreier
David C Driscoll
David Driver
Katharine F Drobile
Ira S Drucker
Jeffrey Drummond
Dan DuVall
Charles R DuVall
Elias J Dudash
Roger L Dudley
J. Bruce Dudley
Colby Duerk
Ted C Duffield
Genevieve H Duffin
Gerard J Duffy
Reid J Duffy
Jerome Michael Dugan
Kevin J Dukles
Joe Dulle
R.P. Dunaway

Mike Duncan
Tom W Dunker
Jonathan Dunkle
Kenneth R Dunn
Robert L Dunn
Saul Dunn
Thomas R Dunne
Frederick B Dunphy
William H Dunstone
Francois Dupuis
Donald Duren
Richard J Durrell
John Duxbury
James B Dworkin
Robert T Dwyer
John Dwyer
Joseph Eacobacci
Frank Eakes
Thomas C Eakin
Joe Earls
Charles Early
Eric P Easterberg
Richard A Easterling
Jeff Eastland
Stephen S Eberly
Ed Echan
John Eckdahl
David Eckdahl
Vince Eckdahl
Thomas G Eckel
Jeff Ecker
Eugene P Ecker
Melvin L Eckhouse
Maria Eckhouse
Allen Eckhouse
Morris Eckhouse
Oscar Eddleton
Ben Eden
Dustin C Edge
Ron Edmonds
Jeff Edmunds
Charles L Edson
Tony Edwards
Kenneth Edwards
Richard S Egan
James E Egan
Christopher Egan
Richard Egenriether
James L Eggler
Bruce W Eggler
Harold J Eggleston
Mike Ehnot
Earl J Eichenlaub
Andrew Eichhorn
Bill Eidmann
Karl H Eikermann
Robert F Eisen
John Eisenhardt
Milton Eisner
Elliott Eiss
William Elander
Stephen P Elders
Richard A Eldred
Robert Elias
Gregory S Elich

Joseph Elinich
Rick Elliott
William D Ellis
Bryan D Ellis
Kenneth C Ellis
Benjamin N Ells
Pierre H Ellyson
Steven A Elsberry
Howard M Elson
Gene Elston
Ralph H Emerson
Lee Emery
Ken Emley
Bob Emling
Gary A Emmett
Joel Emrick
Michael Engaldo
Brad Phillip Engdahl
Gary Engel
Cort Engelken
Frederick E Engelken
John T English
J. Douglas English
Larry Epke
Bob Epler
Wilbur Epstein
Christian C Epting
John Gannon Erardi
Gus Erbes
Roger P Erickson
Christopher G Erikson
Greg Erion
David Ernst
Richard Ernst
Bruce Erricson
Frederick S Ervin
Phillip P Erwin
John Esch
Harold L Esch
Joseph G Eshelman
David S Eskenazi
Gerald N Eskin
Ysidro J Espinoza
Bernie Esser
Donald M Etheridge
Jack Etkin
Joseph M Evancich
David Evans
Robert C Evans
Robert M Evans
Robert W Evans
Daniel P Evans
Barry K Evans
Joshua Evans
Dan Even
Peter Everett
John T Evers
George Ewing
Doak M Ewing
Donald L Fagely
Herb Fagen
John C Fain
Donald S Fairchild
Ron Fairly
James W Falk

Donald M Falk
Edward Falvey
Larry J Farber
Leonard A Farber
Ren Farley
Virgil C Farley
Ted Farmer
Terry M Farmer
William Farmer
Richard Farrell
Vincent D Farrell
Charles K Fasold
Robert Fathergill
Stefan Fatsis
Thomas D Faulkner
Joseph C Favano
Enrico T Federighi
Barry Federovitch
Jim Fee
Herbert Feiler
Alan Feinberg
Harold Feinstein
Bill Felber
Ken Felden
William Feldman
Jonathan H Feldman
Rex A Felton
Ken Fenster
Stephen J Ferenchick
John C Ferguson
John A Ferguson
Richard Fernald
Steve M Fernandez
Paul Ferrante
Michael Fertile
Michael J Feuerstein
Robert S Fick
Russell Field
Scott Fiesthumel
Albert Figone
Jorge S Figueredo
James Filacanevo
Frank F Fincken
Michael Fingerit
Marc Fink
Kenneth Fink
Gordon Fink
Gary Fink
Jan Finkel
Robert D Finkel
Jay Finkel
Arthur Finkelstein
Paul C Finstrom
Daniel A Fiore
Len Fiorito
Lou Fioto
Ira J Fischbein
William E Fischelis
Kenneth A Fischer
Gary Fischer
Robert J Fischer
Erwin G Fischer
William J Fischer
Scott Fischthal
Abraham Fish

Mark E Fishbon
Randy Fisher
Guy M Fisher
Richard T Fisher
Ron Fisher
Michael Fitzgerald
Robert L Fitzgerald
Shaun Fitzpatrick
Dave Fitzsimmons
John D Fix
James K Flack
John Stephen Flack
Barbara G Flanagan
Albert D Flannery
Scott Flatow
Irwin Fleischner
David Fleischner
Wayne G Fleming
Bruce A Fleming
Roy B Flemming
Derwin Flener
F.X. Flinn
J.G. Floto
Joan A Flower
Robert Flynn
John J Flynn
Joseph J Fobel
James E Fogartie
Marshall Fogel
Daniel A Folcher
Tom F Foley
Daniel J Foley
Red Foley
Richard A Fond
Bobby Fong
Thomas H Forbes
Charles F Forbes
Pete Force
Joseph K Ford
David Foreman
Ronald Forman
Larry Forrey
Tom Forsaith
Frank Forthoffer
Jerry Fortuna
Ralph Foss
Ken Fost
Norman Fost
Wilson Foster
Richard N Foster
Joseph W Fowler
Ken Fowlkes
Jeffrey D Fox
Donald C Fox
Raymond W Fraley
Andrew France
David Francis
Charles P Francis
Christopher T Franco
Carl W Frank
Donald G Frank
Howard Frank
Michael Frank
Rich Frank
Jonathan Frankel

Harvey Frankel
Joel S Franks
Charles R Franzen
Daniel Frascella
Jack A Fraser
Malcolm C Fraser
Stuart Frederick
Robert Fredette
Kent Fredrickson
Lewis Freedman
Sumner B Freedman
David Freedman
James Freeman
Harold Freeman
Michael Freiman
Richard Freimark
G Sport French
Kenneth A French
George W French
Anna Daube Freund
J.D. Freund
William H Friday
Steve C Friedman
Michael S Friedman
Robert Friedman
Marty Friedrich
Eddie D Frierson
David L Frishberg
Larry Fritsch
Mark Frobom
Mark E Frohman
Nicholas Fronduto
James Fruth
Dean Frutiger
Richard E Fry
Christine R Fry
David C Frye
Jason W Frye
Larry K Fryer
Robert Fuchs
Fumihiro Fujisawa
Craig Fuller
Robert Fulton
Gregory Funk
Kevin Fura
Rich Furman
James Furtado
Warner Fusselle
Howard N Futerman
Michael V Gabel
Ronald L Gabriel
Melvin Gadd
John H Gaffney
Rudy A.S. Gafur
Bill J Gagliano
Vincent Gagliardi
Robert J Gagnon
Cappy Gagnon
Charlie Gaharan
Greg Gajus
Mike Galbreath
Robert Gallagher
Tom Gallagher
Timothy P Gallagher
Robert H Galle

E. David Gamble
Edward Gammons
Eric Gan
Andrew J Gangliero
Richard Gans
Daniel M Gantt
Abbey B Garber
Steve Gardner
Kathleen M Gardner
Robert A Gardy
Robert W Garfinkle
Steve Garlick
Thomas R Garrett
Warren V Garrison
Robert S Garrison
Terrance W Garstka
Gerald M Garte
Kevin P Garvin
Thomas C Gates
Bill Gates
Robert Gaunt
Gerald Gauthier
Jay Gauthreaux
Ray Gehringer
Frank J Geishecker
Sidney Gelber
Bob Gelzheiser
John Matthew Gendler
Bruce A Genther
Charles J Gentile
Elizabeth George
Michael George
Robert L George
Jeff Georges
Robert C Gerald
Dale H Gerber
Frank B Gerheim
Allen Gerlach
Larry R Gerlach
Catherine Gerland
Kingsley S Gernon
Morton B Gerofsky
Ron Gersbacher
Kevin Gerth
Richard C Geschke
Andy Getch
Carl R Gethmann
Robert E Gettel
William Gettins
Mike Getz
Robert Gewanter
Michael S Geylin
Anthony Gialanella
Michael L Gibbons
Larry Gibbs
Robert Giblin
Jim Gibson
Campbell J Gibson
George Gibson
Steven P Gietschier
Frank W Gifford
Karl Gilberg
Thomas W Gilbert
William C Gilbert
David M Giles

Gerald Gill
Jack W Gill
Robert H Gill
F. David Gill
Jeff Gillard
Eldred Gillard
James R Gillespie
C. Stanley Gilliam
Kenneth B Gilman
John Gilmore
Steve Gilson
Mike Gimbel
Herbert Ginsburg
Daniel E Ginsburg
David Ginzl
Joseph Giovannetti
Jack A Girardi
David Girdany
Sol Gittleman
Michael Giuffre
Horace R Givens
William L Gladstone
Joe Glaeser
Steven Glassman
Richard Glassman
James H Glavin
Dave Gleisner
Michael Glennon
Rush Glick
Lynne Glickman
John D Gluck
Arthur C Glueck
Roger A Godin
Stuart Godwin
Bill Goff
Jimmy F Goggin
Donald L Goguen
Leonard Gold
Robert L Gold
Edward Alan Gold
Jonathan S Gold
David Goldberg
Philip Goldberg
Carl B Goldberg
Richard Howard
Goldberg
Goodwin Goldfaden
Alan Goldhammer
Steven Goldman
Doron Goldman
Henry Y Goldman
Kenneth Goldman
Edward Goldstein
George S Goldstein
Sherwood Goldstein
Dennis Goldstein
Richard Goldstein
Tom Goldstein,
  Publisher
Robert B Golon
Raymond J Gonzalez
Paul Goodemote
George Goodman
Ross Goodner
Charles S Goodwin

Ted A Gooley
David Gordon
Alexander Gordon
Ken M Gordon
Alan M Gordon
James Gorman
Robert G Gorman
Robert T Gorman
Bill Gorman
David A Goss
Glenn Gostick
Arthur Gottheim
John Gottko
Mike Gough
David Gough
Sam Gould
William B Gould
Stephen Jay J Gould
Gerard R Goulet
Andrew F Goydich
Phil Grabar
Dallas S Graber
Ralph S Graber
John Grabowski
Bob Grace
Kevin Grace
Dennis Graham
Michael L Graham
Fred Graham
James S Graham
George Grande
Stephen Grant
Peter H Grant
Karl Grapes
Lawrence P Grasso
Jeffrey R Graubard
Gary R Gray
Walter Dave Gray
Lloyd Graybar
Christopher Green
Ernest J Green
Larry Green
W. David Green
John Green
Larry M Green
Howard L Green
Thornton F Green
H. Daniel Green
Karl E Green
Len I Green
Herbert N Greene
Sanford I Greene
Richard Greene
Wayne Greene
Harvey S Greene
Steven R Greenes
Peter J Greenhill
Daniel Greenia
Gary Greenstein
Hank Greenwald
Paul W Greenwell
Gordon S Gregersen
Barbara Gregorich
Robert E Gregory
John W Gregory

Jerry H Gregory
Jay Gregory
Byron Gregory
Kenneth L Greif
Stephen A Greyser
Sidney Gribetz
George Grice
Ronald K Griggs
Charles B Griggs
Charles Snowden
  Grijalba
Stephen M Grimble
Donald K Grimm
P.J. Grinsell
Duane Groff
Joel Gross
Scott Gross
Douglas A Gross
Stanley Grosshandler
Robert Grove
Gary Growe
Robert S Gruber
Ben Grummons
Kevin Grzymala
Victor Guanowsky
Sante E Guatelli
Richard Gudewicz
Ralph A Guenther
Richard L Guest
John Guilfoyle
Mark Gularte
Clayton R Gum
Jim Gumm
Richard W Gunn
Lawrence A Guren
Brent Gushulak
Joseph Gusky
Milton Gustafson
Mike W Gustafson
John Gustafson
Paul C Gustafson
William F Gustafson
Larry Gusz
Francis S Gut
Frank Gutch
Don Guthrie
Michael S Gutierrez
Dan Gutman
John G Gutowsky
William Guy
John L Guyton
Mark Guziec
Glenn R Guzzo
Allen A Gwinnell
Joe Haardt
Ronald C Haas
Paul Haas
Carl F Haas
Klee Haber
Ken Hackler
Nick L Hadden
John R Haddock
Robert J Haddox
Lawrence Hadley
Bill Haelig

Rudolf K Haerle
Larry J Haffner
Chris Haft
William Hageman
John Frederick
  Hagemann
Louis F Hagenbruch
William K
  Hagginbothom
Bruce T Haglund
Brad Haigh
Howard Haimann
Michael Haines
Dale Hains
Nate Hakman
Peter M Halden
Jeff Hale
Douglas Hall
Edward N Hall
William C Hall
Paul T Hallaman
James Haller
Thomas Halleran
Robert V Hallett
Michael A Halliburton
William P Hallman
Barry Halper
Barry Halpern
Robert Hamalainen
H. Edward Hamalainen
Steve Hamburg
Durward Hamil
Francis E Hamilton
Stanton Hamlet
Bruce R Hammer
Jay J Hammeran
Roger D Hammond
Walter Handelman
Donald Hang
Brock J Hanke
Michael Hanks
David Hanley
Timothy J Hannan
Jerry Hannan
Steven T Hannigan
John T Hannon
Richard Hansen
Thomas A Hanson
Cary Hanson
Tom Hanson
Stuart P Hanson
Thomas L Hanson
James Hanson
Larry Happel
Tim Hardman
Thomas M Harkins
John E Harmon
Richard H Harms
Timothy P Harner
Ira Haron
Michael Harper
James W Harper
Patrick J Harrigan
Mark W Harrington
Michael R Harrington

Tom Harris
Mark T Harris
Ken R Harris
Morley M Harris
John L Harris
Roger Harris
Robert S Harris
Jack E Harshman
Ed Hartig
Michael Hartley
Robert E Hartley
Don Hartline
Steven Hartman
Elwin F Hartwig
Elaine Harvey
Charlie Harville
Elliott Harvith
Ernie Harwell
Charles Harzer
Don Hase
Jeff Haskins
Ed Hasse
Pepper Hastings
David T Hastings
Steve Hatcher
Edward Hathaway
Mason C Haughton
Mike Haupert
Michael Hauser
Mac Havard
Tom Havener
Terrence Havener
John W Hawes
Joel Hawkins
Seth C Hawkins
Roger J Hawks
Donald Hayden
William T Hayes
Mike Hayney
Don J Hazelwood
Michael Hazen
Michael F Head
John B Healey
Paul E Heally
Leslie Heaphy
Dan H Heath
Steven H Heath
Alan W Heaton
Eugene E Heaton
Dan Heaton
John R Hebert
Richard W Hebert
Mayer Hecht
Joseph Heck
George Hecker
Frederick L Heger
Norman M Hegge
Todd R Heidenreich
John E Heiselman
David M Heiser
Dan Heisman
Joseph Heitkamp
Lou Heitke
Thomas R Heitz
Bruce Hellerstein

Diana Helmer
Tim Helms
Joseph P Helyar
Roland A Hemond
Lex Hemphill
Robert C Hemple
Warren S Henderson
Lloyd Hendrick
Dean F Hendricks
Alan B Hendricks
David Hendrickson
Philip G Hendrickx
David Henige
Kevin Hennessy
Peter S Henrici
Paul Hensler
Peter Hepokoski
Paul D Herbert
John O Herbold
James G Herdman
David W Herlinger
Jerry Hermele
E. Kendall Hermes
Christopher M Herndon
G.M. James Herre
George G Herrick
Milt F Herrick
John Herrmann
Ben Herrmann
Rick Herrscher
Deborah Herschaft
Chuck Hershberger
Roger Herz
Ulrich Hesse-
  Lichtenberger
Joseph T Hetrick
William L Hickman
Mark W Hicks
Tom Hicks
Bruce Hicks
Imada Hideyuki
Karl Hiester
Steve Higgerson
Dennis R Higgins
Joseph Hightower
Bret Hildebran
Tom Hildebrandt
Robert W Hill
Tom Hill
Walter Hill
David J Hill
Thomas J Hill
John Hillman
James Hilton
George W Hilton
Charles R Hilty
Robert Himmelein
William F Himmelman
Brenda L Himrich
George G Hines
Weston T Hines
Michael Hinkelman
James B Hinman
Steve Hirdt
Paul L Hirsch

Eric Hirschhorn
Jeff Hirsh
Toyoaki Hiruma
John E Hissrich
Stephen Hitchcock
Arthur D Hittner
Norman Hitzges
William J Hizny
Lucas Hobbs
Gerry Hobbs
David B Hochman
Mark D Hodermarsky
Scott Hodes
Ken Hodges
Larry E Hodges
Martin Hoerchner
Vincent E Hoffman
Herbert S Hofmann
Rolly Hofstedt
John F Hogan
Lawrence D Hogan
DeWayne Hogue
Robert Hoie
Edward J Hoke
Michael Holden
Daniel G Holecy
James Holl
Scott A Holland
William J Holland
Zander Hollander
Harry Hollingsworth
Kris W Holmberg
Tot Holmes
Craig A Holmes
Richard Holody
Kenneth Holt
Gary Holt
James Holt
David Holtz
Jerome Holtzman
John B Holway
Alex Holzman
Louis Holzner
Christopher L Holzner
Brian Honda
David R Hoon
John Hooper
Robert Hooper
Tony Hoover
Michael Hopkins
David Hopkins
William C Hoppe
Robert Hoppe
John V Horgan
Jo Ann Horn
Charles H Horne
John L Horne
Ross Horning
Kenneth E Horowitz
Garrett Horrocks
William Horsey
Scott A Horstmeier
Ken Horton
David Horwich
Jay Horwitz

Robert G Hoskinson
Dan Hotaling
Jon A Hotter
David Hovda
Donald Howard
G. Reed Howard
Mitchell G Howard
Timothy J Howe
David E Howell
Tom Howell
Stephen Hoy
Annie Hoy
Eric Hoyer
Ronald W Hoyle
Michael Hoyt
Brent Hradek
Joseph Hroblak
Robert Hubbard
Marvin Huck
Richard M Huckins
Kenneth Hudson
Ted Hudson
Doug Huffer
Leroy J Huffman
Thomas D Hufford
Mike Hughes
Marty Hughes
William Hughes
Larry M Hughes
David R Hughes
Robert A Hughes
William F Hugo
Marc Hugunin
Gregg Huhn
Tom Hull
David Hullinger
Steve Huls
William A Humber
Joseph R Humphreys
Lou Hunsinger
B. Clark Hunsinger
Daniel T Hunt
Robert James Hunter
Robert Hunter
Peter Hurley
John T Hurley
T. Michael Hurley
John R Husman
Dennis Hutchinson
William Hutton
Allen E Hye
J. Gordon Hylton
James D Hyman
Brad Hyman
Lawrence Hyman
Eduardo A Ibarguen
David Icenogle
Joseph Igoe
Masaru Ikei
Bob Ikins
William Iliff
John Infanger
Ernie Infield
Sherry Inman
Enrico Innocenzi

Peter Paul Insero
Lewis M Irish
Dennis M Irons
Bernie Irvin
Bernard J Irvin
Gregory J Isaackson
Alex Isabel
Carl Isackson
David Ishii
Leonard A Itkin
Akihiro Ito
Alma L Ivor-Campbell
Frederick Ivor-Campbell
Stephen Ivy
John Jablonski
Walter J Jablonski
John Jackanicz
Paul I Jacks
Lester B Jackson
Howard C Jackson
Jerry Jackson
Douglas S Jacobs
Eric Jacobs
Daniel Jacobs
Rollie Jacobsen
Jerry Jacobsen
Mark T Jacobson
Louis Jacobson
Paul K Jacques
Jack Jadick
Steve Jaffe
Kenneth Jaffee
Bill James
John James
Samuel James
Paul Janeczko
Robert S Jankun
Jerome P Janzen
Rich Jaroslovsky
Jon P Jarrett
Paul Jarvey
Gary Jarvis
Joseph E Jarzyk
Bill Jasper
David B Jauvtis
Frank Stephen Jazzo
Harry Jebsen
Peter Jedick
Jef
David S Jeffery
Robert J Jefferys
Joseph Jellinek
Clarence Jenkins
David A Jenkins
David Jennis
Christopher Jennison
Barry Jensen
Donald N Jensen
George Jensen
Peggy Jensen
William Jensen
Greg Jezewski
Jose de Jesus Jimenez
Douglas H Jobling
M. John

Dan Johns
Henry Johns
Gary Johnson
Bruce Johnson
Mark S Johnson
Scott Johnson
Stephen Johnson
Jack Johnson
Edward Johnson
Thomas A Johnson
Rodney W Johnson
Chuck S Johnson
Daniel Johnson
William Johnson
Tom C Johnson
Sharon Johnson
William S Johnson
W. Lloyd Johnson
Glenn E Johnson
Rick Johnson
Cecil M Johnson
Scott Johnson
Stephan G Johnson
Kyle Johnson
Floyd B Johnson
Kenneth A Johnson
Ronald S Johnson
Randall E Johnson
Herbert H Johnson
Richard A Johnson
Frank Johnston
James D Johnston
Barbara M Johnstone
R. William Johnstone
Frank W Jones
Mark Jones
Rick Jones
Eric R Jones
Mark H Jones
H. Lawrence Jones
Howard L Jones
Harold D Jones
Marc A Jones
Robert R Jordan
David M Jordan
Diana M Jordan
George M Joseph
Joseph R Joyce
Harvey Judkowitz
Kim Steven Juhase
Richard Juline
Robert S Junkrowski
Ann T Justice
Clifford Kachline
Shayana Kadidal
Charles G Kagan
Thomas R Kagarise
Gerald L Kahn
Jeff Kahn
Timothy Kain
Robert H Kaiser
Fred Kajiwara
James Kaklamanos
Clay Kallam
Gregory M Kallen

Henry Norr Kalow
Ronald Kaluzok
Joseph Kan
Robert A Kane
Norman H Kane
Frank Kane
Richard Kann
Joli Quentin Kansil
Mark Kanter
Larry Kaplan
Ed Kaplan
Ron Kaplan
A.J. Kaplan
David Kaplan
Mike D Kaplan
Peter J Kaplan
Jim Kaplan
Keith Karcher
Emmanuel J Karides
Dean P Karlos
Chris A Karlos
Bob Karn
Jim L Karn
Alan B Karnath
Thomas L Karnes
Rob Karp
Gene Karst
Gerald Kasiowniak
James Kastro
Nick Kates
Jonathan L Katz
Ira M Katz
Lawrence Katz
Lawrence Kaufman
Charles Kaufman
Richard D Kaufman
Herman Kaufman
Alan Kaufman
Alan Kaufmann
John T Kaup
Jan Kavana
Irvin K Kawarsky
Jeffrey Kay
Shun-ichi Kayada
Thomas B Kayser
Mary Louise Kean
Stephen W Keane
Joseph P Keaney
James R Kearney
Seamus E Kearney
Kevin Keating
Robert W Keeler
John J Keeley
Richard Keenan
Kerry Keene
John C Keesling
Frank M Keetz
John Keever
Robert Keisser
W.J. Douglas Kelcher
Garrett J Kelleher
John A Kelleher
Vincent W Kelleher
Bob Kelleter
Brent Kelley

Robert W Kelley
Jack J Kelley
Kathy Kelly
Dave Kelly
Robert V Kelly
Robert E Kelly
Paul A Kelly
John P Kelly
Robert B Kelly
Mark Kempson
Larry Kempster
Richard F Kempter
Richard Kendall
Bob Kennedy
Wayne Kennedy
Bernie Kennedy
Robert Kenney
Michael J Kent
John Kenyon
David J Keogh
Walter Kephart
Michael Kerbel
Robert Kerler
Al Kermisch
David Kern
Thomas E Kern
Kevin P Kerr
Chris Kerr
John C Kerr
Thomas J Kerrigan
Glen R Kershner
Peter J Kerttu
Kathy Kessler
Leroy Keuler
Mary Kidwell
Dave Kiehle
Robert H Kienzle
Larry Kieran
Robert L Kimball
Larry Kimbrough
Stephen B Kimmell
Jim Kimnach
Gregory P King
Steven A King
J Nelson King
Roger W King
Warren R King
Bill Kingstone
Francis Kinlaw
Henry H Kipp
Allen Kirk
Gerald P Kirsch
Edward Kirwan
Bill Kirwin
Anthony Kissel
Gerald Kissel
Richard H Kitchin
James Kittilsby
Stephen Klatsky
Robert Klein
Joseph Klein
Richard A Klein
Philip C Klein
Andrew Klein
Alan E Kleinberger

Alex F Kleiner
Bruce Kleinhans
Merl F Kleinknecht
David L Klement
David Kline
David J Kline
Carl N Kline
Dwayne Kling
Randy B Klipstein
Art Knapp
Scott Knaster
Christopher A Knepp
Wendy Knickerbocker
Karl W Knickrehm
Rob Knies
Tom Knight
Leonard S Knighton
Andrew Knobel
Roger Knop
Keith Knopf
Theodore Knorr
Elmer Knox
Peter J Koch
John Koch
Ronald B Kocher
Thomas F Koegel
Robert R Koehler
P.T. Koenig
Ted N Koga
Martin Kohout
Kenneth Kolb
Joseph C Koletar
Jim Kolker
Edwin A Koller
Phil Kolodkin
Robert Koltermann
David E Kolva
Robert Kominski
Nick A Komons
Maurice Kondo
Terry Konkle
Leonard Koppett
Donald Korb
William Korbelak
Brian Korinek
Meyer Korman
David Korpiel
Charles P Korr
John A Korsgaard
Harold Kort
James Kossuth
Steven Kotz
John M Kovach
Lawrence Kovacs
Mark Kozaki
Paul Kozlusky
Herman Krabbenhoft
Elliott F Kraemer
Luke Kraemer
Steve Krah
Jay M Kraker
Robert Kraus
Becky Kraus
Jeff Krauss
Kenton Krejci

Harvey Krendel
Jim Kreuz
Stephen Krevisky
Keith Krewer
Dick Kriebel
Michael R Kriner
Richard Krisciunas
Mark A Krohse
Chuck Krome
Dennis R Kroner
William Kross
John Kubes
Walter E Kuczwara
Bruce Kuklick
Stanley F Kuminski
John C Kunich
James Kuntz
Yasuo Kunugi
Tim Kurkjian
Badrig Kurkjian
Norman E Kurland
Lewis Kurlantzick
Norman Kurnick
Robert A Kurtz
Jeff Kurtz
Raymond D Kush
Kenneth J Kuzdak
George Kuzirian
Gerald Kvet
Dennis Kwiatkowski
Gary Kyser
Jeffrey J LaBarge
Gary P LaBrec
Geoff LaCasse
David LaDuke
Steve LaMar
Gary P LaPlante
Sal LaRocca
Ron LaRoche
Michael A LaTona
Ken LaZebnik
Hans Laaspere
Mike Lackey
Al Lackner
Lawrence R Ladd
Bruce C Ladd
Frank B Ladenburg
Paul M Ladewski
George C Ladner
Patrick D Lafferty
Don Lagomarsino
James M Lahey
Jeffrey M Laing
Stephen K Laird
Russell K Lake
Demas Lamas
William Lamb
Jeff Lambert
William R Lamberty
Bill Lammers
Michael Lamone
Anthony Lamonte
Donald G Lancaster
Gary Land
George Land

Pat Landell
Sutton Landry
Mark Landsbaum
Paul Landucci
Timothy B Lane
Clement Paul Lane
A.C. Lang
Allen B Lang
Jack Lang
Scott W Lang
Rob P Langenderfer
Jim R Langford
Jay Langhammer
Mark Langill
James Langlois
Greg Langlois
Donald P Lankiewicz
Jerry Lansche
Herve Lapeyre
Maxwell H Lapides
Rex Lardner
David R Larson
William B Larson
Thomas C Larson
Bob Larson
Tom Larwin
Stephen Laski
Rebecca L Lasky
Vincent T Lathbury
David M Lathrop
Steven A Lathrup
Francis J Lattanzi
Mark A Latterman
Steven K Lauer
Harry Lauritzen
George R Lausch
Vincent A Lauter
Jack Lautier
Glenn Lautzenhiser
Robert Lavelle
Steven Lavoie
William Law
Joe Lawler
David A Lawrence
Lorne M Lawrence
Steven Lawrence
Mark Lazarus
Albert C Lazure
Brian LeBlanc
Walter L LeConte
Charles J LeCorchick
Dennis LePore
Stephen Leach
Tim Leahy
Shebby Lee
Joseph P Lee
James G Lee
Richard Leech
Stuart Leeds
James L Leefers
Irv Lefberg
Roland C Legates
Gary E Legner
Douglas Lehman
Ron Lehmann

Charles Lehourites
G. Philip Lehrman
Ken Leiker
Andrew B Leister
John Leitgeb
David Leiwant
John Lelas
Robert Lemke
Randy Lenser
Paul Lenz
David I Leonard
Kenneth J Leonard
Paul M Lerner
Gary Leshaw
Stanley E Leshinski
Dave Leskovec
Paul Leslie
Ed Lesser
Larry Lester
Richard W Leutzinger
Anthony L Levato
Lewis A Levey
Len Levin
Larry H Levin
Jeff Levine
Barry Levine
Mark Levinthal
William Levis
Jed D Levitt
Daniel R Levitt
Philip G Levy
Robert J Levy
Lee Levy
William Lewers
Warren Lewis
Tony Lewis
Douglas E Lewis
John Lewis
Willard W Lewis
Ethan Lewis
David R Lewis
Allen Lewis
Richard Leyden
Joseph Lian
James D Libbin
John Liberatore
Sports Illustrated
  Library
Mitchel Lichtman
Frederick J Liddle
Mark Lieberman
Ronald G Liebman
Steve Lieder
John Liepa
Arthur L Lierman
Jack Liesner
Robert E Lifson
Jon F Light
Rick Liguori
Thomas Liley
Ralph W Lilge
Timothy E Liljeberg
Kenneth R Lilley
Ed Lilly
Manuel Lima

Jeffery P Lindberg
James Oscar Lindberg
Jorge Lindenbaum
Robert D Linder
Karl Lindholm
Daniel G Lindner
Richard B Lindquist
Rob Lindsay
Donald L Linebarger
Randy Linthurst
Joel Lipman
David H Lippman
Larry Lippmann
Randall L Lippstreu
Charles D Lippy
Lewis Lipset
Kenneth Lipshez
Edward G Lisefski
Raymond T Lisi
Joseph Liss
David L Litogot
Jack E Little
David B Littman
Sandy Litwin
Arthur P Livingston
Fred A Lizzi
Rolando Llanes
Charles W Lloyd
Steven G LoBello
Christopher J
  LoVergine
Thomas A Locker
Alex Lohmann
Nicholas A Loiacono
Robert D Loitz
Frank H Lomax
Fredric M London
Robert Long
Robert L Longacre
Scott Longert
Mario Longoria
Howard B Lorch
Alexander H Lorch
David Lorczak
Gerald D Lore
Julian N Loscalzo
David Lotre
John Lott
Michael S Lottman
Thomas Loughin
William T Loughman
Angelo J Louisa
Warren F Low
  Low and Inside
Charles A Lowe
Samuel Lowell
Lee Lowenfish
Andre Lower
Jay Lowrey
Linda Lowrey
Philip J Lowry
Greg Lucas
Frank L Lucci
Don Luce
Louis J Lucier

Richard F Luebeck
Stanley Lugerner
Michael Luiso
Ted Lukacs
Howard Luloff
David Lund
Robert Lund
Carl Lundquist
Sharon M Lundy
R. Daniel Lunger
Tony Lupien
Jim Lurie
George L Lush
Leonard Lustik
Edward M Luteran
Alyce Lutomski
Charles Lutomski
Kevin M Lynch
Terrance R Lynch
Robert Lynch
Erwin Lynn
David T Lyon
Kirk M Lyons
Philip J Lyons
James G MacAlister
Robert A MacCallum
Neil MacCarl
Kenneth A MacFarlane
Donald MacLean
Norman C MacLean
Henry J MacLean
Douglas MacLehose
Peter M MacPhail
Joseph A MacPhee
Mikko J Macchione
Norman L Macht
Michael Macias
David Mack
William T Mack
Joseph Mackay
James C Mackay
Michael C Mackey
David Mackler
William Madden
Bill Madden
Chris Maddix
Mark L Maddox
Frank A Mader
William Magazine
Gary Magee
Benjamin Magee
Daniel Maguire
Tod Maher
Michael F Maher
Ed Maher
Bob Mahler
Edward G Mahoney
Craig J Mahovlic
Jack A Mahr
John Main
Terence Malley
James V Mallinson
Jim Mallmann
Mitch Mallon
Mary Mallory

Jerry Malloy
Joseph M Malone
Christopher Maloney
Peter Malovrh
Ira J Malter
Chris Malumphy
John Mampreian
David P Mamuscia
Francis Mancini
Alan E Mandell
Jack Mangus
David Mankelow
Donald Mankin
Larry D Mansch
Mark G Manuel
Steve Marantz
Rich Marazzi
Ronald E Marcelle
Skip Marcello
Joe March
Horace G Marchant
Edward L Marcou
James Margarita
John Margarita
Warren A Margolies
David Margolies
David Margolis
Allan Margulies
Anthony Mariani
Steven Mark
Roy Mark
William Markel
Stephen Markman
Frank Markotich
Sidney Markowitz
Murray R Markowitz
David L Marks
David Marks
Kent Markus
Louis M Marmon
Gregory Maronick
Thomas H Marquisee
Richard T Marr
Owen Marredeth
Marriott Lib-Univ of
    Utah
James Marrow
Charles Marsh
Dana X Marshall
Ronald R Marshall
Paul D Marshall
William J Marshall
Paul R Marshall
T. Wayne Marshall
Charles Marshall
Richard Marston
Anthony Clay Marston
James E Martin
Donald Martin
Len Martin
Jack Martin
Michael J Martin
Billy Martin
John Martin
James C Martin

Ricardo Martinez
David Martinez
Francis Martinez
Richard C Martinez
John W Martinsky
Joseph P Martone
Daniel Marucci
Vinnie Maruggi
Frank Marx
Edward J Masek
Bill Maselunas
Rick Mason
Aniello Massa
James Massey
Richard Masson
Michael L Mast
Donald Mastropietro
David Matchett
Brian Mate
David Mateer
Peter Matevich
Jerry Mathers
Paul A Mathews
Steve R Mathias
Bob Mathieu
Michael Mathon
Kenneth Matinale
Lewis Matlin
Michael Matranga
James A Matranga
Hiroyuki Matsumoto
Richard Mattera
Paul Matthew
John Matthew
Jess Matthews
Dennis G Matthews
Herman Mattleman
Steve R Mau
Robert Maurer
Dean Mauro
Thomas J Mawby
Alan Maxcy
James F Maxfield
John Maxymuk
Robert G May
Ralph Maya
Henry Mayer
Robert J Mayer
John Mayeron
Michael P Mayko
Roslyn A Mazer
Thomas C Mazza
Rocko L Mazzaro
Thomas O McAdams
Robert McAfee
William J McAtee
Richard L McBane
Kurt McBee
Kevin McBride
Matt McBride
Michael McBride
Neal McCabe
Peter McCabe
Michael T McCabe
Bill McCaffrey

Michael McCann
James A McCann
John M McCardell
Kevin M McCarthy
William F McCarthy
Peg McCarthy
James C McCarthy
Charles J McCarty
Thomas McCauley
William J McClain
Scott McClellan
Peter L McCloud
Peter McClymont
Kreg McCollum
Wayne McCombs
Ralph McConnell
Robert C McConnell
John McConnell
Carl W McCoomb
Robert McCord
Byron R McCorkle
John McCormack
Frank McCormack
B. Michael McCormick
Terry A McCoy
Julian W McCracken
Gale McCray
Lawrence E McCray
Andrew G McCue
William O McCurdy
Jim McCurdy
Howard G McCutcheon
Robert A McDermott
Frank X McDermott
David McDonald
Chuck McDonald
Jim McDonough
Edward J McEnery
Madison McEntire
Robert P McEwen
Edward G McFarland
Steve McFarland
Paul McGee
Bob McGee
Michael McGerr
Joseph F McGillen
Brian McGinn
Joseph McGivney
Patrick S McGovern
Thomas J McGrath
Paul F McGrath
Robert D McGraw
Kevin G McGraw
Jim D McGreal
Eugene McGuire
Joseph J McGuirk
Ryan C McHugh
Stan McIlvaine
Richard McIntosh
Russ McIver
Chris McKay
Arthur J McKay
Jack W McKee
Brian K McKenna
Gerard E McKenna

Tim McKenzie
Pat McKernan
George F McKiernan
James McKinnon
Mark McKinstry
David McLaughlin
James L McLean
Dennis McLean
G. Roderick McLeod
Edward J McLoughlin
William E McMahon
Steve McManus
James M McMechan
S. Sterling McMillan
Terry McMullen
John McMurray
Michael A McMurray
Dave McNeal
William F McNeil
Ian McNeilly
Nancy Y McNulty
John M McPartland
Donald J McPherson
Steve G McPherson
John McReynolds
Michael McReynolds
Lane L McVey
Douglas M McWilliams
Alden Mead
William B Mead
Charlie Meara
Mendal C Mearkle
Hugh Mechesney
Jeff Meder
Tom Meder
Barry L Mednick
David M Meier
Mike G Meissner
Sig Mejdal
Sigmund Menchel
Arnold Mendelsohn
Philip Meneely
Jorge C Menendez
Tony Menendez
Ed Menta
Dennis Mercer
Clark Merchant
Lowell C Mercier
Joseph A Mercuri
Harold Mermelstein
Robert D Merrilees
George W Merritt
William F Merritt
Charles Merrow
Roberto Mesa
Tom Mesher
Randy C Messel
Scott A Messinger
David J Mestelle
Rosemary Meszaros
John Metz
Thomas Metzger
Ronald Meyer
Evan Meyer
Troy Meyer

Alan Meyer
Eldon Meyers
Larry S Meyers
Stephen B Meyerson
Jerry Mezerow
Court Michelson
Gary L Miessler
Jerry Mikorenda
Lee C Milazzo
Miles Field Renovation
Jerome M Mileur
A. Miley
Michael S Miller
Storm E Miller
Cherie D Miller
Gerald J Miller
Robert Miller
Harriet Miller
Martin Miller
Jay Miller
Arthur K Miller
Sammy J Miller
Bruce Miller
Clyde Miller
Helen Miller
Joe W Miller
Tom Miller
Stanley Miller
Matthew D Miller
Sheldon Miller
William J Miller
Richard Miller
Kenneth Miller
Sherri L Miller
Michael Miller
Leonard G Miller
John J Miller
James W Miller
Robert C Miller
James A Miller
Richard H Miller
Fred F Milligan
Mark Millikin
Ronnie Mills
Dorothy Jane Mills
David Mills
Stephen E Milman
Andrew Milner
Walter J Milner
Robert R Milstroh
Stephen J Minck
Eric Minde
George A Mindeman
Frank A Mindicino
Jay Miner
Minneapolis Public
    Library
Vin Minner
John T Minor
John E Misner
Tim Mitchell
Joseph Mitchell
Robert Mitchell
Stephen L Mitchell
Dave Mitchell

David J Mofenson
Larry Moffi
Guy Mogavero
Kerry A Mohn
Alex Moir
Dan Moir
John Moist
Alan Molin
Rene Molina
Larry T Molloy
Bernard Monostro
Jack Montanaro
Louis Montante
Mike Montfort
Boyd R Montgomery
Hugh Montgomery
H. Wynn Montgomery
Anthony Monti
Robert Moody
Robert A Moody
Bradley Moody
Frank Mooney
Kevin Mooney
Larry Mooney
William J Moore
Shawn D Moore
Steve J Moore
Michael C Moore
Marilyn E Moore
Ross Moore
Ed Moorman
James J Moran
Robert F Moran
David Moreau
Jeffrey W Morey
Kent R Morgan
T. Kent Morgan
Howard R Morgan
Dennis R Morgan
Russell Morgan
Patrick Morley
Edward B Morley
Craig Morooney
Glenn C Morosco
Rick Morris
Jack V Morris
Peter Morris
Gary Morris
Carl N Morris
Stephen F Morris
Kenneth Morrison
Ken Morrison
Dirk Morrison
Brian Morrow
William H Mortell
John Morton
Jeffrey Mosafir
Peter Moscariello
Will Moser
Ralph C Moses
Paul Moses
George Moskal
Gary Moskalyk
Mike Moss
Herb M Moss

Curt Mosser
James Mote
Archie Motley
Paul Motyka
Irv Mouallem
Andy Moursund
Jim Moyer
Alan D Moyer
James Moyes
Anton L Moze
Michael Mozill
David E Mucha
Randy Mudarri
Mike Mueller
Thomas Muldowney
E.K. Muller
Daniel R Mumford
David Mundo
Ronald Mundt
Neil Munro
Robert A Murden
Stephen D Murphy
William C Murphy
J. Elaine Murphy
Lawrence R Murphy
Joseph Patrick Murphy
Thomas P Murray
Clark Murray
John R Murray
Tim Murray
Shawn M Murray
Ritchie B Murrell
Stan Musial
Richard Musterer
J. Paul Muxworthy
Jack Myers
Jim Myers
Fran Nachman
Ernie Nadel
Steven Nadel
Jack Nadelle
Albert Nader
Eric Naftaly
Gary Nagasawa
Yoichi Nagata
David E Nagelberg
Koichi Nagumo
Ernest Nagy
Thomas R Nahigian
Joe Naiman
Samuel G Narotsky
Robert Nash
Mark A Nash
Don Nash
Paul W Nass
Robert G Nassau
Vinny Natale
David H Nathan
Anthony J Nazzario
Richard Nebenzahl
John Neff
Arthur F Neff
David S Neft
Rod Nelson
Walter J Nelson

Robert Nelson
Barry L Nelson
Don L Nelson
Susan Nelson
Tom Nemec
David J Nemec
Raymond J Nemec
Robert J Nemecek
Thomas Nester
Clifford L Netherton
Lance Netland
Maximilian J
    Neuberger
Jeffrey Neuman
Joseph B Neville
Nathanial Newell
Norman D Newell
Richard M Newhouse
William T Newill
Eric Newland
Dale Newlin
Leonard S Newman
David R Newman
Keith Newsome
Anna R Newton
Stephen O Newton
Rob Neyer
Jeffrey Nibert
Chris Nichol
Harry Nicholos
Phil Nichols
Linda Nichols
Sherri M Nichols
Daniel A Nichols
Frederick E Nichols
David A Nichols
Tom Nicholson
Lois P Nicholson
William G Nicholson
Nicki J Nielsen
Daniel Niemiec
Van Nightingale
Robert J Nigroni
Tokuo Nishiyama
William G Nitchals
Jim R Nitz
Edward E Nixon
John Noble
Paul S Noble
A.J. Noftz
John A Nolan
Michael Nolan
Paul F Noll
Eugene Noll
Ruth Nomura
Edward Noneman
Paul A Norem
Andrew North
Stephen H Norwood
Matthew S Novak
Bill Nowlin
Joseph Nunziata
Duane S Nusbaum
Gary Nuthals
Bertil C Nyman

Francis Joseph O'Boyle
Terence C O'Brian
Joseph O'Brien
Joseph O'Brien
Joseph J O'Connell
Pat O'Connell
Thomas O'Connell
Robert E O'Connell
Joe O'Connell
James P O'Donnell
Harry O'Donnell
Maurice O'Dowd
Michael A O'Grady
Donald M O'Hanley
Jon F O'Hare
William P O'Keefe
David T O'Malia
John J O'Malley
Peter O'Malley
James H O'Mara
Bill O'Neal
Tim O'Neil
William E O'Neil
Terry O'Neil
Thomas A O'Toole
J. Ronald Oakley
Tim Obarski
Robert Obojski
Richard Obrand
Sheldon Ocker
James E Odenkirk
Stephen Q Oehmsen
Michael Oestreich
Masakatsu Ogata
Ohio State Univ
    Library
Jon M Ohman
Naoyuki Ojima
Alan Oken
Nelson S Okino
Marc Okkonen
Daniel Okrent
Yoshihiro Okubo
Keith Olbermann
Michael Olenick
Jonathan Oliphant
Mat Olkin
Frank J Olmsted
Steve Olsen
Raymond F Olsen
William H Olsen
John D Olson
Gary M Olson
Harold J Olson
Gordon L Olson
Robert H Olson
Robert C Olson
Greg Olszewski
Paul E Olubas
Chester Omilanowski
James Omitt
Marc Onigman
Carl Opderbeck
Robert D Opie
James Opon

Gene Oppenheim
John Orbison
Barbara S Oremland
Fredric E Orlansky
Jeffrey H Orleans
Gerald L Orlen
James Orner
Jeff Orner
Richard Orodenker
Lee F Ortenstein
Karl Orth
Osaka Taiiku
Daigakutosho
Kenneth L Osborn
Samuel H Osipow
Robert E Osman
Dan Osmond
Edward R Oswalt
Tim Otheos
Charles Ott
Clifford Otto
Phyllis Otto
Dan Ouimet
John W Outland
Joseph M Overfield
James H Overmeyer
James E Overmyer
Michael Overstreet
Santford V Overton
Viola M Owen
Charles A Owen
Thomas S Owens
Harry J Oxford
Burr A Oxley
Nancy B
  Ozsogomonyan
M. Dean Packer
Joseph Paesani
Fred Paine
Vic Pallos
Patricia E Palmer
Pete Palmer
Don K Palmer
Cynthia Palmer
Doug Palmieri
Dan Palubniak
Louis F Panciocco
Mark D Pankin
Herman Pansier
Larry Pansino
Gus Papadopoulos
Anthony J Papalas
Doug Pappas
Richard F Parcells
John F Pardon
William Parizek
Bernard G Park
Donald Parke
Ron Parker
Gary M Parker
Everett Parker
Paul L Parker
James A Parker
Joel Parker
S. Mark Parker

Andy Parkes
Gary Parkinson
Albert G Parnis
Bill Parrillo
Robert Parrott
Clyde Partin
Chuck Partington
Laura Partridge
Cliff Partridge
Gary N Paslow
Gene Pasquariello
Gary R Passamonte
James D Passannante
Jeffrey S Passel
Phil Passen
Clayton Pasternack
John Pastier
Michael N Patchen
Samuel J Pathy
Sharon Patrick
Robert & Sharon
  Patrick
James S Patten
Robert Patterson
Marjorie D Patterson
Robert J Patterson
Theodore Patterson
Walter C Patterson
Charles R Paul
Kenneth R Paulsen
David Paulson
Jerry B Pausch
Charles Pavitt
Dennis Pawl
George G Pawlush
Robert W Payne
Warren S Payne
Martin Payne
Michael Payne
Richard M Payne
David G Paynter
Nicholas Payson
Gary Pearce
Thomas R Pearre
Albert Peckman
John W Peden
James A Peden
Hayford Peirce
Cesar Pellerano
Fred R Peltz
Thomas A Pendleton
Frances J Pendleton
Addison P Penfield
Virgil D Penn
Alfred Pennesi
Robert M Pepe
Gerald Pepper
Peter B Pepper
J.C. Percell
  Periodicals Dept.
Joseph J Perla
Frederick Perlove
Reed M Perlowitz
David L Permut
Michael Perna

Joseph J Pero
Richard L Perry
Steve R Perry
Andrew Perry
Thomas K Perry
Mansco Perry
Claudia A Perry
Blair L Perry
Noel Perry
Konstantine Pertsas
Frank C Perunko
Eric D Peselow
Frank Peters
Anthony J Peters
Brent T Peterson
Robert W Peterson
Greg Peterson
David M Petras
Charles E Petti
Harold Thomas Pettit
James M Pfaff
Fred D Pfening
Allen Pfenninger
Robert P Phelan
Frank V Phelps
Terry Phelps
Jeffrey Philbrick
Wallace L Philips
Todd A Phillips
Blaine Phillips
John A Phillips
John Phillips
Urban Picard
Len Piccione
Deanna L Pierce
Don Piergalski
David A Pietrusza
Patricia Basford
  Pietrusza
Charles E Pikrallidas
Gary Pilat
Doug Pilatzke
Albert J Pinder
Jonathan Pine
Mike Pinneo
William Piper
Joseph C Pisano
Rocco Pisano
Scott Pitoniak
Stephen J Pittari
Allen Pitts
R Plapinger
David O Plaut
Donald G Plavnick
Martin Plax
John Pletsch
William J Plott
Arthur Plourde
Will S Plumley
Charles Plunkett
Gary A Plunkitt
John Plywaczewski
Wayne Poage
Arnold Podair
Peter J Pogacar

Frank Pogoda
Jacob Poleyeff
James M Polhamus
Andrew P Polizzi
Sydney R Polk
Howard M Pollack
Mark Pollak
Paul A Pollard
Donald R Pollins
Donald O Pollock
John Ponchak
Michael W Pool
Melvyn J Poplock
Steven R Popofsky
Harvey Poris
Victor Porraz
Jim Porter
Paul Porter
David L Porter
Barry Posin
Marc Posnock
Donald Post
Alfred Post
Lawrence Potts
Robert Potts
Garth Potts
G. Alan Potts
T.W. Poulton
Ernie Pouttu
Robert Powell
Jim Powers
Brian Powers
Stan Prager
Richard G Prahl
Richard W Pray
Terry Prendergast
William R Presnell
Mark R Presswood
Daniel Price
Jim Price
Don Priestap
Calvin L Pritner
Gregory Proops
Mark Allen Prysant
Joseph A Puccio
Richard Puerzer
Brad Pueschel
Richard A Puff
Anthony F Puglisi
Carmen Puliafito
Jack N Pullig
Marty Pulvers
William F Puotinen
Joseph W Purcell
Jimmie Purvis
Charles Putnam
Lowell Qually
Ray R Queen
Allen H Quimby
Patrick Quinn
Bruce Rabe
B.W. Radley
Roy D Raemer
Roger Raepple
David A Raglin

Joe Ragusa
Bill T Rahm
Jack Raidy
Chris Rainey
C. Frederick Ralston
Mark B Ramsey
Steven Rand
Murray Randall
Wilson T Rankin
Bert M Rappaport
Dan Rappoport
Pete Raschke
James B Rasco
Brian Rash
Timothy J Rask
Bob Rathbun
Jon Ratner
Gary A Ratner
Glen Ray
Leo A Ray
Donald Raycraft
Robert Rayman
Richard Raymo
Neil Raymond
James J Raywood
Mark Rea
Sandy Rea
John W Read
Peter C Read
Michael B Readdy
Billy D Reasonover
Frank Rechtorovic
John J Redfern
Fred Reed
David L Reed
Wallace E Reed
Don C Reed
Friedrich A Reeker
Dennis Reeve
Vic Regan
Kerry Regan
Joe Regan
Raymond Regan
Steven Regan
Elliot Regenstein
Roger Regez
Phil Regli
Edward W Rehak
Steve Reichley
Kevin Reid
Jim Reid
Robert D Reid
Donald Reidell
Todd Reigle
James J Reilly
Larry Reilly
Ronald F Reinke
Robert J Reischer
Jim Reisler
Matthew Rejmaniak
George R Rekela
Thomas G Remington
Bob Remy
William Renaud
Daniel L Rentfro

Ron Replogle
Denis Repp
Michael Resnick
James W Reuter
Claudio Reverberi
John R Reynolds
Bruce A Reznick
Kurt Rheinheimer
Leon E Rhoades
John Rhodes
Greg L Rhodes
Lucius Riccio
David R Ricco
Alan J Rice
Homer C Rice
John P Rich
Kenneth D Richard
Paul Richards
Ron Richards
Richard L Richards
John W Richards
Steven J Richardson
Peter Richardson
Robert Richardson
Gene Richardson
Lance Richbourg
John L Richebacher
Harold Richman
William J Richmond
Gary Richter
S. William Richter
Owen Ricker
John Rickert
Paul G Riding
Robert Rieder
Steven A Riess
Jim Riethmiller
David F Riggs
Peter Rigsbee
Tony Riha
Dennis Riley
Jack Riley
James A Riley
Paul J Riley
John C Ringle
Tracy Ringolsby
Jack Riskin
Michael D Risley
Lance P Rist
Paul D Rittenhouse
Almon S Ritter
Lawrence Ritter
Robert L Rives
Marc A Rivlin
Christopher P Rizzo
William J Roach
Gary Robbins
Donald Robbins
James Robelli
Philip L Roberto
Llewellyn V Roberts
Stephen J Roberts
George Roberts
Len Roberts
James Roberts

John M Roberts
Michael Roberts
Walter C Robertson
George Robicheaw
Mathew Robins
Eugene Robinson
Ray Robinson
Warren C Robinson
Edgar F Robinson
Jeffrey C Robinson
Henri J Roca
Andrew B Rochman
Patrick Rock
Fred O Rodgers
David L Roegner
Douglas N Roesemann
Bruce Rogalska
Barry Rogan
C. Paul Rogers
Chris Rogers
Stephen D Rohrer
Craig Rolfe
Robert A Rolfe
Joseph Rollo
Jerome C Romanowski
David C Romans
Richard L Romeyn
Harry A Romney-
    Joseph
Alberto Rondon
Stephen Roney
Joseph Ronson
Scott Roper
John P Rorke
Charles J Rosciam
Ed Rose
Dennis Rose
Andrew M Rose
John N Rose
Michael J Roselli
Michael H Rosen
Nat Rosenberg
Aaron Rosenberg
Victor Rosenberg
Marc L Rosenberg
Ken Rosenblum
Jason Rosenstock
Robert A Rosiek
Josephine E Rosin
John Q Ross
Daniel J Ross
Joseph Ross
Philip Ross
Richard L Ross
Mike Ross
Jeremy Rossman
Larry T Roth
Don H Roth
David Rothenberg
Steven Rothenberg
Harry J Rothgerber
Rich Rothschild
Mathew V Rothstein
C. Brooke Rothwell
George S Rotter

Theodore S Rouman
Fred Roush
Samuel Rousso
Mark Rowe
Thomas K Rowe
Perry F Rowicki
J.Michael Royster
Thomas Ruane
Tomas Rubalcava
Louis D Rubin
Laurence D Rubin
Charlie Rubin
Conrad S Rubinkowski
Bill D Rubinstein
Lewis H Rubman
Rob Ruck
Kal Rucker
Mark D Rucker
John P Rudolph
David S Rudstein
Jon R Rudzinski
Michael A Rugh
Robert E Ruland
Willie Runquist
Mike Russell
John H Russell
Thomas J Russo
Vincent J Russo
Ballard Rutherford
Bob Rutishauser
Mark Ryan
Tom Ryan
Jim Ryan
David J Ryba
Paul Ryberg
William Ryczek
James J Rygelski
John T Saccoman
Fluffy Saccucci
Charlie Sacheli
Ross De Forest Sackett
Scott Saftler
Daniel K Sage
Rick Salamon
Kevin M Saldana
Tony Salin
Robert H Salisbury
Luke Salisbury
Paul Sallee
David Saltzman
Paul M Salvati
Albert C Salzberg
James A Salzman
Charles E Samec
Donald Samelson
Kenneth Samelson
Philip Samet
Jefferey M Samoray
Gary Sampson
Stephen M Samuels
Martin L Sandberg
Barbara A Sanders
David S Sanders
Michael J Sanders
Tom Sanders

Paul J Sandin
Jay Sanford
Robert M Sanow
Michael Santa Maria
Earl E Santee
Joseph Santry
Charles Sarasohn
James E Sargent
Carl Sargolini
John Sasman
Michael Sass
Eugene Sasso-Maduro
Matthew Sather
Elliot R Satinoff
Lance Sauerteig
Joseph C Saunders
Steven P Savage
Rick Saxton
Kazuo Sayama
William Sayle
Edward M Scahill
Robert Scandiffio
Allen Scanlon
Joseph R Scarola
Michael Schacht
Curtis Schaeffer
Russ Schaeffer
Gary Schahet
Gabriel Schechter
Jerry Scheer
William Scheeren
Lewis Scheider
Michael J Schiavo
Tom Schieffer
Herb Schilling
Robert Schlansker
Barry R Schlenker
John R Schleppi
Lawrence
    Schlernitzauer
Dan Schlossberg
Fred Schlutt
Kenneth R Schmeichel
John R Schmidt
Charles Schmidt
Alan Schmidt
Ray Schmidt
William Schmidt
Robert E Schmierer
Russell Schneider
Amy K Schneider
Bob Schnieders
Mark A Schoen
Leonard Schoenberg
Murray Schofel
Jack Schofield
Clifford Schold
Gregory Scholz
John R Schoon
Art Schott
Richard J Schrader
Mark W Schraf
Paul E Schramka
Ronald Schrank
Stephen Schroder

Frank Schubert
Fred N Schuld
Ronald W Schuler
Richard A Schulman
Elmer L Schultz
Walter E Schultz
David W Schultz
Robert F Schultz
Steve Schultz
Robert F Schulz
Robert D Schumacher
Max B Schumacher
Richard E Schumann
Roy Schuster
Neil M Schwab
Greg Schwalenberg
Wayne S Schwark
Martin Schwartz
Jack Schwartz
John Schwartz
Neil Schwartzbein
Edward M Schwarz
John H Schwarz
Thomas Schwarz
Barry Schweid
Joseph Schweinhart
Joseph A Sclafani
Lynn Scoggin
Charles R Scoggins
Neil Scott
Timothy Scott
John B Scott
David A Scott
John E Scott
Arthur J Screpetis
Vincent F Scully
Spencer Seaks
Michael Searson
Frank Secondo
Corey Seeman
Mike Segal
Richard Segarra
Anthony Segreti
Eugene F Segreti
Philip Seib
Peter S Seidman
David G Selby
Steven Selby
Edward J Seligman
Jamie Selko
James J Sell
Bill Selnes
Ron Selter
Jack Selzer
David S Senoff
Serials Acquisition Unit
Serials Section
Marc L Seror
David Serota
Gene Severson
Steven Shackelford
Dan Shafer
Stephen Craig Shafer
John D Shaffer
James A Shaffer

Mike Shaler
Jeff Shames
Clay Shampoe
Ron Shandler
Larry Shane
Corey Shanus
Stuart Shapiro
Warren Shapiro
Sheldon Shapiro
Paul Shapiro
David Shapiro
Jeff Share
Russell H Sharples
Edward Shatkin
Mike Shatzkin
John Shaw
F. Robert Shea
James Shearon
Lee Shedroff
C. Patrick Sheehy
Kent J Sheets
Barbara Sheinbein
Neil Sheinin
Rob Sheinkopf
Charlie Shelton
Nalown L Shelton
Alan E Shenk
Rowland H Shepard
Robert Shepherd
Samuel A Sherer
Stuart Sheridan
Wilson Sherk
Russell Sherman
Daniel J Sheron
Tom B Shieber
George M Shiffler
Carl Shinabargar
Lester Shindelman
Robert E Shipley
William Shlensky
David B Shoebotham
Robert W Shoemaker
Ed Shoemaker
Richard L Shook
Jeffrey M Shope
William Short
John Shostrom
Thomas G Shrimplin
Jerry A Shroder
Matthew Shugart
Sherman C Shultz
Herbert L Shultz
David W Shury
Timothy B Shutt
Brent A Shyer
Paul A Sicard
Frank Siciliano
Ken D Sidlow
Charles Sidman
Jeffrey A Siegel
Sol Siegel
Howie Siegel
Ira Siegel
Murray H Siegel
Jack M Siegel

Robert Siegmund
Richard W Siessel
Richard Newton Silar
Max Silberman
Steve Sillen
Dan Silverberg
Phil Silvia
Joseph E Simenic
Terry Simeon
Edward J Simeone
Geoff Simkins
Edward Simmer
Tom J Simmons
Tom Simon
Charles Simon
Robert V Simons
William Simons
Eric A Simonsen
Warren K Simpson
William John Simpson
Dick Simpson
Alan Singer
Howard Singer
Jamie Siragusa
Richard Sisler
Seymour Siwoff
John W Sizer
David C Skinner
John Skipper
Douglas A Skipper
Robert Sklar
Ronald J Skocypec
Don Skoller
Gary Robert Skoog
Linda Skory
Ron Skrabacz
Don S Skuce
Jerry Skurnik
Alexander G Skutt
Robert A Skylar
William J Slankard
Stanley Slater
Thomas G Slater
Gary Slatus
John R Slaughter
David Sleight
Steve Sliman
Barry D Sloate
William H Slocum
Richard J Slusarski
Mike Sluss
Robert J Smagula
William F Small
Edward H Small
Ronda Smalley
Robert H Smalley
R.J. Smalling
Steve M Smart
Jim Smietana
Richard A Smiley
Steven G Smith
Carl Smith
James A Smith
Jeff D Smith
Hal M Smith

Ronald E Smith
Thomas H Smith
Robert S Smith
Doug Smith
David Smith
Jeffrey D Smith
Michael C Smith
Rick Smith
Leverett T Smith
Edward N Smith
Bernard H Smith
James D Smith
Fred T Smith
Fred Smith
Talbot M Smith
Kerry L Smith
Duane A Smith
Jerry E Smith
David W Smith
Charles P Smith
Al Smitley
Jerry Smolin
Jeannette Smoot
Ian Smyth
M. Catherine Smythe-
   Zajc
Larry A Sneed
Gary B Snelson
Mike Snodgrass
Brad Snyder
Eric Snyder
George Snyder
Robert A Snyder
Gloria Sobel Smith
Don M Sodergren
Jim Soderlund
Robert E Soderman
Michael Soinski
Mitch Soivenski
Carroll L Sollars
Herb Sollinger
Burt Solomon
Eric Solomon
Greg Solook
Larry Solters
Larry Somer
William Sommer
George Sommerfeld
Paul M Sommers
Ronnie A Sommers
Harvey Soolman
Arnold J Soolman
Troy Soos
Frank S Sopata
Mark A Sorell
Dave Sorem
Tom Soriano
David Sosidka
Fred J Souba
Oscar Soule
Steven D Souza
Mike Sowell
James Sowers
Christopher A Sowick
Virginia Soybel

Paul Soyka
Michael F Spaeth
John E Spalding
David Spaner
Barry Sparks
Michael Sparrow
Lyle Spatz
William Speare
Gary Speidel
Ralph Spelbring
William Spence
Burl Spencer
William D Spengeman
Joseph J Sperino
Michael C Spinelli
Ray Spinney
Greg Spira
Luther W Spoehr
Don J Spoon
Frank A Spooner
Richard Spooner
Resource Centre Sport
   Information
Adrian N Sprick
Arnold J Springer
Art Springsteen
Vincent G Sprinkle
Richard D Spry
Louis J Spry
James Squezello
Joseph St. George
St. Louis Public Library
Steven K St. Martin
Henry Staat
Jeffrey L Staats
Edward W Stack
Charles Howard Stagg
Doug Stagner
Andy Stagno
Alec Stais
Paul D Stanaford
Tom Stanchfield
Roy A Stanfield
Thad Stanford
Mark Stang
Mark W Stangl
Guy M Stanley
C. Vaughan Stanley
Lee Stanley
Joseph E Stanton
Jack Stanton
Jim Starkman
Frank P Staucet
E.W. Staudenmayer
Robert N Stearns
Christopher Steele
Loyal Steelman
Philip J Stefaniak
Dennis Stegmann
Irving M Stein
Walter Stein
Bill Stein
Fred Stein
Charles E Stein
Jerome M Stein

Don Steinbach
Alan Steinberg
David Steinbrecher
Jeff Steindorf
Sumner Steinfeldt
Thomas Steinhardt
Charles I Steinhorn
Richard C Steinmetz
Steven Steinsaltz
C. David Stephan
H. Page Stephens
Marc Stephenson
Andrew Stephenson
Grant C Sterling
Joel Sternberg
Mark S Sternman
Manas Sternschein
Brian Stevens
Bruce Stevens
Robert F Stevens
Frank Stevens
Len Stevens
William Stevens
Edward Stevenson
Kent Stevenson
George W Stewart
Robert S Stewart
Mark L Stewart
William C Stewart
Art Stewart
Perry M Stewart
Wayne Stewart
Mel Stiefel
Thomas Stillman
James Stimac
Rich Stimpfle
Jim Stinson
Jonathan Stoddart
John M Stole
Gary C Stone
William F Stone
Gary Stone
Bruce C Stone
George Stone
Bill L Stone
Robert Stone
Steve Stout
Glenn Stout
Alan Stowell
Robert J Strack
Andy Strasberg
Barry Strassler
Thor Stratton
Brian W Strause
David Strauss
George Strickland
Will Strickland
Steve J Strnisha
David Strong
Tom Strother
Peter J Strouse
Robert Strudwick
Kevin Struss
John Stryker
J. Mark Stryker

Robert A Stuart
Richard D Stueber
Mark Stueve
Grace Caroline Sturges
Kurt Stutt
Stephen Suarez
A.D. Suehsdorf
Thomas M Sukitsch
Steve Suknaic
Jerry Sulecki
Brian G Sullivan
Brad Sullivan
Gerald E Sullivan
James P Sullivan
Kevin I Sullivan
Dean A Sullivan
Henry B Summer
Kevin Summers
Alan C Sunderman
Gene Sunnen
Jeffrey Suntala
William H Suphan
Kenneth Surabian
Bernard Susskind
Mark Sutcliffe
Dennis Sutcliffe
Henry Sutter
Matt Sutton
Paul D Svirbel
Philip V Swan
Richard A Swanson
Paul D Swanson
Louis B Swartz
Terrence J Sweeney
Gayland M Sweet
Paul Sweet
James Sweetman
Merle Swenson
Jerome P Swenson
John M Swiderski
Mike Swierczewski
Charles Swift
John L Swift
William C Swift
Timothy D Swindle
Richard Swiniuch
John M Swistak
Melvin R Syberg
W.K. Symmes
Dick Symons
Anthony Szabelski
Walter Szeremet
Walter Szetela
Mark H Tabakin
Tom Taber
James Tackach
Martin Taft
Steven P Tahsler
Allen E Tait
Hiroshi Takagi
Michio Takeuchi
William S Talbot
Vic Tanenholz
Michael P Tangel
Teddy Tannenbaum

Carl R Tannenbaum
Jim Tarica
Edward J Tassinari
David Tate
William Tatoraitis
H. Lee Tatum
Charles A Tausche
David Taylor
Jerry E Taylor
Richard Taylor
Mervyn S Taylor
Larry S Taylor
John L Taylor
Thomas G Taylor
John Taylor
Tony Techko
Michael Tedesco
Otto Teja
Lee E Temanson
Jerry Tempalski
Brian R Ten Eyck
Steven Tepper
Joseph Termini
James J Tessmer
Richard Testa
James Tester
Wayne Testino
Joseph E Thach
Gerald J Thain
Russell J Thayer
Wilfred Theard
E.A. Thieman
Robert J Tholkes
John Thom
Robert Thomas
Henry W Thomas
David C Thomas
Marshall Thomas
Jeff Thomas
Jerald Thomas
Richard E Thomas
W.L. Thomas
Robert Thomas
Joan M Thomas
Duane L Thomas
Evan E Thomas
David K Thomas
Gordon M Thomas
Ted Thompson
David J Thompson
William H Thompson
Richard J Thompson
Stephen I Thompson
John H Thompson
Keith H Thompson
Timothy M Thompson
Brett M Thompson
Edward J Thompson
John Thorn
James M Thornberry
Richard L Thornburgh
Stew Thornley
Phyllis Thornley
Michele Thrapp
Wade Thrift

Joe Thurman
Ruth Tiemann
Robert L Tiemann
John P Tierney
William Tierney
Thomas W Tifft
Jeff Tilles
Ken Tillman
Tom Tippett
Steven Tischler
Bob Titterton
Yoshinari Tobe
Henry Tobey
Albert Todres
Alfred Toizer
Paul R Tolland
Nick Tomasic
Todd G Tomasic
Antoinette M Tomczyk
Elizabeth Tomczyk
Gerald Tomlinson
James R Tootle
Steve Topolewski
Richard Topp
Barb Topp
Angel Torres
Richard Dixie
   Tourangeau
Eric Towne
Wayne Townsend
Ronald G Toya
Michael Trabert
Robert L Trace
Leo Trachtenberg
Dave Trautman
William K Trautwein
Mark Travaglini
Neal D Traven
Albert S Travis
Chuck Traxler
Roger A Treece
Bill Treese
Charles P Treft
Todd Treichel
Rob Tresso
Edward Trieste
Stephen A Trimble
Jim Troisi
David Trombley
Jim Trout
Barry M Troutman
William Troy
Alan C Truax
W.G. Truitt
Rick Tuber
Mark J Tucker
Oliver G Tucker
Walter D Tucker
Robb Tucker
James Tucker
Wayne C Tucker
Kevin Tulley
Edward J Tully
Bill Tunilla
Wayne Turiansky

Larry Turkish
Ralph J Turner
Charles Turner
Terry Turner
Richard M Turner
Willard F Turner
William Turner
Mark Turnpenny
Ted L Turocy
Peter Tutak
James E Tuttle
Don P Tuttle
Jeffrey R Twiss
Jules Tygiel
Craig S Tyle
Stanley C Tyler
Art Tyler
Takehiko Ueno
Joe Ullian
Harlan Ullman
Bob Underwood
Univ. Of Nebraska
   Library
Richard C Unruh
Charles Upcraft
Ernest Urech
Paula M Uscian
Alain Usereau
R. G. Utley
Leon Uzarowski
James F Vail
J.F. Valente
Anthony Valenti
Joseph J Valenti
Eduardo Valero
Karl Van Asselt
Robert B Van Atta
Steve Van Guelpen
Daniel F Van Horn
Thomas E Van Hyning
Gerard A Van Sickle
Richard C VanWey
Sidney J Vance
Victor F Vance
Tom Vandergriff
James W Varner
Efren E Varona
Charlie Vascellaro
Gerald A Vastano
Paul R Vastola
Mark Vatavuk
John R Vaughn
Terry Vazquez
Joseph M Vellano
Juan Vene
Charles A Venturi
David Venturo
Robert Verhine
James C Verney
John A Vernon
Michael Vickers
Jerry Vickery
Jack Victor
Sandra Vigil
David S Vincent

David W Vincent
Kevin Vincent
Barry Virshbo
Ron Visco
James A Vlasich
Alexander B Vlielander
Art C Voellinger
David Vogel
Michael J Vogel
David L Vogel
Del C Vogt
David Q Voigt
Richard Voldimer
Tom Voll
Philip E Von Borries
J. Von Bushberger
Timothy J Vrana
Gregory J Vranekovic
Vinnie Vrotny
Gerald N Wachs
Craig B Waff
Larry Wagg
Don Wagman
Murray Wagman
Ron E Wagner
R.L. Wagner
Robert J Wagner
Anthony P Wahner
Christopher R Wait
Charles Waites
Brian Waits
Eileen S Waitsman
Howard A Waitzman
Frank H Wakefield
John Walden
Doug Walden
George F Walden
Larry Waldman
Robert G Walker
Robert C Walker
James P Walker
Michael Walker
G. Jay Walker
Hoyt W Wallace
Brian Wallace
David Wallack
Timothy E Wallaert
Jeff M Wallner
Peter A Wallner
Richard E Walsh
Dan Walsh
Thomas Walsh
David Walsh
Patrick K Walsh
Joseph Michael Walsh
Scott Walter
Alan S Walters
Ernest Walther
Edward Walton
Steve Wang
Paul Warburton
Jerry Ward
Ed Ward
Frank J Ward
Mr. Warmth

James Warnock
Bruce W Warren
Ed J Washuta
Eric Wasser
Howard F Wasserman
Luke S Wassum
Robert Waterman
John Watson
James L Watt
George Watters
Jack Waugaman
William Way
Randy Way
Joseph M Wayman
Robert T Wazeka
RS Weatherly
Jack Weaver
Charles Weaver
Robert G Weaver
Michael Webb
Royce Webb
Bill Weber
Roger A Weber
Max Weder
Alan Wedge
William R Wedin
David Wee
Stephen E Weick
Kurt A Weideman
Dale R Weiers
James Weigand
Jack Weigel
Frank Weiler
Donald C Weiler
Ira Weiner
Joan Weiner
Milton M Weinrieb
Stephen Weinstein
Richard Weintraub
Timothy G Weir
Don Weiskopf
Jacob Weisman
Larry D Weiss
Mark A Weiss
Andrew M Weiss
William J Weiss
Ronald L Weitz
Anvil Welch
David Wells
Michael V Wells
Donald R Wells
Michael A Wells
Mike Welsh
Chris Welsh
Glenn Wendler
Paul Wendt
David P Wentroble

Lawrence H Wentz
Brian Werner
Albert F Wessbecher
Robert Wesselhoeft
Paul Westberg
Richard N Westcott
Barry Weston
Glen A Wetzel
Ken Wexler
Clifford E Wexler
Matthew D Weymar
Ken Whalen
Michael L Wheat
Herman L Wheeler
Owen Wheeler
William Wheeler
Jim Wheeler
Hal Whitcomb
Gaylon H White
C. Ronald White
Ken White
Eric M White
Tom White
Jeffery L White
George White
Curt Whiteaker
Lon Whitehead
Donny L Whitehead
Matthew I Whitehorn
Jerry Whitman
G. Whitmore
James R Whittington
Ralph J Wick
Edgar Wickberg
Michael Wickham
Ron Wickline
Edwin J Wicksel
Madeline Wicksel
Doug Wier
Ken Wiklanski
Ed Wikoff
Warren N Wilbert
Robert H Wilcox
Dan Wilcox
Benjamin T Wilcox
Roger Wildin
George T Wiley
Mike Wilhelm
Charles K Wilkins
Phil Williams
Joseph C Williams
Jana M Williams
Robert S Williams
Stephen D Williams
Ed Williams
Frank J Williams
Peter Williams

Robert J Williams
Jack F Williams
Chris Williams
Bruce R Williamson
Mark R Williamson
William E Williamson
Chet Williamson
Al Willis
Mark Willis
Tim Willis
Harry J Willis
C. Norman Willis
James S Williston
Thomas Willman
Arthur Willner
Michael Willoughby
Greg M Willoughby
John Willoughby
Lewis Wills
Danny Wilson
C.P. Wilson
Lyle K Wilson
John Wilson
Charlotte Wilson
Woody Wilson
Walter A Wilson
Chuck Wilson
Robert Wilson
Brian S Wimer
Jerry M Winchell
William T Windham
Ed Winkler
Amy S Winnicki
Ralph F Winnie
Peter Winske
Paul Winston
Graham Winterbone
Michael R Wise
Wes Wise
Richard M Wise
James B Wiseman
Galen A Wiser
Calvin T Wishart
Norbert Wishowski
Mark A Wisniewski
Charles Wiswell
Charles T Witherell
Victor R Witte
Don Wiur
Peter Wlasuk
Theodore O Wohlsen
Tom Wojnicki
Michael Wolf
Karl Wolf
Kenneth E Wolfe
Ronald C Wolfe
Miles Wolff

Larry Wolfson
Sheldon Wolpin
Stewart Wolpin
Tim Wolter
Karla Wolters
Barry Wolven
Loren Woo
Alexander Woo
Robert O Wood
Brian Wood
Allan Wood
Tracy Wood
William Wood
Wayne Wood
C. Eugene Wood
Robert K Wood
Philip Wood
Eric A Wood
William Wood
Edward F Woodcock
Daniel Woodhead
Robert Woodside
Joseph Woolery
Paul K Woolf
Keith Woolner
Frank Workman
Raymond J Worst
Donald L Worthy
Joseph Wouk
Charles B Wride
Russell O Wright
Jerry J Wright
Marshall Wright
Craig R Wright
Jeff Wright
Greg Wroblewski
Jim Wucher
Richard A Wueste
Daniel Wukich
Mark W Wurl
Eric D Wuth
James Wyman
David S Wyman
Paul L Wysard
Lawrence Yaffa
Charles J Yahr
Seiji Yamaguchi
Tadashi Yanagihara
Anthony D Yandoli
Greg Yanta
Peter Yee
Alvin H Yellon
Edward A Yerha
Lenny Yochim
Michio Yorifuji
Charles E York
Mac A Young

Michael D Young
Charles M Young
Andrew Young
James W Young
Donn Youngkin
Rick Youngs
Roy Yoxall
Eric S Yuhas
Paul Zabala
John Zablocki
Paul S Zachar
Richard C Zagrocki
Steve Zajac
John M Zajc
John M Zajc, Jr.
Thomas Zamorski
Peter Zanardi
Brian J Zande
Phil A Zangari
Craig Zanot
Gerard & Donna Zazzi
Lucien Zeffiro
George C Zeller
Dave Zeman
Frederick L Zemmin
Jack Zerby
John Ziegler
Jay C Ziemann
Robert E Zimmermann
Edward B Zimny
Robert Zimring
Dan Ziniuk
David Zink
Joseph S Zinkowicz
Richard A Zitrin
Alvin Zitterkob
Kalvin Zitterkob
Tom Zlatoper
Don Zminda
Thomas Zocco
Michael Zolno
Larry Zorn
Phil Zuccarello
Lauren Ted Zuckerman
Duff D Zwald
Robert William Zwissig
James E Zygaj
Frank de Bruin
Wenceslao de la Cerna
Peter L deRosa

1991 Trivia Contest Champions. David Nemec, Dick Beverage, Bill Carle and Jon Daniels.

Marge Daniels at The Ballpark in Arlingotn, 1994.

June 7, 1996. L to R: Ray Nemec, Art Schott and Mary Schott.

Catherine Smythe Zajc, left, and Maria Eckhouse, right, help out at the Pittsburgh National Convention.

Joe Simenic, Evelyn Begley and Bob Davids, June 7, 1996.

Carl Smith, Norman Arrington and Doug Pappas at the banquet in San Diego.

BIOGRAPHIES

ROSS ADELL, born June 28, 1955 in Jackson Heights, NY and joined SABR in September 1984. His reason for joining was to meet other baseball "STAT" people. Currently he belongs to the Casey Stengel Chapter in New York City. Adell considers the history of the New York Mets to be his field of expertise. He is interested in anything to do with the Mets, game-ending home runs and double digit strike-out games.

He is serving on the Records Committee and has run three regional meetings for SABR. Most memorable experiences to date are Seaver's 300th win, the 1986 World Series, being on Champion Trivia Team and winning in 1996 with Al Blumkin, Dick Thompson and Tom Zocco.

He has prepared two career home run logs for two former major leaguers. These logs gave pertinent information on each home run. He personally gave these logs to Gary Carter and Art Shamsky. Adell assisted in the research for two baseball books, in each case his name appeared in the acknowledgment section: *The Great All-Time Baseball Record Book* by Ken Samelson and *The New York Mets Trivia Book* by Mike Getz. In addition he was asked to provide research by the New York Mets in 1996 to commemorate the 25th anniversary of the 1969 World Champion team. He chronicled the day-by-day details of the 1969 season. This information was used on WFAN radio and subsequently used in the newspaper *New York Mets Inside Pitch.* Finally some of his Met material has been used in recent New York Met information guides.

Adell is single and lives in Flushing, NY where he currently works at Citibank as a clerk.

BRUCE ADAMS, the founder and president of the Bethesda Community Baseball Club (BCBBC), a community non-profit dedicated to improving the quality of youth baseball and softball fields. BCBBC operates the Bethesda Big Train summer college team in the Clark C. Griffith Collegiate Baseball League. The team plays at Shirley Povich Field just outside Washington near Walter Johnson High School. As an elected county official in the early 1990s, Adams led the effort to grant historic designation to Walter Johnson's Bethesda house.

Adams, 51, is the co-author with his wife, Peggy Engel, of *Ballpark Vacations: Great Family Trips to Minor League and Classic Major League Baseball Parks Across America* (Fodor's, 1997). He and Peggy traveled 30,000 miles with their children, Emily, 12, and Hugh, 9, to research the book. Adams is the coach of Hugh's youth baseball team.

TOM ADAMS, born March 8, 1936 in the city of Springer (Carter County), OK. He joined SABR in 1995 to be more involved in baseball. Currently he does not belong to a regional group but attends the Hall-Ruggles meetings. Writing poetry on the subject of baseball is his expertise. He likes to read about baseball played in the 1920s, 1930s and 1940s. Adams is on the Research Committee of baseball songs and poems

and several professional teams have published his poems. One of his greatest moments was reading some poetry to the Hall-Ruggles Chapter.

Adams and his wife, Doris, have been married 43 years and have one son, Larry, and two grandsons, Christopher and Drew. He is a semi-retired minister and works as a substitute teacher. Adams loves to write poetry as well as study military history, particularly the Civil War.

ARTHUR R. AHRENS, born in Chicago, IL on March 12, 1949. He has been a Cub fan since roughly age 7. He attended his first game on Sept. 26, 1959 watching the Cubs trounce the Dodgers, 12-2, at Wrigley Field. He has been a SABR member since late 1971.

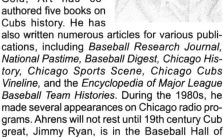

With fellow SABR member and retired *Chicago Sun-Times* sportswriter, Eddie Gold, Art has co-authored five books on Cubs history. He has also written numerous articles for various publications, including *Baseball Research Journal, National Pastime, Baseball Digest, Chicago History, Chicago Sports Scene, Chicago Cubs Vineline,* and the *Encyclopedia of Major League Baseball Team Histories.* During the 1980s, he made several appearances on Chicago radio programs. Ahrens will not rest until 19th century Cub great, Jimmy Ryan, is in the Baseball Hall of Fame.

Ahrens holds a BA degree from the University of Illinois at Chicago. He is a member of Old Timers Baseball Association of Chicago and the Knights of Columbus.

SCOTT C. ALLEN, born Dec. 15, 1973 in Granite City, IL resided most of his life in Collinsville, IL. He became a member of the SABR in 1997 to learn more about the history of baseball and meet fellow historical researchers.

Allen is a researcher of the Negro league teams of St. Louis, MO, specifically the Giants and the Stars. To this endeavor he has written *Organize Your Team: The St. Louis Giants and Black Baseball: 1910-1921.* For this unpublished work he won the 1998 Herbert H. Rosenthal Award for Historical Writing from Southern Illinois University at Edwardsville and the 1998 Robert Peterson Recognition Award from the SABR Negro Leagues Committee. A lifetime St. Louis Cardinals fan, Allen also has a strong interest in the history of the fabled National League franchise. He assisted Bob Broeg and Jerry Vickery in their 1998 book *The St. Louis Cardinals Encyclopedia* by providing a bibliography of materials written about the team.

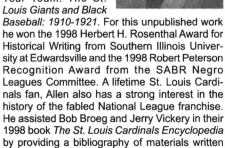

He is active in the Negro Leagues Committee and a member of the Bob Broeg Chapter in St. Louis, MO. Allen's most memorable baseball experiences include attending game three of the 1985 National League Championship Series and games three and four of the 1996 NLCS in St. Louis, meeting Hall of Fame broadcaster, Jack Buck, attending a game at the original Comiskey Park and witnessing Mark McGwire's 61st home run of the 1998 season with his father.

A 1997 graduate of Southern Illinois University at Edwardsville with a degree in history, Allen is currently in graduate school studying American history at Michigan State University in East Lansing, MI. Allen now attends local SABR meetings in Michigan and western Michigan. He enjoys collecting baseball books, memorabilia and attending games.

JIM AMATO, born in 1954 in Cleveland, OH joined SABR in 1996 and is a member of the Cleveland's Jack Graney Chapter. His expertise is baseball of the 1960s. An avid Indian's fan, he also closely followed the Twins and the Tigers of the 60s.

Tony Olivia is by far his favorite player. Also ranking high on his list are Rocky Colavito and "Sudden" Sam McDowell. He enjoys statistical and biographical research and reads anything he can find on the history of the Indians. His most memorable experiences are the countless games he had the pleasure of watching at the old Cleveland Municipal Stadium as a youngster.

Amato is single with four children: Mike (26), Angie (23), Tony (13) and Jimmy (12). He also has three grandchildren: Meredith (3), Travis (1) and Claudia (8 months). Besides his full-time employment, Amato is also a free-lance writer.

PAUL ANDRESEN, born Dec. 18, 1946 in New York City. He joined SABR in 1981 to be among his own kind and is a member of the Northwest Chapter. He served on the executive board as treasurer, 1995-99, and twice as president of NW SABR.

His mentors are Jim O'Donnell, Larry Gerlach and Dick Beverage. Interests include ball parks and book collecting. He has been in over 100 Major League and Minor League ball parks.

Paul is an engineer for Hewlett-Packard and president, Fielder Jones Society. He and his wife Debbie have three children: Matt (20), Marc (17) and Michael (15).

MARTY APPEL, born Aug. 7, 1948 in Brooklyn, NY and joined SABR in 1979. He was on the staff of the Baseball Commissioner at the time and felt it was important to know what the game's most avid fans were thinking. Where better to find fans than SABR. His mentors are Bob Fishel, Lee MacPhail, Gabe Paul, Bill Veeck and Bowie Kuhn.

His interest is in the game's literature, but his expertise is the New York Yankees, Kuhn era, 19th century, King Kelly and the Baseball Hall of Fame. Appel has written 15 books including: 1996 Casey Award winner *Slide, Kelly, Slide* and collaborations with Bowie Kuhn, Lee MacPhail, Tom Seaver (two), Thurman Munson, Eric Gregg, plus *Baseballs' Best: The Hall of Fame Gallery.* He currently serves on the 19th Century Research Committee for SABR. His most memorable SABR highlight was when he conceived the retroactive vote for Rookies of the Year and Cy Young Award winners in 1980, one of the most significant SABR projects in the organization's history.

Appel currently lives in Mamaroneck, NY and has two children Brian and Debbie. He has been the public relations director of the New York Yankees from 1968-77; worked in the Office of the Baseball Commissioner, 1979-80; producer of Yankee Baseball for WPIX-TV, 1980-92; served on the Atlanta Olympic Committee, 1992-93; Topps, 1993-98; and in 1998 founded the Marty Appel Public Relations Company which is still going strong.

SHELDON APPLETON, born in September 1933, saw his first baseball game at the old Polo Grounds shortly before his 6th birthday and was hooked forever. A longtime SABR member, he grew up in New York City in the halcyon days when the city had three teams, frequent subway series, heroes like DiMaggio, Mays, Robinson and Campanella, and announcers like Allen, Barber and Harwell.

A Detroit resident since 1960, he has been a loyal Tigers and Cubs fan and a devotee of statistical analysis. He coached a city champion Little League baseball team and has written many biographical entries for the *Dictionary of Sports Biography: Baseball* and an article on Sam Thompson for the *Dictionary of American Biography.*

In his other life, he has been a professor of political science at Oakland University; husband of Betty; father of four: Vikki, Kevin, Laura and Brad; and grandfather (so far) of one, Erin.

FRANK ARDOLINO, born May 16, 1941 in Brooklyn, NY. Not surprisingly he has a scholarly interest in baseball and joined SABR in 1990. His main interests are the Brooklyn Dodgers, Jackie Robinson and Hawaiian baseball history.

Ardolino has written several articles that have been published in *National Pastime* and *Aethlon and Nine.*

Ardolino is married to June Marie and is a professor of English at the University of Hawaii. He enjoys walking, swimming and has written two books on 16th century English drama.

PRISCILLA (STOCKER) ASTIFAN, has resided in Rochester, NY since 1946. She discovered SABR after yearly visits to Cooperstown and an ongoing intrigue with baseball led her to research the beginnings of the game in Rochester.

She has written *Baseball in the 19th Century* for the *Rochester History* quarterly publication and is finishing a sequel that will include the post-Civil War years through 1877, Rochester's first year to have a salaried team, and is considering a book on 19th century and early 20th century Rochester baseball.

Astifan has been married to Richard for 30 years. They have two sons, Mark (29) and Paul (25). She is self-employed as a writer and researcher.

MEL BAILEY, born in Buffalo, NY in 1933, but grew up in Syracuse following the Chiefs, graduated from Colgate University and entered the Air Force in 1954 as an information officer. He retired in 1975 and has lived in Riverside, CA since then.

He became a sports collector as a 10-year old and also began keeping a roster with uniform numbers. He saw his first major league game in 1948 at Ebbets Field as the guest of Ernie Harwell, a fellow collector who had just taken the Dodgers broadcasting job.

Bailey traded off his scorecard collection in the late 1950s and built a collection of guides. He has always been interested in photography and is a contributing photographer for Baseball

America. Bailey is married to Donna and has three adult sons.

LAWRENCE BALDASSARO, born June 25, 1943 in Holyoke, MA and raised in neighboring Chicopee, home of the A.G. Spalding plant where major league baseballs were produced until 1973. His main research interests are Ted Williams and the history of Italian-Americans in baseball.

He edited *The Ted Williams Reader* (Simon and Schuster, 1991) and has published articles in numerous baseball journals. He is a regular contributor to *Lead Off*, the Milwaukee Brewers magazine.

Memorable baseball experiences are pitching in the 1961 New England American Legion tournament, taking his son to the Hall of Fame induction ceremonies in 1989, throwing batting practice for the Brewers in 1992, and spending time with Ted Williams in his Florida home later that year.

He is professor of Italian and comparative literature and director of the University Honors Program at the University of Wisconsin-Milwaukee. He is married to Judith Ramazzini and has a son, James (23).

TOM BANOCY, born Dec. 29, 1958 in Vienna, Austria. He first joined the SABR in 1990 because of his love of baseball's colorful and interesting past. Due to the fact there is not a Connecticut chapter of the SABR, Banocy joined the Stengel, J. Burkett and Lajoie/Start chapters.

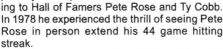

His baseball interest started with baseball cards and memorabilia. Banocy is an expert on statistics, especially those pertaining to Hall of Famers Pete Rose and Ty Cobb. In 1978 he experienced the thrill of seeing Pete Rose in person extend his 44 game hitting streak.

Banocy currently is single and lives in Ridgefield, CT working as a security officer. He has owned and operated a sports collectibles shop. He still actively collects various baseball memorabilia, especially anything pertaining to Pete Rose.

LEON J. BATTISTA JR., born in 1962 in New York, NY, a town filled with baseball history, so there is no mystery to his love of the sport. He joined SABR in 1992 and currently belongs to the Business of Baseball Committee. He is an expert in the fields of arbitration, salaries, and unionization.

Battista is married to Kimberly and they have three children: Matthew, Mollie and Patrick. He is employed as the coordinator of economics at the Bronx Community College of CUNY.

HAROLD W. BEAN, born May 4, 1925 in Anna, IL. His love of baseball was the reason he joined SABR many years ago. As he would say, "Too many to count." Bean's interest in the Hall of Fame eventually led to his expertise in one of baseball's greats, Joe DiMaggio. Bean will never forget the day he saw Mark McGwire hit his 62nd home run.

Bean is single and living in St. Louis, MO making it easy to watch major league teams in person. He has always been fascinated with baseball and football. Before retiring, he was the division chairman for Southwestern Railroads.

DAMIAN BEGLEY, born April 12, 1956 in New York City, NY and joined SABR in 1975 as one of the Society's first 400 members after his sister, Evelyn, showed him a Bob Broeg *Sporting News* article on SABR. Born around opening day in Mickey Mantle's Triple Crown season, he was raised in the lower west Bronx, in the shadow of Yankee Stadium. His baseball interest was solidified when his father took him and his brother to a Yanks-Chisox game in 1962.

As an active member of the Casey Stengel Chapter in New York City, Begley has helped run several regional meetings. A film editor by profession, he has a strong interest in baseball movies, amassing an ever growing list of baseball-related motion pictures. His all-time baseball highlight was sitting in Yankee Stadium on Oct. 16, 1977, the night the Yankees won their first World Series in 15 years.

EVELYN BEGLEY, born in New York City, NY July 7, 1953 in the height of baseball season. On April 2, 1974, she joined SABR to learn more about this wonderful sport. She is currently a member of the New York City Casey Stengel Chapter.

Begley attributes her love of baseball to her mentor, Bob Davids. Her current interests include the Philadelphia A's, Phillies and the New York Giants. In 1983 she wrote an article for *Insiders Baseball* entitled, *Do Walks Always Hurt a Pitcher?* One of her most memorable experiences was assisting with the initial newsletter of the New York Giants Historical Society. She has served on the SABR Nominating Committee and feels her SABR highlights were running a regional and contributing to the growth of the New York City SABR Chapter.

Begley is single, lives in New York City as a teacher and interpreter for the deaf and collects classic movies.

GERALD E. BEIRNE, born in 1936 in Pawtucket, RI, sharing a birthday with Rabbit Maranville, Pie Traynor, George Washington Case and General George Patton on November 11. He joined SABR to meet like-minded people.

A favorite uncle/godfather took him to day games at Fenway Park and Braves Field on the uncle's infrequent days off from firefighting in Pawtucket, RI, home of the

Pawtucket Slaters of the Class B New England League. George Crowe and Johnny Logan were some of the future major leaguers they rated back then.

In 1983 *Yankee Magazine* published his only book (to date) featuring New Englanders by birth or by team. Hence the bridge to SABR which hosted the 1984 National Convention in Providence (1884 Grays!).

His cluster enjoyed the experience so much that their special friendship segued naturally and normally into biannual regional meetings (averaging 85 people) ever since. Baseball history has held together a wonderful group of men, and not enough women, meeting in his church hall. Research papers he has presented are: *World Series Sweeps: There may be More than you Think* and *What Team in One City has the Most Members in the Hall of Fame?*. He has been the pastor of Saint Philip's Catholic Church in Greenville, RI since 1991.

RICHARD W. BELSHAW, born May 8, 1957 in Honolulu, HI. He joined SABR in 1994 after finding a copy of SABR's *Research Journal* in a dusty box on a New York City antiquarian bookstore floor. The discovery coincided with full-time, at-home fatherhood which has prevented active participation in SABR.

By profession he is a painter and writer - having used baseball imagery in visual work and is in the planning stages of a baseball-related work of fiction. He is a big fan of Roger Angell and striving to be an expert in the history of the World Series and to keep track of baseball imagery in visual (fine) art. Belshaw's main interests include baseball's labor and social histories. He is also working on ways to make scorecard keeping more comprehensive, practical and enjoyable. His most memorable moment was swinging Joe Jackson's bat.

Belshaw is married to Julia Gittes, a web designer, and is the father of Emily (5) and Daniel (3). He is very active in the Episcopal Church and AIDS volunteerism.

JAY BENNETT born in Philadelphia, PA, the day after his beloved Phillies won the 1950 pennant. He joined SABR in 1981 to discover more research in baseball statistics. His pursuit of this interest has resulted in baseball publications in *The American Statistician* and various *Proceedings of the Section on Statistics in Sports of the American Statistical Association (ASA)*. *USA Today* highlighted his paper, *Did Shoeless Joe Jackson Throw the 1919 World Series?* Bennett is the editor of *Statistics in Sport* (Arnold, 1998) to which he also contributed a baseball chapter.

Bennett has been married to Lynn since 1975. They have two children, also Phillie fans despite being raised in the New York Metropolitan area. Bennett is a senior statistician with a telecommunications consulting company. He is a past chair of the ASA Section on Statistics in Sports. He enjoys games, especially those simulating sports or military history.

FRANK BETTENCOURT, born Nov. 8, 1924 in San Francisco, CA. He joined SABR in 1992 because of the publications. He is an expert in the Major League Draft. Bettencourt would like to be instrumental in starting a research committee on the Major League Draft.

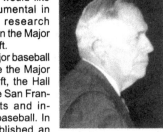

His major baseball interests are the Major League Draft, the Hall of Fame, the San Francisco Giants and instructional baseball. In fact, he published an article on instructional baseball in the *American Baseball Coaches Associated Digest*. Bettencourt enjoys attending the SABR regional meetings and is currently a member of the Northern California Lefty O'Doul Chapter.

Bettencourt has been married for 51 years

and has one son, Mark. He retired from Menlo-Atherton High School as a teacher/coach. He coached the high school baseball team for 46 years and is presently assistant coach at South San Francisco High School. His accomplishments in the field of baseball include being inducted into the Menlo-Atherton High School Hall of Fame as a coach, being the coach for the Northern California Senior All Stars in the 1973 State North/South Senior game, and being a 30-year member of American Baseball Coaches Association.

Some of his awards and honors as a coach include receiving the Certificate of Merit in 1991 from the *Palo Alto Times Tribune*, the 1990 Service Award from the Santa Clara Valley, in 1977 the American Baseball Coaches Association Award Honor, and in 1997 being honored by *USA Baseball* as the Amateur Baseball Coach of the Year for the state of California.

JOHN THOMAS BLACKBURN, born and raised in San Francisco, CA. His dreams are often invaded by recurring visions of McCovey's liner glancing off Richardson's glove and ricocheting into right, as Alou and Mays scamper home.

He joined SABR in 1982 to share his legal addiction with other baseball junkies. He is a member of the Lefty O'Doul Chapter (Northern California) and the Pacific Coast League Historical Society. Currently Blackburn is guiding the Shoeless Ghosts in their inaugural season to oblivion in an All-Time 30-team computer simulation league (although he did coax an opening day no-hitter from Sandy Koufax). In a 12-team head-to-head computer tournament (consisting of the seasons 1959-1970) his Gettysburg Glory are headed to the World Series! This as a result of eight consecutive wins on the road despite key injuries to an already depleted pitching staff. Scanning his bench and peering into the eyes of the eligibles - he selected Jack Kralick, Turk Farrell, Dennis Bennett and Ray Herbert as the new rotation. They responded in superb fashion.

Blackburn is a single, shipping-receiving clerk who resides in San Rafael, a few miles north of San Francisco, and enjoys music, the movies, the Civil War and reading. He is a big fan of Troy Soos and his splendid Mickey Rawlings mysteries.

MORT BLOOMBERG, born on Oct. 26, 1936 in Winthrop, MA. He joined SABR because of his love of baseball and his interest in the Boston Braves. Bloomberg has written a book and articles on the creative process plus occasional pieces on baseball.

He is one of the founding members of Boston Braves Historical Association and one of his most memorable moments occurred during a Boston Braves reunion held in 1996. Bloomberg had the privilege of driving Spahn and Sain to Braves Field for their first glimpse in more than 40 years of what remains of the "WigWam." (Photographic evidence is available upon request.)

He is currently single and living in Chandler, AZ. He has two sons, Jeffrey and Mark, and two grandchildren, Mitchell and Erica. He has worked as a psychology professor and assistant director of merchandise for the Phoenix Firebirds. Presently he is the business manager for Calvin Schexnayder (Arizona Rattlers) who is the num-

ber one receiver in the Arena Football League and also works part-time for the Arizona Diamondbacks, Tucson Sidewinders, Arizona Fall League and several teams in the Cactus League during spring training.

ALAN BLUMKIN has been a SABR member since 1974 and has attended 17 national conventions, including the last 15. He was a member of the SABR Team Trivia Champions in 1989, 1990, 1994, 1995 and 1996. He won the Individual Trivia Championship in 1998.

He has presented the following at the national conventions: Dick Groat and the 1960 World Series; The Yankee Dynasty 1949-1953; The Un-Batting and the Un-ERA Leaders for Each Season (My Citizen Kane); Defensive Replacements (100 or more games, less than 200 Abs, excluding PH appearances); Batters' Strikeouts (100 or more in a season); Players Who Lost Time to the Korean War; and Players Who Were Named After Famous People.

He has done numerous presentations at the New York City and Philadelphia regional meetings. Blumkin has been very active in the New York City Casey Stengel Chapter and received the Meritorious Service Award in 1991. He was also on the Host Committee for the 1991 National Convention in New York City.

His biggest thrills have been the friendships he has developed, his first national trivia championship and his first national presentation. He is 55 years old and currently single.

ROBERT F. BLUTHARDT, born in Boston, MA in 1955 and soon became a fan of both the Red Sox and Fenway Park. He joined SABR in 1981 while a graduate student at George Washington University.

As an intern at the Smithsonian, he wrote a lengthy paper on the history of early 20th century ballparks and was introduced to the Society through then President Kit Crissey. At the national convention in 1982, he helped establish the Ballparks Committee and has served as chairman since 1983. He also chaired the Nominations Committee and makes regular drives to Arlington, TX (250 miles away) to attend the Dallas-Fort Worth chapter meetings.

Bluthardt has coordinated several committee publications, including both the SABR publication and the commercial version of *Green Cathedrals*, a broad overview of all professional, major league ballparks. Also, he led the committee's efforts to publish *City Baseball Magic*, a seminal work of 1989 that makes the case for urban-style ballparks. He is proud of the committee's efforts to assist marker dedications for Hilltop Park in New York, Braves Field in Boston and Roosevelt Stadium in New Jersey. His most memorable SABR moment came at the Milwaukee National Convention in 1984 when he was interviewed by a reporter and appeared on the national network news.

While he enjoys most aspects of the game, Bob maintains a special interest in the ballparks, past, present and future, and he enjoys visiting parks and old stadium sites across the nation.

He is married to a Nebraskan, Valerie Lynn Christensen, and they have a daughter, Carolyn Frances, one and a half years old, who already has seen a few games. He is the director of Fort Concho National Historic Landmark in San Angelo, TX where he has lived since 1982.

ROBERT W. "BOB" BOEHM, born Nov. 7, 1948 in Lincoln, NE. In 1981 he joined SABR to update his personal scoring records and to share his lifetime of baseball memories with others.

He currently belongs to the Southern New England Lajoie-Start and the new group formed in the Boston area. Boehm considers Walt "Woody" Wilson, Bob Tiemann and Pete Palmer his personal mentors. His personal baseball expertise is the 1959-97 World Series, LCS from 1969-97, 1962-98 All Star Games and play-by-play scoring.

He is extremely interested in the Boston Red Sox and serves on the SABR Records Committee. His most memorable experience was attending the 1967 and 1986 World Series and his SABR highlight was attending the 1984 convention.

Boehm resides in Lowell, MA and is married to Dawn and they have an 11-year old named Alyson. He is a physical education teacher in Lowell. The 1998-1999 school year celebrated his 29th year as a teacher. Boehm is the director of the N.E. Fish and Chip and president of the GLOB Club. He has been lucky enough to attend the Summer and Winter Olympics seven times.

ROBERT S. BOGART, born May 17, 1961 in Neptune, NJ. He joined SABR in 1991 because he desired to learn more about baseball history and the baseball camaraderie.

He is a member of the Philadelphia and Baltimore/Washington groups. His major interests are scorekeeping, records, ball parks, and Phillies history. Bogart's baseball expertise is the Philadelphia Phillies. He was fortunate enough to witness Mike Schmidt's 500th career homer and witnessed the nine-run ninth inning at Dodger Stadium to see the Phillies beat the Dodgers 12-11.

Bogart is married to Lauri and they currently live in Glen Rock, PA. They have a son, Ryne Michael, who is named after Ryne Sandberg and Mike Schmidt. His daughter Christy is named after Christy Mathewson. He is employed by the National Security Agency as a senior cryptanalyst. Bogart's hobby is collecting baseball cards and he has every Topps Phillies card made from 1952 to the present.

DEBBI DAGAVARIAN-BONAR, born Oct. 26, 1952 in New York City, NY. She joined SABR in 1981, one of the few women at that time conducting baseball research. She attended her first of many national conventions in 1982 and while there met Bob Wood, son of one of her favorite players, Joe Wood. That led to several meetings and a friendship with Smokey Joe.

Debbi is a member of SABR's Biographical Research Committee and has a particular interest in late 19th and early 20th century baseball. She has published two books on baseball and articles in *The National Pastime,* the *Baseball Research Journal* and other non-baseball periodicals.

Dagavarian-Bonar has been married to Jim Bonar since 1988 and they have one young son, Nicky. She is deputy vice provost of Thomas Edison State College in Trenton, NJ and holds a doctorate in education. Her interests outside of baseball include singing, jewelry-making and old movies.

TIM BOOKAS, born April 28, 1965 in Flushing, NY. He joined SABR in 1996 because of its publications, offers, etc. His baseball expertise is in general trivia and the New York Mets since he grew up three-quarters of a mile from Shea Stadium.

Bookas collects game-worn jerseys, SABERMETRICS and related books, and all Mets paraphernalia. In 1994 he did the pre-season physical exams for the Pittsburgh Pirates.

Bookas currently lives in Southport, CT with his wife, Deanna, and son, John Odyseas. He is a physician with a specialty in family practice. He is a Strat-O-Matic fan and collects baseball cards as a hobby. In 1998 he had 12 straight hits in his softball league.

JOHN MAXWELL BOWDEN, born June 25, 1960 in Salisbury, MD. He could not get enough of the history of our national pastime so he joined SABR Jan. 1, 1992. He is not a member of a current regional group, but would be interested in helping start one.

His expertise is in general baseball history, but he is very interested in the Baltimore Orioles, the early 1900s ball players, such as Cobb and Johnson, and all baseball trivia/records. Bowden is the current director on the board of Eastern Shore Baseball Hall of Fame located at Arthur Perdue Stadium in Salisbury, MD. This is the home of the Delmarva Shorebirds, a Class A affiliate of the Baltimore Orioles in the South Atlantic League.

Bowden is single and self-employed as an accountant to a thriving tax business. His hobby is collecting tobacco cards and he has nearly completed a set of T205.

BOB BOYNTON, joined SABR in 1990 anticipating retirement from UC San Diego the following year. He helped to revive the San Diego Chapter and, as a member of its Steering Committee, since 1991 he has served as secretary every year, but one which was the year he was president.

He was chair of SABR Nominating Committee in 1997 and 1998 and a member of the Sporting-News SABR Baseball Research Award Committee in 1996 and 1997.

Boynton was a member of the Organizing Committee for the 1993 convention in San Diego. He has presented many talks at national and regional meetings with publications in *Baseball Research Journal, National Pastime, NINE* and *Grandstand Baseball Annual* and the *Dictionary of Literary Biography*. His research topics have ranged from biographical to statistical.

JAMES H. BREADY (rhymes with Rosie O'Grady), born Feb. 20, 1919 in Philadelphia, PA. After graduation from Haverford College and Harvard University, he followed his father and mother *(Philadelphia Public Ledger)* into newspaper work. Jim has been writing for the *Baltimore Sun* for more than 50 years: features, book column and editorials.

In 1953, to go with Baltimore's return to the majors, he started a book of local baseball history. The Orioles arrived in 1954; *The Home Team,* self-published, in 1958. Further editions, published by the Orioles, appeared in 1971, 1979 and 1985.

In 1971 Jim was the first Marylander to join SABR. He met Hy Turkin and was good friends with Lee Allen, John Tattersall and (still) Bob Davids. He interviewed Sadie McMahon, Jack Doyle, Bill Clarke, Bill Hoffer and Frank Foreman (of the Old Orioles) and Mrs. John McGraw. By phone he interviewed Cy Young.

Forty years after *The Home Team,* Johns Hopkins University Press published Jim Bready's *Baseball in Baltimore: The First 100 Years,* a much expanded account.

The Breadys include his wife Mary; their sons: Richard, Christopher and Stephen, and their grandson, Alexander.

BOB BRIAN, born Nov. 3, 1925 in San Diego, CA and has a wife, Lee, of 51 years, with sons, Bruce and Brad, and four grandchildren. He has coached high school baseball for 49 years with 20 championships.

For 44 years he has coached American Legion baseball and served a term of five years on the National Committee to write the high school baseball rules book. Brian coached the California All Stars in Oklahoma in 1982 and Florida in 1990. He coached the West Team in the Olympic Festival in 1991, and the American Baseball Coaches Association District named him Coach of the Year in 1972 and 1983.

Other awards and honors include: 1973, 1982, and 1988 Coach of the Year by the National High School Association District 8; California Baseball Coach of the Year in 1982 and 1988; USSA Baseball Association Amateur Coach of the Year for California in 1992; South San Francisco dedicated a baseball field in his name in 1993; member of three Halls of Fame which include The American Baseball Coaches Association, the San Mateo County Sports, and the California Coaches Association.

DENNIS BRICAULT, born in December 1957 in Reed City, MI. He joined SABR in 1987 because he was working in Barcelona, Spain and wanted to keep in contact with baseball. He has always been fascinated with baseball history and statistics.

His interests include the general history of baseball, statistical analysis and European baseball. Two of the highlights of his life include the Tigers' come-from-behind victory in the 1968 World Series and the Tigers remarkable 1984 campaign.

Bricault is single and currently living in Chicago, IL working as the registrar and Director of ESL Programs at North Park University. He is completing a Ph.D in higher education administration at Loyola University in Chicago. He is also the official scorekeeper for the Division III North Park baseball team.

CHUCK BRODSKY, born May 20, 1960 in Philadelphia, PA and his blood still runs Phillies red. He joined SABR in 1997 and is a member of the Baseball Songs and Poetry Committee.

A folk singer and songwriter, Brodsky tours North America year round. His three albums to date contain four baseball songs, including one about a white man playing in the Negro Leagues, *The Ballad of Eddie Klepp*, which has been played at Veterans Stadium and on NPR's *Morning Edition*, and which was the subject of a *Washington Post* feature story. *The Philadelphia Daily News* did a story on his song, *Letters in the Dirt*, about Richie Allen. Brodsky has also written about Moe Berg, Lefty and Richie Ashburn, and has performed concerts at the National Baseball Hall of Fame.

A memorable experience was giving Dick Allen his CD with a song about him on it. He is particularly interested in the folklore, oddball stories and characters of the game and cites Tim Wiles and Bill Plott as mentors.

His hobby is being an ice hockey goalkeeper. Brodsky records for Red House Records (1-800-695-4687). His web site is at www.songs.com/cb.

ISAAC C. "IKE" BROOKS, born March 4, 1948 in Baltimore, MD. He joined SABR in 1993 to learn more of the contributions made by African Americans to the game. His special interest is the Negro Leagues.

He has been very active as a volunteer with the Cleveland Indians Baseball Club as part of their ongoing tribute to former players of the Cleveland Buckeyes, along with other former Negro League players.

He enjoys reading the available articles, books and other material which chronicles the innovations and accomplishment made by this distinguished group of players. Larry Lester, author and historian, has been very helpful in sharing his wealth of knowledge regarding this almost forgotten group.

Brooks' most memorable baseball experience was escorting Leon Day (Newark Eagles, Baltimore Elite Giants) onto Cleveland's Jacobs Field during a pre-game ceremony in July 1994. This event occurred eight months before Mr. Day was elected to the Baseball Hall of Fame.

Brooks and his wife of 28 years, Earline, and their youngest daughter, Erika, currently reside in Shaker Heights, OH. Their oldest daughter, Lisa, and her husband, Hezekiah Brown, reside in Jackson, TN.

JAMES (AUSTIN) BROWN, born in Pittsburgh, PA on January 9, 1924, but was raised in Buena Vista, PA. He joined SABR in 1990 mainly because of his interest in baseball and to locate teams his grandfather pitched for during his baseball career.

His name was Jim (Farmer) Brown and he played 15 years of professional baseball in the minor leagues. Brown sent letters to Joseph Overfield and Bob Hoie after joining SABR and they sent him the information he requested in regard to where Farmer Brown played. Brown's current regional group is the Jack Graney Chapter and he always enjoyed the information and books about baseball he received yearly as a member of SABR.

Brown also played semi pro baseball in the Pittsburgh area and had a tryout with Youngstown in the Middle Atlantic League. Brown also wrote a sports column for a monthly publication back in the 1950s.

Brown has been retired for 12 years after being self-employed for 17 years in the food business. Prior to that, he was a store manager for Bonds Inc. in Cleveland, OH. During World War II, Brown served in the Navy and saw action in the South Pacific and later was on an aircraft carrier at the end of the war. Brown is a member of the South Euclid Methodist Church and is a 32nd Degree Mason and also a Shriner. He was a member of the Cleveland Food Dealers and the Great Lakes Senior Golf Association for many years and his main hobby is playing golf.

Brown is divorced with two children, Bonita and Marty, who are now grown. His grandchildren are Alana, April, Austin and Justin. Brown presently resides in Richmond Heights, OH.

REED BROWNING, born in 1938. Browning has been a member of the History Department at Kenyon College since 1967. Except for his eight years as provost, he has regularly taught early modern European and American history.

He is the author of *The Duke of Newcastle* (1975), *Political and Constitutional Ideas of the Court Whigs* (1982), and *The War of the Austrian Succession* (1993). Prompted by the enjoyment he got from reading about diamond history, he joined SABR in the early 1980s.

He began serious research into baseball history in the early 1990s and has written an unpublished history of the 1924 season. His current project is a biography of Cy Young.

Browning married Susan Lampley, a musician, in 1963. They have one son, Stephen, an attorney, and live with their collie, Trim, in Gambier, OH.

BOB BUEGE, born in Milwaukee on April 29, 1946. His baseball awakening coincided with the Braves' move from Boston to Milwaukee in Spring 1953. It was love at first sight.

Meeting Warren Spahn in 1985 led to a magazine article, which led to Buege's first book, *The Milwaukee Braves: A Baseball Eulogy,* in 1988. He joined SABR that year to help market the book. His first SABR Convention was in Cleveland in 1990, where he received the Cox Award for the best research presentation. He has not missed a convention since, enjoying the fascinating people and wonderful events at each.

In 1994 he published his second book, *Eddie Mathews and the National Pastime,* co-written with the HOF third baseman. Knowing Mathews, his childhood hero, and working with him is Buege's most memorable baseball experience.

Buege is married and the father of two daughters. He writes and also teaches high school in Milwaukee.

JOHN W. BURGESON, born Aug. 19, 1931 in Youngstown, OH. For 50 plus years baseball has been a consuming interest so it was not surprising for him to join SABR in 1995. He has to drive over 300 miles to attend the Denver group since there is not a local one.

His baseball expertise ranges from his sandlot days as a third baseman to coaching Little League for 10 years, leading them to two championships. His main interest is in general statistics for the Cleveland Indians, the 1948 and 1954 Cleveland Indians.

Burgeson published several articles in the *Pine Tar Review.* Burgeson and his wife, Carol Lee, currently live in Durango, CO, have eight children and five grandchildren. He was a physicist in the US Navy and retired from IBM as a computer engineer. He is a Presbyterian Stephen minister. He writes for *Perspectives,* a scientific journal.

ROBERT R. BURNS, born April 1, 1923 in Philadelphia, PA. He joined SABR in 1982 in Baltimore and currently attends the Philadelphia Chapter. His mentor was the late Edward "Dutch" Doyle.

His baseball interests include the Philadelphia A's from 1901-1954 and the Baltimore Orioles from 1954 to now. Burns is a former stockholder of the Baltimore Orioles and enjoyed attending the SABR National Conventions in 1982 and 1995.

Burns and his wife, Ethel M., have five children, nine grandchildren, and six great-grandchildren. He retired from the Scott Paper Company in 1983 and now enjoys collecting sports memorabilia.

HELEN HANNAH CAMPBELL, born in Salt Lake City, UT on Sept. 25, 1915. She is uncertain when she joined, but clearly remembers the reason was Dick Beverage. When asked to choose a mentor she said there were too many to mention.

Currently a member of the Allan Roth Chapter in Los Angeles, CA, her expertise is her father, Truck Hannah's, three decades as a pro. She is very interested in All American Girls Pro Baseball League's five years of history, 1947-1951. Campbell has had the pleasure of attending a couple of SABR conventions.

Campbell is a widow living in Fountain Valley, CA and is retired from the US Marine Corps as a Mgy Sgt after 32 years of service. She collects magnets and miniature spoons. She volunteers one day a week at the following: her HMO; Nixon Library (Docent); Anaheim Stadium with the Booster Club; at FVPD (local Retired Senior Volunteer Program); and both local Marine bases.

BILL CARLE, born Dec. 29, 1955 in Bartlesville, OK has been interested in baseball all his life and joined SABR in March of 1977. He currently belongs to a chapter in Kansas City, MO. Carle was a SABR director from 1988-92 and is the chairman of the Biographical Research Committee. His mentors include Joe Simenic and Bill Haber.

He has many varied interests in baseball, but his expertise is biographical research and Kansas City baseball. He considers some of his most memorable experiences to include the 1985, 1986 and 1993 SABR Conventions as well as in 1993 he was a member of the winning trivia team and received the Bob Davids Award.

Carle's written works include biographies for Jake Beckley and Kid Nichols for *Baseball's First Stars,* History of the Kansas City Royals for the *Encyclopedia of American League Team Histories* and book reviews for *SABR Review of Books*.

He is single and employed as database analyst for AT&T.

BO CARTER, born Feb. 19, 1952 in Sheffield, AL, hometown of Heinie Manush. He joined SABR in February 1992 for the historical fun and fellowship. He currently belongs to the Dallas-Fort Worth Chapter (Hall-Ruggles) and considers Howard Green and Wayne Poage his mentors.

Carter played youth league and high school baseball from 1962-68. He is interested in college baseball, historical data, and college players who are in the pros. Carter's written works include the 1994 National SABR Convention Program and editing four sports books.

Two highlights in his life are the 1994 SABR Convention in Arlington and the 1996 ALDS at The Ballpark in Arlington.

Carter is married to Dr. Joanne Pryor-Carter and they live in Carrollton, TX. His employment history includes being media relations person for the following: Vanderbilt from 1970-74; Mississippi State University from 1974-86; Southwest Conference from 1986-96; and the Big 12 Conference from 1996 to the present.

JOHN B. CARTER, born May 1950 in Corner Brook, Newfoundland, Canada joined SABR in 1983 as a result of his deep interest in baseball, particularly in baseball statistics and history.

He has attended all but one convention (San Diego 1993) since 1987. Most of these he attended with his son, Bob, an annual event which has provided experiences and memories of those that will last lifetimes.

His interest and modest expertise relates to the World Series. He was at Skydome in Toronto in October 1993 when Joe Carter became the second player in history to win the World Series with a home run.

Carter is married to Linda. He has a daughter, Wendy, in addition to his son, Bob, and a stepson and daughter, Michael and Paula. He is a chartered accountant and is the managing partner for Atlantic Canada for Ernst and Young.

M.D. "MIKE" CARTER, born Aug. 21, 1948 in Spokane, WA and is currently the treasurer for the Northwest SABR in Seattle, WA. He joined in 1986 because of his love for the game and to further his knowledge of the national pastime.

He has 30 years experience of umpiring amateur baseball, working high school, Legion, PONY and youth leagues. Carter's interests include umpiring and reading box scores. He serves on the Umpire and Rules Research Committee, and wrote *Why Umpire?*, unpublished, which will be presented at the 1999 Spring Northwest SABR meeting.

His most memorable experiences were watching Don Newcombe pitch, cut the mustard, LA Dodgers issued first W-2.

Carter is single and lives in Mukilteo, WA where he is a contract administrator/bookkeeper for CAE and Associates. He had the pleasure of working the 1998 State High School Tournament on the plate when four children went yard with two slams. His hobbies include philately, football official, and history.

JAMES CASEY, born Dec. 14, 1950 in Washington, DC, grew up a Washington Senators fan through both incarnations of the team. He joined SABR in 1997 to learn more about the history of the game which is something he reads about a great deal.

He has no mentors and is not currently serving on any committees, though being on an Old Ballparks committee would definitely be a pleasure as well as researching into how the reduction of the strike zone following the 1968 season affected pitching and batting performances.

He has continued to play hardball in adult amateur leagues which is a source of great pleasure. He has had the great good fortune as a pitcher to have pitched and won several memorable games, including a league championship, a complete game 1-0 shutout in a regional tournament and two victories in an annual 4th of July tournament in Cooperstown.

More of his great pleasures are to see Cal Ripken's 2,131st consecutive game, Mark McGwire's 60th and 61st home runs last season, the game Cal Ripken sat out to break his streak, and the pleasure of seeing games in all of the current Major League stadiums except Seattle, Phoenix, Milwaukee, Houston, and Cincinnati.

Casey is married to Melanie, has no children and works as a travel agent in Arlington, VA. Baseball is his primary hobby. He is a member of the Bob Davids Chapter of the Baltimore/Washington area and looks forward to rooting for a new Washington Senators team next year.

PETE CAVA, born July 26, 1946, Staten Island, NY. Because of a life-long interest in baseball, he joined SABR in 1982 and currently belongs to Lou Criger Chapter. His mentor is Dr. Peter Bjarkman.

His expertise is Indiana born Major Leaguers; Olympic baseball; New York Yankees and New York Mets. His interests are Cuban and Japanese baseball, World War II baseball, baseball books and the Biographical Research Committee. A memorable experience was coaching his son's team to a Little League title.

Written works include *New York Mets (Encyclopedia of ML Baseball Team Histories - NL)* and *Ring Lardner (Dictionary of Literary Biography)*.

Married since 1976 to Molly Menagan, they have a son, Andy, and daughter, Nancy. He is the executive director of International Sports Associates and is currently working on an encyclopedia of Indiana-born Major Leaguers.

B. BENJAMIN CAVALLO, born Oct. 9, 1927 in Mansfield, MA. He is a graduate of Bentley College and Northwestern University. He joined SABR in the early years to learn more about the game and the men that played it. He is an expert on the careers of Ted Williams, Bob Doerr, Ike Delock and Eddie Pellagrini.

He has an extensive library on baseball and has been an avid collector of all baseball material. His biggest

disappointment was when his offer to purchase the Red Sox in the late 70s was rejected by Jean Yawkey.

Cavallo was an insurance broker for 41 years, is a director of the Bosox Club, Peoples Saving Bank of Brockton, Good Samaritan Hospital and People Bancshares. He has been married to Jeanne for 25 years. They have one son, Benjamin, a graduate of Emory University and a MBA candidate at Boston College.

JIM CHARLTON, born Nov. 1, 1939, in New York City. He joined SABR in 1988. Memorable experience was pitching a no-hitter in high school and losing the game. He is interested in baseball history and is on the Records Committee.

Charlton has written more than 30 books, the most recent is *Who, What, Where of Baseball* and *Writers Quotation Book*.

He and his wife, Barbara, have four children: Kevin, Tim, Anne and Meg, and one grandchild, Tyler. He has been employed with various publishers and is now a book packager and agent.

J. PARKER CHESSON JR., born Aug. 19, 1941, in Hertford, NC. He grew up across the road from Hall of Famer, Jim "Catfish" Hunter in rural Perquimans County. He played high school and semi-pro baseball and continues to be an avid fan. Memorable experience was playing with "Catfish" Hunter and against Gaylord Perry.

Chesson is a member of the Carolina Chapter of SABR and lives in Durham, NC, just a few miles from the home of the Durham Bulls. He is now doing research on baseball in northeastern North Carolina during the first half of this century, with special emphasis on the semi-pro Albemarle League.

Chesson has been married to the former Wynda Chappell for 38 years. They have two daughters, Daphne, 31, and Melanie, 27. He was a teacher, dean and president of College of The Albemarle in Elizabeth City for 28 years and now heads the Employment Security Commission of North Carolina.

RALPH JERRY CHRISTIAN, born Sept. 18, 1944 in Mount Airy, NC. He joined SABR in 1994 due to a renewed interest in baseball and its history inspired in large part by Jose Maria Esquer, an exchange student from Mexico, who lived with him and his wife Victoria in their Des Moines, IA home during the 1993-94 school year. His primary research interests are Iowa baseball history, 19th century baseball and the Negro

Leagues. He has presented papers on these subjects at the national conventions in Kansas City and San Francisco, and the Negro League Conference in Harrisburg. He is on the 19th century and Negro League Committees. His most vivid baseball memories are attending a House of David game in his home town, meeting Ernie Shore, and attending his first major league game at Wrigley Field.

Christian has been married to Victoria

Josephine Gabrys for 30 years. In addition to Jose Esquer, their extended family includes Key Fujimura, also from Mexico; Mauricio Palomeque of Ecuador; and Konrad Malendowicz, Marcin Bania, Mateusz Schmidt, and Zbigniew Bania of Poland. He is the architectural historian for the State Historical Society of Iowa. In addition to baseball research, his hobbies include collecting baseball materials, especially films and recordings.

CHARLES T. CLARK, born Jan. 20, 1934 in Clear Lake, WI and is a life-long baseball fan. He is president of the Burleigh Grimes Museum. Clear Lake is Burleigh's home town and Clark was a close friend of Burleigh for 35 years. Clear Lake is also the hometown of Gaylord Nelson, father of Earth Day.

Memorable experiences were the many times he went to Coopertown with Burleigh for induction ceremonies. Clark is also a great fan of Bob Feller, Mel Harder, Herb Score, Bob Lemon and the Cleveland Indians.

Clark has been married to Ardeth for 46 years, and they have four children: Mary, Thomas, John, Charlie, and eight grandchildren. His hobby is collecting all baseball items.

"DICK" CLARK, born in 1946 in Detroit, MI. He attended his first Tiger game in 1953 and remains a devoted fan. Dick has been a SABR member since 1980 and is a member of the Fred Smith Chapter.

He attended his first National Convention in 1983, became the Negro Leagues Committee chair in 1985 and continues to be in that position. He co-authored articles for *The National Pastime* and *The Baseball Research Journal.* He is co-editor of SABR's *The Negro Leagues Book.* Dick is also an active member of the Minor Leagues, Umpires, Scouts, Ballparks, and Bibliography committees.

Dick received a SABR-MacMillan Award in 1990. He is a long-time collector of baseball books and publications. He is a graduate of Eastern Michigan University and lives with his wife, Marilyn, in Ypsilanti. They have a son, Kris, and two granddaughters, Macy and Kelsey. After many years as a motorcycle accessories salesman, he now serves as a computer system administrator in Troy, MI.

DICK CRAMER is a scientist geek type, whose work has been split almost evenly between chemistry and baseball, with statistical research using computers and leadership roles in small technology businesses as common threads. The only hot streak of Joe Lonnett's career somehow led him to the Turkin-Thompson encyclopedia and an addiction to baseball statistics. Even his penchant for computer programming began with a baseball simulation program.

In 1972 a classified ad in the Sporting News brought him to SABR, where he soon found that his obsession with "what the statistics meant" was shared by someone else - Pete Palmer. They became SABR's initial Statistical Analysis

Committee. Having someone else to exchange ideas with means a lot in research, and several "SABRmetric" studies resulted that are summarized in the first Thorn/Palmer collaborative book, The Hidden Game of Baseball. He was also active in SABR affairs, collaborating with Ben Weiser to organize a SABR national meeting in Philadelphia and to put out a second SABR National Pastime periodical. During a 1975 stint as SABR's vice-president, several SABR executive meetings were held at his suburban Philadelphia home, located midway among Bob Davids, Bob McConnell, Dave Voigt and Cliff Kachline.

STATS, Inc., will be familiar to many SABR members. He was a founder of STATS in 1981, and its refounder when STATS was reincorporated in 1985 to bring in John Dewan and Bill James. From 1984-87 he was the only person active in the business. From 1981-92 he wrote the vast majority of the programs that STATS used. In the early 1990s most daily box scores were generated by his Playball program. As the STATS co-principal with John Dewan from 1987 to roughly 1991, he also participated in most of its critical early sales, in particular the first, to USA Today, and others such as ESPN, the Associated Press, and an investment and disinvestment by Paul Allen. However his involvement with STATS effectively ended with the year 1995.

JEFF CREAMER, born Dec. 16, 1956 in San Rafael, CA. Because of his love for baseball and its history, he joined SABR in 1996. He is currently a member of the Lefty O'Doul Chapter in northern California.

His main interest is the Deadball Era, 1900-15. He has played amateur baseball for 25 years (still playing) and has played on a re-created Deadball Era team.

Jeff and his wife Barbara have two children, Kirsten and Brett. Employed as meter reader for Pacific Gas and Electric Co. His hobby is collecting baseball and football cards.

GARY COLLARD, born Nov. 10, 1961 in Dallas, TX. He joined SABR in 1996 because of his love for baseball and is currently a member of Hall-Ruggles Chapter, Dallas-Fort Worth, TX.

His expertise is Sabermetrics/statistical analysis and Baltimore Orioles. He is on the Statistical Analysis Research Committee.

Memorable experiences include Arlington, TX, National Convention, and the 1995 All-Star Game. He is a software developer with i2 Technologies. Hobbies are fantasy baseball, baseball card collecting and bowling.

Gary is divorced and has twin sons, Jeff and John (born in 1982).

HARRINGTON E. CRISSEY JR., born Feb. 21, 1945 in Schenectady, NY. He joined SABR at the invitation of John Tattersall a few weeks before the 1974 convention in Philadelphia. His early SABR mentors included Tattersall, Bob Davids and Cliff Kachline. Crissey was president of SABR (1980-81) and has been coordinator or co-coordinator of the annual Philadelphia regional meeting since 1978.

He has also served as chairman of the SABR Nominating Committee. Crissey is the author of three books on WWII era baseball: *Teenagers, Graybeards and 4-Fs,* Volume I and II (1981, 1984) and *Athletes Away* (1984).

Crissey married Yelena Sergeeva, a Russian figure skater, in 1992. He teaches English to foreign adults for English Language Services at St. Joseph's University in Philadelphia. Crissey is a retired commander in the Naval Reserve. His hobbies include sports history, classical music and geography.

STEFAN "STEVE" CSIK, born Sept. 28, 1956, in Hochhause, West Germany. He wanted more information on baseball so joined SABR in 1991. He is currently a member of the St. Louis chapter.

His interest is traveling to different ball parks and so far has been to roughly 100 Major and Minor League ball parks.

He is a member of the Ball Parks, Umpires and Rules and Pictorial History committees.

He is a self-employed accountant and holds professional designation of CPA, CMA and CIA. His hobby is collecting baseball stadium photos and postcards and schedules. He is married to Karen.

JOHN CHARLES CULLINANE, born May 31, 1965, Dorchester, MA. He joined SABR in August 1998 to help out in Research, and is currently a member of Lajoie-Start Chapter. Expertise is baseball and trivia; interests are baseball records, biographical research, statistical analysis, book collecting and Boston Red Sox. Mentors are his parents, Marjorie and John Cullinane.

John was a delegate to the Massachusetts Democratic Convention in June 1998. He is a member of the Friends of the Hall at Cooperstown. His uncle is Frank Malzone, former Boston Red Sox third baseman and currently a scout with the Red Sox. Frank was baseball's first coveted Gold Glove Award winner in 1957.

John's hobby is collecting baseball cards, reading and listening to music. He has written a song (not about baseball) and is waiting to hear from the Library of Congress for the copyright.

Single, he has worked as health aide, dishwasher and researcher.

STEVE CUMMINGS, joined the world the same year the St. Louis Browns won their only pennant. He caught "Baseball Fever" in the Summer of 55 and learned its symptoms from Red Sox announcer, Curt Gowdy, on radio station WHDH. An uncoordinated fastball pitcher through high school, he really should have become a baseball announcer instead of a clinical psychologist.

He began his love affair with the Cincinnati Redlegs when he heard a Ted Kluszewski home run over crackling air waves. A diehard fan of the Big Red Machine, Dr. Cummings built the most extensive collection of Reds memorabilia in the nation. When he came across Grobani's *Bibliography of Baseball Literature* in 1977, he decided to collect all the baseball books ever published. His garaged archives number almost 5,000 volumes.

Steve has written for *Spitball Magazine, The Diamond Angle, Sports Collectors Digest,* and *Vintage Baseball Memorabilia* over the years. He has attended four national conventions and has been a SABR member since 77. His most memorable experience consisted of observing the intense politicking at the Albany (1989) Convention. However, nothing has ever exceeded blood-rushing excitement than rooting Ken Griffey Jr. to score the winning run in the fabulous five-game playoff series against the Yankees in 95.

He has two daughters, Rachael Rose and Tasha Alexandra, the former named after Pete, of course. His dream is to write the "Great American Novel," with baseball and collecting as a continuing metaphor.

JON DANIELS, born and raised in St. Louis. He is a life-long Cardinal fan and has a special interest in the St. Louis Browns and Stan Musial.

In 1968 he moved to Chicago for graduate work at Northwestern University and still resides there. He joined SABR in 1980 at the urging of Bob Roach, owner of the 1944 St. Louis Browns Bar. In 1981 he attended his first national convention and has missed only once since. During 1981 he and his wife, Marge (see separate biography), became the first husband and wife to both be members of SABR.

Daniels served as chairman of the Audit Committee from 1986-89 and is on the Bibliography Committee. For 15 years he has been preparing the trivia quiz for the Emil Rothe Chapter. He is the second person to win both the team (1991) and individual (1996) trivia contests at the National Convention.

Daniels attends 40 major league games and many minor league games each year. He has been going to Sarasota, FL, for spring training every year since 1977 plus several trips to Arizona for spring training and the fall league. He has been present at two no-hitters (Hooton and Morris), Mike Schmidt's 4-HR game, Lou Brock's 3,000 hit game and Stan Musial's last game.

Daniels, age 51, is a CPA and specializes in work for nonprofit associations.

MARGE DANIELS, went to the Toronto Convention with her husband, Jon, in 1981 as part of a larger trip. She was amazed at how much

baseball she had absorbed from him in their eight years of marriage. She really enjoyed herself. At the banquet the organizers thanked "their better halves" for helping. She knew they were going to become very active in this fledgling group (1500 members), but she was not going to do it as a "better half." She approached vice president Jerry Gregory (charged with growth) about joining. She did not fit any of the then "criteria" for membership. She was not a researcher, etc. She just attended about 30 games per year. Jerry responded with "that's current research" and "perhaps you can assist with administration - organize a regional meeting." She had her membership check ready but Jerry said to just mail it in.

SABR headquarters was in Cooperstown then, their next vacation stop. They went to the library where they found the curator and SABR Board Member, Cliff Kachline. Bob Davids and a half dozen SABR researchers were also there. Cliff, always plugging for new members, asked Jon when he was going to get her to join. She pulled out her prewritten check and floored both Cliff and Bob. They became the first SABR couple.

A dozen years later she reminded Jerry of his comments to her and said "I developed and organized 12 regional meetings for 60+, co-organized the 1986 National Convention (479), assisted with computerization of the membership, wrote a regional meeting manual, was major force in by-laws revision, and served as director on the Board for four years. Is that good enough?" Jerry just laughed.

Marge, age 50, is a non-practicing RN and has resided in the Chicago area most of her life.

LEONARD ROBERT "BOB" DAVIDS, born March 19, 1926, Kanawha. IA. He served in the Army Air Force, 1944-46, with service overseas on Okinawa. He re-

ceived a bachelor of journalism degree in 1949, a master of arts in history in 1951 (both from University of Missouri) and a PhD in international relations from Georgetown University in 1961.

Dr. Davids began his federal civilian career in Washington with the Department of Defense in 1951; 1952-58, was assistant editor then editor of the *Navy Civil Engineer Corps Bulletin*; April 1953, was the Navy information officer for Operation Hardtop, a Navy Seabee experiment to snow-pack an airfield runway on the ice cap of Northern Greenland. While in the Arctic, he journeyed with the Thule Air Base Commander and the Danish Governor of North Greenland to an Eskimo village to present a gift on behalf of the Navy Civil Engineer Corps to Ootah, who had accompanied Civil Engineer Robert E. Peary, Matthew Henson and three other Eskimos on the 1909 North Polar expedition.

Davids transferred to the Atomic Energy Commission in 1958 and was on special assignment in 1964 compiling Presidential documents on nuclear energy for the John F. Kennedy Memorial Library. Received a Congressional Fellowship in 1968, spent the next year working in the offices of Sen. Mark Hatfield and Rep. Robert Taft Jr. Traveled to Cincinnati in 1969 to participate in ceremonies marking the 100th anniversary of professional baseball. Returned to AEC later in 1969 to prepare the Weekly Report to the White House; also served as a speech writer for AEC Chairman Glenn T. Seaborg, and later, Dixy Lee Ray, who served until the agency was dissolved in January 1975. Joined The Energy Research and Development Admin., later became special events coordinator. In 1981, he retired from federal service at age 55.

As a writer/historian, he published many articles on Congressional history in *Roll Call*, the Capitol Hill publication, 1960-75. Similarly, he wrote many articles on baseball for *The Sporting News*, 1951-65.

In April 1971 he started a monthly newsletter called *Baseball Brief* and invited subscribers to an organization meeting in Cooperstown, NY, Aug. 10, 1971; 16 baseball historians and fans came and adopted the constitution for SABR. What was expected to be a cozy research group with its own publications operated out of the Davids' northwest Washington home for 10 years as he prepared and mailed the *SABR Bulletin* and *Baseball Research Journal*. Substantial growth took place and by 1986 there were more than 6,000 members around the world, annual conventions were attended by up to 400 members and baseball book publishing flourished. The Bob Davids Award, the Society's highest honor, be-

came an annual award in 1985, and the Baltimore-Washington Chapter was named for him in 1986.

Throughout this period Mr. Davids was actively involved in numerous community activities. He was commissioner of the Washington-area Church Fellowship Softball League, 1961-87; donated 9-1/2 gallons of blood to the Red Cross (prior to heart bypass surgery in 1982); prepared and served meals at Shepherd's Table in Silver Spring, 1988-99; was an active member of the Washington Christian Reformed Church, 1953-69, and helped organize its daughter church in Silver Spring in the latter year where he served three years as a deacon and head usher 1969-99.

He married Yvonne Revier, a Pentagon administrative assistant, in 1953 and has one daughter Roberta Davids-Hagen of Cabin John, MD and two grandsons.

WILLIAM G. DEANE IV, born April 23, 1957, in Poughkeepsie, NY. He joined SABR while visiting the Baseball Hall of Fame during his honeymoon in 1982. Deane now lives just four miles from Cooperstown in Fly Creek, NY, with his wife, Pam, and daughter, Sarah. He is an avid slow-pitch softball player, with three MVP awards to his credit.

Deane's mentors include Bob Davids and Pete Palmer, and his main area of expertise is baseball statistics. He is a member of SABR's Biographical Research, Statistical Analysis and Records Committees. Deane has authored nearly 200 baseball articles and six books, including *Award Voting*, winner of the 1989 SABR-Macmillan Award. He served as senior research associate for the National Baseball Library & Archive from 1986-94. He has since done consulting work for Topps Baseball Cards, Curtis Management Group, STATS, Inc. and Macmillan Publishing, among others.

PAUL DEBONO, born July 22, 1961, in Eugene, OR. Joined SABR in 1990. Member of the Negro League Committee. Joined as a result of doing research on the Indianapolis ABCs, a Negro League baseball team. First heard of SABR as a result of correspondence with Robert Peterson. Author of *The Indianapolis ABCs: A Premier Team in the Negro Leagues* (McFarland Publishing, 1997).

His area of expertise is Negro League baseball history in Indianapolis, IN. Graduate of Indiana University at Indianapolis. Debono is single and is a freelance writer with regular full-time employment as a real estate title abstractor. Other interests include fishing, backpacking and computers.

VICTOR DEBS JR., born in New York City in 1949. He joined SABR in 1992 and enjoys reading its annual publications and monthly newsletters. Debs has written several baseball books, including *Still Standing After All These Years*. His articles have appeared in *National Pastime*. His favorite hobby is speaking with former major leaguers. His most memorable baseball experience is witnessing Bobby Murcer's four consecutive homers in a doubleheader at Yankee Stadium in 1970.

Debs is a retired teacher. He is a member of the Authors Guild and American Society of Journalists and Authors. He is a staff member of Rutgers University's Continuing Education program where he teaches a baseball history course. Debs has been married for 19 years to Lola, a successful clothes designer. Their daughter, Jacqueline (18), began matriculation at the University of Pennsylvania in the fall of 1999. Debs considers his family his greatest accomplishment.

WILLIAM C. DELLINGER JR., born Oct. 5, 1933, in Chelyan, WV. Joined SABR in January 1999. The first major league baseball that he remembers was listening to the 1945 World Series, Chicago versus Detroit, Peanuts Lowery and Hank Greenberg. It was the day of the third game and he was 12-years-old.

The next season his father taught him how to keep score. You learn many of the nuances of the game by keeping score. When to expect a bunt. Who should cover which base and when. How a runner can take an extra base on a throw.

He has memories of a few games at Crosley Field and Griffith Stadium (Ewell Blackwell and Eddie Yost); the many games at Watt Powell Park in Charleston, WV; The outfield terrace, just like in Crosley Field; Joe Nuxhall, the traveling Negro League teams and Wayne Terwilliger.

He played on a baseball team or a softball team, or both, every summer, from the time that he was in the sixth grade until he left the U.S. Army. Many of those teams were average at best, but a few were pretty good. He remembers winning the Junior High School Conference Championship in softball. They won the State High School Baseball Championship. His team won an intramural softball championship and an Army battalion softball championship. He usually played first or third, but sometimes second base. The thrill of being part of something bigger than yourself and that feeling of esprit de corps that comes from playing on a team are memories that will last a lifetime.

The Army sent him to Germany. He got there near the end of softball season. After playing badly in his first game, at third base, he watched several before playing in his second game. To his surprise, he was sent to left field, without having practiced there. It was to be his first outfield play since Junior High School. He was playing on a totally dirt ball field, 330 feet down the third base line, where a misplayed ball would roll forever. Pressure!

They were tied going into the bottom of the third. Their leadoff hitter that inning was truly their leadoff hitter. At his first at bat, he had appeared to be a good, speedy runner. He singled, bringing up the number two hitter in the lineup. A definite bunt situation. Then, as many third basemen know, a player who is going to bunt will look to see where the third baseman is playing. He looked. He was not very large and batting number two, so Dellinger was playing a medium, short left field.

The ball was pitched and the batter squared around. The sacrifice bunt was nearly perfect. Their (Dellinger's) third baseman fielded the ball, falling down, while making a good throw to first. The runner from first had rounded second and headed for third, without breaking stride, as Dellinger is sure he had done before.

When the batter had started to square around, Dellinger took off for third base. Their first baseman was surprised to see him nearing the third base bag, but got off a good throw. On a mildly close play, the runner was out. A double play, 5-3-7.

"Where did you come from?" asked the former runner. Dellinger didn't say it out loud, but as he trotted back to left field, the answer was obvious to him. He came from the man who taught him how to keep score - his father.

He is married to Joyce Ann and has one son, William David. He is a retired industrial engineer.

MERL LINDBERGH DEMOLL, born in Alexandria, VA, July 25, 1927. He is a graduate of Waynesboro (VA) High School, playing varsity baseball and tennis.

Joined SABR in March 1996 and currently belongs to the Triple Play Club; Friends of Rickwood (oldest ballpark in America); and Friends of the Hall of Fame. Former member of The Dugout Club, Birmingham. His mentors are Louis E. DeMoll Sr. (his deceased father) and Clarence "Tommy" Thomas (deceased St. Louis Cardinals scout and baseball school instructor). Baseball interests: National League - Atlanta Braves; College baseball - University of Alabama.

Employed Jan. 21, 1952, in the Works Manager's Office, he later worked in the Time Office and Mono-Cast Dept. before being transferred to the Publicity Dept. in February 1959. In January 1970 he was appointed editor of the *Acipco News.* He was assigned to the Manufacturing Division—later the Human Relations Division—in January 1986 and continued in duties as '*News* editor together with the development of the *Acipco Bulletin.* Earlier, he was associated with the baseball team for three years as scorekeeper-reporter, 1954-56.

Highlights and memorable experiences: Waynesboro (VA) High School letterman, 2nd baseman (1944); scorekeeper, ACIPCO team, 1954-56 (National Amateur Baseball Federation Tournament, Youngstown, OH, 1954); and "extra" in movie *Cobb,* 1994. DeMoll is married to the former Mary Jo Orr. He retired as publications editor, American Cast Iron Pipe Co. (ACIPCO) after 38 years service. Fulfilled life-long dream in September 1999 with birthday visit to Cooperstown.

MICHAEL E. DEMPSEY, born Oct. 5, 1949, in New London, CT. Joined SABR in 1982, finally bowing to several years of recruiting by Joe Favano turns out he was right, SABR is everything he said it was. Dempsey is a member of the Lajoie/Start Southern New England regional group and belongs to the Ballparks and Minor League Committees which dovetails well with his interest in photography. He has taken several trips tracking down and photographing past and present minor league parks and sites of same, the earliest site still in use possibly being (now) Mercer Field in New London, CT ... one of (he believes) nearly 200 locations visited. His SABR most memorable experience was the Albany Convention (oh well...). He is single and shares his life with 19 cats (with the question of who's trained who still up for debate).

CHRISTOPHER (CHRIS) JOHN DEVINE, born June 10, 1984, in Springfield, MA. Joined the SABR in November 1998 as it seemed like a great opportunity and fun (interested in research as well). His favorite player is Barry Bonds.

Baseball expertise: Books (biographies/autobiographies). His baseball interests include biographical books, baseball trivia and baseball drawings.

Devine is single and currently a student. He sells drawings (business name C.J. Drawings). Hobbies include collecting baseball bios/autobios, baseball drawings and playing baseball and hockey.

MICHAEL DEVIVO, born May 10, 1967, in San Jose, CA. Joined the SABR in March 1999 desiring to meet others who share a passion for the history of baseball. He would like to form a San Francisco group. Baseball interest(s): San Francisco Giants/NY Giants; biographies; and photography. Baseball/SABR highlights and memorable experiences: Any game at Candlestick; meeting Willie Mays; and meeting Johnny Bench.

DeVivo is married to Christine. Employed by California Bank & Trust as real estate portfolio manager. Hobbies: Scorekeeping Giants games; reading the box scores; reading and collecting baseball books (and American Civil War books); backpacking in the Sierras; golf; and wine.

DAN DISCHLEY, born Dec. 2, 1944, in Poughkeepsie, NY. Founding member of SABR (1971). Reason for joining: To straighten baseball's records. His baseball expertise is the Cincinnati Reds (general history and individual player photos). Dischley is a member of the Bio Committee.

He has published a baseball memorabilia magazine, *The Trader Speaks,* for 15 years.

Memorable experiences: Worked security for 1969 and 1973 World Series.

Dischley is divorced and has four children: Stephanie, Edward, Paula and Shaun; and two grandchildren, Marcel and Michael. He is currently retired.

TED DI TULLIO, born in Bronx, NY, May 8, 1930. Joined SABR in April 1973, Casey Stengel Chapter. Di Tullio has three five-inch thick statistical books on (1) batters, (2) pitchers and (3) teams, coaches, managers, umps, DS, AS, CS and WS.

Member of four SABR committees including Records, Umpire, Latin-American and Biographical. 21 consecutive nationals (1977-97).

His father was a stone mason who made the Gehrig Stone in 1941 and Ruth Stone, 1949, in Yankee Stadium. His uncle made the Huggins Stone in 1932.

Yankees contacted him in 1982, the 50th anniversary of the Huggins Stone, with a Yank twist on his list of Yanks who played only for them for 15 years. The Yankees acknowledged him and SABR.

Wrote many lists for SABR publications through the years. He's the only fur designer in SABR.

Di Tullio is a widower with three children: Diana (38), Maryann (28) and Mario (23); and three grandchildren, so far: Eric (10), Danielle (8) and Paul (1-1/2).

JOE DORINSON, born Nov. 15, 1936, in Jersey City, NJ. Joined the SABR March 15, 1997, after meeting Sabrites at Babe Ruth (1995) and Jackie Robinson (1997) conferences. Currently a member of the Casey Stengel Group. His mentors are Lyle Spatz and Terry Malley. Baseball expertise: Book on Jackie Robinson, studies of NY Yankees including Babe Ruth and Joe DiMaggio.

Written works: *Jackie Robinson: Race, Sports and the American Dream.* His memorable experiences include the conferences in 1995, 1997 and 1998 (Arizona).

Dorinson has been married to Eileen Susan for 31 years and has three children: Hilary Beth, Paula Michelle and Robert Greg. He is a professor of history at Long Island University.

PATRIC J. DOYLE, born Aug. 19, 1943, a native of Rochester, NY, now lives in Leawood, KS, a suburb of Kansas City. A SABR member since 1985, he is active in the Minor League and Biographical Committees. He is currently active in the compilation and computerization of player career statistics with an emphasis on minor league data. His long-term goal is a computerized database containing the yearly performance of every  major and minor league player to have played professional baseball.

Doyle has been married to his wife, Bonnie, for 24 years. They have three children: Brian (20), Karen (18) and Lauren (16). A retiree of Marion Laboratories, Inc., he is involved in a number of church and community activities.

MIKE DUGAN, a lifelong resident of Hot Springs, AR. Born July 17, 1954, he is a graduate of Henderson State University where he later served as sports information director for 10 years. He was also baseball information director for the Arkansas Intercollegiate Conference and host to 10 All-Star games and regional tournaments.

He joined SABR in 1987 to associate with people with same interests. Dugan has a  keen interest in the Cotton States League and is putting the finishing touches on a book on the Hot Springs Bathers. He is also hoping to form an Arkansas chapter of SABR members during 1998-99. His primary hobby is collecting baseball books, guides, yearbooks and videos. His goal is to own a biography for each member of Baseball's Hall of Fame.

Dugan has been married to Susan for 20 years. The couple has a daughter, Mary Kate born in 1992. He has been general manager of Merritt Wholesale since 1990.

JOE DULLE, born Jan. 3, 1937, in Jefferson City, MO. Joined the SABR in 1994 and is a member of Hall-Ruggles Chapter. His mentor is Carroll Beringer.

Baseball interests: Ballparks: Architecture, design and layout and photography (as a part of urban history and development).

SABR highlights and memorable experiences: Has attended five SABR National Conventions.

Dulle is married to Mary and has one son, Joe T. and one daughter, Caroline Dulle Smith. He is owner of Joseph K. Dulle Co., property development and management in the Fort Worth Stockyards National Historic District. Current interests/activities: Fort Worth Sports Authority Board of Directors, Fort Worth Convention & Visitors Bureau Executive Committee and immediate past chairman of the board, Live Theatre League of Tarrant County Board of Directors and immediate past president, North Fort Worth Business Association Board of Directors and past president, Jubilee Theatre Board of Directors and past president and Casa Mañana Musicals, Inc., Board of Directors.

CHUCK EARLY, born in Toledo, OH, in February 1947. Joined SABR in 1993 to learn more about 19th century baseball, minor league ball and the baseball park history. Early is sports director and promotions director of WNIX Radio in Greenville, MS, and stays close to the game as play-by-play voice of the Greenville Bluesmen of the Texas-Louisiana League.

Early has been an Indian fan since 1957 and is a public speaker about the grand games past. He hosts a Saturday morning baseball show on WNIX. He has been named Sportscaster of the Year three times by the Mississippi Association of Broadcasters. Early is also heavily involved with the Special Olympics program and other civic and sports organizations. His hobby is collecting baseball books and minor league Indian memorabilia. Most memorable broadcasting experience was broadcasting a perfect game by Bluesman Ken Krahenbuhl.

Early remains an eligible bachelor waiting for that perfect lady to help him cross home plate.

RICHARD A. EASTERLING, born April 17, 1935, in Nelsonville, OH. Joined the SABR in September 1993 as a gift from a friend. Current regional group: Jack Graney - Cleveland.

Major baseball participation has been as fan and participant. Cleveland Indian fan for well over 50 years. He has seen the Tribe through good years, bad years and now  good years again. Played baseball in high school, college and amateur. Coached in youth and amateur leagues. Umpired for 30 years in youth, high school, college and amateur leagues.

Memorable experiences: Tour of Jacobs Field under construction.

Easterling has been married to Betty for 37 years and has three children: Mark, Jill and Paul; one daughter-in-law, Peggy; and one granddaughter, Rachel.

He is a retired insurance agent and is a part-time drivers training instructor. Hobbies include boating and golf.

THOMAS G. (TOM) ECKEL, a SABR member since 1978, Eckel was born Feb. 25, 1953. He married Jane Harper in 1975. They have two children, Jason, a sophomore at Michigan State and Jennifer, a high school senior and accomplished gymnast. Eckel has a MS degree in chemical engineering from Purdue and is currently the director of engineering and manufacturing with Storopack, a world leader in protective packaging supplies.

While working for DuPont in West Virginia from 1978-82, Eckel was the statistician for the AAA Charleston Charlies, where he compiled their first media guide and assisted the HOF in correcting records of former Charleston players. He collaborated with local sportswriter Mike Whiteford and political cartoonist Taylor Jones - performing research for their book *How to Talk Baseball*, which they graciously dedicated to Eckel.

Moving to Wilmington, DE, Eckel volunteered as a proofreader and inputter for Project Scoresheet. Striking a friendship with David Smith, he has participated in Project Retrosheet - locating and copying old scoresheets, inputting games and verifying numbers.

After a transfer to Cincinnati, Eckel became the book review editor for *Spitball*, the leading literary baseball magazine.

On an ongoing basis, Eckel scours old book stores and interacts with various SABR members to add to his 7000+ volume collection of baseball books and publications. Because his wife is a direct descendent of the founders of Harper's Publishing, he collects old baseball woodcuts from *Harper's Weekly*. Finally, Eckel "collects" baseball parks. To date he has seen games in 35 major league and 74 minor league stadia.

ALLEN ECKHOUSE, born in August 1989 in Mayfield Heights, OH. He joined SABR in 1991 and has attended numerous SABR conventions and regional meetings. He is a member of the Jack Graney Chapter in Cleveland, OH.

His hobbies are Pokemon, WWF wrestling, and playing N64. He is the son of Morris and Maria Eckhouse and grandson of Melvin Eckhouse and Joanne and Tony Valenti.

MARIA ECKHOUSE, born in Washington, PA. She joined SABR in 1991 and has attended numerous SABR conventions, regional meetings and other functions.

She has been married to Morris Eckhouse since October 1986 and they have one son, Allen.

MORRIS ECKHOUSE, born in October 1959, Cleveland, OH. He joined SABR in 1985, was founding president of the Jack Graney (Northeast Ohio) Chapter of SABR, 1987-90, and was hired as SABR executive director in 1990.

From 1979-90, Eckhouse authored, co-authored, or contributed to numerous baseball books, including *Day By Day in Cleveland Indians History* and *This Date In Pittsburgh Pirates History*. From 1987-90, he was executive director of Cleveland Sports Legends Foundation.

He is a graduate of Ohio University (1982, BS in communications) and Shaker Heights High School (1978). Eckhouse has been married to Maria Valenti since October 1986. They have one son, Allen.

OSCAR EDDLETON, joined the SABR shortly after seeing a *Sporting News* article in 1977. His SABR research in the early years was confined mostly to the origin and development of night baseball. *Under the Lights* was published in the 1980 Research Journal. Recently he has undertaken a major league ballpark chronology 1901-to date which is available from Len Levin's SABR research library. His article on the 1937 All-Star Game, which he attended as a teenager, appeared in the 1997 *National Pastime*.

He and his wife, Alice, have been married for 51 years. They have attended eight SABR National Conventions and enjoyed them immensely. He is a retired Episcopal minister with 30 years of service in Virginia and North Carolina.

ROB EDELMAN, born March 25, 1949, in New York City. He joined SABR in 1995 and was delighted to present the restored version of Babe Ruth's 1920 feature film *Headin' Home* at the 1997 annual.

He has published two baseball books, *Great Baseball Films* (Citadel Press) and *Baseball on the Web* (MIS: Press). His most recent book, *Meet the Mertzes* (Renaissance Books), co-authored with his wife, Audrey Kupferberg, is a biography of *I Love Lucy's* William Frawley (who was a notable baseball fan) and Vivian Vance.

Edelman has contributed essays to *Total Baseball* and *The Total Baseball Catalog*; lectured on baseball films in the New York State

Council for the Humanities' Speakers in the Humanities program; and presented baseball film and baseball-on-the-Internet programs at the National Baseball Hall of Fame & Museum.

Additionally, Edelman is the author/editor of dozens of film-related books, references, essays and newspaper/magazine articles.

BRUNO EGLOFF, born March 2, 1940, in San Cristóbal, Venezuela. He is an economist graduated in Switzerland and received a diploma as a certified public accountant from a Venezuelan university. In addition to lecturing in economics at Universidad Simón Bolívar in Caracas, he is acting as president for the Venezuelan operation of RadioShack.

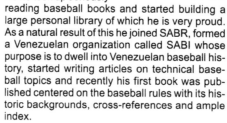

Relatively late in life he took up seriously reading baseball books and started building a large personal library of which he is very proud. As a natural result of this he joined SABR, formed a Venezuelan organization called SABI whose purpose is to dwell into Venezuelan baseball history, started writing articles on technical baseball topics and recently his first book was published centered on the baseball rules with its historic backgrounds, cross-references and ample index.

A current project is participating very actively in the building of a museum with a Hall of Fame for Venezuelan baseball glories and an adjoining library with complementary video and audio sections. All this will be an integral part of a mall built around a unique theme: Baseball.

JOHN J. EISENHARDT, born Aug. 30, 1917, in Bristol, PA, near Philadelphia. Joined SABR in September 1981 to learn anything new or old of baseball in baseball research society.

He saves all SABR bulletins, SABR *National Pastime*, and *Baseball Research Journal*, and often refers to them for information. You never know when you will find something new in SABR bulletins.

Jimmy Foxx was his boyhood hero. He saw him play for Philadelphia A's and Boston Red Sox, and thanks to the SABR Bulletin, found out a group was looking for support to build a life-size statue of Jimmy Foxx in his hometown of Sudlersville, MD. Eisenhardt sent them a donation and thanks to SABR members and Foxx fans they built the statue of him in Sudlersville, MD, Oct. 25, 1997.

Married to Anna since 1948, still living in same town, Port Jefferson Station, NY. Has two sons, John and Joseph, and twin daughters, Laura and Mary. Collects TSN, baseball registers, guides, encyclopedia, SABR, journals, etc.

STEVEN A. (STEVE) ELSBERRY, born May 7, 1946, in Sacramento, CA. Joined the SABR in 1983 for publications (originally). Currently belongs to Halsey Hall Chapter. Baseball expertise: Pinch-hit grand slam homers. His baseball interests include records, Hall of Fame, trivia and books. Member of the Statistical Analysis Committee. Elsberry was treasurer of Lefty O'Doul

Chapter (Northern California) for 12 years. SABR highlights and memorable experiences: 14 conventions in 15 years.

Elsberry is divorced and has one daughter, Karen. He is a retired senior accountant. Currently works in the accounting department for a small civil engineering firm. His significant other is Lyn Moller.

HAROLD LESTER ESCH, born July 30, 1921, in Milwaukee, WI. Due to a family health problem spent about equal time between Milwaukee and Orlando, FL. Seldom missed a spring training game in Orlando with the Dodgers (1934-35) and the Senators beginning 1936. Member of the *Orlando Sentinel* sports staff for a number of years and worked as official scorer for Orlando's Class D club prior to returning to Milwaukee.

Following Army service in WWII was with the Milwaukee Brewers American Association for three years and compiled and had published a club yearbook in 1947. Maintained one of the early "Sports Record Bureaus" supplying baseball data, stats, etc. upon request. Having privileged an access to the press box during his many years of spring training was a great thrill to rub shoulders with the likes of Shirley Povich, Bob Addie, Burton Hawkins, Wirt Gammon, Arch McDonald, not to mention press representatives with visiting clubs. Joined SABR in the inaugural year and has maintained an active interest in a number of the committees ever since.

Esch has been a permanent resident of Mount Dora, FL, since 1982.

BERNIE ESSER, born in December 1930 in San Francisco, CA. He worked for Lockheed for 37 years, retiring as vice president of operations of the Fleet Ballistic Missile Program. He served 14 years as a city councilman of Millbrae, three years as mayor. Upon retiring from civic service he began collecting baseball books.

His library consists of over 2500 hardbound books and another 2000 paperbound pieces. Originally if a book was about baseball he bought it. The objective then was quantity. Today quality rules but he hasn't found a way to trash any of the collection.

In 1982 he began getting autographs of players in the books. In this pursuit he became friends with Joe DiMaggio and has over 70 books and 20 magazine covers autographed by Joe.

He joined SABR in the '80s and has been active on the Bibliography Committee.

Married for 47 years he has two boys, one daughter and three grandchildren.

JENNIFER ETTINGER, a full-time artist lives in Vancouver, BC. Approximately half her work is composed of baseball images, where she concentrates on portraits of stars from the past. She was inspired to work in this area by her father, Ab. Ettinger, who was a successful pitcher in the Nova Scotia Senior Men's League in the 1940s and 50s. She graduated from Emily Carr College of Art and Design in 1993. Since then she has had numerous shows of her work and is presently represented at Gallery "E," Camden Yards, Baltimore. She did a slide presentation of her work at the 1998 SABR Convention. Being Canadian, she occasionally strays to hockey

paintings and has done two book covers in that area. She is married to SABR member Max Weder.

TERRY M. FARMER, born March 29, 1946, in Springfield, MO. Joined the SABR in mid-late 1970 to gain access to various SABR publications. Baseball expertise: 1950s and 1960s baseball players and teams; collectibles related to them. He currently follows the Cardinals and Rangers.

Baseball/SABR Highlights and Memorable Experiences: Played baseball for Preacher Roe's town team in West Plains,

MO, after Preacher retired from Brooklyn in 1955.

Farmer is married to Darlene. He is a retired history teacher from Columbia Public Schools. Hobbies: Has a huge baseball card collection from 1949 to present.

WILLIAM R. (RUSS) FARMER, born Nov. 11, 1952, in Morris, IL. He joined the SABR to learn about the game and to have access to the latest information published. Baseball expertise: Baseball book collecting. His current interests include books, Chicago Cubs and team histories. Baseball experience: When he was six and went to Wrigley Field for the first time.

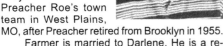

Farmer is married to Corinne and has one child, Caitlin. He is principal of Saratoga Elementary School. Hobbies include collecting baseball books.

PAUL D. (PETE) FEURER, born in December 1944 and lived in Marion, IL, until college. Proximity to St. Louis made him a lifelong Cardinals fan. He joined SABR to obtain all the history available in SABR publications. He has a library of over 400 baseball books, enters baseball pools and serves as announcer for local Little League games.

In his lifetime, Feurer has been a baseball player, umpire and coach. He would love to attend

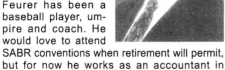

SABR conventions when retirement will permit, but for now he works as an accountant in Calgary, Alberta, Canada.

Feurer and his wife, Judi, have two daugh-

ters who are also baseball fans. It isn't always "fathers and sons."

Feurer enjoys baseball's timelessness, its statistics, its historical generational linkage and its unpredictability. To him the time between pitches, when a fan can think of what may occur next, provides hundreds of golden moments in an afternoon at the ballpark.

AL FIGONE, born March 4, 1938, in San Francisco, CA. He was a teacher-coach at the high school and college levels until 1990. Since that time, his time has been primarily devoted to teaching undergraduate and graduate courses in Kinesiology at Humboldt State University, Arcata, CA.

Figone joined SABR in 1983 because of his lifelong interest in all aspects of baseball. His interests are focused primarily on the

gambling scandals which have surfaced in Major and Minor League baseball and specific legal issues involving player-management relations. He has presented over 35 papers at various professional conferences and has had over 41 manuscripts published. In 1987 he authored: *The Mental Aspects of Baseball: A Coach's Handbook.* Figone is a member of the Bay area Lefty O'Doul Chapter of SABR. His PhD degree was completed at the University of Utah specializing in the areas of applied sport psychology and sociology of sport.

SHYA M. FINESTONE, born Nov. 2, 1954, in Montreal. He joined the SABR in 1998 because he loves baseball and for the trips. Baseball expertise: Umpiring, Montreal Expos and Jackie Robinson. Current interests include ballparks.

Married Debra in 1985. She is a medical doctor. They have three children: Leona (1987), Nathaniel (1989) and Hannah (1993). Em-

ployment/Positions: C.A., C.F.P., senior partner - Finestone Chan. Hobbies and noteworthy accomplishments: Can speak Hebrew, read and chant the Torah.

LEN FIORITO, born Feb. 19, 1943, in Seattle. Joined the SABR in 1972 when he became interested in the whereabouts of former players of the 1950s. Fiorito is currently a member of the Pacific Northwest Chapter. Baseball expertise: Baseball in the 1950s. He began communicating with SABR member Rich Marazzi of Ansonia, CT, in 1977 and in the early 1980s they co-authored the books *Aaron to Zuverink* and *Aaron to Zipfel.* He has twice traveled to Cooperstown to visit the Baseball Hall-of-Fame and to the "Field of Dreams" in Iowa. He enjoys communicating with players of the 1950s and has written a *Where Are They Now* column for *Oldtyme Baseball News.* He is currently working with Marazzi on updating *Aaron to Zuverink* for a future re-printing. Fiorito is a member of the Biographical Research Committee.

Fiorito has been married to Patti since 1971. They have a daughter, Gina (22), and a son, Steve (17). He is employed in the transportation department at the *Seattle Times.* Hobbies: Traveling.

MIKE FISCHER, born in Detroit in 1963. He cannot recall a time when he was not a diehard Tiger fan. Among his favorite Tiger memories, he counts the final series against Boston at the close of the 1972 regular season, watching "The Bird" talk to the ball throughout 1976, the dramatic series against Toronto at the close of the 1987 regular season, and anything having to do with Mickey Lolich, his all-time hero and favorite player.

A SABR member since late 1997, Fischer specializes in the history of baseball in Detroit. He is currently a labor and employment lawyer in Milwaukee, where he resides with his wife, Elaine, a high school teacher. On many summer nights, the two of them can be found suffering through yet another Brewer loss at County Stadium—when they aren't off on one of their annual pilgrimages to "the Corner" at Michigan and Trumbull.

JIM FLACK, born Feb. 11, 1937, in Brooklyn, NY. Joined the SABR in 1984 to get information otherwise inaccessible. Currently a member of Baltimore/Washington Bob Davids Chapter. His mentor is Bob Davids. Baseball expertise: History of University of Maryland baseball. His interests include the history of intercollegiate baseball.

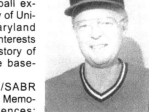

Baseball/SABR Highlights and Memorable Experiences: 1986 Washington, D.C. program on Senators & Homestead Grays.

Married (since 1960) to Jan LeMessurier and has three grown children: James K. III, Hilary and Jake. Employed by the University of Maryland, assistant baseball coach.

JOAN A. (JO AN) FLOWER, born Aug. 7, 1929, in Brooklyn, NY. She preferred participation rather than spectator sports in high school - primarily softball, field hockey and bowling. Joined the SABR about 1992. Reason for joining: Research for writing, Women in Baseball, Expansion. Currently a member of the Rocky Mountain Chapter. Baseball interests include research on women in baseball East Coast and has closely followed Rockies since draft day. Committees involved in are Women in Baseball and Ballparks.

Written works: *Those Guys Drove Us Crazy,* newsletter 1995-97 and *Colorado Women's Baseball* (including Ladies Pro League until it folded).

She feels her writings about the Rockies differs from others because it's from the point of view of a fan without media credentials.

Other projects planned: (1) A comparison of the inaugural Arizona Diamondbacks with the 1993 Rockies, including notes on ballparks involved; (2) a photo tour of Major and Minor League ballparks visited; and (3) women's baseball on the East Coast.

She has been a widow since 1972. Currently retired and is a freelance writer/photographer. Noteworthy accomplishments: Historical novel *Monsieur Verite* 1975 and amateur radio.

JAMES E. FOGARTIE, born June 20, 1924, in Brookhaven, MS. Joined the SABR in 1982 or 1983 because of a life-long interest in baseball. Baseball expertise: New York Yankees ('27-'30s), Lou Gehrig, college baseball. Enjoys reading about baseball. Written works: Christmas stories.

Married to Vivian M. and has four children and five grandchildren. He is a retired Presbyterian minister.

WILSON B. (BUD) FOSTER, born Aug. 26, 1926, in Burlington, VT. He became interested in playing baseball when he was about 8-years-old, but did not become interested in Major League baseball until he was 11. He did not support any particular team until 1942, when Mel Ott was named manager of the Giants. Living in the panhandle of Connecticut it was expected that you supported one of the New York teams. During the summer of 1956 Foster and his family moved to Denver, CO, and in 1958 moved to Littleton, CO, a suburb of Denver. He became a Denver Bears and Zephyrs fan until the Rockies came into existence.

He is interested in collecting books and almost any memorabilia and is currently putting together scrapbooks on Major League baseball beginning with the Rockies, his major source of information being the Denver newspapers. He has many memorable baseball experiences, but it is difficult to top the joy of the Bobby Thomson home run in 1951. Giant fans had the enjoyment of bragging rights over the Dodger fans. He does not remember when he first heard of SABR or joined.

Foster and his wife, Phyllis, celebrated their 50th Wedding Anniversary in February 1999. They have five children: Bill, Ken, Barbara, Patricia and Leslie; and five grandchildren. Employment as pipefitter, construction and maintenance. They are retired and wonder: How come they are so busy? Hobbies include baseball books, baseball memorabilia and pictures.

CHRISTOPHER T. FRANCO, born July 23, 1962, in Edison, NJ. Still an avid baseball fan, he credits his interest in the early years of baseball to the dice game, Strat-o-Matic. He started replaying seasons with various Hall-of-Fame players of the past when he was 13-years-old. His baseball memorabilia collection is impressive and specializes in Babe Ruth items. "Sometimes I walk into my library and it looks like I own every book ever written about baseball between the years 1915-35. I guess you could say I'm an expert on this period." Franco founded the SABR Goose Goslin New Jersey Chapter in 1992 but had to leave New Jersey and the chapter in 1997 when he accepted a job promotion which moved him to South Carolina.

Married to his wife, Jeannine, since 1995 with a baby due in the spring of 1999. He is currently employed by Amcan Specialty Steels in Hartsville, SC, as their southeast regional sales manager. He is also an active member of the Professional Football Researchers Association

MICHAEL FRANK, a baby boomer who joined SABR around 1980. Though a self-employed consulting pension actuary who doesn't take long vacations, he's seen virtually every MLB, NFL, NBA and NHL team play at home, with a second go-round for new stadia. He's been on the Ballparks Committee since it had a dozen people.

Though he doesn't call himself a researcher, Frank has helped others with ideas and items from his collection, and wrote a paper on MLB teams policies on freebies for kids. He's been to two Nationals (Brown and New York City), some New York Regionals and ballparks dinners when Bob Bluthardt came east. An Indians fan, he drove the retired 1980 Yankee bullpen car for 17 years.

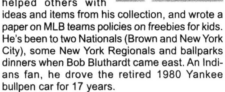

Single, he does mostly administrative work for a Little League, another area of his expertise, though he wishes kids played all day on their own like when he was a kid.

MEL R. FREESE, born Jan. 10, 1933, in St. Louis, MO. He is married to Martha and has a son, Charles; a granddaughter, Tanya; and a great-grandson, Evan. Joined SABR in December 1998 to have fellowship with other baseball fans and researchers. Member of Bob Broeg Chapter. Baseball expertise: Historical research. McFarland has published two of his books. *Charmed Circle,* a history of 20-game winners in the 20th century and *Magic Numbers,* a history of great hitting feats of the 20th century. Unpublished are four books: one on hitters, another on pitchers, a third on the first 50 years of the American League and the fourth on Mark McGwire.

Freese retired in 1989 as director, marketing services for Calgon. During that time he taught economics for 25 years at St. Louis University. Currently teaches part-time at Webster University in St. Louis.

KEVIN J. FURA, born in February 1961 in Reading, PA. He joined SABR in 1990 happy to find an organization that loved the game of baseball. His collection of baseball books has topped the 350 mark and his extensive autograph collection is well over 1,000. Old ballparks and uniforms are among his varied interests along with a love of good baseball trivia. His favorite personalities are Casey Stengel, Ted Williams and Christy Mathewson. If he were commissioner for

a day, he would ban the DH and tear out any and all Astroturf.

Kevin and his wife, LeeAnne, reside in Allentown, PA, along with their three children: Regina (11), Daniel (9) and Audrey (7). He is the accounting department chair at Allentown Business School. He is currently pursuing a Master's degree in U.S. History.

RONALD L. (RON) GABRIEL, born in 1941 in Brooklyn, USA, demanding to be born in a Brooklyn pennant-winning year. At about age 5, his father, Lou Gabriel, showed him the league standings in the evening newspaper each night to follow the Brooklyn Dodgers daily. In early 1974 he joined SABR, realizing SABR could provide an important vehicle in baseball's historic preservation. He served as SABR's vice president, 1989-91.

Gabriel has attended 24 conventions, including the last 18, has given numerous presentations, and serves on the Ballparks and Business of Baseball Committees. On Nov. 9, 1974, SABR's first regional meeting ever, was held at his home and museum (Cooperstown South). Gabriel is active in the Bob Davids Chapter. His memories include games at Ebbets Field, especially World Series, and trips to Cooperstown. He was present at the 1953-56-62-84 Hall of Fame inductions, and has witnessed World Series games in six different decades. On Oct. 4, 1975, at 3:44 p.m., the 20th anniversary minute of Brooklyn's World Series victory, Gabriel founded the Brooklyn Dodger Fan Club as a catalyst to bring together Brooklyn Dodger fans with whom he exchanged memories.

As president since 1975, Gabriel publishes a quarterly newsletter, including special editions where he updates his *This Date in Brooklyn Baseball History* by listing nearly 400 significant events during the April-October period. He contributed articles to SABR's original *National Pastime,* and wrote several biographies for *Biographical Dictionary of American Sports: Baseball.* In June 1984 Gabriel was inducted into the Brooklyn Dodger Baseball Hall of Fame as a charter member. He has given baseball interviews on four different continents.

Gabriel resides in Chevy Chase, MD. Other hobbies include: travel, genealogy and tennis. Having taken early retirement as a Federal Government executive, he now heads Gabriel Government Group (its GGG logo is from Ebbets Field's scoreboard), a management consulting firm. He also worked in the advertising and drug industries and academia, primarily in human resources and statistics. Gabriel has BS and MBA degrees from the Kenan-Flagler Business School of University of North Carolina at Chapel Hill and a PhD degree in management from American University. He is the only person in the U.S. to serve on the last four Democratic Presidential Inaugural Committees.

RUDY A.S. GAFUR, born April 30, 1941, in Guyana, South America. He emigrated to Canada in 1972 and in 1977, at age 36, saw his first baseball game. He joined SABR in 1993 to learn more of baseball history and is a member of the Toronto Chapter.

A student of baseball history, Gafur's focus is the National Baseball Hall of Fame. The Negro Leagues and Ty Cobb are among his other baseball interests. His mentor is former New York Yankees shortstop, Tony Kubek. In 1995 his book *Cooperstown is My Mecca* was published.

Gafur works for an aircraft company. His hobbies include baseball history, writing and philately. Married for 38 years, he resides in Toronto with his wife, Niza; children: Shelley, Nicky, Shahab, Sharon and Michelle; and grandchildren: Dairl, Brooke and Mallorie.

Gafur's dream of introducing baseball to his native Guyana was realized in 1996 when, with a $7,000.00 donation of equipment from Little League, Inc., he and others conducted clinics throughout the country.

CAPPY GAGNON, born March 10, 1944, in Fort Bragg, NC. After moving to Washington, D.C., late in 1976, Gagnon read a Bill Madden column in *The Sporting News* about SABR founder Bob Davids. Gagnon soon became a regular member of Davids' *Newsletter* "folding, stuffing and mailing" crew.

During the next 20 years, Gagnon served on several SABR committees, chairing the "Collegiate Committee" for a number of years. In 1981 he located six missing ballplayers for the Biographical Committee, for whom he has also written several bios.

Recruited to the SABR Board by Davids, Gagnon has served as vice president, president, treasurer and director (four years). As president (1984 and 1985), Gagnon instituted the first contested elections for SABR office; developed the Trivia Contest format; and created the Bob Davids Award.

While traveling on business and living in several parts of the country, Gagnon located a missing 1880s ballplayer's obit in London; founded two SABR chapters (Los Angeles and South Bend, IN); and won SABR trivia contests in three cities (Los Angeles, Seattle and Portland).

Gagnon has published more than 50 articles of his baseball research, including a half dozen for various SABR publications. From 1988-90 he sent more than 3,000 letters to universities, verifying the college attendance and academic achievements of more than 7,000 Major Leaguers.

As a Babe Ruth League pitcher-first baseman, Gagnon won a two-hitter in his debut, and once went four for four. There were few field playing highlights. In 1965 he was the field announcer for Notre Dame baseball. As a high school baseball coach, his 1968 team defeated national powerhouse Sarasota (FL), featuring future Major Leaguer Hugh Yancy.

He received national awards from the Big Brothers of America (1973) and the National Association of Counties (1985 and 1986). He received the Exemplary Service Award from the Los Angeles County Sheriff's Dept. in 1984.

From 1980-90 Gagnon provided personal protective services for 33 of the most recognized persons in the entertainment field.

Gagnon currently serves as the director of stadium personnel for the University of Notre Dame (1966 grad). He is working on a book *Anson to Yaz*, featuring the baseball contributions of the 70 Major Leaguers from Notre Dame. His most cherished SABR achievement is his friendship with Bob Davids.

THOMAS R. GARRETT, born June 5, 1950, in Portsmouth, VA. Joined the SABR in 1991 to learn more about baseball from those who really know its history. His mentors are Rev. William Duvall (deceased), Dick Clark, Jim Riley, Larry Lester, Todd Bolton and Jeff Eastland. Garrett's baseball expertise: The baseball career of Walter "Buck" Leonard. Baseball interests include Negro Leagues and Minor League baseball in Norfolk and Portsmouth, VA.

Garrett is a member of the Negro Leagues Committee. He is a contributor to *The Twentieth Century: Great Athletes*, Pasadena, CA, Salem Press, 1992 (20-volume set written for middle school students).

Baseball/SABR Highlights: Interviewing Buck Leonard several times; the first SABR Negro League Committee Convention in Harrisburg, PA; and attending the HOF induction of Leon Day.

Garrett is married to Carol and has one son, Andrew. Presently a principal in Portsmouth Public School Dist., has been a special education teacher, specialist and supervisor; adjunct faculty at Old Dominion University. Hobbies: Collecting local baseball images collectibles and the study of the Negro Leagues.

JAY GAUTHREAUX, born Dec. 21, 1961, in New Orleans, LA. He became a SABR member in 1981 through the urging of friend and mentor, Arthur Schott. In January 1993, Gauthreaux, along with Arthur Schott and Rick Dempsey, organized the Art Schott/ Pelican Chapter which boasts over 25 members.

Gauthreaux is a member of the Ballparks and Minor League Committee, where his interests are with the ballparks in New York, and the New Orleans Pelicans and New Orleans Zephyrs, respectively.

His written works have appeared in *Oldtyme Baseball News*, *Bleacher Creature* newsletter, New Orleans Zephyrs programs, 1995-97, South Louisiana *Sports Scene*, SABR 21 Convention and 1995 Research publications.

He has worked with the Zephyrs batting coach as an "unofficial statistician," compiling daily hitting records on the Zephyrs in 1994-95.

His most memorable experience is being involved with baseball and people associated with the sport. He has an impressive collection of baseball books and memorabilia, and roots passionately for the Yankees, Cubs and Zephyrs.

PHILIP EVAN GAWTHROP, born March 28, 1949, in Prince George County, MD. He joined SABR in 1998 because he loves the game of baseball, especially old-time baseball history. He was raised in Hillsmere Shores just outside Annapolis, MD, and now lives in Crofton, MD. He's a big guy, 6 feet 4 inches tall and weighs 295 lbs., with brown hair and hazel eyes. He attended Annapolis High School and then college at Ohio Institute of Technology (graduating in 1972 with a Bachelor's degree in electronic engineering technology).

His full-time job is an electronic engineer/ radio frequency spectrum manager for the U.S. Dept. of Commerce but he has a unique part-time job (a hobby so to speak); he's been an umpire in excess of 27 years and in 1984 he was selected to umpire the USSSA Men's Class "C" World Series in softball. For the past 10 years

he's been umpiring baseball (all levels); currently he's an umpire for two associations doing high school/college baseball (Anne Arundel Umpires Association in Anne Arundel County, MD, and the Southern Dist. Umpires Association in the Maryland counties) around Washington, D.C. Baseball is very much like life; if you can teach kids of today the fundamentals of baseball and sportsmanship that goes along with the game then those kids stand a very good chance of becoming hardworking and honest citizens of tomorrow.

Gawthrop married Brenda Faye Thomas Jan. 25, 1985. They have two children, Mitchell Bennett (Sept. 10, 1985) and Andrew Thomas (May 25, 1990).

VINCE GENNARO, born in 1951 (on Whitey Ford's birthday) in Paterson, NJ. While he did not join SABR until 1995, he has had a long standing love affair with baseball. He played semi-pro baseball in the Metropolitan League in northern New Jersey in the early 1970s. A knee injury redirected his energies to Seton Hall University and later the University of Chicago, where he received his MBA. In the mid-90s his baseball spirit was reignited while living in Cleveland, experiencing the rebirth of the Indians. He was even inspired to attend an Indians' fantasy camp ... which resulted in two subsequent knee surgeries, taking his grand total to seven.

He recently published an article in the *Baseball Research Journal*, "The Best Cleveland Indians Team Ever." Today, Gennaro is a division president at Pepsi-Cola in Purchase, NY.

His wife, Karen, is a psychiatrist, and they have a 12-year-old daughter, Danielle (born on Stan Musial's and Ken Griffey Jr.'s birthday). A distant second behind Gennaro's passion for baseball, are his interests in golf and wine.

LARRY R. GERLACH, born Nov. 9, 1941, in Lincoln, NE. Joined the SABR in 1978 to associate with others interested in baseball history. Member of the Utah Chapter in Salt Lake City. Expertise: Umpire biographies and history. Gerlach's interests include general history and biographies; the Minor Leagues, especially Pacific Coast League; the Negro Leagues; and the business of baseball.

Committees: First chair of the Umpires and Rules Committee; also member of Minor Leagues, Negro Leagues and Business of Baseball Committee. Offices held include director, 1991-97 and president 1997-99.

Gerlach's works include *The Men in Blue: Conversations with Umpires* (1980, 1994) and numerous articles, most recently "Baseball's Other 'Great Experiment: Eddie Klep and the Integration of the Negro Leagues" (1998).

Highlights: Attending the national conventions and talking with friends, old and new.

Gerlach is married to Gail and has two sons, T.J. and Jonathan. He is professor of sport history, University of Utah and NCAA faculty athletics representative. Hobbies are baseball history research, following University of Nebraska football and cooking.

MIKE GETZ, born Dec. 29, 1938, in Brooklyn. He has contributed to *Baseball Digest*, *Baseball Bulletin* and *Diamond Report*. He joined SABR in 1980 and was one of the chief organizers of the first New York City Regional. Listed in *Who's Who in U.S. Writers, Editors and Poets,* Getz is the author of books on the Cardinals, Mets, Yankees and Brooklyn Dodgers. His many radio appearances include "The Art Rust Show" (WABC), "In the Public Interest" (WHN), local college radio at Kingsborough (WKRB) and Brooklyn College (WBCR). Getz has lived in Brooklyn all his life except for two years in the U.S. Army. He is proud of the fact that he played ball on diamonds in all five boroughs of New York. Having won a talent contest at New York's Raleigh Hotel, he still has hopes of singing the National Anthem at Shea Stadium one day. He lives with his wife, Lois.

Getz worked out with San Diego Padres AA farm team (one day), ran in Madison Square Garden and at the Penn Relays, played piano and sang at the 25th anniversary of Brooklyn Developmental Center, and has been a guest performer at a night club in Sun City, AZ.

STEVEN P. GIETSCHIER, born July 21, 1948, in New York, NY. Joined the SABR in 1987 to commune with other baseball historians. He is currently a member of Bob Broeg Chapter. Baseball expertise: Archivist for *The Sporting News.* Member of Records, Bibliography, Business of Baseball, Negro Leagues and Umpires and Rules Committees. He served on the Board of Directors in 1997-99.

Written works: Editor, *Cooperstown Corner: Columns From The Sporting News,* by Lee Allen.

Gietschier is married to Donna P. and has two daughters, Katie and Sarah, and one grandson, Andrew. He has been employed as archivist for *The Sporting News* since 1986.

WILLIAM C. (BILL) GILBERT, born in Denver, CO, in November 1935. A SABR member since 1984, he has made research presentations at the last five conventions. He is on the Statistical Analysis, Records and Business of Baseball Committees and has had articles published in both *The Baseball Research Journal* and *The National Pastime.* As the leader of the Houston Chapter for 10 years, he organizes two or three meetings each year.

Gilbert has contributed to numerous baseball publications including *Baseball's Top 100,* a winner of the Sporting News Award in 1995. He has worked on Tal Smith's salary arbitration staff for six years after retiring from a 35-year career in engineering management with Exxon.

Gilbert served 14 years in Little League baseball as a manager and administrator and still plays competitive softball and tennis. He has been married to Evelyn for 37 years. They have four children: John, Paul, Susan and Patrick; and three grandchildren: Allie, Caleb and Evan.

DANIEL E. GINSBURG, born Jan. 13, 1956, in Pittsburgh, PA. He is a charter member of SABR who enjoys networking with other researchers. His mentors are Lee Allen and Cliff Kachline. Baseball expertise: Gambling scandals. His baseball interests are the 19th century and Hall of Fame.

Written Works: *The Fix Is In* (McFarland, 1995) and various articles.

Ginsburg has been married to Teresa for 17 years. He is the retired president of Draft Worldwide (ad agency) and part owner, Norwich Navigators (Eastern League). Ginsburg has compiled one of the finest collections of Baseball Hall of Fame/star player autographs. His collection was donated to the Elliott Museum (Stuart, FL). He is part owner of Champagne de Meril (Aÿ, France).

ARTHUR (ART) GLUECK, born Oct. 15, 1924, in Brooklyn, NY. His favorite team is the Los Angeles Dodgers. Baseball expertise: He feels he is well versed in all aspects of baseball. He has been published twice this year in local magazine, *The Sullivan Scene.* Glueck is currently researching material for two Major League baseball articles he is planning to write.

At present his area is represented by the Catskill Cougars of the unclassified Northeast League. Though its classification is lowly there is a plethora of former Major League and Triple A players representing the League.

Glueck is married to the former Lillian Gordon. Earned BA and MA degrees at Long Island University. He is a retired language arts teacher with the New York City Board of Education. Interests: Sports, current events, politics and music.

JOE GLYNN, born June 23, 1961, in Carbondale, IL. Joined the SABR in 1995 due to his interest in baseball history. He is a member of Kentucky Regional Chapter. Baseball expertise: Louisville, KY baseball history before 1900. He is interested in 19th century baseball, Minor Leagues. Glynn is a member of the 19th Century Committee.

Written works include *Baseball's First Big League Strike* and *A Red-Letter Day in the History of Baseball* which he hopes will be published.

Baseball/SABR Highlights & Memorable Experiences: Presenting his paper *Baseball's First Big League Strike* at the 1997 SABR National Convention.

Glynn is single and is employed as clerk, Geography Branch, Census Bureau, Jeffersonville, IN. Hobbies include writing and coin collecting.

ROGER A. GODIN, born July 7, 1938, in Tarrytown, NY. Joined the SABR in 1977 due to his interest in baseball history. He is a member of the Baltimore Chapter. Baseball expertise: 1922 St. Louis Browns. His interests include St. Louis AL, Minnesota Twins and unique Minor League teams.

Written works: *The 1922 St. Louis Browns: Best of the American League's Worst.* Baseball/SABR highlights and memorable experience is getting his book published.

Godin is divorced and has two sons, Chris (27) and Terry (25). He retired March 31, 1998, as curator, U.S. Army Ordnance Museum.

He is the author of 51 biographical essays of American hockey players appearing in Green-

wood Press' *Biographical Dictionary of American Sports.* His essays on Hobey Baker and Moose Goheen will appear in the *American National Biography* to be published by the Oxford University Press in 1999.

A member of the Society of International Hockey Research (SIHR), Godin's short essay "American Participation on Stanley Cup Winning Teams" appeared in the Spring 1997 issue of the organizations' *Hockey Research Journal.* He presented a monograph "The Warroad Lakers, 1947-1997" at the Society's fall 1997 meeting in Kingston, Ontario.

Along with Donald M. Clark he has written "Hockey in the United States: The Canadian Influence," an essay that will be published in the *Encyclopedia of Ethnic Sports in the United States* in 1998.

Godin was the executive director, United States Hockey Hall of Fame, 1971-83 and director-curator of that facility 1985-87. He holds a Bachelor's degree from Pennsylvania Military College, 1961 and a master's degree from Ohio University, 1971.

CARLOS RUBEN MORALES GONZALEZ, born March 3, 1966, died June 14, 1995, at the age of 29. Posthumous member of the Puerto Rico Chapter of SABR. His mentors were Eligio (his father); Orlando (Peruchin) Cepeda recently nominated or selected to the Baseball Hall of Fame of Cooperstown, NY; the policeman, Mr. José Rodriguez; and Mr. Tolentino (of the Little League of Caguas, PR).

Baseball expertise: He began playing baseball at the early age of 12 years at "Villa Nueva" Little League at Caguas, PR in 1978. He also played at Santo Domingo, Venezuela; Chicago; Davenport, OH; and New York City; representing his island, Puerto Rico, and the Little League. Also he helped many kids in the fundamentals and discipline of how to play good and "baseball sense" baseball.

Baseball interests: His great interest was to play with the Atlanta Braves. Three or four months before his death he wrote a letter directly to Mr. Ted Turner, requesting him to invite Gonzalez for a "try out" and/or to practice with the Braves team at the Big League. He was a left handed player, with great speed running, fielding and throwing the ball. Mr. Schuerholz assigned a scout located in Puerto Rico to offer him a "try out" to be held around June or July 1995, but he never obtained such opportunity to demonstrate his natural ability to play baseball at the big show. The reason "the driver of a truck killed him on June 14, 1995, the same month that he was waiting the great opportunity of his life. Life is a real mystery. He used to tell his dad (Pai) "Pai, life is brief (short). Look at Clemente, he died exactly after his 3,000 hits at the Big League, because the destiny was it." Gonzalez believed greatly in the profession of the Holy Bible.

He wrote a few works related to children's comic books. Also, three of his works were approved at the American International Publishers, just a few months after his death. Irony of Life?

Baseball/SABR Highlights & Memorable Experiences: The summer of 1980 when he enrolled at the Orlando Cepeda's Baseball Academy in Puerto Rico and when he was representing his island of Puerto Rico, playing baseball at Santo Domingo, Venezuela, Chicago and New York.

They were the happiest days of his short life in this world. "Thanks Pai (Dad) for giving to me such short, but unforgotten, period of time. God bless you."

Gonzalez studied at the universities of Cayey, Interamericana and at Columbia College, Caguas, PR. He was fully engaged in comics cartooning, in writing works related with children in how to save lives in an aircraft accident and so forth. He was operating his own enterprise of video machines and computers. *Submitted by his father, Eligio Morales Sosa.*

RAYMOND J. GONZALEZ, born Oct. 27, 1919 in Havana. He loves baseball and joined SABR in August 1971. He has played the game, umpired and been score keeper, but his main interest is records and analysis.

Member of Records Committee. He has all Yankees games recorded, home run records, triple plays and thousands of other statistics. He is married to Aleida and is a retired accountant. Accomplishments include his baseball books (by the thousand) and the records he has kept through the years.

DAVID A. GOSS, born July 22, 1948, in Joliet, IL. Baseball interests include eye and vision problems of players, history of baseball at Indiana University and the Chicago Cubs.

Written works: A report on the history of spectacle lens wear by Major League baseball players. *Sports Vision 1996*; 12(2): 10-11. Eye and vision problems of some early major league baseball players. *Indiana Journal of Optometry 1998*; 1(1): 10-13. The relationship of eye dominance and baseball batting: a critical literature review. *Journal of Behavioral Optometry 1998*; 9(4): 87-91. 1892 Indiana collegiate championship game. *The National Pastime 1998*; 18: inside back cover. Book reviews of *I Was Right on Time, Play for a Kingdom, Wait Till Next Year: A Memoir,* and *A Great and Glorious Game: The Baseball Writings of A. Bartlett Giamatti.* Sunday *Herald-Times,* Bloomington, IN, 1997, 1998. Those days on the country diamond remain golden. *Country Extra 1996*; 7(3): 23. Book review: Why Michael Couldn't Hit—And Other Tales of the Neurology of Sports. *Journal of Optometric Vision Development 1997*; 28(3): 191.

Goss is married to Dawn and has one child, Brad. He is professor of optometry, Indiana University, Bloomington, IN.

DR. JOHN GOTTKO, born July 30, 1953. Joined the SABR in 1983 because of his love of baseball. Currently a member of NWSABR. His mentor is his grandfather, an old-time (1900-60) Brooklyn Dodger fan. Baseball expertise: Presentations at regional and national SABR meetings; book review for *Nine.* His interests include statistics, Brooklyn Dodgers, business of baseball; and baseball films. Gottko is a member of the Business of Baseball Committee. He also belongs to Brooklyn Dodger Fan Club (Ron Gabriel). He has served as president for one term of NWSABR.

He is employed in academics and holds a PhD in marketing and international business. Hobbies include reading, traveling, movies, skiing, golfing and tennis.

DR. JOHNIE GRACE, born Sept. 7, 1946, in Jasper, AL. Has been a member of the SABR from 1982-86 and 1993-present. He joined because of his love of the game.

Baseball expertise: Strat-O-Matic League, "Dixie Baseball Association," now in 29th season. His interests include statistical analysis, oral history and biographical research.

Baseball/SABR Highlights & Memorable Experiences: Table Game League (APBA, Strat-O-Matic for 39 years).

Grace is married to Karen and is employed in school administration. Hobbies: He has completed 29 full seasons of his "Dixie Baseball Association," a draft league using Major League players. He has detailed statistical records, including career records. He used APBA and Strat-O-Matic from 1960-90, now he uses Diamond Mind Computer Baseball. He collects baseball books and has over 250 hardback non-fiction and over 50 fiction.

Noteworthy accomplishments: Recently completed his Doctorate degree in school administration. Retired from public education in 1995 (27 years) and started a private Christian school (Cornerstone Christian School) now in its third year with a capacity enrollment and more than 75 individuals on a waiting list for entrance.

KEVIN GRACE, assistant head of the Archives & Rare Books Department at the University of Cincinnati where he directs the Baseball Research Collection. He teaches courses at University of Cincinnati on the social history of baseball and on sports and society. A member of SABR since 1984, he has been a consultant for documentaries on Crosley Field, Waite Hoyt, the 1919 Black Sox scandal, and Indianapolis' Bush Stadium, and for various books on baseball history. He has received several research grants for studies of African-Americans in baseball, urban ballparks and women in baseball. In addition to subject research guides, his articles and stories have appeared in the *Baseball Research Journal, Fan, Elysian Fields Quarterly,* and *Spitball,* among other journals and magazines. His current research interests are focused on a biography of Garry Herrmann, baseball and American vice, and the historic and contemporary relationship between baseball and the tobacco industry.

DR. DANIEL GREEN, born Feb. 4, 1934, in Scranton, PA. Joined the SABR in 1985 to learn. His mentor is Ted Williams, Bosox. Green wanted to be his cf but beaned in 1950. Baseball expertise: Baseball humor/trivia, buying a team, Bosox, ST/Snuff in baseball. Green is a member of the Collegiate Baseball Committee.

He has held the office of president, Wisconsin Dental Association and president, Wisconsin Council of Prof. Chm.

Written works include *Your Dental Health,* 19 articles in prof. ADA on dental practice. Memorable experiences were giving papers at Kansas City and Louisville and paper at Indiana State Baseball symposium.

He has been married for 40 years to Dr. Cornelia Green and has two children, Scott Alan (35) and Mary Ann (33). He has been in the general preventive dentistry field from 1960-present. Hobbies include golf, traveling (45 countries) and *Who's Who in the World.*

HOWARD GREEN, born Jan. 24, 1921, in Swenson, TX. Founding president (1991) Hall-Ruggles Chapter, convention coordinator SABR-24, joined 1979 at the suggestion of Clifford Kachline. Authority on Texas baseball, 16-year panelist on 50,000 watt WBAP Sports Trivia Show. Also chairman, Selection Committee, Texas Baseball Hall of Fame. Former sports writer. Served 10 years Texas Legislature, eight years as Tarrant County

judge. Founding president, both Longhorn and Gulf Coast (Texas-Louisiana) Leagues. With two other veterans, obtained Abilene franchise (West Texas-New Mexico League) in 1946. Co-owner, general manager, three seasons. Also, headed Big State and Gulf States Leagues. Served in 1955 B, C, D representative, National Association Executive Committee and Major-Minor Executive Council.

Contributed to SABR publication, *The National Pastime.*

Green and wife, Mary, reside in Fort Worth and have two daughters, two grandchildren and two great-grandchildren. (Widely known actor, Ethan Hawke, of stage and screen is grandson.)

LARRY GREEN, born March 21, 1940, in Ludlow, MA. He rejoined the SABR in 1997 because of the great source of baseball information. Baseball expertise: Great teams of the past. His interest is in great teams of the past statistical analysis of player performance.

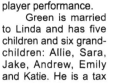

Green is married to Linda and has five children and six grandchildren: Allie, Sara, Jake, Andrew, Emily and Katie. He is a tax supervisor. Green is a sports gaming hobbyist.

PAUL W. GREENWELL, born April 25, 1950, in Washington, D.C. Joined the SABR in 1976 to expand/preserve history of baseball. Currently a member of the Dallas/Ft. Worth Chapter. His mentor is Art Schott. Baseball expertise: High school/college player. His interests are 1901-30 Orioles and ballparks. Greenwell has served as vice president of the Dallas/Ft. Worth Chapter.

He has had several written pieces in annual SABR publications.

Greenwell is married to Kelly and has one child, Kate. He is a partner in an investment counseling firm. Hobbies include racquetball and billiards.

ROBERT J. GRIFFIS, born Nov. 10, 1937, in Binghamton, NY. Joined the SABR in November 1996 due to his interest in baseball history and research. Baseball expertise: General knowledge of late 1940s-60s and current Eastern League. General baseball interest in comparative statistics by decade, 1940s-current.

Baseball/SABR Highlights & Memorable Experiences: Attended games three and four of the 1996 World Series in Atlanta.

Griffis is married to Carolyn and has three children: two living, Kevin and Karen, and one deceased. He retired Jan. 1, 1996, from the state of Virginia after 31 years as director of economic research and chief economist. Former president, two terms, Board of Directors of Virginia Association of Economists and two terms on Board of Directors of Southern Regional Science Association Earned his BA degree in economics at Harpur College (now Binghamton University), Binghamton, NY, and his MA degree in economics from Southern Illinois University, Carbondale, IL. He has attended Hall of Fame induction, Induction Week, at Cooperstown, NY, every year since 1991. He has also attended spring training (mid-March/April) in Ft. Myers and Port Charlotte every year since 1991. Hobbies include hunting, fishing and autograph collection (has all living and several deceased Hall of Famers plus Major-Minor stars from 1940s-present, 350+ autograph balls, pictures, plaques and scorebooks).

STEPHEN M. GRIMBLE, born Oct. 25, 1944, in Dallas, TX. Joined the SABR in the early 1990s to learn more about baseball history and statistics. He is currently a member of the Philadelphia Chapter. Baseball expertise: Statistical analysis and history 1900-65. His interest is in statistics.

Written works include *Setting the Record Straight: Baseball's Greatest Batters* published by Cedar Tree Books Ltd., Wilmington, DE.

Grimble is married to Eliete and is vice president and university treasurer at the University of Delaware.

STANLEY LOUIS GROSSHANDLER, SABR member #50 was born in Youngstown, OH where he played high-school football and American Legion baseball. He received a BA from the College of Wooster where he was a member of the football team and a MD from Ohio State University.

Stan served as a captain with the U.S. Eighth Army in Korea.

He is a board certified anesthesiologist who has taught at The Medical College of Wisconsin and the University of North Carolina. He also presented a course on Sports History at North Carolina State University.

Stan has held several SABR offices and written articles for SABR publication. He has published over 250 articles on all sports in magazines, newspapers, and game programs.

Stan and his wife Mary have five children: Lynn Holt (Taylor and Connor), Cathe Barnhart (Kyle and Erica), Todd and Ronnie (Mrs.), Lisa and Scott.

KEVIN J. GRZYMALA, born Dec. 4, 1959, in Buffalo, NY. Joined the SABR in January 1998 because of the research opportunities and knowledgeable people. He is currently a member of the Lefty O'Doul Chapter. His mentor is Joe Overfield. Baseball expertise: Baseball and ethnicity; 19th century baseball. His interests are in 19th century baseball, neighborhood ball and immigrant participation. Grzymala is a member of the 19th Century Committee and Negro Leagues Committee.

Written works include "Baseball and Ethnicity: A Case Study of German-Americans in Buffalo, NY, during the 19th century."

Baseball/SABR Highlights & Memorable Experiences: Presenter at 1998 convention.

He has been married for seven years to Hiromi and has a newborn daughter, Ayano. He is a teacher and is working on his Doctorate degree. Hobbies include writing, neighborhood coaching and researching.

ROBERT GUAGLIARDO, born Sept. 13, 1956, in Brooklyn, NY. Joined the SABR in December 1997. His membership was a gift from his late mother-in-law who knew his deep love of the game. Baseball interests: Umpires, rules and their evolution, ballparks, the Yankees, and late 19th/early 20th century players.

Written works: Monthly column in *On the Base Paths*, "The View in Blue."

Baseball/SABR Highlights & Memorable Experiences: Has been a player in the Richmond Men's Senior Baseball League since 1992. Has held every officer position including commissioner, treasurer, secretary and president in the league and was editor of *On the Base Paths* for two years. Biggest thrill was hitting a triple off the fence against his old team, with the manager who traded him playing third base in his first game against them. Currently an umpire for high school and local amateur baseball leagues.

JOHN GUILFOYLE JR., born July 12, 1961, in Queens, NY. He joined SABR in 1990 and is a member of the Ballparks Committee. He attended his first game at Yankee Stadium in 1968 and has been to over 100 since then. He considers himself an expert on the stadium. His most memorable day was Mickey Mantle Day in 1969. Guilfoyle recently visited the Baseball Hall of Fame and the stadium's Monument Park for the first time.

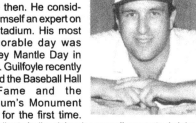

He collects ballpark books as well as seats, bricks, photos, postcards, etc. He is still bitter about the 1994 strike and occasionally has nightmares about the Yankees playing in New Jersey.

Guilfoyle and Barbara have three children: Katherine (12), Colleen (11) and John (7). He coaches Little League and plays softball three times a week. Guilfoyle is a police officer in Nassau County, NY.

WILLIAM F. GUSTAFSON, born May 20, 1926, Chicago, IL. He was one of the original 16 to join SABR and belonged to the Lefty O'Doul Chapter. His expertise is pre-WWII baseball. Wil-

liam has held the office of national vice president. He has many written works. Memorable experiences were the 1971 and 1996 reunions.

He is divorced and has a son William, daughter, Mrs. Mary Ann Sawyer, and three grandchildren: Shane Gustafson; Matthew and Kevin Sawyer. Retired Professor, Dept. of Human Performance, San Jose State University. He is still going and enjoys popular music.

JEFF HALE, born April 29, 1962, in St. Marys, Ontario, Canada, site of the Canadian Baseball Hall of Fame and Museum. He joined SABR in 1991 to increase his knowledge about a game that he has always adored. As a baseball writer for the London (Ontario) *Free Press*, Hale covered the now-defunct London Tigers of the Class AA Eastern League from 1991-93. He has also reported on the American League Championship Series of 1989, 1992 and 1993 and covered the World Series in 1992 and 1993. A life-long fan of the Cincinnati Reds, Hale counts interviewing Johnny Bench in 1989 as a hallmark of his baseball life. He is currently a member of the editorial board at *The Free Press*.

H. EDWARD HAMALAINEN, born Dec. 8, 1925, in Detroit, MI. Joined the SABR in 1983 due to his interest in baseball. Currently a member of the Fred Smith Chapter.

Has attended the Detroit Tigers fantasy camps every year since 1995. He does not play but receives a uniform and all the goodies that come with it. At the last banquet he received the new Tiger dugout jacket with his name embossed on right front chest for attending five fantasy camps.

Met Mr. William Rogell in 1997 and sat with him at the banquet. Had picture taken with him, had 8x10 made and mailed it to him. Received it back in one week, autographed, plus baseball cards from Rogell's playing days. This past winter he autographed a ball for Hamalainen, "1935 World Series Champs." Eldon Auker also signed it.

Has a dozen baseballs autographed every year of all the Tiger players, plus former Tiger players, who attend the Tiger alumni dinner, like Ned Garver, Virgil Trucks and J.W. Porter. He mailed Hamalainen one of his playing days cards.

Hamalainen has attended SABR conventions since 1984 except for 1985. He is not a writer like many of the members but enjoys their writings that are published in various SABR books.

His wife, Rose Mary, died Sept. 15, 1991. They had two sons, Edward J. and Richard P. Hamalainen retired from Chessie System R.R. after 34 years as switchman.

REX DANIEL HAMANN, born Oct. 21, 1957, in Madison, WI, and currently lives in Milwaukee, WI. He became a SABR member in 1996 in order to foster his various baseball interests, including the history of baseball in Milwaukee and Wisconsin, ballparks, the Chicago Cubs and the Minor Leagues. Hamann's ultimate baseball fantasy is to build a replica of Borchert Field, home of the former American Association Milwaukee Brewers.

Hamann is currently doing research on the 1943 Milwaukee Brewers, and is pursuing his interest in the inaugural year of Milwaukee County Stadium and the 1953 Braves. Long range projects include a comparative analysis of the Chicago Cubs, a biographical work on the life and career of former Cub Phil Cavarretta, and a statistical compilation of the American Association Milwaukee Brewers. He has a particular interest in the geography of baseball, tracing the geographical paths, from birth to death, of the players of his favorite teams. He has written *The Evolution of Location: Wisconsin Minor League Cities, A History in Maps*, 1902-1996, unpublished.

Hamann is a teacher in the Milwaukee Public Schools. Hobbies include baseball memorabilia and truck restoration. He has earned his master's degree.

TOM HANRAHAN, born Dec. 21, 1960, in Hawthorne, NJ. Joined the SABR in March 1998 as an outlet for exchanging information and research. Baseball expertise: Statistical analysis. Baseball interests include scoresheet baseball (fantasy/simulation). Evaluating players and what makes teams win.

Written works: Three articles in the *Baseball Analysts* in the 1980s. *Platooning Groundball/Flyball* in February 1999 BTN. Unpublished work on *Catchers - Defense Improves With Experience.*

Baseball/SABR Highlights & Memorable Experiences: Going to Fenway Park on his honeymoon.

He and his wife, Janet, have three children: Sara (13), Ashley (11) and Justin (9). He is a weapons system analyst for the U.S. Navy. Hanrahan serves as a church elder with many teaching and preaching duties.

ED HARTIG, born Jan. 28, 1965, in Blue Island, IL. Joined the SABR in 1992 for research exchange and network with other baseball fans. Expertise/interest(s): Chicago Cubs and Wrigley Field. He provides historical research for the team's publications, media guides, etc. He also writes for *Vine-Line* (the Cubs' monthly newspaper) and gives tours of Wrigley on weekends when the team is on the road. Hartig is a member of the Ballparks and 19th Century Committees.

Baseball/SABR Highlights & Memorable Experiences: In general he enjoys providing historical research and then seeing it put to good use. He has helped writers from the *Chicago Tribune, Chicago Sun-Times, ESPN: The Magazine, Sports Illustrated, The Sporting News,* a handful of books, and even a couple of TV/video productions.

Hartig has been married for almost nine years to Gail Lynn Hartig and has two children, Alex (3) and Maddie (newborn). He is employed as a research statistician with Nalco Chemical Company in Naperville, IL.

EDWARD (TED) HATHAWAY, born July 14, 1961, in Minneapolis, MN. He joined SABR in 1988 when the SABR National Convention was in town. In addition to writing essays and articles on baseball for SABR and other publications, he has devoted most of his energies to the Bibliography Committee's *RBI - Research in Baseball Index,* an electronic catalog to baseball literature. Hathaway first proposed the project in April 1990. He has since been co-director and principal director of the project, responsible for the development of cataloging tools, attracting and training of volunteers, cataloging literature for *Research in Baseball Index,* and the sale and distribution of the database.

Hathaway has been married to Pam Haiden since 1985 and has a daughter, Julia. He is a reference librarian for the Minneapolis Public Library.

THEODORE M. HAUSER, born June 3, 1943, in Alton, IL. Joined the SABR in 1995 to further his interest in baseball. He is currently a member of the Kansas City Chapter. Baseball expertise: Minor League stadium projects; Minor League research; and economic impact studies. His interests include the history of baseball and Minor League baseball.

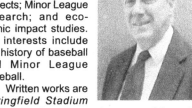

Written works are *Springfield Stadium Project, Eastern Kansas League* and *Impact of Minor League Baseball.*

Baseball/SABR Highlights & Memorable Experiences: Attending SABR conference and regional meetings.

Hauser is married to Dr. Karen Hauser and has eight children: Jennifer, Christopher, Erika, Mathew, Shad, Elizabeth, Andrew and Trudy. Employment in city planning and city management in Iowa, Kansas and Missouri. Hauser's hobbies are meteorology, political science, tornado research and astronomy.

STEVEN H. HEATH, born Jan. 10, 1943, in Salt Lake City. Joined the SABR due to his interest in baseball history. Baseball expertise: Walter Johnson and Babe Ruth pitching games.

Baseball/SABR Highlights & Memorable Experiences: Talks on Babe Ruth's pitching games at Hofstra University Babe Ruth Conference.

Heath is married to Donna and has four children and six grandchildren. He is a professor of mathematics at Southern Utah University. Hobbies include reconstructing past baseball games.

MONTE HESS, born July 7, 1930, in Fresno, CA. He has been a rabid baseball fan from the time his uncle took him to see the Oakland Oaks play a game at the old Emeryville ballpark in 1939. With the help of his friend, Fred Imhof, Hess increased the size of his baseball library in the early 1960s from a few books to a roomful of material, including a collection of *The Sporting News* dating back to 1929. His interests include the early days of baseball, the players rebellion of 1890 and the game's relationship to antitrust law. He has written the article *In Defense of Justice Oliver Wendell Holmes and Good Baseball* and is working on a book covering the same antitrust issue.

Hess is a retired city planner. He and his wife, Kay, have been married 40 years. They have five children: Theresa, Greg, Mark, Jennifer and Scott; and, to date, five grandchildren.

J. THOMAS HETRICK, born Sept. 22, 1957, in Ft. Belvoir, VA. Joined the SABR in 1987 for research networking. Currently a member of Bob Davids Chapter, Baltimore-Washington. Baseball expertise: 19th century. His interests include expansion Washington Senators, especially 1968-71. Member of the 19th Century and Bibliography Committees.

Hetrick has written *MISFITS! The Cleveland Spiders in 1899* and *Chris Vonder Ahe and the St. Louis Browns.*

Baseball/SABR Highlights & Memorable Experiences: Witnessing a triple play in Washington, D.C.

He is married to Mi Ae and has one daughter, Alicia (5). Employed in electronic security. Noteworthy accomplishments: Finally convincing his father to take him to a game at age 10.

TOMMY D. HILL SR., born June 25, 1949, in Bucyrus, OH, but has lived in Upper Sandusky, OH, all his life. He has been a baseball krank all his life so what better organization to belong to than SABR. He is on the 19th Century and Pictorial History Committees. Tom and his wife, Marnie, enjoy collecting baseball and Civil War memorabilia. They have been married for 30 years and have two sons, Stephen (29) a student

at Ohio State doing his Master's in dietetics and Tommy Jr. (27) a police officer in Ontario, OH. Hill has been included in two published books about 19th century baseball by David Nemec. He also had an article about tips on dating old photographs sent in to SABR. Hill has worked for the Ohio Dept. of Transportation for 28 years and is looking forward to his retirement.

GEORGE WOODMAN HILTON, bought *The New York Times* to read on the bus from New York to Cooperstown, and discovered in it that SABR had been founded the previous day. He joined immediately, being one of the second wave who followed the founders into membership. His reason for going to Cooperstown was work on what became his *The Annotated Baseball Stories of Ring W. Lardner 1914-19*

(Stanford: Stanford University Press, 1995), which won *The Sporting News*-SABR Baseball Research Award for the year.

Hilton is professor emeritus of economics at UCLA where he once taught an interdisciplinary course, Baseball in American Society. A White Sox fan, he noted in 1959 that Bill Pierce had set the club record for victories by a left-handed pitcher, a fact that he brought to Bill Veeck's attention. On Dec. 11, 1964, as a shareholder in the Milwaukee Braves, he introduced the resolution for retirement of Warren Spahn's numeral, 21.

WESTON HINES, born Jan. 6, 1960, in Exeter, NH. He joined SABR in the summer of 1983 to build upon his lifelong passion with others who love baseball. He is currently a member of the Kansas City Chapter where he has lived for seven years. Hines loves 20th century baseball history, baseball statistics and prefers following many Major League teams.

He has written one article submitted to the SABR research library, which discusses the pros and cons of whether Roger Clemens was worthy of his multi-year contract upon signing with the Blue Jays, and he has several unfinished projects. The highlight of his SABR experience was attending the Kansas City National Convention in 1996.

His baseball hobbies include reading and taking pictures at major league games. Hines graduated from Southwest Missouri State University in 1988 with a MBA degree. His hobbies include golf, bowling and photography. Hines is single.

LOWELL I. HINKLE, born July 26, 1936, in Toledo. Joined the SABR in March 1997 because of his lifelong interest in baseball. Currently a member of the Roger Bresnahan Chapter in the Toledo area. Baseball expertise: Started baseball pitching career in 1950 with Monclova, OH, Little League and had a record of 15-3. Highlights were pitching in the eighth grade against two adult teams, the Federation Team-Metcalf Oil and against the Blissfield, MI, American Legion team. Named to the All Ohio Baseball Team 1954 and was Anthony Wayne High School's Most Valuable Player, 1954, with a pitching record of 18-1. ERA-1.12. Attended Washington Senator's Rookie Baseball Camp in Winter Garden, FL, after high school graduation.

Pitched for seven years on class AA Federation teams. Pitched for McMacklin Buick in the Ban Johnson League, Collinsville, IL. Worked out under the direction of Joe Becker, manager of the Charleston Senators and later pitching coach for the LA Dodgers.

On Feb. 20, 1999, he was inducted into the first Anthony Wayne High School, Whitehouse, OH, Hall of Fame.

Baseball/SABR Highlights & Memorable Experiences: Meeting Mel Parnell at SABR convention in Louisville.

Hinkle is married to Shirley and has three children: Lisa, Lori and Luan; and has seven grandchildren: Justin, Jeremy, Jordan, Jenae, Haley, Tyler and Evan Lowell. Employed with the Bostwick-Braun Co. as vice president/director of transportation until his retirement in December 1997. Hobbies include baseball memorabilia and attending games.

FR. JOHN HISSRICH, born Feb. 21, 1960, in Pittsburgh, PA. Currently a member of Forbes Field Chapter. Baseball interests include Pittsburgh Pirates, ballparks and World Series.

Fr. Hissrich is parochial vicar at St. John Vianney Parish. Hobby: Collecting hobbies.

JAMES PHILLIP HOLL, born April 7, 1931, in North Canton, OH. A SABR member since 1986, Holl was weaned on Minor League baseball as a Knot Hole Gang youngster watching the old Columbus Red Birds where his heroes were Preacher Roe and Johnny Antonelli. He is an active member of the Minor Leagues Committee where his research efforts have included a published book, *The Canton Terriers 1936-1942,* and contributory articles to the *Journal of Minor League History,* the *Minor League Register* and the *Encyclopedia of Minor League Baseball.* Holl is also active in the Jack Graney Regional Chapter where he enjoys biographical research on Minor League and Negro League players and teams in Ohio and currently has an obsession with finding out whatever happened to Bade Myers and Peggy Moore.

Holl, a recently retired urban planner, resides in North Canton, OH, with his wife, Pat. They have two grown children, Jeff and Jenni.

CHARLES H. HORNE, born Sept. 22, 1933, in Mexico, ME. Joined the SABR in 1972 (1972-78; 1981-present) for exposure to knowledgeable baseball people. Current regional group: Southern New England Chapter (mailing list). Baseball expertise: Trivia (on the decline). His baseball interests include trivia/anecdotes, chronology, and statistical analysis.

Written works are a baseball crossword quiz book (1977) and Baseball's *You Could Look It Up* (1973).

Memorable experience: As co-host of weekly radio talk show (1977-78).

Married Marlene May 24, 1969. Currently retired after 27 years as purchasing agent for HVAC Service Co. His hobby is golf. (Nothing noteworthy about his golf game!)

SCOTT HORSTMEIER, born Aug. 30, 1970, in Cincinnati, OH. Joined the SABR in 1998 because of his love and support of baseball. Currently a member of the Cincinnati Chapter. His mentor is Matthew Evans. Baseball expertise: Negro Leagues and Cincinnati Reds. His interests include anything dealing with the game. Horstmeier is a member of the Records, Biography and Negro Leagues Committees.

Ever since he can remember he has loved baseball. He was fascinated with the mystique of the players, the smells and sounds of the game and the competitiveness it instilled. When he was little the neighborhood kids would play every day all summer long. Even though he did not have a lot of natural ability for the game he would still play and envision himself in "The Show" doing wonderful things. He can remember his first "real" baseball game. It was at Riverfront Stadium to see the Reds and the Cardinals. He even got to sit down in the blue seats, the first section on the field. He was amazed and can still see images from the game that he carries with him and holds dear.

He still loves the game, even to the point where most people don't understand why. The game has enraptured him and always will.

Horstmeier is single and is a teacher with the Mt. Healthy City Schools. Hobbies include sports, reading, traveling and history.

RALPH L. HORTON, born Oct. 16, 1921, in St. Louis. After graduating from Southeast Missouri State College, he served in the Navy for four years in WWII and two years in the Korean War, rising to the rank of commander. He began a 35-year career in the sporting goods industry with the Rawlings Sporting Goods Company in 1952. While at Rawlings he was responsible for introducing the Gold Glove Awards in 1957. A SABR member since 1976, he served on a number of committees and wrote several articles for SABR journals. After retiring from *The Sporting News* in

1986 he started Horton Publishing Company which reprinted old baseball guides and record books. He is the author of *Baseball's Best Pitchers* and *Rating Relief Pitchers.*

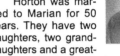

Horton was married to Marian for 50 years. They have two daughters, two granddaughters and a great-grandson. Horton passed away on Oct. 28, 1998.

THOMAS D. HUFFORD, born Sept. 13, 1949, in Radford, VA. He was one of SABR's 16 founding members in Cooperstown, Aug. 10, 1971, and served the organization as secretary in 1976. Hufford's interests are biographical research, Minor Leagues, Latin American baseball, umpires, coaches, the Appalachian League and the Atlanta Braves. While in college, Hufford worked for his hometown Pulaski Phillies, and was their ballpark organist in 1972. He was president of the Atlanta Braves 400 Club (booster club) in 1991-92 and was a consultant to the Braves as a member of the Atlanta Stadium Design Team during the design of Turner Field.

Hufford graduated from Virginia Tech with a degree in architecture and urban planning. He and his wife, Nan, live in Marietta, GA. Hufford mixes his hobbies of baseball and genealogy. Two of his cousins, Bert Hamric and Ed "The Pitching Poet" Kenna, were Major League players.

DAVID P. HULLINGER, born Jan. 31, 1928, in Berwyn, IL (Chicago). He joined SABR in 1992 to see if he wanted to be a member. His expertise is 19th and early 20th century rules, fields and equipment. He is especially interested in pitching distances and pitchers who hurled at more than one distance. Although not a trivia buff, he is fascinated by off-beat trivia. Hullinger is the author of *Ball Park Numbers,* a random walk through a baseball season in which no games were actually played because of a postulated players' lockout: All things were equal. (It also postulates a third Major League.) It was discovered that it's easier to win a pennant than to finish at .500! Other written works include *Mediocrology* and *Casey Exegesis.*

Hullinger denies being a statistician. He is a retired mechanical engineer, with no hobbies but reading, writing and arithmetic. He is widowed with two grown sons, Paul and Andrew, and one grandson, Isaac.

WILLIAM HUMBER, born Sept. 9, 1949, in Toronto. A SABR member since 1978, was the first Canadian board member (1982). His childhood memories are of Maple Leaf International League games. His major interest is Canadian baseball and among his 10 books to date are *Cheering for the Home Team: The Story of Baseball in Canada* (1983), *Diamonds of the North: A Concise History of Baseball in Canada* (1995) and *All I Thought About was Baseball* (1996).

He helped organize the Toronto SABR Conference in 1981 and was subject knowledge specialist to the Royal Ontario Museum's baseball show in 1989. Since 1979 he has taught Baseball Spring Training for Fans at Seneca College. It provides a forum for baseball talk without the pressure of academic evaluation. In 1998 he led Seneca's 20th annual trip to Cooperstown for 50 dedicated fans.

He and his wife, Cathie, live in Bowmanville, Ontario with their three children: Brad, Darryl and Karen. Humber is chair of technology at Seneca College in Toronto.

CHARLES L. HUNNICUTT, born June 12, 1938, in Sulphur, OK. Joined the SABR in 1996 because he is a die-hard baseball fan. Currently a member of the South Carolina Chapter. Baseball expertise: General knowledge. His interests include 1960-70 Pittsburgh Pirates.

Baseball/SABR Highlights & Memorable Experiences: A very close cousin pitched many years for Pirates, Padres and White Sox.

Hunnicutt is married to Yvonne and has two children, Carrie and Sarah. He is employed by Lockheed Martin as vice president and general counsel. Hobbies: Sports nut and reading.

JOHN R. HUSMAN, born June 16, 1942 in Toledo, OH. He joined SABR in 1982 to learn more about baseball and is a member of the Roger Bresnahan/Mudhens Chapter in Toledo, OH. His mentor is Fred Ivor-Campbell; his expertise is in the New York Knickerbockers, Daniel Adams, early rules, J. Lee Richmond, and perfect games. His interests are in 19th C baseball, civil war and pre-1871 baseball, 19th C in general and Worcester National League.

He enjoys research on 19th C, biographical and ball parks and is chairman of the 19C Committee. John has written about 20 articles in various periodicals. His memorable experience was bringing vintage base ball to SABR conventions. John is the founder of Great Black Swamp Frogs BBC (1860 rules re-creation team, president 8 years) and founder and first president of the Vintage Base Ball Association (VBBA).

John and wife Sandy have two children, Marianne and Michelle, and two grandchildren, Sophia and Isabelle.

JOSEPH GORDON HYLTON, born May 29, 1952, in Pearisburg, VA. Joined the SABR in 1986 for a source of sophisticated information. Baseball expertise: Legal history and 19th century. Member of the 19th Century and Business of Baseball Committees.

Written works: *Jackie Robinson and American Civil Rights Laws*, Marquette Sports Law Journal 1998.

Hylton is married to Monica Walker and has four children: Veronica, Joseph, Elizabeth and Caroline. He is professor of law, Marquette University; director of National Sports Law Institute in Milwaukee, WI.

JOHN F. INFANGER JR., born in Chicago, IL, Nov. 16, 1936. Retired from AT&T Co. with a little over 30 years service. A dedicated bachelor.

Joined SABR in 1991. Raised in a large family of baseball fanatics, he has been reading and watching baseball all of his life. Presently has a library which includes over 500 baseball books. He also has hundreds of baseball publications and thousands of newspaper articles. Has accumulated 16 file cabinet drawers of baseball "notes." In the past couple of years he has written an occasional baseball article. Two have been published in *Oldtyme Baseball News* (three others are pending).

Infanger is a member of the Emil Rothe, Chicago SABR Chapter. Through correspondence with baseball authors and responding to SABR-ites with "research needs," he has met a large number of fine people. A voracious reader, his baseball books represent about 20% of his library.

ERNEST S. (ERNIE) INFIELD, grew up during the Great Depression on a farm near Wooster, OH. He became interested in baseball by reading a sample copy of *The Sporting News*. He saw many Cleveland Indians games during the prewar period.

Volunteered for the U.S. Marine Corps during WWII. Member of the Fourth Marine Div. (Marshalls, Saipan, Tinian and Iwo Jima). Top combat experience was witnessing the flag raising on Iwo Jima. Wrote for the division paper. Formed a regimental baseball league from scratch and covered the games with a daily report. Following the war he and four others (now deceased) formed the Wayne County Hot Stove League, which spawned a Little League. He also formed an independent countywide basketball league and served as its coordinator. After 20 years as a sales executive he became director of news services for The College of Wooster where he pioneered the forming of The Downtown Rebounders, a large basketball booster's club. Became interested in SABR through correspondence with Bob Davids. Joined in 1977. Became close friend of the late Gene Murdock. Began writing weekly column, "Ramblin' Round The Infield," for the *Wooster Daily Record* in 1951. Won a number of national awards for publications produced at the college. Elected to Wayne County Sports Hall of Fame in 1980. Named a newly formed conference of Div. III colleges in 1985 (North Coast Athletic Conference). In 1994 the community honored him with a special day, only the second Wooster citizen to be so chosen. Followed Bob Feller's career closely, furnished Feller with game-by-game record of his career and built a sizable baseball library.

Despite three open heart surgeries he continues to operate a farm and write a weekly column. He and wife, Emily Kuhles, were married in 1947. Their daughter, Linda, now Mrs. Mark Wakefield, resides in South Euclid, OH, and has a small son, Jared. Infield is a member of the Jack Graney Chapter.

ALMA LUCY IVOR-CAMPBELL, born March 11, 1937, in New Bedford, MA. Joined the SABR in 1993 because she enjoyed the annual conferences with her husband and family rate dues were initiated. She is a member of the Southern New England (Lajoie/Start), Rhode Island Chapter. Baseball interests are 19th century, current Red Sox and vintage baseball games.

Baseball/SABR Highlights & Memorable Experiences: Seeing Yaz get 400th home run, visiting and touring New Camden Yards and researching baseball history at Cooperstown with her husband. Annual conference highlights: Tour of Metrodome in Minneapolis (1988), the first Seymour Medal event (1996) and performance of *Matty* (1998).

Married to Frederick Ivor-Campbell. She is a library staff member, currently head of circulation at a university library.

FREDERICK IVOR-CAMPBELL, born in 1935. His first baseball research led to brief biographies of Pete Reiser and Larry Doby for a junior high English class, but over three decades passed before he again researched the game.

With Cliff Kachline's encouragement he joined SABR in 1981 and at John Thorn's invitation he wrote his first SABR article for the 1985 *National Pastime*. Since then he has contributed to numerous SABR publications and several baseball and biographical encyclopedias, including *Total Baseball* and *Biographical Dictionary of American Sports*. He chaired SABR's 19th Century Committee from 1992-98 and since 1991 has compiled *Nineteenth Century Notes*, the committee's oft-cited newsletter. As general editor of *Baseball's First Stars* he earned one of The Sporting News-SABR Awards for 1996. From 1992-96 he was a SABR director and in 1998 was elected SABR's vice president.

He and his wife, Alma, were married in 1957.

HERBERT HENRY JOHNSON, born July 1, 1918, in Plainfield, NJ. Joined the SABR in 1976 for conviviality-fellowship. Member of the Southern Florida Chapter. His mentors are Fred Lieb and Larry Ritter. Baseball expertise: Minor Leauges, Baseball Records, Biblography and baseball in Europe. His baseball interest is European baseball with favorite being "Italian Cuban Series" in Italy. Johnson's written works include numerous articles in *Int'l. Herald Tribune* and *Rome Daily American*.

He is single and has one son, Larry Bracken, who attends Pensacola Junior College in Florida. Self-employed, 45 years in Paris, France - international insurance.

It always happens that he is stimulated and euphoric as a fan and sometime reporter for the Italian Baseball Press and the Italian Baseball Federation (Intl.) of Rome, Italy, in observing Italian baseball. The Italian baseball culture is much different than the American. They tend to root for the player not teams. They will readily jeer a hometown boy if he makes an obvious error. Day games begin at 4 p.m. ... nothing may interfere with the Italian dinner hour, noon to 3 p.m. Night games start at 7 p.m. or 8 p.m. Fine restaurants prevail at most all Italian stadiums! The parks are quite modern with average attendance from 3000 to 4000. A great rivalry is Turino-Milano (geographical neighbors). With an 80-game schedule they possess a 23-man roster. Each team is allowed three non-Italians. They produce Americans, Canadians, South Americans and other Europeans. Fans are very volatile and passionate.

MARK L. JOHNSON, born in September 1932 in Newman Grove, NE, (near Richie Ashburn's hometown of Tilden, NE). He joined SABR in 1997 after reading about SABR in the *Baseball Collector* magazine. He is currently a member with the Halsey Hall Chapter in Minneapolis. He fell in love with baseball after reading a comic book in the 1940s about Mel Ott and during this period drove to Lincoln to see Connie Mack's Phila-

delphia team and to Omaha to see Eddie Dyer's St. Louis team in exhibition game action. He will be attending and scoring his 1000th major league game this summer, has caught nine foul balls and has a collection of more than 600 baseball books.

Johnson has been married to Thelma for 41 years. They have three daughters and seven grandsons (two short of a baseball team). He is retired from Augsburg College and residential real estate.

STEPHEN JOHNSON III, born in April 1950 in Oberlin, OH. He joined the SABR in 1992 to learn more about the game and enjoy fellowship with other baseball fans. He is currently a member of the Jack Graney Chapter in Cleveland, OH. His mentors include Fred Schuld and Larry Gerlach. He is an expert on the career of umpire Charles Frances Berry and has a general interest in umpires. He also enjoys biographical and historical baseball books. He is on the Umpires and Rules Research Committee as well as the Bibliography Committee and is an officer-at-large with his local chapter. His written works include *Umpires of the 1928 and 1929 Seasons*, as yet unpublished. He enjoys attending National Conventions. His most memorable experience is of a chapter tour of Jacobs Field under construction.

Johnson has been married to Mary Ann for 21 years. They have two daughters, Courtney (16) and Sarah (14). He is the director of bands in the Oberlin, OH, school district. His hobby is collecting baseball books.

W. LLOYD JOHNSON, born Jan. 23, 1951 in OKC. He is an established baseball historian, writer and consultant. He formed a baseball information, research, consulting and mail list company called Double Play in July 1992. He is currently editing the *Complete Book of the Negro Leagues* (Hastings House), compiling George Brett hit data for Year of Sports and leading the database project of professional player statistics for the Museum of Minor League Baseball, located in Memphis, TN, two blocks from famous Beale Street.

Johnson also writes books. Recently published works are the *Total Baseball Catalog* and the *Baseball's Book of Firsts*. Other works include *Baseball: A Pictorial Tribute, The Minor League Register, Who's Who in Baseball History,* and the *Encyclopedia of Minor League Baseball*, second edition. Other books included *Baseball's Dream Team* (second edition), *Unions to Royals: The Story of Professional Baseball in Kansas City, The Baseball Timeline* and portions of *The Whole Baseball Catalog, Total Football* and *Who's Who in African-American History*. The *Encyclopedia of Minor League Baseball* won the prestigious SABR-Macmillan Award for the year's best baseball research book. It was also nominated for the Casey Award, best baseball book of the year. The current *Baseball's Book of Firsts* was a "pick of the week" by Amazon.com for sports books and the subject of an extensive radio publicity campaign.

Formerly the executive director (1985-89) and president (1991-92) of the Society for American Baseball Research (SABR). He chaired the SABR National Convention in 1996. Between stints with SABR, Johnson, along with John "Buck" O'Neil and Larry Lester, founded the Negro Leagues Baseball Museum (1989) and served as its first director and executive director (1989-92). He also brought the RBI program (Revitalizing Baseball in the Inner City) to Kansas City in 1992. Johnson served as a paid consultant for Florentine Films on Ken Burns' Baseball documentary, shown around the country on PBS.

As senior research associate (1985) for the National Baseball Hall of Fame and Library, Johnson helped to found the Leather Stocking Base Ball Club town ball team. The Club has been chronicled in *Sports Illustrated* and on *The Today Show*. He has also worked as a consultant for ABC-TV on the Pete Gray story entitled, "Quitters Never Win," for the Kansas City Parks and Recreation Department; the Johnson County Historical Museum; the Show-Me Baseball Camp in Branson, MO; and the Veterans Committee of the Baseball Hall of Fame.

For seven years (1987-93), Johnson taught a class on baseball history at the University of Missouri at Kansas City. Guest speakers for the class included baseball author and historian, Bill James; Kansas City Royals radio broadcaster, Denny Matthews; Negro League historian, Phil Dixon; Tom Heitz, the librarian at the National Baseball Library of the Baseball Hall of Fame and famed Negro League raconteur John "Buck" O'Neil.

He and his wife Connie have two sons, Shaun and Christopher, and one granddaughter, Kay Leigh.

RICHARD W. JULINE, born March 21, 1915, in Warren, PA. He joined the SABR in 1973 and is currently a member of the Allan Roth Chapter in Los Angeles. He has been a baseball fan since the mid-1920s. He has attended three SABR National Conventions: San Diego, Louisville and Burlin-game; and made presentations at the former two. He has had articles published

in the 1974 and 1997 *Baseball Research Journal*, and has presented several papers at Allan Roth SABR quarterly meetings. He is now embarked on compiling a book on *Pennant Winning Playing Managers*.

Juline has been married to Mary for 59 years as of July 6, 1999. They have three daughters: Annette, Kathryn and Jane; a son, Jeffery; seven grandchildren; and one great-grandson.

Juline is a retired salesman, editor, publisher, statistical analyst and accountant. He managed an amateur baseball team in the Sunset League in Warren, PA, in 1934. A graduate of the University of Michigan, 1938. He has been an editor for the *Haysco News* in Erie, PA, and *Export-Import News* in Los Angeles. A former owner of Llewellyn Publications in Los Angeles where he published and edited books, among which was *The California Quarterback* (1962), a record book on all California university and college football teams. He now resides in Stanton, CA. His hobbies are baseball research, Fantasy baseball and football. In his spare time he has devoted 54 years in community activities with the Lions service clubs where he has resided.

CLIFFORD KACHLINE, born in Quakertown, PA, Cliff began his journalistic career at age 20 with the nearby *Bethle-hem Globe-Times* in 1942. Later that year he became sports editor of the *North Penn Reporter* of Lansdale, PA. The following April he went to St. Louis to join *The Sporting News*, then known as *The Bible of Baseball*. He spent 24 years there as a writer and editor. During much of that period he re-

searched and wrote most of the material appearing in the annual *Official Baseball Guide*.

Cliff left TSN in April 1967 to become public relations director of the North American Soccer League. Two years later he was named historian of the National Baseball Hall of Fame, a position he held through 1982. A founding member of SABR, he served as its first executive director from 1983-85. He and his wife Evelyn have been married 50 years and have two daughters.

FRANK (BUD) KANE, born Nov. 29, 1929, in St. Louis, MO. Joined the SABR in 1982 after reading an article in *Sporting News*. Hooked on baseball at age 7 when his uncle began taking him to Sportsman's Park for Browns and Cardinals Sunday double headers. He is currently a member of the St. Louis Bob Broeg Chapter. His mentors are Bob Broeg and Jack Buck. Baseball expertise: Browns and Cardinals history and World Series history. Kane's baseball interests include baseball history, ball parks and rules. He is a member of the Umpire and Rules Committee and has served as secretary of Bob Broeg Chapter. He is a charter member and treasurer for the St. Louis Browns Historical Society.

Written works include an article in *The National Pastime* about the first St. Louis night game and a column, *Raisin' Kane* for the Browns Fan Club newsletter.

Baseball/SABR Highlights & Memorable Experiences: Meeting Connie Mack and attending various SABR conventions. He was especially impressed with visiting the site of League Park and Ray Chapman's grave in Cleveland.

Kane is married to Jane Ellen and has eight children, 12 grandchildren and one great-granddaughter. He retired after 40 years in the trucking business. Hobbies: Visiting kids, life member of VFW and Korean War Veterans Association He and Jane live in Webster Groves, MO.

MARK FRANKLIN KANTER, born May 8, 1956, in Trenton, NJ. Joined the SABR in 1985 because he has had a love of Major League baseball ever since Jim Bunning pitched his perfect game against the Mets on Father's Day in 1964. SABR provides him with the opportunity to exchange ideas on baseball history and statistics. He has had the opportunity to do original research and present it at National Conventions and local regional meetings. His research has also been published in the 1997 *Baseball Research Journal* for which he is grateful.

Kanter is currently a member of Lajoie/Start Chapter of Southern New England and Casey Stengel Chapter of New York City, NY.

Baseball Expertise: He played Little League baseball as a child and continues to play softball in an adult league. His interests include history, Philadelphia Phillies, statistics - "competition evaluation" and trivia. Kanter is a member of the Statistical Committee.

His written works include "What Has Divisional Play Wrought?" in the 1997 *Baseball Research Journal*.

Baseball/SABR Highlights & Memorable Experiences: Being published in the 1997 *Baseball Research Journal* and having his name and the title of his article on the cover of the 1997 *Baseball Research Journal*. Being a member of the 1997 and 1998 SABR Team Trivia Champions.

Also being a member of the 1985 Southern New England/Rhode Island Team Trivia Champions. Being at the 1993 and 1983 National League pennant clinching games for the Philadelphia Phillies.

Kanter is married to the former Lynne Frances Glickman who is also a member of SABR. He has worked for the Naval Undersea Warfare Center in Newport, RI, as an industrial/ergonomics engineer since 1984.

ADAM KATZ, born April 26, 1982, he has been a baseball fan as long as he can remember. His favorite team is the Florida Marlins, despite the fact that he has lived in San Francisco his whole life. He is also an Oakland A's fan, but he decided that he wanted to be a fan of a franchise since they started, hence the Marlins fixation. His favorite player is the ex-Mr. Marlin, Jeff Conine. As you can see, he is the anti-bandwagon fan, and is disappointed with the current states of his favorite teams. There is a light at the end of the tunnel, but with both teams threatening to move, it just may be an oncoming train. He joined SABR this year and has learned more than he could have imagined, mostly through the daily SABR-L digest on the Internet. You can email him at adam@neglekt.lick.pvt.k12.ca.us.

LAWRENCE S. KATZ, born March 26, 1947, in Detroit, MI. He joined the SABR in 1983 because of his general interest in the game. He is currently a member of the Fred T. Smith (Michigan) Chapter and is a member of the 19th Century Committee.

Katz is the author of *Baseball in 1939: The Watershed Season of the National Pastime*, McFarland & Company, Inc., Jefferson, NC, and London (1995). His articles have appeared in *Sports Collectors Digest* (1989), SABR's *The Baseball Research Journal* (1990 and 1998) and SABR's *The Perfect Game* (1993).

In 1998 he performed the National Anthem with the Wayne Renaissance Choir at a Detroit Tigers baseball game at Tiger Stadium. He has been a featured guest on several television programs and has spoken to a variety of community and academic groups on the topic of baseball.

He is a biographee in *Contemporary Authors* (1997) and Marquis *Who's Who in American Law* (1996-97).

Katz has been a practicing attorney since 1973. He lives in West Bloomfield, MI, with his wife, Karen, and their two sons, Mitchel and Steven.

CHARLES KAUFMAN, born Dec. 31, 1952, in Dallas, TX. Joined the SABR in 1994 due to his appreciation of baseball history. His mentor is Fred Schuld. Baseball expertise: Playing careers of Bibb Falk and Tex Hughson. His baseball interest is collecting autographed or vintage memorabilia.

His written works include "Baseball Mastermind: Bibb Falk" in *The National Pastime* (1999).

Kaufman is married to Jennifer and has two children, Heather (15) and Brian (12). He is a

former newspaper editor/writer (16 years) and has been owner of Kaufman Communications since 1989.

TOM KAYSER, president, Texas League of Profession Baseball Clubs. Over the course of his 23 years in baseball, Tom Kayser has been involved in virtually every facet of the game since starting his career in Pittsfield, MA, in 1976 as the business manager of the "AA" Berkshire Brewers. Kayser became one of the youngest Minor League team owners when, at the age of 27, he purchased the Holyoke Club of the Eastern League two days prior to the 1980 season.

A 1974 graduate of Point Park College in Pittsburgh, PA, Kayser returned to Pittsburgh in 1981 as assistant Minor League director of the Pittsburgh Pirates, where he worked for Branch B. Rickey, currently the president of the Pacific Coast League.

Prior to his election as the president of the Texas League in February 1992, Kayser also worked for the Cincinnati Reds, Calgary Cannons and Rockford Ligntning of the CBA.

Since joining the Texas League, Kayser has been working on various research projects: the history of the Texas League All-Star game; the history of the Dixie Series; the 100 most interesting/historic games in Texas League history and a complete catalogue of all Texas League no-hitters.

Born in Hinsdale, IL, in 1952 Kayser is single and has lived in San Antonio since 1993.

GARRETT J. (GARY) KELLEHER, born Feb. 13, 1937, in Bayside, New York City. He joined SABR in 1983 and soon after began working on the first New York City regional, which was held in Shea Stadium in June 1984. This led directly to the formation of the Casey Stengel Chapter. Kelleher has written articles on Kid Gleason and Lou Gehrig that have appeared in SABR publications. He has also written articles about Bobby Doerr and, with his wife, Virginia, was a guest at Doerr's Cooperstown induction. Kelleher is also known for his New York Giants expertise. He resides in Suffern, NY, is an alumnus of Manhattan College, received a MBA degree from St. John's University and is a CPA. His son, Garrett, is a student at Holy Cross College, Worcester, MA. Kelleher is presently vice president, Finance, for Family Golf Centers, Inc. but looks forward to retirement in the very near future so he can once again give quality time to SABR as well as appear in theatrical productions (Passion II).

FRANCIS KINLAW, a SABR member since 1983, has authored articles which have been published in yearbooks and programs of professional baseball clubs, newspapers and magazines. He also reviewed books about baseball for the *Greensboro News and Record* for six years and authored poems which appeared in the *Flatbush Faithful*.

Mr. Kinlaw provided oral presentations at SABR National Conventions in 1987 and 1997, and has contributed to two popular books and three of SABR's convention publications. He is an active member of three Research Committees with SABR: Ballparks, Pictorial History and Business of Baseball.

Mr. Kinlaw resides in Greensboro, NC, and has been a member of the SABR Carolina Chapter since he and others organized it in 1985. He is also a student of the history of college basketball and football, and has written extensively on these subjects.

RICH KLEIN, born June 11, 1960, in Hackensack, NJ. He is currently a member of the Hall-Ruggles Chapter. Baseball expertise: Trivia and sports cards. His baseball interests include trivia, sports cards and memorabilia.

Written works appear in *Beckett Almanac of Baseball Cards & Collectibles* (co-editor of all three editions).

Baseball/SABR Highlights & Memorable Experiences: Two time Trivia Team Champion.

Klein is single and is a baseball book editor with Beckett Publications.

MERL FREDRIC KLEINKNECHT, born April 13, 1940, in Crestline, OH. He joined SABR in 1971. His area of expertise has been the Negro Baseball Leagues. John Holway has exerted the greatest influence on Kleinknecht's research efforts. He enjoys collecting baseball statistics. His most memorable experiences include meeting Negro League players at SABR conventions.

Kleinknecht is a founding member of the SABR Negro Leagues Committee and served two terms as committee chairman in the 70s. He has had articles published in a variety of publications. His research efforts have been recognized by the Ohio Baseball Hall of Fame and the SABR Negro Leagues Committee.

Kleinknecht has been married to Bonnie for 38 years. They have two grown sons, Jon and Derek, five grandsons and a granddaughter. He is retired from the U.S. Postal Service with 37 years service and currently compiles and publishes high school sports record manuals.

TED KNORR, BR, TL, born March 17, 1951, in Pittsburgh, PA, raised in and longtime resident of Lancaster, PA, currently resides in Harrisburg, PA. His daughter, Ellen Marie, turned 9 Sept. 20, 1998. Employed by the Commonwealth of Pennsylvania as an economic development analyst.

Lifelong baseball fan ever since his grandmother bought him a Brooklyn Dodger uniform. Fantasy baseball buff since cutting teeth on spinner baseball (Cadaco-Ellis), graduated to APBA Major League Baseball Game in 1962. Attended all five National APBA Conventions. Thought he was the greatest baseball trivia expert in world until he was humbled at his first SABR convention; still cocky enough to claim supremacy in central Pennsylvania. Favorite teams are the Pittsburgh Pirates, Pittsburgh Crawfords and the Harrisburg Giants.

SABR member since 1981; attended his first National in '84. Has attended a dozen nationals and many regionals. Member of Negro League Research Committee. Principal organizer of the SABR Negro League Committee Conference held in Harrisburg in August 1998. After 25 years of regionals, this was SABR's first "Topical" with a keynote speech, player panel, trivia contest and 12 research presentations all devoted to the field of Negro League baseball. Approximately 100 attended some of the events with 55 researchers registered.

HERM KRABBENHOFT, born in Detroit the same day Zeb Eaton hit a pinch grand slam for the Tigers. Joined SABR in 1981. In 1986 he founded *Baseball Quarterly Reviews* which provides authoritative reports and comprehensive summaries of in-depth baseball research on topics of historical interest and statistical significance. His research endeavors have included the most complete study on leadoff batters, extra inning homers, Babe  Ruth (the pitcher) vs. Ty Cobb (the batter), Warren Spahn vs. Stan Musial, President George Bush's baseball career at Yale, Hall of Fame pitchers vs. Hall of Fame pitchers, ultimate clutch hitters, etc.

Krabbenhoft has received the Macmillan-SABR Baseball Research Award twice: (1) in 1991 for *Baseball Quarterly Reviews* and in particular for his ground-breaking research on ultimate grand slam homers, which presented the complete story for those relatively few players who hit a bases-loaded home run in the last of the ninth inning to overcome a 3-run deficit and catapult their team to a dramatic victory; (2) in 1995, in collaboration with fellow SABR member, Jim Smith, for the *Baseball Quarterly Reviews* Triple Play Project, which documented every triple play in major league history.

Krabbenhoft has given many presentations on his research at SABR meetings, including 14 SABR National Conventions. A member of SABR's 19th Century, Statistical Analysis and Baseball Records Committees, he has contributed many items to their newsletters. In addition, his research has been published in *Baseball America, The Sporting News, Baseball Digest, Baseball Weekly, USA Today* and several newspapers across the country.

An industrial research chemist (PhD degree, Michigan in 1974—Go BLUE!) with numerous U.S. patents and scientific publications, Krabbenhoft and his wife, Patti, and daughters, Mary and Jean, attended the game where Nolan Ryan gained his 300th career victory.

STEVE KRAH, born Dec. 22, 1963, in South Bend, IN. Joined the SABR in 1994 because of his all-around baseball and history interest. He is a member of the Michiana/Lou Criger Chapter. Baseball expertise: Played nine years as a boy, including high school. His baseball interests include Lou Criger, dead ball era and Philadelphia Phillies.

He wrote an article entitled "The Limestone League" which appeared in *The National Pastime.*

Baseball/SABR Highlights & Memorable Experiences: Attending SABR 27 in Louisville and starting Criger Chapter in 1998.

Krah is single and is a sports writer for *Elkhart Truth.* Hobbies: Music. He has been awarded the Indiana Baseball Coaches Award three times.

RON KRAMER, born Oct. 17, 1946, in Pittsburgh. He joined the SABR in 1996 and is currently a member of the Forbes Field Chapter. Baseball expertise: 50s and 60s. His baseball interests include *Sporting News,* guides, registers, films, cards, etc.

Kramer is married to Donna and has one son, Bryan. He is a consumer loan specialist and Three Rivers Stadium usher.

TONY LAMONTE, born May 24, 1948, in Houston, TX. Joined the SABR in 1987 because of his love of baseball. He is currently a member of the Houston Chapter. Baseball expertise: On 1964 Colt League W.S. Champions and two years of college baseball. His baseball interest is in the LA Dodgers. Lamonte is a member of the Ballparks Committee.

He and his wife, Diane, have three children: Chris (23), Eric (20) and Lori (16). Employment as an engineer for Reliant Energy for 27 years. Hobbies: Collects baseball memorabilia, cards, publications, autographs and books.

JAY LANGHAMMER, born May 3, 1943, in Shreveport but has since lived in Omaha, Detroit, Dallas and Fort Worth. He joined SABR in the early 1980s and is in the DFW Hall-Ruggles Chapter. After earning a radio-TV degree from TCU he spent four years in the Air Force and six years in broadcasting. Since 1977 he has sold convention exhibits for Freeman Exhibit of Dallas. Langhammer has written sports features for many national fraternity magazines and collects books and cards. His greatest baseball experience was attending a 1985 Yankees fantasy camp in Fort Lauderdale.

Langhammer's wife, JoAnne, is an elementary school teacher and his 19-year-old son, Jeff, attends University of Texas at Arlington. Langhammer compiled Major League players lists for Southwest and Big 12 conference media guides and has written features for the Big 12 championship program.

HERVÉ F. (FRANK) LAPEYRE, born April 9, 1947, in Paris, France. He came to the USA in 1960. Graduated from Western High School in Washington, D.C. in 1965. He fell in love with baseball during his high school days.

In 1966 he went back to France and became a social worker.

In 1978 he founded a baseball club in Tours. Since that time he has worked with the French Baseball Federation.

In 1988 he joined SABR to learn more about the game. His mentor was Matts Novak. In 1990 he wrote the only book on baseball in French. He started in 1996 a SABR France section. Currently he is working on a book on French baseball history.

Lapeyre has been married to Janine for 27 years. They have four children: Yann (27), Frank (22), Kevin (16) all baseball players and a daughter, Corine (26).

He works as a social worker with young delinquents in Tours. His hobbies are sports, books and travel. He will be happy to receive any SABR members who wish to visit France.

RICHARD SPENCER LAWRENCE, born on the eve of the Great Depression, Nov. 27, 1929, in Chicago, IL. In 1933 the family moved to southern California. While listening to the 1941 World Series he became a devout Dodger fan. In 1958 his DREAM came true when the Dodgers came west to Los Angeles and he was at the Los Angeles Coliseum for that first historic game against those hated Giants.

In 1982 he joined SABR in order to maintain a closer connection to the history of THE game. When he retired in 1989 he relocated to San Jacinto, which is equal-distance between beautiful Dodger Stadium and "The Q" in San Diego. He is a member of the Ted Williams Chapter in San Diego. His most memorable moment in baseball came on Aug. 7, 1988, when he and his youngest son, Grayson, completed their tour of all 26 Major League ballparks; their quest took seven years to complete. Known as "Dodger Dick" to his baseball friends, he enjoys collecting baseball books and corresponding to other baseball addicts.

He has been married to Sweet Marie for 44 years; they have four adult children: three boys and a daughter.

JAMES L. LEEFERS, born Oct. 20, 1955, in Carlinville, IL. He joined SABR in 1994 out of his love for baseball and the desire to learn more of its history. He is a member of the Bob Broeg Chapter in St. Louis, MO. He is a lifelong St. Louis Cardinal fan and is also interested in the Hall of Fame and baseball records. He enjoys the monthly meetings of the Bob Broeg Chapter where the Hall of Fame sportswriter regales his fellow members with his vast storehouse of anecdotes and knowledge.

Leefers has been married to Tina (a Lou Brock and Todd Zeile fan) for 20 years. They have two sons, Adam (16) who wants to be a Major League umpire and Matthew (11). He is a draftsman for a small agricultural manufacturing firm. His hobbies include collecting baseball cards and memorabilia.

MEL LEHAN, born in May 1944 in Vancouver, B.C. Canada. As a youth his interest in keeping statistics on his Vancouver Mounties PCL team led local baseball radio announcer, Jim Robson (now in the Hockey Hall of Fame), to hire Lehan to assist him in broadcasting away games. In those days of the early 60s, away games were re-created through the use of tele-type machines transmitting the pitch-by-pitch situation, and  through prerecorded crowd and bat sounds on newly invented cassette tapes re-creating the ballpark atmosphere.

At that time the Vancouver Mounties were the farm team of the Baltimore Orioles. Lehan has maintained a 40-year love affair with his Orioles. He flew to Baltimore in 1995 to see Cal Ripken's 2131 game and in 1998 after contracting cancer he had the wonderful experience of meeting and playing catch with Cal at spring training.

Through the years his love of baseball and

its stats and history has always been a part of his life. He has accumulated thousands of baseball books and artifacts with an emphasis on statistics. Now that he is retired, he joined SABR and hopes to assist in creating a thriving local SABR chapter. Another hope is to put together a complete all-time register of Triple A Vancouver Mounties and Vancouver Canadians baseball players with their stats and records.

Lehan has been a public school teacher and a neighborhood and community organizer for the past 30 years. For this activity he has been honored as Kitsilano's "Good Neighbor of the Year" and "Citizen of the Year." He and Barbara have been married for 27 years and have three wonderful daughters: Shaina (20), Kathleen (17) and Mira (11).

LARRY LESTER, one of the country's leading authorities on the Negro Baseball Leagues. His second book on the subject, *The East-West Game: Black Baseball's National Showcase* is to be published by the University of Nebraska Press.

His first book, in collaboration with Dick Clark of Ypsilanti, MI, simply titled: *The Negro Leagues Book* (1994), is billed as "the most complete collection of information on baseball's Negro Leagues ever published." Lester serves as co-chairman of the Negro Leagues Committee for the prestigious SABR in Cleveland, OH.

As one of the original founders of the Negro Leagues Baseball Museum in Kansas City, MO, he served as their research director and treasurer for four years. Lester was instrumental in the development of their licensing program that has become the Museum's primary source of revenue. He also wrote the hang tag information that adorns caps and jerseys in shopping malls across America.

He served as the Museum's senior editor for their quarterly newsletter *Silhouettes,* and their annual yearbook *Discover Greatness!.* The Museum's first major exhibitions were developed from Lester's personal collection of photographs, news clippings and memorabilia. Likewise, Lester developed the traveling Negro League exhibit that showcases each year at Major League Baseball's FanFest during All-Star Week since 1993. A comparable exhibit has unveiled at various museums across the country and is sold-out by Smith-Kramer Fine Art Services through the year 2001.

His writings on African-Americans have appeared in *The National Pastime, Biographical Dictionary of American Sports, American National Biography, The Ball Players, World Book Encyclopedia* and the *Dictionary of American Negro Biography.* Recently, he wrote three dozen biographies for Major League Baseball web page; *www.majorleaguebaseball.com,* which included a special section on Jackie Robinson's 50th Anniversary of breaking baseball's color barrier. His comprehensive life history of Jackie Robinson's journey became part of the New York Mets Opening Day Program in 1997.

Other works include his photographs on General Mills' 75th Anniversary of the Negro Leagues *Wheaties* box (1996). Also the development of the only CD-ROM on the subject, *The Negro Leagues Dream Teams,* by Computerized Educational Resources (1995).

Lester has been a contributing researcher for several books on black baseball, including: The

Biographical Encyclopedia of the Negro Baseball Leagues (1994), *The Negro Baseball Leagues: A Photographic History* (1993), *The Negro Leagues: 40 Years of Black Professional Baseball* (1993), *When the Game Was Black and White* (1993), *Playing America's Game: The Story of Negro-League Baseball* (1993), *The Forgotten Players: The Story of Black Baseball in America* (1993), and several other publications, including the 1997 Official Major League Calendar and the 1998 Baseball Calendar by Pomegranate.

Lester has made appearances in the following films: *Behind the White Foul Lines* (1991) by CNN, *Ain't Seen Nothin' Like It Since* (1994) by PBS, *Outside the Lines: A League Second to None* (1994) by ESPN, *No League of Their Own* (1995) by NBC, with contributions to HBO's *Journey of the African-American Athlete,* Ken Burns' *Baseball* documentary, along with hosting numerous player panels.

Lester campaigns annually for worthy Negro League players for induction to the National Baseball Hall of Fame in Cooperstown, NY, through his company NOIRTECH RESEARCH, INC. He and his wife, Valcinia, and their daughters: Tiffany, Marisa and Erica Joi, live in Raytown, a small community outside of Kansas City, MO, where he can be reached via email: BuletRogan@aol.com.

LEONARD (LEN) LEVIN, born March 4, 1931, in Providence, RI. Joined the SABR in 1977 because of his interest in baseball history. Currently a member of Southern New England (Lajoie-Start Chapter). Baseball expertise: Rhode Island teams and Boston Red Sox. His interests include attending games and researching. He is a former National secretary and presently chairman of the Regional Chapter. He has had many articles in the newspaper (his former employer). Winner of Bob Davids Award in 1997.

Levin is married to Linda and has two children, Sara and Rachel. Employed as editor, Quincy, MA, *Patriot Ledger.*

DANIEL R. LEVITT, a SABR member since 1983, has only recently begun to enjoy the full benefits of the association through attendance at the National Conventions. Levitt is a past president of the Halsey Hall Chapter in Minnesota and actively participates on the chapter's 19th century historic baseball club, the Quicksteps. His interests include statistical analysis and baseball records: he is a member of both research committees.

As published in the 1996 *Baseball Research Journal,* Levitt considers his most valuable research contribution the discovery that Ferdie Schupp deserves recognition as the single season ERA record holder for his 0.90 ERA in 1916. Levitt lives with his wife and son in suburban Minneapolis.

DICK LEYDEN, born May 21, 1943, in Washington, D.C. Joined the SABR in 1994 to be part of a nationwide research group. Currently a member of the Larry Gardner Chapter (Vermont). Baseball expertise: Baseball cards, Vermont baseball history and pre-1900 baseball. His interests include baseball as played before 1920 and St. Louis Cardinal history.

Leyden is a contributor to *The Green Mountain Boys of Summer* and is a writer of two as yet

unpublished books, *A Leper in the Bleachers* and *The Complete History of the Northern League* (Vermont-New York-Canada).

He is a baseball artist as well as doing wildlife and portrait art. Hobbies: Organic gardener and fly-fisherman.

MARK LIEBERMAN, born Aug. 28, 1948, in Brooklyn, NY. Joined the SABR circa 1983. Why he joined SABR: Sabermetrics. Baseball interests include statistics, Joe Jackson and Rotisserie.

Lieberman is married to Candace and has two children, Charles and Rachel. Employed as senior vice president Dime Savings Bank of New York. He is a trustee of Brooklyn Public Library.

JOHN LIEPA, born Feb. 26, 1945, in Oldenburg, Germany. Joined the SABR in 1987. Why he joined SABR: Professional historian who loves sports history (where else would he go?). His mentors are Lou Gehrig, Roberto Clemente and Jackie Robinson. Baseball expertise: 19th century Iowa baseball, Calvin McVey and Iowa and the Minor Leagues. Liepa is a member of the 19th Century Committee.

Written works include papers presented on Calvin McVey - Iowan and 1869 Red Stockings and 19th century Iowa baseball.

Baseball/SABR Highlights & Memorable Experiences: Guest of George Steinbrenner - Yankee Stadium (1995); Mattingly's last home game; and three-hour interview with Buck O'Neil.

He has been married to Dianne for 28 years and has one son, Torey (22) and one daughter, Hillary (18). College professor (28 years) Des Moines Area Community College. Member of History Society of Iowa; life-long runner (18 marathons; 2:41 P.R./22 years - never missed a day). Collects historic newspapers "Dewey Defeats Truman," "Lincoln Assassination," etc. He also collects 19th century baseball cards.

THOMAS LILEY, born Sept. 29, 1948, in Topeka, KS. Joined the SABR in 1989. He is married to Nancy and has one daughter, Noël. Liley is a college professor.

KEN LIPSHEZ, an administrator in the Eastern League for eight seasons (1981-88), was born in 1952 in New Haven, CT.

Lipshez was an administrative aide for the West Haven (Connecticut) A's in 1981. In 1983 he was director of public relations for the Waterbury Reds. He moved to the Glens Falls (New York) White Sox in 1984 where he was the assistant general manager, prior to becoming general manager of the Glens Falls Tigers throughout the club's existence (1986-88).

Lipshez, who earned a journalism degree from Southern Connecticut State University in 1982, turned to sports writing in 1991. He wrote in Bristol, CT, until 1995 when he became an Eastern League beat writer in New Britain for the New Britain Rock Cats. He is an occasional contributor to *Baseball America.*

He is currently researching the history of Minor League baseball in New Britain which goes back to 1884.

Member of SABR for two different terms, first in 1984 but allowed membership to lapse in 1988. Was member of Northeast New York Chapter. Rejoined in 1996.

He and his wife, Lisa, have been married for nine years. He has one son, Jason (12) and a stepson, Jason (16). Employed as sports writer for *The New Britain Herald*. Hobbies: American history (with particular interest in Theodore Roosevelt, his life and times), classic movies and television (interests include James Cagney, Errol Flynn, Charles Laughton and the TV show "Bonanza").

MARIO LONGORIA, born Jan. 10, 1948, in San Antonio. Joined the SABR in 1991. Reason for joining: Baseball history & research. Baseball expertise: U.S. born Latino Major League players. His interests include biography, 20th century and Mexican-American players. He is a member of the Latin America Research Committee.

He has written numerous articles about Latino athletes in collegiate/pro football, Olympics, boxing commentary, collegiate/Major League baseball. In particular, articles about Oakland As' Horacio Pina, New York Yankees' Celerino Sanchez and the defunct Southwest Conference baseball.

His articles have been published in Latino publications *Nuestro* (D.C.), *ProMex Sports* (San Antonio) and *Primera Fila* (sports supplement - *New York Daily News*).

In 1997 his research on Latino pro football athletes was published by the Bilingual Press at Arizona State University. The book is titled *Athletes Remembered: Mexicano/Latino Professional Football Players, 1929-1970*.

To date he has nearly completed the manuscript on the biography of the first U.S. born Latino Major League player. He is Vincent Nava, who caught for the Providence Grays (1882-84) and the Baltimore Orioles (1885-86). Nava's historical significance is equal to Cuban born Major Leaguer Esteban E. Bellan (1871-73). The two were the first Latinos in organized baseball.

Baseball/SABR Highlights & Memorable Experiences: The camaraderie and help from SABR members.

He is married to Noemi R. and has four children: Cynthia, Marisol, Gerald and Gabriel; and one grandson, Desmond. Employed by the United States Automobile Association Insurance Co. as a training instructor. He collects sports books/magazines on Latino athletes.

ANGELO J. LOUISA, PHD, born near Bridgeville, PA, Oct. 12, 1951, earned his BA degree, magna cum laude, in history from Saint Vincent College in 1973; his MA degree in early modern European history from Duquesne University in 1975; and his PhD in Tudor-Stuart English history from the University of Minnesota in 1985. Since 1973 he has taught at the college and university level for 16 years (1973-79, 1982-88 and 1994-present), served as the assistant to the Minnesota state director of the National History Day program for four years (1979-83) and was the executive and financial director of *The College Football Statistics Quarterly* for six years (1988-94). Highlights of his career include being named

to *Outstanding Young Men of America* in 1981, receiving the Outstanding Teacher of the Year award from Metropolitan State University in 1986 and publishing 58 biographical entries in *The Harper Encyclopedia of Military Biography* in 1992.

A baseball fan since the age of 4 and a SABR member since 1984, Dr. Louisa is new to the field of baseball writing. His first contributions were biographical entries on Christy Mathewson and Cy Young (along with one on Chris Evert) for *The Encyclopedia of Sport in American Culture*. He is currently working on two articles on baseball managers, and is interested in biographical research, statistical analysis, the Hall of Fame and the Pittsburgh Pirates.

Dr. Louisa is married to Pamela Acre and resides in Omaha, NE, where he is a faculty member in the department of history at the University of Nebraska at Omaha.

DOUGLAS B. LYONS, of Scarsdale, NY, born Sept. 29, 1947, in New York City is the co-author of *Out of Left Field*. A SABR member since 1996 he is interested in odd facts, such as home plate weddings; plaques, monuments, statues, etc., to ball players; baseball-related license plates; ball players in halls of fame besides Cooperstown; ball players married to athletes; and ball players' odd off-the-field jobs. He is a member of the Casey Stengel New York City Chapter.

His most memorable baseball experience was sitting in the Yankees' dugout at Yankee Stadium. Lyons is a criminal lawyer.

WILLIAM H. LYONS, born March 5, 1947, in Fitchburg, MS. Joined the SABR in 1995 because of his interest in baseball history. Baseball expertise: History of the Boston National League Baseball Club. His interests include the history of professional baseball in New England and Minor League baseball.

Baseball/SABR Highlights & Memorable Experiences: Attending the three game series between the Atlanta Braves and Boston Red Sox at Fenway Park in 1997 and meeting Boston Braves outfielder Tommy Holmes and pitcher John Sain at the Boston Braves Historical Association dinner and program following one of the games.

He is married to Karen V. and has one daughter, Virginia L. Lyons Brown, and one son, Kevin M. Lyons. Employed as professor of law, University of Nebraska College of Law. Hobbies and noteworthy accomplishments: Collecting baseball books, other baseball memorabilia, reading, historical geology and bicycling.

JIM MALLINSON, born March 27, 1962, on Long Island, NY. A lifelong baseball history buff, he joined SABR in 1982 to gain more knowledge and to interact with others who shared similar interests.

For nine years Jim managed tournament teams and held several Board of Director posts in the Levittown Pony/Colt Baseball League. This was followed by two years in a similar capacity with the Floral Park Teenage League.

He has been a player in the 19th century re-creation Vintage Base Ball League of Old Bethpage, NY, since 1984 and was named manager of the "Bellmore Seminoles" entry in 1994.

He is the author of the A.G. Mills biography in SABR's *Baseball's First Stars*, has written for *Vintage and Classic Baseball Collector* magazine and was a sports columnist for the *Levittown Tribune* newspaper.

Mallinson's interests include collecting 19th century Victorian baseball trade cards, reading baseball history books and completing his partial card sets of the 1960s and 1970s. He has been married to Lori since 1992. They have one 5-year-old child named Jimmy who will be managed by his daddy in the upcoming "T-Ball" season.

JEFF MANDELL, born March 31, 1979, in New York City. Joined the SABR in October 1998 due to his passion for baseball. He is currently a member of the New York Chapter. Baseball expertise: New York Yankees, Mets, collectibles, cards and autographs 1980-99 and films. His interests include ballparks, cultural references, films, New York baseball, societal influences and getting Pete Rose into the Hall of Fame. Mandell is a member of the Ballparks Committee. He is single.

LARRY D. MANSCH, born Feb. 12, 1958, in Slayton, MN. He won 10 varsity letters in four different sports at Slayton High School, and won six more, including three in baseball, at Hamline University in St. Paul. He graduated from Hamline in 1980 with a degree in public administration, and then attended Creighton University's School of Law. For 14 years he has been the senior attorney with the public defender's office in Missoula, MT. He is also a judge advocate general in the Montana Army National Guard. In July 1999 he entered private practice in Missoula.

Mansch received a SABR gift membership from his brother-in-law, Bill Lamberty, in 1993. Together the two are planning the formation of SABR's Montana Chapter. A member of the Biographical Committee, Mansch is primarily interested in baseball in the deadball era. His mentors include Lawrence Ritter and Fred Schuld. He is the author of *Rube Marquard: The Life and Times of a Baseball Hall of Famer*, published in 1998, and hopes to complete projects on Tris Speaker, Jim Thorpe and Babe Ruth in the future.

Mansch has been married to Kim since 1987. They have four children: Bethany (10), Lincoln (9), Abigail (7) and Madison (5).

MARK G. MANUEL, born July 15, 1951, in Peoria, IL. He joined SABR in 1993 while beginning his research into the career of his grandfather, Mark G. "Moxie" Manuel. His interests include the Cotton States League, Southern Association, the Chicago White Sox and the Deadball era. He thoroughly enjoys SABR publications and SABR-L. He hopes someday to be able to meet Alaska's four other SABR members and to publish articles on ambidextrous players and

pitchers who have thrown double-header shut outs. His article *That Ball's on the Queer!* was published in the 1997 *Baseball Research Journal.*

Manuel has been married to Diana for 22 years and they have two sons, Caleb (16) and William (9). He is a guidance counselor at Kenai Central High School in Kenai, AK. He enjoys reading, especially about the Deadball era.

ALFRED (SKIP) MARCELLO, born March 19, 1932, in Columbia, PA. Joined the SABR in 1986 because he is in-

terested in anything about baseball. His mentor is Richard (Max) Bishop, his college baseball coach. Baseball expertise: The Major Leagues from the mid-1930s to the mid-1950s. His interests include the Minor Leagues. He is currently researching the career of Cecil Travis.

Baseball highlights: Attending his first Major League game at Shibe Park between the New York Yankees and the Philadelphia Athletics during the 1939 season. In attendance at Cal Ripken's record breaking game.

He has been married to Hilda Sue for 46 years and has one son, Doug and two granddaughters, Emily and Sarah. Marcello is a retired high school principal. Coached basketball and baseball and also was an athletic director. Hobbies and noteworthy accomplishments: Baseball is his hobby.

OWEN MARREDETH, born May 22, 1922. Baseball was discovered in 1932 in Waukegan, IL, when the Cubs won the National League. With a church group he saw a World Series game but was not one of the 150,000 who saw the Babe home run point. Suffered again in 1935, 1938 and 1945 ... still suffering. He never could hit so his only baseball claim was his dad who played semi-pro in the early 1900s. Many good players did not play pro as more money could be made with a steady job and playing usually on weekends. Stats are his game but only to bat around with friends. Years ago he tried to join the SABR but had no published data. His daughter, Gail, secured his membership about five years ago.

Marredeth is married and has three daughters. He says, "My dad's expertise died with him, but, if possible, my youngest daughter, Meg, is a baseball nut like dad."

KEVIN LEE MARSH, born April 29, 1966, in Torrance, CA. He joined SABR in June 1995 to enjoy fellowship with other baseball fans. He is currently a member with the Allan Roth Memorial Chapter in Los Angeles, CA. His general interests are in Minor Leagues, statistical analysis and ballparks. He has a large collection of photographs of Minor and Major League ball-

parks. His most memorable experience and noteworthy accomplishment was when he toured the country for 80 days in 1995, visiting 50 Minor League ballparks. He gave a speech and showed pictures about the 1995 trip at an Allan Roth Memorial Chapter meeting in May 1996.

He has also visited 28 Major League ballparks, 21 of them on baseball tours in 1990 and 1991.

Marsh has been married to Maria for nine months. He is a driver for a foster care agency.

JOHN M. MARTIN, born April 11, 1953, in Little Rock, AR. Joined the SABR in August 1998. He has a lifelong interest in baseball stemming from

his mother and aunt's deep interest in the game. He was taken as a child along to the local Minor League parks. It was at Traveler's Field in Little Rock that he discovered he was near-sighted when he couldn't read the scoreboard! He lived within a short distance
from the field and on summer nights, when not at the game, he could hear the cheers from backyard. He remembers climbing trees in the outfield to shag balls and see what he could of the game. He was at the game the night Richie Allen integrated baseball in Arkansas and remembers the tension, the protests and the excitement of that game and that season. He is currently compiling an all-time roster of the Little Rock team, from beginnings in 1895 to the Texas League club.

His interests include Minor Leagues, Southern Texas League and is beginning research on Cotton States League.

Martin is married to Kathy and has three children: Matthew (12), Sarah (10) and Kathryn (8). He is an engineer and formerly in transportation. Hobbies: Baseball and railroad historian, research and photography.

ALAN A. MAY, born April 7, 1942, in Detroit, MI. Joined the SABR in 1995 as student of games and statistics. He is currently a member of the Michigan Chapter. Baseball expertise: Fan. He is interested in the period 1945-55.

May is married to Elizabeth and has two children, Stacy and Julie, and two grandchildren, Carly and Katie. He is employed as an attorney at law. Hobbies: Collector.

ROBERT MAYER, born and raised within walking distance of the Polo Grounds and Yankee Stadium, where he caught baseball fever in the 1940s and '50s. He is a nostalgist whose articles in *Baseball Digest, The National Pastime, The Baseball Research Journal* and *USA Today Baseball Weekly* reflect those pre-expansion days. Reared on the Polo Grounds homers of Mel Ott, the tumult of Jackie Robinson's early days

and the Yankees' run of championships, Mayer came of age on Bronx street corners debating the merits of Willie, Mickey and The Duke. (His pick: Mays.)

After college and service in Korea, Mayer began a lifetime career as a teacher, guidance counselor and child study team consultant. He is currently employed as an educational consultant in New Jersey and is a coordinator of volunteers one day a week at a soup kitchen in New York.

Mayer jumped the Hudson River and settled in New Jersey after meeting Pat O'Brien, whom he married 30 years ago. They have two daugh-

ters, Pam, who teaches K-1 in New York City and Kara, a therapist. Their son-in-law, Dave, is a financial forecaster.

A former good-field, no-hit infielder, Mayer bats and throws right. He has two Polo Grounds seats and collects ballpark postcards, *Baseball Magazine* and a variety of sports ephemera.

ROBERT "SKIP" MCAFEE, born in December 1937 in New York City. He joined SABR in 1979 and is a member of the Bob Davids Chapter (Washington and Baltimore). His baseball interests include terminology, bibliography, indexing baseball books and baseball in movies. He has edited the newsletter of the Bibliography Committee since 1988, and is active in the Umpires and Rules, Nineteenth Century, and Women in Baseball committees. He was SABR treasurer (1987- 90) and developed the SABR policy manual. Since 1994, he has chaired the committee to select presentation paper awards at SABR National Conventions. He was editor of *The New Dickson Baseball Dictionary* (1999) and is a contributor to Research in Baseball Index (RBI) project.

McAfee is married to psychiatrist, Laurice, and has two daughters, Clancy and Megan. He was a member of the executive staff of three professional societies, including executive director of the American Society for Horticultural Science from 1988-93, at which time he retired. His hobbies are collecting baseball books, administering and umpiring in softball leagues and weightlifting.

ROBERT (BOB) MCCONNELL, born Jan. 18, 1925, in Seattle, WA. Has lived in Wilmington for 46 years. He is married to Mildred and has

two sons, Daniel and David, and three grandchildren. Power plant engineer (retired) with Delmarva Power & Light Company.

One of the founding members of SABR. Served as secretary-treasurer 1971-72; member of Board of Directors for 11 years; and first recipient of Bob Davids Award.

Presently on the following committees: Baseball Records, Bibliography, Biographical Research, Minor Leagues, 19th Century and Umpires & Rules.

McConnell is a member of the Philadelphia and Washington-Baltimore regional chapters. He has attended all, but one, National Conventions. Co-editor of *The Home Run Encyclopedia*; author of *Going For The Fences: The Minor League Home Run Record Book*; has written several articles for *The Baseball Research Journal*; and has contributed to many publications by SABR members.

JOHN MCCORMACK, born in Arlington, MA, May 21, 1917. New York City resident 1919-53; Dallas, TX, thereafter. Columbia College, Business and Law Schools graduate. Member Texas and New York bars. Texas Instruments retiree; handled its legal matters in 44 countries. Naval supply officer 1941-45. At Pearl Har-

bor Dec. 7, 1941. Married Catharine O'Brien in 1950 (she died in 1968); had five children. Married Janet Sachs in 1991.

Reared as a Giant fan. Polo Grounds moments: Hack Wilson tripling, 1924; John McGraw opening day, 1932; Carl Hubbell besting Cardinals 1-0 in 18 innings, 1933; Hub fanning American League sluggers in 1934 All Star Game; Mel Ott's final home run, 1945; and Bobby Thomson's blast winning 1951 playoff. Joined SABR in 1976. Member Hall Ruggles Chapter. Served as National vice-president 1984-85.

Expertise: 1920-41 Golden Age. His interest is in the game generally. Has been published in *The Baseball Research Journal, The National Pastime, The New York Times* and *USA Today Baseball Weekly*.

Hobbies: Tournament contract bridge, travel and reading.

DAVID MCDONALD, born March 24, 1947, in Barrie, Ontario. Joined the SABR in 1991 because of his life-long interest in baseball history. Baseball expertise: Canadian-born players and integrated baseball in 1800s.

Perhaps first writer to take a comprehensive look at the contributions of Canadian-born Major Leaguers in a series for the *Toronto Globe and Mail*, 1981.

Was writer for master of ceremonies, Donald Sutherland, at the 1982 Major League All-Star Game Gala in Montreal.

Wrote a first-hand account of top-level Cuban baseball for *The Canadian Review*, 1976.

Has written about the integration experiment in the International League in the late 1880s ("Jim Crow Comes North") for the Canadian baseball anthology *All I Thought About Was Baseball* (1996).

Has written about the black experience in baseball before Jackie Robinson (1997) and the career of Hack Wilson (1998) for the *Ottawa Citizen*.

Has contributed short items to *The Baseball Research Journal* and *The National Pastime*.

Employment as freelance writer, TV producer and broadcaster.

MADISON MCENTIRE, born May 26, 1968, in Marshall, AR. Joined the SABR in January 1992 because he loves baseball and reading. Baseball interests include general baseball history and trivia and historic ballparks. He is working on a baseball trivia book that he hopes to have published someday.

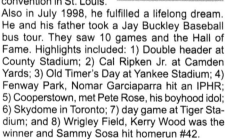

Baseball/SABR Highlights & Memorable Experiences: Attended 1992 SABR convention in St. Louis. Also in July 1998, he fulfilled a lifelong dream. He and his father took a Jay Buckley Baseball bus tour. They saw 10 games and the Hall of Fame. Highlights included: 1) Double header at County Stadium; 2) Cal Ripken Jr. at Camden Yards; 3) Old Timer's Day at Yankee Stadium; 4) Fenway Park, Nomar Garciaparra hit an IPHR; 5) Cooperstown, met Pete Rose, his boyhood idol; 6) Skydome in Toronto; 7) day game at Tiger Stadium; and 8) Wrigley Field, Kerry Wood was the winner and Sammy Sosa hit homerun #42.

He married Crissy June 8, 1991, and has a daughter, Mackenzie (2). McEntire is senior design engineer at Garver Engineers in Little Rock, AR. Hobbies: Reading, playing and umpiring softball.

WILLIAM EDWARD MCMAHON, born Sept. 25, 1937, in Chicago, IL. Because recommended in James' Abstract, he joined SABR in 1986 and is a member of Cleveland chapter.

A fan since 1946, he has played baseball through high school and coached Little League games. His interest is in the Cubs, 19th century, Minor Leagues. Research Committees are 19th century, Minor League and Retrosheet.

William has written articles in *Nineteenth Century Stars, Baseball's First Stars, Bill James Statistical Abstract, Encyclopedia of Sports Biography*.

Married to Mary Louise Owens and they have two children, Coleman and Elizabeth (Mrs. Morrill). A professor of philosophy at University of Akron and retired in August 1999. Hobbies include baseball history and memorabilia, naval history and stamp collecting.

WILLIAM F. MCNEIL, born Feb. 26, 1932, in North Attleboro, MA. Joined the SABR in 1994 for exchange of information. Baseball expertise: Dodgers, baseball in general. His interests include the Dodgers, Negro Leagues, Japan Leagues and pre-1960 Winter Leagues.

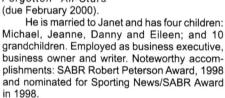

His written works are *Dodger Diary; King of Swat; The Dodgers Encyclopedia; Ruth, Maris, McGwire and Sosa; and Baseball's Forgotten All-Stars* (due February 2000).

He is married to Janet and has four children: Michael, Jeanne, Danny and Eileen; and 10 grandchildren. Employed as business executive, business owner and writer. Noteworthy accomplishments: SABR Robert Peterson Award, 1998 and nominated for Sporting News/SABR Award in 1998.

JOHN MCREYNOLDS, born in May 1944 in Modesto, CA. He grew up a fan of the Modesto Reds of the California League. As a high school right-hand pitcher he was a soft tosser. He remains a devotee of the Minor Leagues, of baseball in Latin America, of the Negro Leagues and of the San Francisco Giants. He is a member of the Allan Roth Chapter of SABR where his mentors are Karl Knickrehm, Joe Wayman and Fred Peltz. His research into Jackie Robinson cohort Nate Moreland won the SABR-Macmillan Award for 1997. An unabashed hero worshipper, McReynolds' biggest thrill was meeting Orlando Cepeda, Bill Weiss and Smokin' Joe Frazier, another big hitter.

McReynolds has been married to Barbara for 30 years. They have two daughters, Victoria (20) and Christine (17). McReynolds is a sports writer with the Santa Maria, CA, *Times* and a freelance writer and producer.

JOHN MCMURRAY, has been an active member of several SABR committees since he became a member of the organization. He currently directs the *Player Image Index* project for the Pictorial History Committee and he has also cataloged more than 800 articles to date for the Bibliography Committee's *Research in Baseball Index* project. McMurray has attended SABR National Conventions in Cleveland, Kansas City and in San Francisco. He enjoys the study of sports collectibles and has written many articles for publication on older baseball cards. Oral history is another great interest of his: McMurray has interviewed dozens of players from several different

eras and has written many *Where Are They Now?* articles about former Major Leaguers.

McMurray counts the study of baseball business issues and pictorial history research among his interests. He enjoys reading about early 20th century baseball and is a devoted fan of the Cleveland Indians.

DOUGLAS M. MCWILLIAMS, born Oct. 6, 1937, in Oakland, CA. Joined the SABR about 20 years ago because of his interest in history/ good publications. He is currently a member of the Lefty O'Doul Chapter/San Francisco Bay Area. His mentor is Dick Dobbins who taught him to love photography and baseball. Baseball expertise: Photography, Oakland As 1968-present comprehensive collection. His interests include

Oakland baseball history 1880s-present photos, roster, ephemera, etc. McWilliams is a member of the Minor League and Pictorial Committees. He has served as coordinator, convention publication 1998 at San Francisco.

Baseball/SABR Highlights & Memorable Experiences: 1) Collection of 30,000 plus color negatives of most all Major Leaguers 1969-89 has been accepted by The National Baseball Hall of Fame and Library; 2) photographer for Topps Baseball Cards, 1971-94 on the West Coast and Arizona (spring training); and 3) putting together the convention publication about Northern California baseball history in 1998. He was especially impressed with the willingness of writers to produce articles that he felt were needed. They are a wonderful bunch!

McWilliams has been married to Mary for 39 years and has two children, Susan and Evan, and three grandchildren: Hanna, Austin and Brandon. He was head of industrial scientific photography at the University of California from 1960-91 and is currently retired. He has a collection of complete run of Oakland A's uniforms.

J. JEFFREY MEDER, born May 16, 1951, in Columbus, OH. He is currently a member of the Pacific Northwest Chapter. Baseball expertise: History. His interests include the 1920s, '30s and '40s.

He and his wife, Debe, have two children, Josh (17) and Benjamin (15). Former CEO, Western Drug Distributors. For the past nine summers he and his best friend, Rick, have spent a week of vacation visiting Major League baseball cities. Their first trip was to Chicago.

During the suspended season of 1994 they spent the week in Cooperstown visiting the Hall and playing golf at Leatherstocking. He would vote their trip to Kansas City as the best. They were visiting the Negro Hall of Fame when they were introduced to Buck O'Neil. After a personal tour they took a side trip to the gravesite of Satchel Paige where Buck continued to tell them stories of the Negro Leagues. Then it was off to Buck's favorite barbecue joint, Gates and Sons. They ran into Buck at the Kansas City game that night. What a first-class guy.

RON MENCHINE, fell in love with baseball and ball parks the first time his father and grandfather took him to a game at Oriole Park in Baltimore. The year was 1939, he was 5-years-old and baseball was celebrating its 100th anniversary.

Fascinated with architecture, he began to write major and minor league teams asking for pictures of their stadiums. In the late 1940s, he started writing major league players to ask for autographs and nearly all of them replied with postcards. In those days before Baltimore had a major league team, he adopted the Orioles' affiliate, the Indians, as his favorite. Postcards sent to him by Indians greats like Mike Garcia, Bob Lemon, Bob Feller, Early Wynn and Al Rosen remain prized possessions to this day. He will never forget the thrill of receiving an autograph postcard from his boyhood hero, Lou Boudreau, in 1949.

He spent four years at the University of Maryland, where he laid the foundation for his future career by broadcasting Terrapin sporting events on campus radio station. For three glorious years, he chronicled the Washington Senators games on radio and was devastated when owner Bob Short moved the team to Texas following the 1971 season.

Memories with the team will be with him forever: pitching coach Sid Hudson introduced him to the finest restaurants in American League cities; introducing Del Unser and Bernie Allen to Maryland's hard-shell crabs; talking baseball with Hall of Famers Ted Williams and Nellie Fox; discussing finance with Jim Hannan; learning about snowmobiling from ace pitcher Dick Bosman; enjoying the antics of Eddie Brinkman, Jim French and Tim Cullen who always made Frank Howard the butt of their jokes; and laughing with Joe Grzenda.

As he traveled the country with the Senators, he was able to meet many top postcard collectors (John Sullivan, Frank Nagy, Dick Dobbins, Buck Barker, Ed Budnick, Ray Medeiros, Pat Quinn, Jim Rowe, George Tinker, Mel Bailey and many others) who helped him enhance his collection greatly and became good friends.

PHILIP M. MENEELY, born in Punxsutawney, PA, in 1953 and began listening to baseball during the Pirates' 1960 season. His love of baseball comes from Bob Prince, Bill Mazeroski and Roberto Clemente. He joined SABR in 1985 because of the Bill James Baseball Abstracts and his desire to learn from others who think about baseball daily. He contributed regular statistical columns for *Inside Sports* and wrote articles on relief pitchers and the effect of catchers on a pitcher's ERA in the *Bill James Newsletter* as well as an (unaccredited) article on teenage stars for the Seattle Mariners magazine. While a faculty member at the Fred Hutchinson Cancer Research Center in Seattle, he was asked by the Mariners to find Fred Hutchinson's uniform number for a "Turn Back the Clock" promotion of the Seattle Rainiers. He is a genetics professor in the biology department of Haverford College in suburban Philadelphia.

He and his wife, Debra, have been married for 19 years and have two children, Alison (17) and Andrew (14). Hobbies: Mystery novels and American history.

TONY MENENDEZ, born July 29, 1965, in San Juan, PR. His baseball interests are Latin America and Florida Marlins. Since 1988-present he has been baseball sportswriter and columnist of El Vocero de Puerto Rico.

Menendez is married to Maria Mercedes. Employed by Florida Marlins as season and group sales account executive.

ELDON H. MEYERS, born Jan. 13, 1937, in Ionia, IA. Joined the SABR in 1975 to learn more about the history of baseball and research being done now. Baseball interests include St. Louis Cardinals history and baseball autographs.

Meyers married Lynne in 1969 and has one daughter, Carmen (22). He is a retired middle and junior high school mathematics teacher.

COURT MICHELSON, born Jan. 30, 1952, in Chicago, IL, and grew up in Wheaton, IL. He joined the SABR in 1981. His hobby of gathering information concerning unusual records and occurrences in baseball culminated several years later (with the assistance of many SABR members and former players) in *Michelson's Book of World Baseball Records*. He has also written articles pertaining to sports  history, various baseball subjects and local history and is a contributor to *The Guinness Book of World Records*. His research on another former Wheaton resident, Red Grange, led to the inclusion in both the National and Illinois High School Sports Record Books of Grange's early football exploits. Michelson is a graduate of the College of DuPage and Aurora University. He played baseball in high school and in college competed in track and field as a sprinter. He was also a two-time state collegiate powerlifting champion.

Michelson lives in Naperville, IL, with his wife, Ruth, and sons, Eric and David. He is employed by the U.S. Postal Service and is a member of the Sons of the American Revolution.

BRUCE MILLER, born in Louisville, KY, Jan. 15, 1947. He graduated from the same high school as Pee Wee Reese and bowled in youth leagues at Pee Wee's Bowling Lanes. A professional engineering career has taken him coast to coast and to Germany. Stops included Williams, AZ, where he and then high schooler, Billy Hatcher, were named to the same all-tournament team and Severna Park, MD, where he coached future Minor Leaguer Scott Neuberger. He's been working on a book on racial prejudice and other shames in the rules for electing to baseball's Hall of Fame.

Miller and his wife, Martha, celebrated their 30th anniversary in June 1999. They have two sons, Ty (25) and Corey (21). His current position is head of natural resources and environmental affairs at the Marine Corps Air Ground Combat Center, Twenty-Nine Palms, CA. Besides baseball his hobbies include the Boy Scouts and horseback riding.

KENNETH B. MILLER, born Sept. 19, 1948. Joined the SABR in 1983. Baseball expertise: Games, simulations and software.

Baseball/SABR Highlights & Memorable Experiences: Played in 100th anniversary game of World Series and saw Mantle hit longest homerun of his career.

He is married to Diane and is president of Miller Associates. Former chairman, Cooper-Hewitt National Design Museum; member Smithsonian National Board; member, Board of Directors, American Libraries, American Library Association.

RAY MILLER, born Aug. 10, 1951, in Havertown, PA. His family moved to the Chicago area when he was 2, thus sealing his fate as a hard-core Cubs fan. He joined SABR in 1994 to pursue lifelong interests in baseball history and old ballparks. A resident of New England for the past 25 years, he has been active in the Southern New England Lajoie/Start Chapter in Rhode Island. He is especially interested in the history of the National League, MLB franchise histories, Major League uniforms and caps, and 20th century MLB stadia. He is on the Ballparks and 19th Century Committees. His written works include: "Pre-1900 National League Franchise Movement" (*The National Pastime*, #17, 1997); "Here's a Belated Salute to Four Old Ballparks" (*Baseball Digest*, September 1996); and "Great Clouts: Top Home Run Performances in America's Classic Ballparks" (*The Baseball Research Journal*, #26, 1997). His most memorable experiences to date have been attending the 1995 Cubs Convention in Chicago and the annual meetings of the Boston Braves Historical Association

Miller has been married to Paula Price since 1980. They have two children, Austin (12) and Hannah (9). He teaches Russian language and literature at Bowdoin College in Brunswick, ME. His hobbies include music (writing and performing) and he likes to collect baseball books, ball caps and ballpark photos.

TOM MILLER, born Jan. 9, 1951, in Somerset, KY. Long time resident of Kentucky, moved to Cincinnati after high school. Became interested in baseball from following the Big Red Machine in the early 1970s. He joined SABR in 1980.

He is interested in baseball records of all levels, biographical research and 19th century baseball. He is a member of Bibliography and Biographical Research Committees. He has done research on Rookie League leaders and yearly regulars at each position for all teams.

He collects baseball books and publications and plays computer baseball games. He has attended nine National SABR Conventions.

He currently lives in Dalton, GA, where he works for the Mohawk/Aladdin Carpet Mill.

Miller has been married to Judy for nine years. Other interests include traveling and science fiction.

MARK R. MILLIKIN, born April 16, 1951, in Baltimore, MD. He began playing in Little League, mostly at pitcher, by 1958 when he moved to Randolph, MA, a suburb of Boston. He saw his first Major League game in June 1961 at Fenway Park. As a boy his baseball idols were Ted Williams and Brooks Robinson. Topps baseball cards in 1958 and 1959 introduced Millikin to all the Red Sox and Major  League stars. Millikin and his family moved back to Baltimore in October 1962. He attended many Orioles' games at Memorial Stadium from 1963-69. During this time, Millikin read weekly issues of *The Sporting News* and became addicted to baseball statistics. Millikin's proudest accomplishment associated with baseball is the full-length biography he authored, "Jimmie Foxx: The Pride of Sudlersville," published by Scarecrow Press, Inc. in 1998.

Millikin graduated from Perry Hall High School (Baltimore County) in 1969 and received a BS degree from the University of Maryland, College Park in 1973. He received a MS degree in marine biology from the College of Charleston (South Carolina) in 1983.

He joined the SABR because he is an avid baseball fan and researcher. Currently a member of the Bob Davids Chapter. Baseball expertise: Baltimore Orioles, Jimmie Foxx, Home Run Baker and Brooks Robinson. His interests include biographies on baseball players and officials and baseball statistics.

Millikin is currently single and has one daughter, Melissa and one son, Luke. Employed as fishery biologist (1974-84) and fishery manager (1984-present). Noteworthy accomplishments: Certified Fisheries Scientist.

ANDREW MILNER, born March 7, 1968, in Norwich, NY. He joined SABR in November 1984 to study baseball statistics. He is currently a member of the Phila-delphia Chapter. His mentors include Cliff Kachline and Lloyd Johnson. His interests include baseball literature, the Phillies and baseball trivia. While a student at Syracuse University (class of 1990) he was a contestant on ESPN's "Super Bowl of Sports Trivia" quiz show. Milner has written for *The SABR Review of Books* and *The Cooperstown Review* and he has contributed to many reference texts. His most memorable SABR experiences include presentations at three SABR regionals and attending the 1989 and 1991 National Conventions.

Milner is single and is currently an editor at Surgent and Associates in Devon, PA. He also writes online for *sportsjones* magazine and is a critic for the Philadelphia *City Paper*. He lives in Bryn Mawr, PA.

MICHELLE MINSTER, born Aug. 10, 1982, in New Jersey. She joined SABR in 1997 after learning about it through an article in the local paper. She has been interested in baseball since 1994. She enjoys reading any books about baseball, especially biographical books and books about the Yankees, her favorite team. Last year she won an honorable mention in a Jackie Robinson essay contest sponsored by the Hall of Fame. Ms. Minster often attends games at nearby Yankee Stadium and it is her goal to one day visit every Major League ballpark.

Because she just recently joined SABR she has not yet had a chance to attend any National Conventions, but she hopes to do so soon. She also wants to get more involved in SABR activities.

She will graduate high school in 2000 and hopes to attend college and pursue a career as an actress.

DAVID H. MITCHELL, born Sept. 28, 1934, in Cherrydale, VA. Joined the SABR because of his lifelong interest in baseball. Currently a member of the Los Angeles Chapter. His mentor is Vic Pallos. Baseball interests include ballparks, Angels and original Washington Nats. Mitchell is a member of the Ballparks Committee.

Baseball/SABR Highlights & Memorable Experiences: Bibliography and collection of stadium books.

He is married to Joan and has five children: Susan, Dean, Carol, Colleen and Cynthia; and eight grandchildren. Employed as an aerospace engineer for 40 years. Hobbies: Travel, photography and YMCA.

DAVID HUGH (DAVE) MITCHELL, born Dec. 10, 1959, in Orlando. Joined the SABR in December 1995 to expand his knowledge of baseball. Baseball expertise: Years of watching and one season coaching Little League. His interests include the Minors (especially in Florida), spring training, Twins and Astros.

Baseball/SABR Highlights & Memorable Experiences: Hearing Buck O'Neil speak at '96 convention.

Mitchell is single. He is a graphic designer for a printing company and a freelance cartoonist. Hobbies: Collects baseball books/memorabilia and self-publishes comics.

LARRY MOFFI, born in 1946 in New York City and now lives in Silver Spring, MD. Educated at Southern Connecticut State University, Trinity College and the Iowa Writers Workshop. He is the author of *This Side of Cooperstown: An Oral History of Major League Baseball in the 1950s* (University of Iowa Press, 1996) and *Crossing the Line: Black Major Leaguers, 1947-1959,* (McFarland, hardbound, 1994); University of Iowa Press (paperback, 1996), as well as three collections of poetry.

Formerly assistant director for the Cracker Jack Old Timers Baseball Classic (1982-85), he served as managing editor of the *World of Baseball* book series (1987-89). Moffi presently makes his living as a freelance writer and editor, including serving as managing editor of *CommonQuest: The Magazine of Black/Jewish Relations.* He is presently working on a photography book on baseball around the world with photographer Geoffrey Clifford.

DAVID A. MOREAU, born Sept. 6, 1958, in New Orleans, LA. Joined the SABR in 1994 and is currently a member of the Arthur Schott/Pelican Regional, New Orleans Chapter. Baseball expertise: Head baseball coach, Jesuit High School since 1983. He is a member of the Ballparks Committee.

Baseball/SABR Highlights & Memorable Experiences: Attended final games of World Series since 1987.

Moreau is married to Rosalyn and has one stepson, Steven. He is head baseball coach and teacher at Jesuit High School.

ROBERT PATRICK MORRIS, born July 26, 1957, in Manhattan, New York City. Graduated from Rochester Institute of Technology, Rochester, NY, in engineering. Then moved to Dayton, OH, in 1982 to work for DOE at Mound Lab. Morris grew up to love baseball and wants to learn more about it so he joined the SABR in 1995. He still enjoys the 19th century and Negro League players. He is currently a member with Lee Allen/Waite Hoyt Chapter in Cincinnati, OH. He is working on William (Dummy) Hoy and Luther (Dummy) Taylor lifetime in baseball.

Morris has two sons, Jonathan (14) and Steve (13) and a daughter, Megan (11). Employment: Thaler Machine, CNC Machines. His hobby is collecting National pastime things, old baseball items, game used items and autographs of players.

RALPH C. MOSES, born Nov. 11, 1954, in Chicago, IL. Joined the SABR in 1988 to further his study of baseball history. Currently a member of Emil Rothe Chapter. Baseball expertise: Lou Gehrig, player rankings and Chicago Cubs. His interests include biographies, records, 19th century, Negro Leagues, Cubs, the 50s and 60s. Written works include articles on Bid McPhee, Roy Thomas and Vada Pinson published in *The National Pastime* and *Baseball Research Journal.*

Baseball/SABR Highlights & Memorable Experiences: He was at Wrigley Field in 1965 for Jim Maloney's no-hitter and in 1984 for Ryne Sandberg's greatest game.

Moses is married to Ann S. Walker. He is a licensed clinical social worker. Hobbies: Creating his own "baseball den" in his home.

MIKE MUELLER, born May 28, 1959, in Mt. Vernon, IL. Joined the SABR in 1985 because he can't get enough of baseball history. Baseball expertise: History in general. He is a 1983 journalism graduate from University of Illinois. Player/manager of Lakeland, FL, Tigers in Men's Senior Baseball League, 1989. Baseball interests: All (big Cub fan).

Written works include, *These Were Four Worst Teams in Major League, Baseball Digest,* March 1983 (his very first freelance article published).

Baseball/SABR Highlights & Memorable Experiences: Met Jack Brickhouse, 1983; caught foul ball (Nolan Ryan pitch) at Busch Stadium in May 1981.

Mueller married Denise A. Baker March 9, 1985. He has been a freelance writer/photographer since 1991. Hobbies: Aviation history, model planes. He has written/photographed about 30 automotive history books.

TIM MUELLER, born Oct. 2, 1967, in Upland, CA. Joined the SABR in June 1983. His mentors are Bob Stewart and Jim Herman. Baseball expertise: Baseball in Nevada. His interests include Western, California and PCL Leagues. Written works: Work in progress on baseball in Nevada.

DANIEL R. MUMFORD, born March 25, 1952, and is a lifelong resident of Ocean City, MD. He graduated from the University of Maryland at College Park and is a 1976 graduate of the University of Maryland School of Law in Baltimore. He is a deputy state's attorney for Worcester County, MD. He has an interest in cemeteries and the gravesites of notable people, particularly base-

ball players, and he has traveled extensively throughout the U.S. and abroad in pursuit of this interest. He has written articles on Bill "Swish" Nicholson, Pie Traynor, the Boston/ Milwaukee/Atlanta Braves and the 1944 World Series between the Browns and the Cardinals that have been published in a local newspaper, and he collaborated on articles about Jimmie Foxx and Frank "Home Run" Baker. He has been married to Liz since 1983. He also enjoys fishing and is a part-owner with his family in Oyster Bay Tackle in Ocean City and Fenwick Tackle in Fenwick Island, DE.

ROBERT W. (BOB) MUSE, born June 10, 1949, in Montebello, CA. Joined the SABR in 1998 for baseball historical knowledge. He is currently

a member of the Ted Williams Chapter in San Diego. Baseball expertise: Old baseball parks. His interest is in old baseball parks and he is a member of the Baseball Parks Committee.

Baseball/SABR Highlights & Memorable Experiences: Was related to Ted Williams via marriage with cousin (Soule).

He is engaged to Marina Paddock. Employed at Space Electronics Inc. in inventory control. Hobbies: Sports mainly and all kinds of history.

ROBERT A. MURDEN, born in Virginia in 1951. He joined SABR in 1984, being overjoyed to find a group combining his two loves of baseball and research. He is primarily interested in statistical analysis. Murden has two articles in *The Baseball Research Journal*, one analyzing players with 80 extra-base hits in a season (1986) and the other studying whether career years exist or affect pennant races (1989). He also has additional research in the SABR Research Library.

Murden is a physician on the faculty at the Ohio State University School of Medicine. He performs medical research on Alzheimer' Disease, hypertension and doctor-patient relations. He has been married to Isla, an occupational therapist and educational book (OK Publications) distributor, for eight years. They have three wonderful children: Robbie (13), Nick (7) and Chelsea (3).

ERNEST A. NAGY, born May 1, 1927, in Hamilton Square, NJ. Joined the SABR April 25, 1979, after seeing an article in *Stars & Stripes*. He is currently a member of the Bob Davids Chapter. Baseball expertise: Burial locations of members of Hall of Fame. His interests include Hall of Fame, lifetime records and early organized baseball.

Nagy has written works regarding the Hungarian Revolution of 1956.

He is married to Helen and has one son,

David. Employed as foreign service officer (diplomat) for 34 years. He is currently retired. Hobbies: Popular music of 30s-40s and video film collection.

JOE NAIMAN, joined SABR in 1980 at the age of 16. He attended his first regional meeting in Los Angeles in 1981, and while in college gave his first regional presentation in 1983 at a Chicago regional meeting. When the San Diego Chapter was formed in 1986 Naiman became secretary-treasurer of the chapter, and in 1991 Naiman was named convention coordinator in anticipation of the 1993 National Convention. After the SABR XXIII duties were complete Naiman became the local contact for the chapter. He has given research presentations at the 1992 and 1994 National Conventions on the 1941 Cheyenne Indians and Shoeless Joe Jackson's 1919 regular season, respectively. Naiman works fulltime as a freelance journalist. He lives in the San Diego suburb of Lakeside and has three children: Clifford, Bridget and Sarah.

GARY L. NAMANNY, born Oct. 27, 1955, in Oakland, CA. Joined the SABR in May 1998 to get a better price for SABR 28 and a love of baseball. He is currently a member of the Northern California Lefty O'Doul Chapter. Baseball expertise: Statistics, history and fantasy (rotisserie).

Namanny is a member of the Statistical Analysis, Baseball Records and 19th Century Committees.

Baseball/SABR

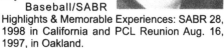

Highlights & Memorable Experiences: SABR 28, 1998 in California and PCL Reunion Aug. 16, 1997, in Oakland.

He is married to Gayle. Employment as computer operator, programmer and analyst specialist. Hobbies: Fantasy baseball, softball and playing casino blackjack.

DAVID SAMUEL NEFT, creator and editor-in-chief of *The Baseball Encyclopedia* (Macmillan, 1969). He has also co-authored 18 other sports books, including *The Sports Encyclopedia: Baseball* (St. Martin's, 19th ed., 1999) and *The Sports Encyclopedia: Pro Football* (St. Martin's, 17th ed., 1999). He is co-editor of *Total Football* (Harper Collins, 2nd ed., 1999).

Neft, 61, is a native New Yorker. He has a BA degree, MBA degree and PhD degree in statistics from Columbia University. He is currently vice president of research for Gannett Co., Inc. where he also participated in the planning for *Baseball Weekly*. His wife of 34 years, Naomi, is co-author of *Where Women Stand: An International Report on the Status of Women in 140 Countries* (Random House, 1997). Their son, Michael, 27, is content manager at Associated Press Megasports and co-author of *The Sports Encyclopedia: Baseball*. Debbie, 24, is a research assistant in pediatric psychopharmacology at Massachusetts General Hospital.

BARRY L. NELSON, born Dec. 22, 1952, in the Bronx. Joined SABR in January 1981 because

he was and is a baseball statistics junkie. Member of Northeast New York Regional. Baseball interest is the Giants, New York and San Francisco. Expertise is statistical analyses of individual seasons by team and position.

SABR highlight was the 1989 convention which he helped organize and on which he did considerable work.

Happily divorced, three beautiful children - son was all-star Little League and Babe Ruth, daughters all-stars softball. Health and safety officer for the great state of New York and a volunteer firefighter. Addicted to Baseball Fantasy Leagues.

DON NELSON, born July 3, 1934, in Mackinaw, IL. Nelson is a Cubs fan (go, Sammy!), was a Cubs fan (he remembers Harry), always will be

a Cubs fan (will Kerry come back?). He's been backing these lovable losers since 1943. It's a little like a nagging cough that resists treatment and won't go away. Even the church slow-pitch coed softball team he still pitches for is a consistent loser. Nelson has at least one accomplishment: he's

the author of *Baseball's Home Run Hitters*. It's amazing how many people are impressed that you once wrote a book, even though it was published 15 years ago, read by few, never made any money. Today, his passions-besides the ever-losing Cubs—are his wife, two daughters and two grandchildren; Frank Lloyd Wright; and the Civil War, where, at least he's backing a winner: "I'm a Grant man," he says.

NEIL C. NELSON, born Sept. 6, 1945, in Decorah, IA. Member of SABR's Biographical Research Committee and is currently doing research on the development of leadership qualities among Major League baseball players. He received his doctorate from the University of Maryland, where he focused his study and research on the history of religious thought. He taught at the University of Maryland and George Mason University and, for many years, has been an analyst with the U.S. Department of Education. He was a Cubs fan during his youth in Northeast Iowa but transferred his primary loyalty to the Orioles when he moved to Maryland, where he lived for almost 30 years. Since moving to the Kansas City area in 1996 he has been devoted to the Royals and is excited about their prospects under "owner-designee" Miles Prentice. Dr. Nelson is married and has two children.

SCOTT NELSON, born Sept. 30, 1927, the very day that Babe Ruth hit his 60th home run, an accomplishment now pretty much lost in the wake of the feats of Mark McGwire and Sammy Sosa.

Nelson especially enjoys developing statistical baseball material and has had two articles in SABR's *Baseball Research Journal*. His first memory of a sports happening was a radio account of Gabby Hartnett's pennant-clinching "homer in the gloamin'" for the Chicago Cubs in 1938. He is a member of the Records Committee.

Nelson and Marge, his wife of 43 years, have four children and 11 grandchildren. He is a retired high school English and journalism teacher in Mankato, MN, where he was sports editor of the daily paper for 11 years.

In addition to his interest in sports, Nelson enjoys compiling family histories and is currently working on his church's history. Summers are spent at the family lake cabin in Northern Minnesota.

DAVID NEMEC, born sometime ago, in Cleveland, OH, BB/TR 6' 1-1/2", 184 lbs. Nemec grew up in Bay Village, OH, and played without distinction at Ohio State under Marty Karow. After a brief 23-year retirement, Nemec resumed his playing career in 1988 and showed he'd lost nothing to Father Time by again performing without distinction for the past decade in the San Francisco Bay Area Men's Senior Baseball League. His career highlight to date was serving as player-manager for the Oakland Oaks in 1993 when they won an "Over 40 Division" National Championship.

In the off-season Nemec is a novelist and baseball historian. His many books include *Great Baseball Feats, Facts & Firsts, The Beer and Whisky League* (the first history of the American Association during its tenure as a Major League) and *The Great Encyclopedia of 19th Century Major League Baseball.* His latest book is *The Great Baseball Book of Knowledge.*

Nemec is a member of the Lefty O'Doul Chapter. Baseball expertise: 19th Century and Minor Leagues. Member of 19th Century, Biographical, Minor League Rules and Records Committees. He has written over 20 books on baseball.

Baseball/SABR Highlights & Memorable Experiences: 1998 The Sporting News-SABR Baseball Research Award.

JEFFREY NIBERT, born Nov. 18, 1959, in Meyersdale, PA. Joined the SABR in 1990 to learn about 19th century baseball. Baseball expertise: Former Major Leagues and franchises. His interests include 19th century baseball, women in baseball and Pittsburgh Pirates history.

Baseball/SABR Highlights & Memorable Experiences: Attending spring training in Arizona and the 1998 National Convention.

Nibert is married to Joan and has one son, Timothy and one daughter, Jenna. Employed as a process engineer at Intel Corp. Hobbies: Sports history, spectator sports, scouting, hiking and personal finance.

LOIS NICHOLSON, born Sept. 3, 1949, Dover, DE. Because of her interest in baseball she joined SABR in 1992 and is a member of the Bob Davids Chapter. Mentors are Norman Macht and Jack Kavanagh.

She is a writer and her main interest is children's baseball literature. She is a member of the Education Committee and held the office of Ex. Bd. Director, 1998-2002.

Nicholson is single and an elementary school librarian. She has written *Babe Ruth: Sultan of Swat, Booker T. Washington: Modern Moses* and numerous other books for children. Her hobby is teaching kids about the history of baseball.

DAN NIEMIEC, born Aug. 15, 1968, in Warren, OH. Joined the SABR in 1991 to meet other baseball enthusiasts and to have access to the research of the greatest collection of baseball minds ever assembled. Baseball expertise: Statistical analysis. His interests include statistical analysis, Pittsburgh Pirates, Ty Cobb, Babe Ruth, baseball books, baseball on stamps and measuring luck factors in baseball. Niemiec is a member of the Statistical Analysis Committee. His written works include 1997 *Baseball Research Journal*: "Measuring Luck in Batting Average."

Baseball Highlights & Memorable Experiences: 1) Attending Babe Ruth Centennial Celebration at Hofstra University in 1995; 2) playing catch at the Field of Dreams with his wife; 3) going to the Baseball Hall of Fame; 4) going to a day game at Wrigley Field and then taking the subway south to see a night game at Comiskey Park; 5) seeing his article published in the 1997 *Baseball Research Journal*; and, 6) whenever his 2-year-old daughter insists on wearing the Baseball Hall of Fame shirt he bought her, the "Baseball Nightshirt" as she calls it, to bed.

Niemiec is married to Nicole and has one daughter, Colette (2) and another due in February 1999. Employed as statistical analyst at Alliance Data Systems in Columbus, OH. Hobbies: Stamp collecting, watching baseball, playing guitar and "playing" with baseball.

JIM NITZ, born Sept. 12, 1961, in Milwaukee, WI. Joined the SABR in the 1980s because it is a great research resource. His interests include the Chicago Cubs and White Sox, plus areas of expertise: AAGPBL, Happy Felsch, Milwaukee, Fort Wayne and Indy Ball Parks. Nitz is a member of Ballparks and Women in Baseball Committees.

Written works include *Milwaukee Chicks, Borchert Field* and *AA Milwaukee Brewers,* articles published in *Milwaukee Magazine, Milwaukee Journal* and *Milwaukee History.*

Nitz married Wendee in November 1983 and has one son, Jeffrey Ryne (13) and one daughter, Bethanee Grace (8). He is vice president of Nitz Do It Best Hardware. Hobbies: President, Elmbrook Little League.

BILL NOWLIN, born Feb. 13, 1945, in Boston. Joined the SABR for access to baseball research. He has been a baseball fan since childhood when his father, once a Fenway hot dog vendor, introduced him to the game. A lifelong Ted Williams fan, Nowlin co-authored *Ted Williams: A Tribute* with Jim Prime. He more recently co-authored *Fenway Saved* with  Mike Ross and Jim. Nowlin has also contributed numerous articles to the Red Sox magazine, *Boston Baseball, Fan* and *Nine.* He's working at this point on books about the Jimmy Fund and Johnny Pesky. Baseball expertise: Ted Williams, Fenway Park, Johnny Pesky and Red Sox. His interest is in the Red Sox.

Co-founder Rounder Records, America's leading roots music label which has released over 2,000 albums of bluegrass, blues, Cajun, reggae, folk and other off-the-beaten path musics.

Nowlin collects Ted Williams memorabilia exclusively. Living in Cambridge, MA, and Austin, TX, he's married to Yleana Martinez and they have a young son, Emmet Raul, born in 1991. He is a retired professor.

ROBERT OBOJSKI, joined the SABR in 1978, then rejoined in 1998 after several years lapse. Baseball expertise: General but likes to work with stats and Minor Leagues. He has many written works including *Bush League History of Minor League Baseball* (Macmillan, 1975).

Obojski is widowed. He is a full time freelance writer. Hobbies: Sequel to *Baseball's Strangest Moments* (Sterling) coming out in 1999. *Baseball's Strangest Moments* came out in 1988 and is still in print. The sequel is entitled *Baseball's Zaniest Moments.*

RICK OBRAND, born Oct. 15, 1946, in Los Angeles. Joined the SABR in 1981 to expand his baseball knowledge. Currently a member of Allan Roth Memorial (Los Angeles) Chapter. His mentors include Bill Schroeder and Braven Dyer Jr. Baseball expertise: High schools and players from Los Angeles. He has several published articles and a book *Baseball in Los Angeles Schools* (unpublished).

Baseball/SABR Highlights & Memorable Experiences: Meeting so many great people.

Obrand is married to Xiomara and has two children, Daniel (17) and David (14). He has been a teacher in Los Angeles for 30 years. Hobbies: All sports.

TERENCE C. O'BRIAN, born Nov. 17, 1962, in Corning, NY. Joined the SABR in 1992 to belong to an organization that included the best baseball researchers in the world. Baseball interests include 19th century baseball and the Minor Leagues. He was listed under the acknowledgment section of the second edition of the *Encyclopedia of Minor League Baseball* for contributing info on several leagues in the early 1900s.

O'Brian is married to Marla and has one child, Tyler, born Jan. 9, 1998. He is a customer service representative.

DR. JAMES E. ODENKIRK, born May 31, 1928, in Mansfield, OH. He played semi-professional baseball for seven years, had a tryout with the Cleveland Indians in 1951 and coached baseball for 11 years at the high school and college level. Odenkirk is a charter member of the Arizona SABR and has been a member of SABR since 1983. He joined the SABR because of his interest in baseball history. Odenkirk is a member  of the Umpire and Rules Committee. He has presented several papers at SABR meetings and is author of *Plain Dealing,* a biography of Gordon Cobbledick, Hall of Fame baseball writer for the Cleveland *Plain Dealer.* He served as director of the Diamonds in the Desert International Baseball Conference (March 1998). Offices held: Vice president, Arizona SABR, Flame Delhi Chapter. A memorable experience was interviewing Bill Veeck in the right field bleachers of Wrigley Field shortly before his death.

Odenkirk is married to Benita and the father of two sons, Tom and Jim. He also has one grandson, Thomas James. He is a retired professor from Arizona State University and currently teaches American History at Boise State University. Odenkirk has been a dedicated Cleveland Indians fan since 1936.

BILL O'KEEFE, born in Chicago Jan. 29, 1958. He joined SABR about a decade ago to be part of the kind of cutting edge baseball research SABR is known for. A member of the committees on 19th Century and Negro League Baseball, he hopes to aid them in their research. He is currently in the preliminary stages of writing a book of series of articles on an all-star team for the ages. He owns a baseball library of over 200  books and magazines and is a die-hard Chicago Cubs fan.

He is married to his wife of 23 years, Karen Renee, and has a 22-year-old daughter, Jennifer, along with a 200 lb. St. Bernard named Khan. He is retired on disability after a career as a market director for a pizza franchise in the upper Midwest. His goal is to have a book published or see his Cubs win, he'll take either, but both would be grand.

MARC OKKONEN, born July 21, 1933, in Muskegon, MI. Joined the SABR in 1985 for support in research project (baseball uniforms). Baseball expertise: Major League uniforms, early 20th century Major League ballparks and Minor Leagues in Michigan. His interest is baseball history in general. Member of Pictorial History, Minor Leagues and Ballparks Committees. He has served as a board member of the Mus-  kegon Area Sports Hall of Fame. Written works include *Baseball Uniforms of 20th Century, Baseball Memories* series, *Federal League, Minor League Baseball Towns of Michigan*.

Baseball/SABR Highlights & Memorable Experiences: SABR/Macmillan Research Award 1989.

Okkonen is divorced. He is a retired publications consultant, freelance artist and writer. Hobbies: Numerous booklets on local (Muskegon) history.

YOSHIHIRO (KOYO) OKUBO, born in March 1935 in Tokyo, Japan. When he was 15 he attended a "Lefty O'Doul Kids Day." Seals beat Tokyo Big-Six All-Star in an extra-inning contest.

It was the beginning. He felt a great interest in Minor League baseball. A graduate of Tokyo University, he had been a longtime associate as a civil engineer with Kajima Corp., the contractor of the new San Francisco downtown ballpark.

Between the business trips to U.S. he searched for the Minor League ballparks and researched the history at local libraries. While a visitor to the Cooperstown Library, he met Cliff Kachline and willingly joined the SABR Aug. 15,

1981. The situation was told by Cliff rather comically on the front page of the newsletter.

Has been married to Hiroko for 40 years, they have two daughters, Yuko and Haruko. Haruko resides in Walnut Creek, CA, with her husband, Kevin Kodama.

Now almost retired, they visit the U.S. at least once a year to see ball games around the Bay, to enjoy California cuisine and to play golf.

KEITH OLBERMANN, hosted the World Series and the All-Star Game for NBC, the pre-game show for Fox's game of the week, has broadcast for Fox Sports News, ESPN, NBC Nightly News, CNN, ABC, UPI and a boatload of local radio and television stations, and has written for *Sports Illustrated, Time, Newsweek, The New York Times* (both sports and news) and the *Los Angeles Times*, as well as having followed up that 1973 best-giver-away on coaches with a book about ESPN. But he knew he'd "made it" when the work Bob Richardson and he did on Irving Lewis, a 1912 Boston Brave who never made it into a game but did make it onto a baseball card, was published in the SABR Journal.

FRANK J. OLMSTED, born Feb. 28, 1951, in St. Louis, MO. Joined the SABR in 1978 due to his passion for baseball. Currently a member of the Bob Broeg Chapter, St. Louis, MO. Baseball expertise: Biography. His interests include St. Louis Cardinals and baseball literature.

Written works: Since 1982 he has contributed hundreds of articles and entries for four volumes of *Biographical Dictionary of American Sports*, David 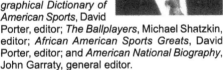 Porter, editor; *The Ballplayers*, Michael Shatzkin, editor; *African American Sports Greats*, David Porter, editor; and *American National Biography*, John Garraty, general editor.

He has been married 24 years to Mary (Zupetz) Olmstead and they have two children, Abby and Justin. He was an associate professor of theology at Benedictine College, Atchison, KS (1975-84), and has been pastoral director and theology teacher at De Smet Jesuit High School, St. Louis, since 1984 and an instructor in theology for Paul VI Institute, St. Louis since 1985. He was ordained a deacon in the Roman Catholic Church in June 1999.

RAYMOND FRANCIS OLSEN, born Nov. 25, 1958, in San Rafael, CA. He joined the SABR in 1993 after receiving information on the society in a letter from San Francisco Giants broadcaster, Hank Greenwald. His membership has enriched a lifelong interest in virtually every aspect of the game. He is an expert in ballparks, World Series opponents and statistics within many record categories. General interests include broad-  casters and biographical histories. Currently researching the San Francisco Giants 1966 season.

Attended first game at Candlestick Park Sunday, Aug. 28, 1966, seeing Gaylord Perry lose to Los Angeles by a 5 to 2 margin; witnessed a sensational catch by Willie Mays in right-centerfield

off the bat of Cincy' Bobby Tolan in April 1970 and also Mays' 3,000th hit July 18, 1970.

Single. U.S. Navy 1976-82. Served on personal staff of Adm. H.E. Shear, commander-in-chief Allied Forces Southern Europe, Naples, Italy, 1977-79. Employed as title examiner. Currently attending Diablo Valley College in Pleasant Hill, CA. Hobbies include singing in Concord United Methodist Church Chancel Choir and collecting official team pocket schedules. Resides in Martinez, CA.

RICHARD S. ORDER, born Aug. 14, 1956, in Worcester, MA. Joined the SABR in February 1999 to network, to facilitate publication of his baseball and law-related novel and to keep informed on baseball scholarship and research. Baseball expertise: Little League coach. His interests include Anti-trust and baseball, the Negro Leagues and the origins of baseball. He has written an unpublished novel blending the popular genres of baseball and the lawyer mystery/thriller.

Married Denise in 1983 and has two children, Jonathan (10) and Daniel (8). Order is a trial attorney and principal, Updike, Kelly and Spellacy in Hartford, CT.

JEFFREY L. ORNER, born July 13, 1952, in York, PA. Joined the SABR in 1975 for history and stats. He is currently a member of Bob Davids Chapter. Baseball expertise: Baltimore Orioles. His interests include history and stats.

Baseball/SABR Highlights & Memorable Experiences: Conversation with Ernie Banks at local sports show.

Orner is single and resides in York, PA.

JOSEPH N. OVERFIELD, born April 7, 1916, in Buffalo, NY. Joined the SABR April 8, 1972, due to his interest in baseball history. His mentors are Lee Allen, Bob Davids and John Thorn. Baseball expertise: Buffalo Bisons, Jim Galvin and Deacon White. He is a member of the 19th Century and Biographical Committees. Written works include *100 Seasons of Buffalo Baseball* and over 40 articles for SABR publications.

Baseball/SABR Highlights & Memorable Experiences: Saluted by SABR in 1986.

Overfield is a widower with one son, James H., three grandchildren and three great-grandchildren. He is a retired executive vice president-director, Monroe Title Ins. Corp. Hobbies and Noteworthy Accomplishments: Buffalo Baseball Hall of Fame, honored by Buffalo Historical Society in 1991.

SANTFORD (SANDY) OVERTON, born Sept. 15, 1949, in Rocky Mount, NC. Joined the SABR in the early 1990s to learn and appreciate what Afro-Americans contributed to the game of baseball. Baseball interest is Negro Leagues. He is currently working on Negro Leagues trivia book.

Baseball/SABR Highlights & Memorable Experiences: Meeting and talking with former Negro

League players such as Mahlon Duckett, Stanley Glenn and Gene Benson.

He has been married to Joan Lasota for 11 years. Employment as research scientist/educator for last six years. Currently plays in New Jersey Over 40 Baseball League and has played in last two Roy Hobbs World Series. He is truly ambidextrous, he switch hits and throws lefty and righty.

JOHN F. PARDON, born Jan. 30, 1938, in East Meadow, NY. A charter member of SABR, he was one of the 16 researchers who met in Cooperstown, NY, Aug. 10, 1971, to form the Society. He has held several positions including vice president, secretary and director; chaired the Minor League Committee; and is a member of several committees, including: Ballparks, Biographical Research, Business of Baseball,

Latin America and 19th Century. He is a member of the Casey Stengel Chapter in New York City and was the recipient of the chapter's Meritorious Service Award in 1995. A longtime researcher of Minor League cities, in 1972, with assistance from SABR member Jerry Jackson, he put together *The Cities of Professional Baseball* an 80-page product. He has attended 24 National Conventions and many chapter meetings. Several of his articles have appeared in SABR publications and he is active in establishing an archival program for the Society. He has been honored with a "SABR Salute" in the 1997-98 Directory and was the recipient of *The Bob Davids Award* in 1998.

A former sports writer in Ossining, NY, and Asheville, NC, he is now retired from the Dept. of Veterans Affairs. As a youngster he lived in Ossining (next to Sing Sing Prison) and as he learned later, in the same neighborhood as baseball's oldest living ex-Major Leaguer, Chet Hoff, born in 1891. Pardon is an elder in his church, likes classical music and history.

ROYSE (CRASH) PARR, born Sept. 11, 1935, in Elk City, OK, home of the nation's last great semi-pro town baseball team. He joined SABR in 1997 when he retired as an oil company attorney to co-author the first baseball history book for any state, *Glory Days of Summer: The History of Baseball in Oklahoma,* published in 1999 by the Oklahoma Heritage Association He is an expert on the pre-1950 sandlot/semi-pro baseball era in Oklahoma

which produced national and international championship teams and many notable Major Leaguers. Parr is a member of SABR's Minor League Committee.

He has been married for 38 years to Sheila Ann, a freelance writer. They have four grandsons and two sons, Clint and Reagan, who changed their father's life by sending him to Randy Hundley's Chicago Cub Fantasy Baseball Camp in 1994.

JOHN PARROTT, born July 22, 1954, in Avoca, PA. Joined the SABR in 1995 because "baseball is life." Baseball expertise: National League in 1950s. His interests included Boston, Milwaukee

and Atlanta Braves. He has written *The Promise: An Odyssey of Americans and Their National Pastime* (as yet unpublished).

Baseball/SABR Highlights & Memorable Experiences: Living in Atlanta during the 1991 miracle season.

Parrott is a college professor at Kutztown University, Kutztown, PA. Noteworthy accomplishments: Lifetime .432 hitting average.

JOHN PASTIER, a ballpark consultant, architecture critic, and president of SABR's Northwest Chapter. He has written for the *Baseball Research Journal* and *The National Pastime,* and earned the 1996 *Baseball Weekly Award* for the best research presentation at SABR's National Convention.

Pastier has been an officer of the Allan Roth Chapter and is an active member of the Ballparks, Business of Baseball and Internet Committees. In addition to participating in National Conventions, he has attended chapter meetings in Los Angeles, Cleveland, London, Vancouver, Seattle, Portland and Tacoma, giving more than 20 presentations on ballparks and player performance.

He has advised on the design of Orioles Park at Camden Yards, Seattle's Safeco Field and Minor League parks in Trenton and Somerset County, NJ. He has delivered ballpark lectures throughout the U.S. and in Canada and has written 30 articles on ballparks and baseball for professional, general-interest and baseball publications. He has visited 47 Major League stadiums and nearly 200 other ballparks in the U.S., Canada and Japan. In 1990 he was awarded an NEA Fellowship for ballpark design research and is working on a ballparks book.

MIKE PATCHEN, born July 8, 1952, in Portland, OR. Joined the SABR to help in research. Patchen is currently a member of the Rocky Mountain Chapter. His interest is in Wyoming connected players, players who live or lived in Wyoming, both Major and Minor Leagues. He has written an article for the SABR *Research Journal* entitled "Wyoming Players in Majors."

Baseball/SABR Highlights & Memorable Experiences: Attended the first three Rockies regular home games.

Patchen is married to Mary Kay and has three children: Chris, Jon and Lizz and one grandchild, Nicholas. He is employed as an attorney. Hobbies: Collects Wyoming connected players cards and memorabilia - all sports.

DAVID PAULSON, born Nov. 28, 1931, in Baltimore, MD. Joined the SABR in 1983 because he's a baseball fan. Currently a member of the Bob Davids Chapter. His interest is in oral history and he is a member of the Oral History Committee.

Baseball/SABR Highlights & Memorable Experiences: Playing in 1860 baseball game in 1998.

Paulson is married to Barbara and has three children: Melyssa, Michael and Rebecca. He is a retired pharmacist. Hobbies and noteworthy accomplishments: Collecting autographs and first day covers and donated 26-1/2 gallons of blood.

CHARLIE PAVITT, born Jan. 11, 1952, in Queens, NY. Joined the SABR in 1983 and is currently a member of the Baltimore/Washington Chapter. Baseball expertise: Statistical research. He is a member of the Statistical Analysis Committee. He has written several articles which have appeared in *Baseball Analyst* and *Baseball By The Numbers.*

FRED R. PELTZ, a native of California, Peltz's first taste of Major League baseball was in the late 1930s, watching Pie Traynor's Pittsburgh Pirates' spring training in San Bernardino, CA. In 1947 while playing Junior League ball he earned a trip to the World Series in New York and witnessed Jackie Robinson in his debut year.

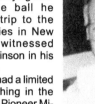

Peltz had a limited career pitching in the Sunset and Pioneer Minor Leagues from 1948-51. In 1954 he played with Dave Bristol on Army's XVI Corps championship team in Japan.

Before retiring from newspaper advertising in Riverside, CA, Peltz learned of SABR from co-worker Andy McCue. Peltz credits McCue with introducing him to the wealth of available resources and camaraderie of SABR.

He is currently working on an oral biography and article about one of his former managers.

Peltz has been married to Sue for 46 years and they currently live in San Clemente, CA. They have five children and six grandsons.

ADDISON P. (ADD) PENFIELD, born Sept. 6, 1918, in Meriden, CT. He joined SABR in 1987 at the urging of a fellow broadcaster and is a member of the Carolina (Durham-Raleigh) Chapter. He authored a paper for SABR on one-time Philadelphia Athletics pitcher "Colby Jack." He was a student and friend of Coombs when the North Carolina Hall of Famer coached at Duke. Penfield was play-by-play announcer for the Rochester Red Wings in the late 40s and for the Greensboro club of the Carolina League in 50s and 60s. He began his play-by-play radio career with broadcasts of Duke baseball while an undergraduate in 1938. He has served on SABR's Oral History Committee and is a lifetime fan of the St. Louis Cardinals. He remembers attending game 2 of the 1932 World Series (Yankees vs. Cubs) at Yankee Stadium and chasing down foul balls off the bats of Ben Chapman and Riggs Stephenson.

Penfield has been married to Virginia Cameron for 59 years. They have two adult sons, Add Jr. and Cam W. and two adult daughters, Nancy P. Wease and Sandra P. Suggs. Semi-retired, Penfield is a part timer at WKXR Radio, Asheboro, and marketing specialist for Regional Consolidated Services, an Asheboro non-profit. Hobbies and noteworthy accomplishments: 60+ years of broadcasting Duke football in five different decades, swimming and walking.

GEORGE J. PETERSEN, born in November 1957 in Los Angeles, CA. He joined SABR in 1995 because of his passion for the game and desire to learn from others that shared that passion. From 1995-97 he was a member of the Breshahan/Mudhens Chapter of Toledo, OH. Petersen is particularly interested in the socio-psychological and organizational aspects that influence team leadership. He is currently conducting research that examines leadership in collegiate

and professional baseball teams. His favorite book is *The Mental Game of Baseball* (1995) by H.A. Dorfman and Karl Kuehl.

Petersen has been married to Jennifer for 15 years. They have two sons, Eli (13) and Jacob (8). Both sons are very involved in competitive baseball and Jennifer is a self-proclaimed "Baseball Mom." Petersen is an associate professor (PhD) in the department of educational leadership and policy analysis at the University of Missouri-Columbia. His hobby is "eating, sleeping and playing baseball."

FRANK VAN RENSSELAER PHELPS, born in New York, NY, in 1917; married Helen Richter in 1951; has one son, Frank Jr.; graduate, Trinity

School, New York City in 1936 and Hamilton College, Clinton, NY, in 1940; military service: 161st Medical Battalion, 5th Army in North Africa and Italy during 1942-45; employment: Metropolitan Life, Group Insurance Div. in New York (1940-53) and Cleveland, OH (1953-68) and, as regional supervisor, Philadelphia, PA (1968-82) retirement. Phelps joined SABR in 1973 and served as treasurer, 1979-80; director, 1980-84; founder, Bibliography Committee in 1984 and chaired it for 10 years; won Bob Davids Awards in 1991; and was principal compiler of *The Index to the Sporting News Baseball Register 1940-95*, published 1996, by the Bibliography Committee. Phelps has maintained a strong lifetime interest in the history, records and literature of baseball and lawn tennis, particularly, and of many other competitive sports. He has contributed about 100 biographies to *Biographical Dictionary of American Sports* and 22 to *American National Biography*. Many authors of sports books have acknowledged his assistance.

DAVID PIETRUSZA, served as SABR president (1993-97) and secretary (1997-98). During his presidency SABR reached record member-

ship levels, held the line on dues increases, first moved on to Internet (sabr.org and SABR-L), undertook new merchandising initiatives, instituted its ongoing donors program as well as its endowment fund, first visited Latin America, produced *SABR Presents The Home Run Encyclopedia* (Macmillan) and published *The Negro Leagues Book*. As secretary he co-sponsored SABR's special dues rates for younger members.

He is editor-in-chief of *Total Sports* and served as co-editor of *Total Baseball*, the official encyclopedia of MLB, and managing editor of *Total Football*, the official encyclopedia of the NFL.

Pietrusza also co-edited *The Total Baseball Catalog*, *Total Braves*, *Total Indians* and *Total Mets* and has written *Judge and Jury: The Life and Times of Judge Kenesaw Mountain Landis*, *Lights On!* (nominated for the 1997 Casey Award), *Minor Miracles*, *Major Leagues* and *Baseball's Canadian-American League*.

He co-edited *Total 49ers*, *Total Cowboys*, *Total Packers*, *Total Steelers* and *Total Quarterbacks*.

For younger readers he has written *Top 10 Baseball Managers*, *The New York Yankees*, *The Los Angeles Dodgers*, *Michael Jordan*, *The Phoenix Suns* and *The Boston Celtics*, *The End of the*

Cold War, *The Invasion of Normandy*, *The Battle of Waterloo*, *John F. Kennedy*, *The Chinese Cultural Revolution*, *Smoking* and *The Roaring Twenties*.

In 1994 Pietrusza served as a consultant for PBS's Learning Link on-line system and wrote and produced the documentary *Local Heroes* for PBS affiliate WMHT—film that eventually helped lead to the election of George Davis into the Hall of Fame.

Born in Amsterdam, NY, Nov. 22, 1949, in 1986-87 he served on that city's Common Council. He holds a MA degree in history from the State University of New York at Albany.

He lives with his wife, Patricia, in Scotia, NY.

PATRICIA BASFORD PIETRUSZA, a SABR member since 1993. Born in Sheboygen, MI, she has lived in New York state since the early 1970s.

She has attended the 1993 SABR Convention in San Diego. Her most memorable moment in baseball occurred on July 17, 1990, at Fenway Park when she witnessed the Minnesota Twins turn a record two triple plays against the Boston Red Sox—both Gaetti to Newman to Hrbek. She has attended Major League games in 13 ballparks as well as Minor League games in at least 24 parks.

A staff member for New York State Senator Hugh T. Farley (Schenectady), she is married to author and former SABR president, David Pietrusza, and lives in Scotia, NY. She bats and throws left-handed.

SCOTT PITONIAK, from the time he was knee-high to a Louisville Slugger, Pitoniak has been smitten with baseball. Born in Rome, NY,

April 10, 1955, Pitoniak grew up worshipping Mickey Mantle. An inability to handle the curve ball ended Pitoniak's dreams of succeeding The Mick in centerfield, but that didn't dull his passion for the game. Winner of more than 70 national and state writing awards, Pitoniak has spent the past 14 years working as a sports columnist for the Rochester, NY, *Democrat and Chronicle*. The Syracuse University graduate writes often about baseball. A member of SABR since the mid-1980s, Pitoniak has authored two baseball-related books, *Silver Seasons: The Story of the Rochester Red Wings* and *Playing Write Field: Selected Works by Scott Pitoniak*. His main areas of research interest are the Minor Leagues, the Yankees and anything Mantle. He has contributed several stories to SABR publications through the years, including pieces on the longest game in professional baseball history, a 33-inning marathon in the summer of 1981 between the Red Wings and Pawtucket Red Sox, and Herb Washington, the designated runner for Charley Finley's Oakland A's. Among his greatest baseball thrills: coaching his son's Little League team; watching Mantle take batting practice at the Stadium in 1966; witnessing in person Joe Carter's World Series-ending homer, and smacking three hits off Hall of Fame pitcher

Bob Feller in a charity game. Pitoniak lives in Rochester with his wife, Susan; their children, Amy and Christopher; and their cocker spaniel, Sadie.

HOWARD M. POLLACK, born June 13, 1928, in Philadelphia, PA. Joined the SABR to share experiences with others of like mind. Currently a

member of the Philadelphia Chapter. He has been a member of the Pictorial and Bibliography Committees. Pollack has written a dozen books and hundreds of articles, but most of them are medical.

Baseball/SABR Highlights & Memorable Experiences: Presented research papers at three local and two national SABR meetings.

He and his wife, Shanlee, have been married for 48 years. They have three sons, all physicians and all devout baseballers; three grandchildren and two step grandsons. Pollack is a retired radiologist and was professor of radiology at the University of Pennsylvania School of Medicine (20 years) and Temple University (18 years). His hobbies are baseball history, collecting books on sports quotations (he has 76 of them) and visiting sports museums and sports Halls of Fame around the world (he has been to more than 100).

ROBERT E. POTTS, born Aug. 24, 1936, in Jersey City, NY. Joined the SABR in February 1972 to learn more about baseball history. Cur-

rently a member of the Casey Stengel Chapter. His mentor is Ben Marmo, former Philadelphia Phillies scout and *Paterson News* sportswriter. Baseball expertise: Semi-pro baseball in North Jersey. His interests include amateur and semi-pro baseball, Negro Leagues and Minor Leagues. He is a member of the Negro Leagues and Minor Leagues Committees.

Baseball/SABR Highlights & Memorable Experiences: Honored by USA Baseball in 1987 as Amateur Coach of the Year in Atlanta, GA.

Potts is single and is recreation supervisor, city of Clifton, NJ. He has been owner/manager, Clifton Phillies semi-pro team for the past 45 years.

DANIEL PRICE, born Jan. 10, 1957, in Brooklyn, NY. Joined the SABR in 1991 because of his love of baseball and for research. He is currently a member of the Casey Stengel Chapter of New York. Baseball expertise: Giants of the late 30s, Yankees and Mets. His interests include history of old ballparks and Minor Leagues from 1937-40. He is a member of the Ballparks Committee.

Baseball/SABR Highlights & Memorable Experiences: Trips to other regionals and meeting the ballplayers on various panels.

He is married to Joanne and is employed as manager, Bell Atlantic.

JIM PRICE, born March 9, 1938, in Los Angeles, CA. A lifelong baseball fan, Price has spent his entire career as a sports writer, editor, publicist and announcer. He joined SABR in 1979 and became the founding president of Northwest

SABR. An expert on pro ball in the Pacific Northwest, Price won a Macmillan-SABR Award for a retrospective article on the bus crash that killed nine members of Spokane's 1946 Western International League team. He is a member of the Umpires and Rules and Minor Leagues Committees.

He has been an official scorer and public address announcer in the California, Northwest and Pacific Coast Leagues and a play-by-play broadcaster in the PCL. He spent most of the 1970s as announcer and publicist for horse racing tracks in Spokane, Portland and Arizona and most of the 1980s as sports information director at Eastern Washington University. Since 1990 the California native has been a copy editor for *The Spokesman-Review* in Spokane, WA.

An avid investor and historian, he is the author of an upcoming comprehensive history of Spokane baseball. A Stanford University graduate, Price, and his wife, Ann, have a son, Jon, a 1999 college graduate. Hobbies: Reading, gardening, wine and collecting baseball reference books.

SCOT PRICE, born April 1, 1970, in Kingsport, TN. Joined the SABR in 1996 to learn more about baseball history and to help preserve its history. Baseball expertise: Steve Garvey, 20th century baseball history and baseball cards. He loves everything about baseball (with the exception of the DH and Astroturf). Price is a member of the Oral History Committee.

Baseball/SABR Highlights & Memorable Experiences: Visiting Hall of Fame and meeting Bob Feller and going to spring training.

He is married to Kellie and has one child, Ashleigh. Employed as senior technician on computer help desk, Holston Valley Hospital. Hobbies: Collects baseball memorabilia.

JASON D. PYLES, born Jan. 28, 1974, in Cumberland, MD. Joined the SABR in 1997 for the baseball experiences SABR provides. He is currently a member of the Forbes Field Chapter (Pittsburgh). His mentor is Dave Pyles. Baseball expertise: The Cincinnati Reds. Pyles' interests include the history of baseball in eastern panhandle of West Virginia and western panhandle of Maryland. He has written a research paper "The Five Greatest Cincinnati Reds of the 20th century."

Baseball/SABR Highlights & Memorable Experiences: Being on the field at Three Rivers Stadium right after the '94 MLB All-Star Game.

Pyles is single and is employed as a school psychologist and is junior varsity baseball coach at Frankfort High School. Hobbies: Collecting baseball memorabilia.

JAMES B. RASCO, born Nov. 17, 1941, in Little Rock, AR. He grew up in DeWitt, AR, and graduated from Hendrix College. Rasco was invited to join SABR in 1982 by Cliff Kachline, who Rasco met while doing research at the Hall of Fame Library in Cooperstown. He is an expert on the career of his good friend, George Kell, and the era from 1947-57, especially post-season All-Star selections. He is a past president and the permanent historian of the Arkansas Sports Hall of Fame. Rasco collects baseball, basketball and football films, publications and memorabilia and has formed the National Museum of Sports History, Inc. to hold his collection.

Rasco married Pam Dunaway in 1964. They have two daughters, Laura and Lisa. Rasco has been a CPA in Little Rock for the past 35 years and for the past 25 years has headed the firm of Rasco, Burris & Winter.

LAURENCE W. REILLY JR., born March 21, 1952, in Brooklyn, NY, not far from Ebbets Field. He joined SABR in the early '80s because he's a baseball fanatic and wanted to enjoy his passion with others of the same ilk. He loves any and all baseball books, especially those of a historical nature. He is a member of the Ballparks Committee. His ambition is to retire at a young age and write about historical aspects of the game.

His most memorable baseball experience is attending the 10-inning no-hitter of Francisco Cordova and Ricardo Rincon at Three Rivers Stadium July 12, 1997, the first stop of a baseball tour he took with his family.

Reilly has been married for 25 years to Ginny. They have a daughter, Kate (16) and a son, Dave (14). He is a chemist at Cauldron Process Chemistry in Malvern, PA.

GEORGE REKELA, a 1965 graduate of the University of Minnesota School of Journalism, Rekela, a native of Kenney, MN, joined the Halsey Hall Chapter of the SABR in Minneapolis in 1987. After serving the Halsey Hall Chapter in various committee positions, he was elected the chapter's vice president. Then, in July 1996, was elected president of the chapter. He also serves as editor of the chapter's monthly newsletter, the *Holy Cow*. He has authored numerous sports books including *Tower of Power: the Hakeem Olajuwon Story; Karl Malone, Star Forward;* and *State Champions.* He also authored the 1998 special *Stadium Game* edition of *AEC Magazine.*

Rekela is married to the former Judy Aslesen of Crystal, MN. He has three daughters, one son, one granddaughter and one grandson. He is the executive editor for Chapin Publishing, New Hope, MN, publishers of the weekly *Construction Bulletin Magazine.*

NORM RICHARDS, born June 19, 1952, in Quincy, IL. Joined the SABR in February 1995 to share his love of baseball history with others. He is currently a member of the Bob Broeg Chapter, St. Louis, MO. Baseball expertise: College baseball coach for 10 years. His interests include bio-

graphical information on players' hometowns, high schools and Minor Leagues. He submitted a list of Major Leaguers from Beaumont High School to *Baseball Digest* which took first place.

Baseball/SABR Highlights & Memorable Experiences: Each monthly meeting of their chapter is a highlight because of Bob Broeg (he gets to be with Broeg for three hours!) and attending SABR 28 in 1998 in Frisco.

Richards has been married to Linda for 20 years and has one son, Brent (16) and one daughter, Allison (13). He is a scout for the Houston Astros and college consultant. Hobbies and noteworthy accomplishments: College Coach of the Year (four times) and JFK assassination researcher.

OWEN RICKER, born in December 1939 in Spirit River, Alberta. He joined SABR in 1973 after having helped Bill Haber trace some Canadian-born players and meeting Bob Davids in 1972. He began doing baseball research at an early age and has presented papers on baseball at Operations Research conferences and at national and regional SABR meetings. He is a member of the Statistical Analysis, Minor Leagues, Biographical Research and Business of Baseball Committees and has attended 13 National Conventions. He is currently researching the Western Canada League which operated between 1907 and 1921.

Ricker married Celia in 1962. They have a daughter, Laurie (34) and a son, Darryl (32), who was a SABR member as a teenager. He is professor emeritus of administration, University of Regina, where he taught for 28 years. He has an extensive collection of baseball books and other memorabilia and plays baseball simulation games.

STEVEN RIESS, written works include *Touching Base: Professional Baseball and American Culture in the Progressive Era* (1980). He retired in 1999 from the University of Illinois Press.

JAMES A. RILEY, born July 25, 1939, in Sullivan County, TN. He joined SABR in 1979 and currently serves on the SABR Executive Board and as president of the Central Florida Chapter.

He has authored six books, including *The Biographical Encyclopedia of the Negro Baseball Leagues,* and has contributed to several compilations and magazines, including *The Baseball Encyclopedia* and the official *All-Star Game Program.*

In recognition of his scholarship on the Negro Leagues he has been a guest lecturer at the Smithsonian in Washington, D.C. and is a member of the Florida Humanities Council Speakers Bureau. He has also served as an editorial consultant, appeared in television documentaries and maintains an award-winning website.

Riley, a two time recipient of the SABR-Macmillan Research Award, is director of research for the Negro Leagues Baseball Museum.

He and his wife, Dottie, have two sons and reside in Rockledge, FL.

LAWRENCE S. (LARRY) RITTER, born in Brooklyn May 23, 1922. He attended Indiana University (1939-42). Following graduation he spent four years in the U.S. Navy (1942-46). After the war he attended the University of Wisconsin where he received a PhD degree in economics in 1951. Subsequently he taught at Michigan State University and New York University and also spent several years as an economist with the Federal Reserve Bank of New York. In 1991 he retired from New York University after 31 years on the faculty.

He has been a member of SABR since the mid-70s. Publications include *The Glory of Their Times* (1966); *The Story of Baseball* (1983); *The Babe: The Game that Ruth Built* (1988); *Lost Ballparks* (1992); *Leagues Apart* (1995); and *East Side, West Side* (1998).

He was married to Claire Fliess (1942-52) and to Elisabeth Fonseca (1977-89). Both marriages ended in divorce. He has one son, Stephen, born in 1948.

RAY ROBINSON, born Dec. 4, 1920, in New York City. Joined the SABR because of his love of baseball. His interests include biography, history and watching day baseball on TV and at the park. His published books include: *Iron Horse: Lou Gehrig In His Time; Matty: An American Hero; Oh, Baby, I Love It* (written with Tim McCarver); *The Home Run Heard 'Round The World; Yankee Stadium: 75 Years of Drama, Glamour and Glory; American Original: Will Rogers; Rockne of Notre Dame; The Mario Lanza Story;* and *Baseball Stars* (series, 1958-75). He is also a contributor to the *New York Times, American Heritage, Diversion, Washington Post, New York Daily News, Baseball Weekly, The Sporting News, Yankees Magazine, New York Observer, Columbia College Today, USAir Magazine* and *Fifty Plus.*

Robinson has been married to Phyllis (author and editor) for 50 years. They have three children: Nancy, Steve and Tad; and four grandchildren. He is a retired magazine editor (*Coronet, Good Housekeeping, Seventeen* and *TV Guide*). Hobbies: Tennis, swimming, reading and writing. He has been a nominee for the Casey Award.

HARRY ROTHGERBER, born in 1947, a life-long resident of Louisville, KY. A SABR member since 1983, Rothgerber was co-chair of the successful 1997 SABR National Convention in Louisville. He serves on the Executive Committee of the Kentucky SABR Chapter and his articles have appeared in several SABR publications.

His book concerning the life and times of young Babe Ruth is scheduled for 1999 publication (McFarland) and Rothgerber is currently working on a biography of Joe McCarthy. He enjoys researching the Louisville Colonels and Pee Wee Reese remains his personal hero.

A criminal justice professional, Rothgerber is an attorney who serves as first assistant to the local felony prosecutor. He holds degrees from Bellarmine College, Spalding University and the University of Louisville, and he has received numerous awards and honors. Rothgerber's hobby is collecting sports programs and Babe Ruth publications. He has three children: Hank, Jessica and John.

C. BROOKE ROTHWELL, born Oct. 10, 1949, in Detroit, MI. Joined the SABR in March 1981 because of his love of baseball. He has been a member of the Allan Roth Chapter for 12 years. His mentor is Joe Wayman. Baseball expertise: Semi-pro Chicago Bruins 1978 and writer of baseball fiction/poetry. His interests include 1959-63 Dodgers, 19th century baseball, Babe Ruth, gloves, memorabilia, uniforms, books and swing music. Written works are *Never Before Collected Works of Babe Ruth, Spitball,* and *Grandstand Baseball Annuals.*

Baseball/SABR Highlights & Memorable Experiences: Meeting Cappy Gagnon, knowing Joe Wayman and meeting Hank Greenberg.

He has been married to Janine for 25 years (with fidelity). He has one daughter, Elora Ann. Employed by USPS as a mail handler. Hobbies and noteworthy accomplishments: Collecting old radios, growing roses and successful love-making to one woman.

THOMAS K. (TOM) ROWE JR., born in Richmond, VA, a week before the improbable Whiz Kid Phillies began playing the Yankees in the 1950 World Series. He became interested in baseball during the late 1950s and has built extensive collections of baseball cards and other photographs and reference books. He has photographed Minor Leaguers in Richmond and Norfolk since the mid-1970s, has compiled trade

lists independently since the 1960s and is an expert on Major League uniforms. He joined SABR in 1979 at the urging of his late friend and SABR member, Brook Treakle, a Cleveland Indians buff, to have greater access to historical articles and records. He is a lifelong Yankee fan.

Rowe is married to Randi Hicks Rowe and lives in Alexandria, VA. He worked at the Newport News, VA, *Daily Press* newspaper for 26 years before becoming an editor at the Bureau of National Affairs in Washington in 1998. He has a daughter, Megan, born July 4, 1983, hours before Dave Righetti pitched a no-hitter.

TOMAS RUBALCAVA, born Oct. 21, 1970, in Wadolajora, Jilisco, Mexico. Joined the SABR in 1987 because he was curious about the organization. His baseball interests include the Dodgers, statistics, baseball cards and video games.

Baseball/SABR Highlights & Memorable Experiences: Going to Dodger Stadium for the first time.

He is single and is employed as an insurance officer.

BILL RUBINSTEIN, born Aug. 12, 1946, in New York. He was educated at Swarthmore and Johns Hopkins and has lived most of his adult life outside the USA, especially in Australia (from 1976-95) and the UK (since 1995). He is currently professor of modern history at the University of Wales-Aberystwyth, and follows baseball regularly. He has contributed a number of articles to SABR publications and also to *Grandstand*

Baseball Annual, where he publishes an annual quiz. He has been a member of SABR since about 1981 and is interested in all aspects of baseball history. Eventually he hopes to write a long book examining modern statistical methods of assessing baseball greatness (by Pete Palmer, Bill James, etc.) to see how good they are. He is married and has one son. Phone number: (h): 44-01970-615281; fax: 44-01970-622676; email: wdr@aber.ac.uk.

BARRY RUCKER, born Nov. 30, 1947, in Denver, CO. Joined the SABR in January 1999. He is currently a member of the San Diego Ted Williams Chapter. Baseball interests include computer baseball games, statistics and history.

Baseball/SABR Highlights & Memorable Experiences: Saw Maris homer in 1965 and McGwire homer in 1998, live.

He is married to Estela and is employed as a library clerk. Hobbies and noteworthy acknowledgments: World's worst golfer, yet had a hole-in-one once.

MARK RUCKER, born on Chicago's south side and was raised a White Sox fan. He played ball from age 3 to present, has been a member of SABR since 1983 and served on board of directors from 1990-93. He started a publishing company, Transcendental Graphics, in 1986. Initially he built image bank covering the 19th century, then expanded holdings into the modern era. He provides images for most SABR publications; is co-author of pictorial biographies, including *The Babe: A Life In Pictures* and *Ted Williams: Seasons of the Kid.* Also, a picture consultant for Ken Burns' Baseball documentary series; a major contributor to ESPN's SportCentury project, a number of MLB projects, plus hundreds of other books, magazines, films, videos and card sets. In 1999 he co-authored first pictorial history of the game in Cuba, *Smoke: The Romance and Lore of Cuban Baseball.* Family includes son Kriston, daughter Caitlin and wife Alison Moore. They live in Boulder, CO.

BALLARD (ROCKY) RUTHERFORD, born in Shelbiana, KY. Joined the SABR in 1997 for history research, especially Minor Leagues. His mentors are C. Wayne Gilbert, Al Campanis, Golden Holt and Gerry Waring. Baseball expertise: Sports writer *Macon News, Macon Magazine.* His interests include Major and Minor League players before first strike (1971). Written works: *Aunt Maudie's Kuntry Cookbook* (1995).

Baseball/SABR Highlights & Memorable Experiences: When he was signed with Brooklyn organization in 1956.

He is married to Faye Leilani and has three children: Sherrie Ferrell, Cindie Bailey and Michael Rutherford; and two grandchildren, Katie Ferrell and Caitlin Sabine. He is a retired technical writer. Hobbies: Collects old player photos and cards and baseball history.

DAVID S. SANDERS JR., born in June 1926, in Kellogg, ID. He joined SABR in 1975 and helped to organize the first regional meeting in Southern California. His earliest baseball memories are of playing ball in the streets of Baltimore and reading daily stories of the 1934 World Series. He began following the Dodgers and the Hollywood Stars in 1941 and lately has become interested in the San Diego Padres. As a member of the Allan Roth and Ted Williams Chapters he has especially enjoyed meeting Hank Greenberg, Wally Berger and Dave Garcia and being reunited with old shipmate Roy Smalley Sr. He has published articles on sports writing in *The National Pastime* and *Dictionary of Literary Biography* and baseball poems in *Spitball*.

Sanders has been married to Mary Frances since 1948. They have three children: Scott, Bonnie and Peter; and six grandchildren. He is emeritus professor of English at Harvey Mudd College in Claremont, CA, and has written about such American writers as John Dos Passos, John Hersey and Ernest Hemingway.

MICHAEL J. SCHELL, born July 17, 1957, in Bloomington, IN. He joined SABR in 1997 due to his interest in baseball research and is a member of the Statistical Analysis Committee. He has authored *Baseball's All-time Best Hitters* (Princeton University Press, 1999). The book describes four adjustments to batting average (league batting average, league talent, ballpark and late-career declines) and presents the 100 best hitters for

average. Gwynn barely edges out Cobb as the best "hitter." Schell met Gwynn on the occasion of Gwynn's 8000th at-bat (the onset of the late-career decline) and received a used bat from Gwynn. David Stephan and Peter Palmer provided helpful information for the book.

Schell is an avid Reds fan. He is an associate professor of biostatistics at the University of North Carolina at Chapel Hill. He has authored over 50 articles on statistical methods or cancer research. His hobbies are stamp collecting and traveling.

JOHN ROGERS SCHOON, born Aug. 29, 1931, in Michigan City, IN. He joined the SABR in 1985 to learn about baseball. Schoon is a member of the Bob Broeg Chapter. His mentors are Harry Brunt, Dan Krueckeberg and Erv Fischer. His interest is in the slugging career of Dan Quisenberry. He assisted with the 1992 Convention.

Schoon married Sarah Legg June 1, 1957, and has two sons, John and Nate, and two grandchildren, Jessica and Matthew. He is a retired PE teacher and has been a Busch Stadium usher for 12 years. Hobbies: Stamp collecting.

ARTHUR O. SCHOTT, born July 9, 1918, in New Orleans. He was the 26th member to join SABR and the first from the South, having become a member immediately after the Society was organized in 1971. He joined because of his interest in baseball history. Currently a member of the Schott/Pelican Chapter. Baseball expertise: Babe Ruth, New Orleans Pelicans and New York Yankees. His interests include the Cincinnati Red Stockings 1869 and in any and all historical and statistical baseball presentations or compilations. Schott is a member of the Ballparks, Minor Leagues and 19th Century Committees. He held the office of vice president in 1978.

His written works include two books: *70 Years With The (New Orleans) Pelicans - 1887-1957* and *Let's Go To Bat.* He has written some 300-plus columns entitled *A Schott From the Bleachers,* which have appeared in the *New Orleans States-Item* and the *Times Picayune* newspapers. His articles have appeared in several national publications and he often makes radio and television appearances.

Baseball/SABR Highlights & Memorable Experiences: Meeting so many baseball researchers. Named *Louisiana's Official Baseball Historian* Aug. 1, 1973, by then Lt. Governor (of Louisiana) James E. Fitzmorris. This is an honorary title, with no fee included.

In his 67 years of baseball research he has assembled one of the finest private libraries of baseball books and data, dating back to 1869. He and his wife, Mary Grinnen, celebrated their 50th Wedding Anniversary Sept. 11, 1998. They have been blessed with seven sons, six grandsons and six granddaughters. Employed for 49 years in family meat packing business. Hobbies and noteworthy acknowledgments: Baseball research, on panel for anniversary of Babe Ruth's 100th anniversary, Hall of Fame, University of New York.

SCOTT E. SCHUL, born Feb. 27, 1966, in Buffalo, NY, and was raised in Kane, PA. He joined SABR in 1995 at the invitation of Marc Okkonen. His purpose in joining was to further his research in baseball's pre-1920 "dead ball" era. He takes special interest in Rube Waddell. Schul is also interested in 1970s-era baseball, the decade in which he came of age as a baseball fan.

Schul is an attorney with and share-

holder of Bernstein, Shur, Sawyer and Nelson in Portland, ME. He practices primarily in the areas of executive compensation, taxation and general commercial law. He has been married for over 10 years to his wife, Linda, and has one daughter. Schul also serves as a High Councilor in the Augusta Maine Stake of the Church of Jesus Christ of Latter-Day Saints and can be found every opening day at Fenway Park.

JAMIE SELKO, born Dec. 21, 1948, in Brooklyn, NY. Joined the SABR in 1976. His mentors are Vern Luse and the three Bobs - Davids, Hoie and McConnell. Baseball expertise: Minor Leagues, stats, trivia, baseball in the movies, high school histories of Major Leaguers and Major Leaguers who played other sports. His interests include the same as previously mentioned plus autographs, SABR and its members. He is a member of the Minor League, Biographical Research, Ballpark, Pictorial History and Umpires Committees. He has written numerous articles for *National Pastime* and *Research Journal.*

SABR highlights: Being on four trivia championship teams; meeting and getting to know the three Bobs; sitting around with Bill Carle, John Thorn, Pete Palmer and Jeff Neuman. Sitting around with Dick Thompson, Scott Flatow and Alan Blumkin.

He married Nancy Aug. 22, 1971, and has six children: Eden, Rose, Miryam, Ariel, Ioana and Zachery; and two grandchildren, Isabel and Valentina. Employment: Shiloh Christian Commune, 1970-76; forestry work, 1975-81; U.S. Army-Intelligence, linguist, 1981-92; early retirement with disability; 1992-until the end of time, home dad. Hobbies and interests include collecting books on sports, paleontology, WWII and the holocaust, language reference, little Golden books, natural history, especially, endangered species, movie reference, Tolkeiniana, Jane Duncan. Also collects soda bottles, 1961 baseball cards, stamps (Third Reich, France, Antarctica). In the service earned nine decorations. At one time, spoke Swedish, Danish, Russian, French and German. Has written for philatelic publications. Bench pressed 400 pounds on his 45th birthday. Working on several books - one on baseball, one on Sci-fi movies, one on philately and WWII. Has single panel cartoon ("Face to Face") he is trying to get syndicated. Working on a graphic arts project he would like to get published (Philatelica Baseballica Fantasia).

WARREN M. SHAPIRO, born Dec. 19, 1958, in Queens, NY. Joined the SABR in 1991 (approximately) for the love of America's pastime. Currently a member of Casey Stengel Chapter. Baseball expertise: Business of baseball. His interests include broadcasting, business, Minor Leagues and expansion.

Shapiro is single and is president of Sports Research Consultants.

NALOWN L. SHELTON, born July 21, 1931, in Dierks, AR. Joined the SABR in 1994 because of his love of baseball books. He is currently a member of the Bob Broeg Chapter of St. Louis Region. Baseball expertise: High school baseball coach. His interest is the Baltimore Orioles, his favorite team, because they used to be the St. Louis Browns and he used to own a bit of stock in the Baltimore Orioles.

Baseball/SABR Highlights & Memorable Experiences: Going on a Jay Buckley baseball tour to Hall of Fame and getting to see several games in several different ballparks.

He is married to Mary Ann and has one daughter, Lori Bucholz and three grandchildren: Nicky (9), Jerry (5) and Susan (2). Shelton is a retired guidance counselor from Central High School in Breese, IL. Hobbies: Collecting baseball cards and memorabilia and hardback books.

DAVID SHINER, born in Tiberias, Israel, July 26, 1951. He joined SABR in 1995 after years of being told by friends that he should be a member. His current regional group is the Emil Rothe Chapter in Chicago. He has written a lot of baseball articles and essays, which have appeared in the SABR *Research Journal, Fan Magazine, Nine: A Journal of Baseball History* and *Social Policy Perspectives,* and various other

magazines. He is currently working on a book on baseball's superstars.

Shiner is very happily married to Nancy Wallace. He has been academic dean at Shimer College since 1976. Hobbies and noteworthy accomplishments: Chess, musical performance and acting.

TOM SHRIMPLIN, born Jan. 18, 1952, in Junction City, KS. Joined the SABR in 1990 because he has always been interested in baseball. Currently a member of the Kansas City Regional Chapter. Baseball interests include Minor Leagues, especially Three-I League and Kansas City teams. He is a member of the Biographical Committee.

Baseball/SABR Highlights & Memorable Experiences: Attending convention in Kansas City and helping Lloyd Johnson acquire information for Minor League book.

Married to Becky and has two children, Aimee and Ben. Employed at Hiawatha Community Hospital as director of pharmacy services.

SIMMS SHUBER, born Feb. 28, 1933, in Toronto. Joined the SABR because of his profound interest in the game. Baseball expertise: Excellent - the game, history, strategies, in detail. Baseball interests: Been to every World Series since 1972; spring training since 1965; the game and how it's played.

Baseball/SABR Highlights & Memorable Experiences: His daughter and now his grandson at many memorable games. The ritual of passage.

He is married to Florence and has one daughter, Leslie and two grandchildren, Zachary and Cassandra. He is president of Cantol Ltd. - Cantol Inc., Barrister. Hobbies: Sports events, worldwide.

DAVID SHURY, the walls of Shury's study are lined with plaques and certificates of appreciation. His basement is filled with over 1000 baseball files. Since retirement from his law practice in 1994 he has devoted his days to the history and organization of baseball - his lifetime avocation.

Shury was instrumental in expanding the Saskatchewan Baseball Association and in re-organizing the Canadian Federation of Amateur Baseball. He was the driving force behind the formation of Canada's First National Senior Baseball Team. He helped form the Western Canada Baseball Association

He founded the Saskatchewan Baseball Hall of Fame and Museum and has written histories of the sport. He was the first life member of Baseball Canada. He conducts free legal clinics for the Salvation Army and has been honoured by the Canadian Paraplegic Association Shury, confined to a wheelchair since 1969, has never let his disability hinder his intense volunteer activity.

Shury has been awarded the Saskatchewan Volunteer Medal.

JOSEPH E. SIMENIC, born Aug. 4, 1923, in Kostanjevac, Yugoslavia. He joined the SABR Aug. 10, 1971, to meet other researchers with interests similar to his. He is currently a member of the Jack Graney Chapter, Cleveland, OH. Baseball interests include 19th century biographical research and Cleveland Indians history. He is a member of the Biographical and 19th Century Commit-

tees. He served as SABR vice president in 1973 and Biographical Committee chairman 1983-84. Simenic is co-author of *Cleveland Indians Encyclopedia.*

Simenic is a widower with two sons, Steve and Tom, and three grandchildren: Joe, Jenna and John. He is a retired secretary to publisher and editor, *The Plain Dealer.*

ERIC SIMONSEN, born Sept. 29, 1945 in Buffalo, NY. Because of his interest in baseball and related research, he joined SABR and was one of its first 25 members. He is a member of the New England - Rhode Island chapter.

Eric's main interest is Buffalo Bisons and general baseball. Held office of national treasurer and served on board of directors. Accomplishment was being the founder of Rhode Island Men's Senior Baseball League in 1987.

Eric and his wife, Suzanne, have two daughters, Anne and Kara. Employed as chief operating officer of a financial corp.

WILLIAM JOHN SIMPSON, born May 15, 1935, in Chicago, IL. Joined the SABR in 1981. His mentor is Jay Langhammer, as to area of expertise indicated below. Baseball expertise: College fraternity men in baseball. His interests include the Federal League and Minor Leagues during WWII. Simpson is a member of the Biographical Research Committee. He is presently writing history of Theta Chi Fraternity.

He has been married to Mary since 1976. Employed as an attorney 1978-90 (retired) and editor, previously.

ROBERT A. SKYLAR, born Nov. 27, 1950, in New York, NY. Joined the SABR in 1986 because of his love of baseball and statistics. He is currently a member of the Los Angeles Allan Roth Chapter. Baseball expertise: Strategy and analysis. His interests include statistics, oddities, strategy and Fantasy Leagues.

Baseball/SABR Highlights & Memorable Experiences: SABR publications, visit to Hall of Fame and watching Willie Mays play.

Skylar is married to Lisa and has two children, Jessica (16) and Katherine (12). He is the senior consultant of Econ One Research, Inc., economic research and consulting firm. Hobbies: Playing softball and basketball and participating in baseball Fantasy Leagues.

JIM SLATTERY, born Dec. 21, 1947, in Jersey City, NJ. Joined the SABR in 1997. Baseball expertise: Baseball Hall of Fame, members committed to memory. He is a frequent visitor of Baseball Hall of Fame and uses their research library.

Baseball/SABR Highlights & Memorable Experiences: Member of the Friends of the Hall of Fame and contributor to Negro Leagues Baseball Museum.

He has been married to Maureen for 25 years. They have two children, Brian (23) and Laura (19). Employed as banking staff officer, presently retired. Hobbies: Baseball board games and baseball books.

EDWARD H. SMALL JR., born in October 1932 in Brooklyn, NY, and grew up on Long Island. An avid Yankee fan and baseball card/memorabilia collector, joined SABR in 1978 to enhance overall knowledge of the Yankees, Dodg-

ers and Giants and their farm teams, "cup of coffee" players, and the Majors/Minors of the 30s through 50s. Also interested in writing about the Brooklyn Bushwicks, New York's premier semi-pro team of the 30s.

He is a retired civil engineer and has been married to Beryl for 43 years. They have two sons, two daughters and five grandchildren.

Other historical interests include postcard collecting and membership in aviation and Civil War historical groups.

WILLIAM F. (BILL) SMALL, born March 28, 1935, in Rutland, VT. Joined the SABR in 1993 because baseball is his #1 hobby. Currently a member of the Larry Gardner Chapter, Burlington, VT. Baseball expertise: Game of baseball and baseball umpiring. Played baseball for about 30 years - high school, American Legion, U.S. Air Force, semi-pro Los Angeles, CA, semi-pro Vermont and Over 40-Year-Old Senior Baseball in Vermont 1987-98. He was a baseball umpire for 35 years from 1963-99. Coached youth baseball for 16 years. His interests include any books on baseball umpires.

Baseball/SABR Highlights & Memorable Experiences: The first meeting of SABR and finding out that there are so many other people interested in baseball. Sitting down in a dug-out in the Los Angeles Semi-pro Leagues next to and playing with and against Major League, Minor League and future professional baseball players in the Los Angeles Winter Leagues 1963-66.

His first marriage lasted 22 years. He is currently married to Mari Anne Allen. Small has four children: Phil, Therese, Cisca and Joe. Employment with USPS. Hobbies: Baseball, baseball umpiring and NASCAR auto racing. Noteworthy acknowledgments: He umpired at the 13-year-old boys Babe Ruth National Tournament in 1989.

JAMES D. SMITH III, born in 1951, a San Diego native. At age 9 he "discovered" baseball in the sports section of an almanac, beginning a life-

long enjoyment (on and off the field). He joined SABR in 1982 at Cliff Kachline's invitation, a Turkin and Thompson initiate (thanks, Tom Shea). While in New England he organized three Boston regionals and currently serves on the San Diego Chapter's Steering Committee.

Smith's SABR committee work and publications reflect 19th century, biographical and PCL research (notably Padres). A participant in the Providence 1984 World Series centennial game, his visit with Joe Hauser at Minneapolis 1988 inspired memorable contacts with other old-timers like Jimmie Reese.

Smith and Linda married in 1972, blessed by children: Ben, Andy and Becca. Holding a Harvard doctorate in church history, he is pastor of Clairemont Emmanuel Baptist Church and adjunct faculty at Bethel Seminary and the University of San Diego.

MARK B. SOMMER, born Jan. 8, 1958, in New York, NY. Joined the SABR in 1998 to better understand the game's history. His interests are varied and eclectic including baseball records, biographical research, statistical analysis, ballparks, Hall of Fame, 19th century, socio-economic aspects, biography, book collecting, collegiate baseball, oral history, baseball education, New York Mets, All-Star games, Japanese baseball, European baseball, amateur - semi-pro, pictorial history, scouts, Hoboken, NJ, baseball history, American colonial period references to baseball and Jewish baseball players and related baseball people. Sommer is a member of the Baseball Songs & Poems, Business of Baseball, 19th Century and Ballparks Committees.

He is a college instructor of humanities at Stevens' Institute of Technology.

ELIGIO MORALES SOSA, born July 9, 1934, in Aguada, PR. Joined the SABR Jan. 1, 1995, to improve his knowledge of baseball matters, etc.

He is currently a member of the Puerto Rico Chapter. His mentor is Jose Manuel Cora (died in 1989), who is considered the "father of the Little Leagues" in Caguas, PR. His son, Joey, recently retired from the big leagues and his son, Alex, belongs to the Dodgers Organization. Baseball expertise: 50 years as baseball fan. Also as manager, coach and general manager from the Little Leagues in Caguas, PR, to the class Double A baseball amateur, including his beautiful island, Puerto Rico, Santo Domingo, Venezuela, Chicago and New York, respectively, organizing different baseball teams. His interests are in scouting and Negro Leagues history, etc. He has written sports articles of Little Leagues in Puerto Rico.

Baseball/SABR Highlights & Memorable Experiences: The fact that he is planning to attend the 1999 National Baseball Hall of Fame inductions in Cooperstown, NY, to salute personally his good friend and Puerto Rican, recently nominated to the Hall of Fame, Orlando "Peruchin" Cepeda.

Sosa is married to Cielo and has four children: Hector E. (40), Victor M. (died at 14 in 1976), Carlos R. (died at 29 in 1995) and José E. (16-1/2). Carlos was waiting for a "try out" from the Atlanta Braves the same month he died in a car accident. Cepeda taught him most of the fundamentals of baseball. Sosa is an agronomist, retired in 1994 from the Farmers Home Administration (28 years as assistant county supervisor in Puerto Rico). He is still working as a broker of real estate properties and is expecting to study law at the School of Law, Eugenio Maria De Hostos, Mayaguez, PR. Hobbies: Collecting baseball books, videos of baseball, etc.

CHARLES HOWARD STAGG, born Oct. 24, 1946, in Kinder, LA. Joined the SABR in 1987 because of his appreciation of baseball statistics. Baseball expertise: Pitching statistics. His interests include college baseball (Rice University Owls) and professional baseball (St. Louis Cardinals). Written works in *Baseball Research Journal*, Number 21, *Control Pitching - A Learned Behavior.*

Baseball/SABR Highlights & Memorable Experiences: Publishing article in *Baseball Research Journal* with son as co-author.

He is married to Carla and has three chil-

dren: Howard, Charla and Loren Jay. Employed as environmental scientist for U.S. Army. Hobbies: Practice with youngest child (play pepper) and collects baseball books.

DAVE STALKER, born in Watertown, WI, Jan. 27, 1961. He has lived in the Everett, WA, area since June 1986. He joined the SABR in 1998 because of his love for the game and its history. Stalker has special interest in the career and life of Fred Merkle. His other area's of research interest are the 1908 season, the Chicago Cubs and the history of baseball in Watertown, WI, and surrounding area.

Stalker is married to Lori. They have three children: Angie (18), Nick (17) and Candace (14). He spends his vacation time traveling to different baseball stadiums, with the goal of getting to all of them. His lifelong hobby has been collecting baseball cards. The last several years he has been working on putting together a baseball card set from 1911, the beautiful T-205 gold border set. Stalker has been employed for 12 years at P.F. McDonald in Seattle, WA. He holds an inside sales position.

MARK STANG, born Jan. 8, 1955, in St. Cloud, MN. He joined SABR in 1990 after visiting the Hall of Fame research library in Cooperstown to start his uniform numbers project. He is currently a member of the Waite Hoyt-Lee Allen Chapter of SABR in Cincinnati, OH. His greatest reward of SABR membership has been the fellowship of other fans of the history of the game. His area of expertise is Major League uniform numbers. His first book, *Baseball By The Numbers* (Scarecrow Press, 1996) serves as the definitive source book for the history and evolution of player uniform numbers, and received the 1991 Macmillan-SABR Baseball Research Award. Stang is currently completing research on his next book, a biography of Chattanooga Lookouts owner, Joe Engel, dubbed the "Barnum of the Bushes" for his crazy promotional stunts. He is also a nationally recognized collector of vintage baseball memorabilia, specializing in flannel uniforms.

DENNIS STEGMANN, born June 23, 1958, in St. Louis, MO. Joined the SABR in 1992 and is currently a member of the Bob Broeg St. Louis Chapter. His interests include St. Louis Cardinals, Negro Leagues and statistical analysis. Offices held: Member, Board of Directors, Bob Broeg Chapter SABR. He has written articles, reviews and cartoons in several publications.

Stegmann is married to Cheryl and has three children: Ben, Jeff and Scott. He is a letter carrier. Hobbies: Doing broadcasting work at radio information service in Belleville, IL.

C. DAVID STEPHAN, born May 23, 1933, in La Porte, IN. Joined SABR in 1986 because of sabermetric cooperation. He is currently a member of the Los Angeles Chapter. His mentors are Joe Wayman and Vic Wilson. Baseball expertise: Hitting streaks, 50-hit months, sabermetrics and why players DNP. His interests include sabermetrics. He has had written works included in *Grandstand Baseball Annual* and is writing the *Dodger Encyclopedia.*

Baseball/SABR Highlights and Memorable Experiences: Many World Series and All-Star games.

He is married to Patricia (Hobson) and has two children, Larisa Angelique Natalya and Annelisa Christiana. He is retired after 35 years in the aerospace industry. Hobbies and noteworthy accomplishments include traveling and working with gifted children.

DAVE STEVENS, born in a galaxy far away ... uh, actually Baltimore, in the mid-20th century. He is on the 19th Century and Biographical Research Committees. Stevens' presentation on *John Montgomery Ward and Kansas City Baseball* at the 1995 National, may hold a record for the fewest attendees and for running into the Saturday night banquet.

His mentors include Fred Schuld and Dave Biesel. The story of how SABR enabled Stevens to write *Baseball's Radical for All Seasons* (Scarecrow Press 1998), a biography of Ward, appears elsewhere in this book. Stevens hopes to write a biography of Cap Anson.

Stevens has been a college history instructor and a social worker with homeless people, refugees and prisoners. The lifelong Orioles fan lives with his wife, Taffy, and his dog, Callie Ripken, in Chicago. His hobby is running up other SABR members' long-distance bills.

JOHN J. STODOLA, born Feb. 11, 1956, in Marinette, WI. He joined the SABR because he likes baseball. He is a member of the Statistical Analysis Committee.

Stodola is married to Laurie and has three children: Kristen, Philip and Angela. He is a teacher of math.

A.D. SUEHSDORF, born in Glen Ridge, NJ, Dec. 26, 1916. He graduated from Princeton University in 1938 and had a 41-year career as writer or editor for newspaper, magazine and book publishers. He joined SABR in 1979, has written regularly for *The National Pastime* and *Baseball Research Journal* since getting started (with big-league help from Vern Luse and Cliff Kachline) in 1980, and has been copy editor of both journals since 1995. Chaired the Publications Committee (1991-92). Wrote *Great American Baseball Scrapbook* (1978), has contributed articles to *Baseball History*, entries to *Biographical Dictionary of American Sports: Baseball, Baseball Chronology, Ballplayers, Total Baseball* and *American National Biography* (Oxford). Recipient of Bob Davids Award (1994).

16-Team Baseball Memories: Elegant pitching by Grove, Hubbell and Pennock; Foxx homer into upper left-field deck at Comiskey; a Maranville belt-buckle catch; L. & P. Waner; and Ruthian bases-full homer off Lloyd Brown before 56,000 one Memorial Day at the stadium.

GERALD E. SULLIVAN, MD, born Nov. 22, 1937, in Lexington, KY. Joined the SABR many years ago because of his love of baseball. He is currently a member of the Kentucky-Louisville Chapter. Baseball expertise: Collectibles, especially vintage cards, rules and history. His interests include collectibles, books, rules and history.

Sullivan is married to Joy Sue and has two children, Gerald E. and R. Thomas. He is a physician, ophthalmology.

BILL SWANK, played American Legion and high school baseball in Farmington, MN, during the 50s. Unable to hit the curve ball, he signed with the San Diego County Probations. He retired in 1994 after a 31-year career as a supervising probation officer. He has a BS degree in business administration from San Diego State College with a minor in history.

In addition to SABR he is also a member of the Pacific Coast League Historical Society and has campaigned for years to get San Diego's first Major Leaguer, deadball era slugger, Gavvy Cravath, elected into the Baseball Hall of Fame.

Swank, along with fellow SABR member, James D. Smith III, wrote an article about the original Lane Field Padres for *The Journal of San Diego History* and he served as the local historian for the "Runs, Hits and an Era" exhibition at the San Diego Historical Society in 1995. He coauthored with Dr. Ray Brandes *The Pacific Coast League Padres,* a two-volume history of the Lane Field era which was published by the San Diego Padres Baseball Club and the San Diego Baseball Historical Society in 1997. His own book, *Echoes from Lane Field,* was published in 1999.

He built a scale model of Lane Field, the home of the Padres from 1936-57. It was on display at the San Diego Hall of Champions in 1997 and 1998. Swank has appeared on television, radio and in news articles as an expert on early baseball in San Diego. He is happy to help others with research about the original San Diego Padres.

BARRY SWANTON, born Sept. 26, 1938, in Winnipeg, Manitoba. He joined the SABR in 1997 to learn more about the game. Swanton is a member of the NWSABR. Baseball expertise: Mandak League. His interests include Cleveland Indians, Negro League baseball and Mandak League. He is vice president of Competition Manitoba Baseball Association

Baseball/SABR Highlights & Memorable Experiences: Coached a number of years in the Manitoba Junior League.

He is married to Irene and has three children: Kelly, Dean and Jane. Swanton is retired.

W.K. (KIRK) SYMMES, born Dec. 30, 1923, in Oak Park, IL. Joined the SABR in 1990 because he was looking for a picture of 1937 New York Giants. He has autographs of 25 members of that team. The Baseball Hall of Fame did not have a picture of the team. A friend said, "Write SABR." Symmes did, joined, ran a research notice, a member in Hawaii sent him a team picture for five dollars. He thinks the bulletins, research journals and special publications are wonderful reading from cover to cover. Baseball interests: Ballplayers of the 1930s when he was an avid

Chicago Cub fan. Baseball trivia. The Asheville Tourists, Class A Sally League: the best entertainment value anywhere!

Memorable experiences: In 1968 took son and friends to day game in Atlanta Braves ballpark for his 8th birthday. Told him they would sit in the bleachers and talk to the outfield, a la Wrigley Field. Turned out the bleachers were in the upper deck so far from the field they could not see the catcher's signals. It was bat day. Boys with Hank Aaron bats wanted Joe Torre bats and v.v. Atlanta Tourist ballpark much more fun for young baseball fans.

Married to Gay and has three children: Will (member of SABR), Martha McLaughlin and Sarah Cotugno (husband a Yankee fan). Retired after 35 years in computer marketing. Hobbies: Woodworking; second career in retirement: teaching at a college for seniors (recognized in *Wall Street Journal,* June 1, Encore edition).

ANTHONY JOSEPH (TONY) SZABELSKI, born Jan. 4, 1965, in Chicago, IL. Joined the SABR in 1986 because of his love of baseball and research. Baseball expertise: Baseball photos, Minor Leagues and Negro Leagues. His interest is in Cubs photo collecting. He is a member of the Pictorial History, Minor League and Negro League Committees.

Baseball/SABR Highlights & Memorable Experiences: Being mentioned in SABR *Bulletin* for photo contributions.

He is married to Gwen and has three children: Amy, Ryan and Emily. Employed as food and beverage manager, Wynscape Nursing Home. Hobbies: Has photos of all Major Leagues, back to 1930, many others before that.

MICHIO TAKEUCHI, born Jan. 1, 1939, in Nagoya, Japan. Joined the SABR in July 1972. Baseball expertise: Manager of college women's baseball team. Vice president of Japan National League of College Women's Baseball. Member of the Biographical Research, Negro League, Ballpark and Women's Baseball Committees. Written works include *The Rise of Baseball in Meiji, Japan* and *Japanese Women's Baseball Before WWII* (both in paper).

She is married to Fumiyo and has two children, Satoshi (20) and Atsushi (18). Employed as professor of Kinjo Gakuin University, Nagoya, Japan.

MICHAEL P. TANGEL, born Dec. 21, 1947, during the 1947 blizzard in Greenpoint Brooklyn, NY. Presently he resides at 11 King Arthur's Ct., St. James, NY. He joined SABR in 1987 because of an ad in *The Sporting News.* He is a mini-season Mets ticket holder and likes the Yankees also. He is currently a member of the Casey Stengel Chapter

in New York City. His mentors include Norman Macht, John Husman and Robert L. Harrison (author and poet). He was an umpire of USSSA softball and plays 19th century baseball at Old Bethpage Village Restoration.

Tangel is currently a fifth grade teacher in Middle Country School District #11 since 1970. He was drafted during his first year of teaching and served in Vietnam. One of his proudest achievements in "The Nam" was tutoring eight "grunts" who successfully completed their high school equivalency diplomas. Since 1993 Tangel has played and umpired 1866 and 1887 baseball. One is underhand pitching (1866) and the other is overhand pitching (1887). In 1995 with the sponsorship of the Middle Country Teachers Association, Mickey "The Lip" started the Huntington Suffolks Baseball Club. The group of Middle Country teachers plays in the Old Time Base Ball League at Old Bethpage Village Restoration. The Suffolks also play many charity games for children with debilitating diseases.

Tangel has a collection of over 300 baseball books, many dealing with how the game was played in the 19th century. He has joined the 19th Century Committee of SABR. He is currently working on a project entitled *Old Time Base Ball Chatter During the 19th Century Game.* It will be used by players to liven up any 19th century game. He enjoys attending National Convention. He has been to Minnesota, Washington, D.C., New York City and Cooperstown. His most memorable experience is Norman Macht's 1998 Baltimore Bash Tour. Tangel has been married to Joan Marie for 20 years. They have one child, Matthew James. Tangel will retire from teaching in 2003. He will be busy bringing old time baseball to schools on Long Island. His hobby is collecting baseball memorabilia, books and the Long Island Ducks (year 2000 baseball team).

MGEN LARRY S. TAYLOR, USMCR (Retired), born March 28, 1941, in New York, NY. Member of Magnolia (Atlanta) Chapter SABR. Baseball expertise: Contributor '84 Bill James baseball abstract (Atlanta Braves analysis). Contributor *Hornsby Hit One Over My Head - A Fan's Oral History of Baseball* by David Cataneo (Chapter *The Magnolia in Center Field*). Written works: Baseball columnist *The Hudspeth Report* (Atlanta), 1988-92; columnist *Atlanta Braves Revista Mundial* (*World Magazine*) 1993-94.

Taylor is divorced and has one son, Keith. He is a 747 captain for Northwest Airlines. Noteworthy accomplishments: Major general (retired) U.S. Marine Corps Reserve.

DAVID C. THOMAS, born Jan. 11, 1956, in Harrisburg, PA. Joined the SABR in 1992. Reason for joining: Publications. Baseball expertise: Amateur draft. His interests include draft, Minors, records and amateur baseball. He is a member of the Minor League Committee. He has had one article in *Minor League History Journal* #2, two in *Baseball Research Journal,* three football research articles published, one regional, one national.

Baseball/SABR Highlights & Memorable Experiences: Jim Palmer no-hitter in 1969 (Vida Blue's first game he believes).

Thomas is married to Cathy and has two children, Jocelyn (14) and Drew (11). He is vice president of sales, Electrical South (Greensboro, NC). Hobbies and noteworthy accomplishments: Running, high school sports research, U.S. patent for electronic connector and contributor to second edition of *Encyclopedia of Minor League Baseball.*

STEW THORNLEY, born July 23, 1955, in Minneapolis, MN. Joined the SABR in 1979 because of his love of baseball. Currently a member of the Halsey Hall Chapter. Member of the Ballparks and Umpires and Rules Committees. He has been two-time president of Halsey Hall Chapter. Written works: Author of more than 20 books for adults and young readers. Most are sports related although one, co-authored with Brenda L. Himrich, is a science book about uses of electricity in medicine. Baseball books include *On to Nicollet: The Glory and Fame of the Minneapolis Millers* and *Holy Cow! The Life and Times of Halsey Hall* as well as biographies for young readers on Cal Ripken, Deon Sanders, Frank Thomas, Alex Rodriguez, Greg Maddux and Roberto Alomar. In addition, collaborated with Minnesota Twins broadcaster, Herb Carneal, on his autobiography.

Baseball/SABR Highlights: Recipient of the SABR-Macmillan Baseball Research Award in 1988 for his book, *On to Nicollet.* Recipient of the Baseball Weekly Award in 1998 for the best research presentation (subject was the Polo Grounds) at the SABR convention in San Francisco.

Married to Brenda Himrich. Employed as health educator, Minnesota Department of Health.

ROBERT L. TIEMANN, born Feb. 19, 1950 in St. Louis, MO. Always interested in history and baseball, he was SABR's 400th member when he joined in 1976. Using a chronological approach, he compiled daily game scores for the major leagues starting with 1876, graphing the pennant races up to the present day.

This study gave him an especially strong knowledge of early baseball and he has served as chairman of the 19th Century Baseball Committee, helped edit two volumes of player biographies, and spearheaded the project to produce modern box scores and statistics for the National Association, 1871-75.

A St. Louisan, Bob has done comprehensive studies of pennant races, winning and losing streaks, home and road records, ball parks, pre-1901 attendance and managerial changes. The author of histories of the Cardinals and Dodgers, he has attended a dozen national conventions, shared two SABR research awards and, at age 42, was honored with the Bob Davids Award in 1992.

Robert is single and works as a bank teller.

GERALD TOMLINSON, born Jan. 24, 1933, in Elmira, NY. A long-time fan of the Elmira Pioneers, with a continuing interest in the history of the NYP-Eastern League, he joined SABR in 1979 as a result of an inquiry about the Minor League career of James (Rip or Ripper) Collins sent to Cliff Kachline, at that time historian at the National Baseball Hall of Fame and Museum.

Tomlinson helped design the covers for the small-format 1982 and 1983 *Baseball Research Journals* and in 1986 suggested to then-president, Cappy Gagnon, the idea for a research guide, which became *The Baseball Research Handbook* (title and foreword by John Thorn), published by SABR in 1987. He has attended many National Conventions.

Tomlinson has been married to Alexis (nee Usakowski) for more than 30 years. They have two sons, Eli, who owns a computer store in Scranton, PA; and Matthew, a graduate student in anthropology at the University of Pennsylvania. A writer and small-press publisher who lives at Lake Hoptacong, NJ, Tomlinson's recent publications have been in the mystery and true-crime field.

RICHARD B. (DIXIE) TOURANGEAU, nick-named for 1930s movie star Richard Dix and Brooklyn's "People's Cherce," Tourangeau was born in Webster, MA, July 3, 1947, the day Cleveland signed Larry Doby. Tourangeau first visited Cooperstown in 1976 and witnessed the Ernie Banks-Joe Sewell induction in 1977. In 1980 he met Hall librarian, Cliff Kachline, and

joined SABR by 1981. Almost simultaneously a publisher friend gave Tourangeau charge of the *Play Ball!* baseball calendar (1981 debut) now one of the longest continuously published collectibles. Tourangeau headed a group to elect Arky Vaughan to the Hall of Fame and promoted Nellie Fox for the same honor. He has written for *The National Pastime* and has gathered tidbits from the Boston Public Library for several SABR friends. Tourangeau has seen games at 30 Major League ballyards including the final games at Memorial Stadium and old Comiskey Park. Since the mid-1980s he has journeyed twice-yearly the 242 miles to Cooperstown from his Boston home (a mile from both Fenway Park and the old Huntington Avenue Grounds). He has attended several National Conventions and has given many research presentations at Southern New England's Lajoie-Start Regional sessions.

Sharing Tourangeau's hobbies of baseball, travel (49 states, 190 national park areas), camping, photography, softball (.450), golf and the Celtics (since 1956) is Marilyn Miller (computer wiz). Tourangeau has worked for the National Park Service since fall 1983. His baseball publications number more than 1,000 and his card collection is substantial. Since Hall of Fame Day (June 12) 1986, Slater (acquired via street waivers), World's Greatest Pussycat, has ruled Tourangeau's apartment.

RICK TUBER, became a SABR member after hearing about the organization from author Darryl Brock. His book *If I Never Get Back,* is one of Tuber's favorites.

Tuber is a television film editor, currently working on the show, *Martial Law.* He won an Emmy for his work on *ER.* An avid Yankee fan, Tuber also plays softball once a week. His son, Peter, who is now pitching in high school, was a member of the Northridge Little League team that played in the 1994 Little League World Series in Williamsport, PA. He is married to the daughter of Brooklyn Dodger great, Pete Reiser.

WALTER DUNN TUCKER, born Oct. 5, 1931, in Richmond. Joined SABR because of his love

of baseball. Baseball expertise: 1930s, 40s and 50s. His interests include records. He has written letters to local paper correcting errors.

Baseball Highlights & Memorable Experiences: Seeing Ted Williams and Stan Musial hit home runs and playing semi-pro baseball.

Tucker is married to Jacqueline R. and has two sons, Andrew and Bruce, and one grandson, Bryan. He is a retired banker and naval reservist. Hobbies: Reading history and Navy League of the U.S.

HARLAN ULLMAN, born Oct. 24, 1962, in Columbus, OH. Joined the SABR in 1994 because of his love of baseball history (especially ballparks) and SABR publications. He is currently a member of Jack Graney Chapter, Cleveland, OH. Baseball expertise: Ballparks and ballparks on postcards. His interests include ballparks on postcards (especially antique) and Cleveland Indians. He writes a column called *The*

Scouting Report for *Ballparks & Ballplayers,* a baseball postcard hobby newsletter published six times a year.

He has been married to Susan for 11 years and has one daughter, Julia (3). Employed as a radiologist in Akron, OH. Hobbies: Collecting baseball park postcards and Indian season ticket holder (shared).

R.G. (HANK) UTLEY, born March 22, 1924 in Concord, NC. He has been a SABR member for many years. His childhood hero was Hank Greenberg, hence his nickname "Hank." From his Greenberg collection he has donated seven photographs to Ted Williams' Hitters Hall of Fame and nine photographs plus two scrapbooks to Cooperstown. His personal collection includes 50 Greenberg photograph negatives. Utley's book, *The Independent Carolina League, 1936-1938, Baseball Outlaws,* was published in 1999. Utley donated over 50 vintage photographs of the "outlawed professionals" to the Minor League archives in Cooperstown. He has made research reports at the 1997 SABR National Convention and the 1998 Cooperstown Symposium on Baseball and American Culture. He has an extensive book collection.

Utley has been married to Jean for 48 years and they have two children, Linda and Robert, and five grandchildren: Sam, Kelly, Matt, Jessica and Nicholas. Utley is a retired textile engineer. Hobbies: Baseball research and history.

EDUARDO VALERO, born July 29, 1925 in San Juan, PR. He is a sportswriter and historian and joined SABR in 1981. Eduardo is chairman of Latin-American Committee. His expertise is Latin-American Major and Minor Leagues and Negro Leagues.

Interests are amateur and international baseball. He has written over 900 newspaper articles on history of baseball - international.

Eduardo is president, International Promotion and Press Service. He is single and has three children: Eduardo, Carlos and Ricardo.

ALEXANDER VASICH, born Oct. 8, 1957, in Milwaukee. Joined the SABR in 1995 to learn more about the game. Baseball expertise: Old ballparks and baseball board games.

Baseball/SABR Highlights & Memorable Experiences: Most memorable is visiting Wrigley Field.

Vasich is single. Hobbies: Collecting old ballpark models and board games.

DAVID QUENTIN VOIGT, born Aug. 9, 1926, in Reading, PA. At Syracuse University in 1962, he earned his Ph.D degree in social science with

a dissertation on the commercialization of Major League Baseball during the 1880s. Subsequently he continued his MLB research and writing as a professor at Albright College, where he taught courses in sociology, anthropology and MLB history.

He is the author of eight books and more than 200 articles on MLB, including *American Baseball* (3 volumes), *America Through Baseball, Baseball: An Illustrated History* and *A Little League Journal.* His latest book, *The League That Failed,* appeared in 1998.

Voigt joined SABR in 1972 and became its president in 1974. He was later honored with a SABR Salute and by the Grandstand Baseball Annual. In April 1999 fellow baseball historians staged a symposium in honor of Emeritus Prof. Voigt at Albright College.

He has been married to Virginia Louise for 48 years. They have two sons, David J. (high school baseball coach) and Mark W. (a player turned lawyer), and two grandsons, David Grady and Gregory David. He is currently at work on the fourth volume of his American Baseball opus.

DAVID WALKER, mathematician and teacher, turned to keeping score and statistics early when an injury ended his dream to play: 14H 7HR in 15AB. When their Blue Sox manager needed help, Walker gave him new statistics "ability to get on," "production with men on," "player win average," "progressive ability to produce" and "performance help."

In 1982 he formulated a way to compare Ruth to Maris. The mathematical comparison to the rest of the league: Walker Comparison Factor. Cliff Kachline at the National Baseball Hall of Fame accepted the resulting lists, "provable top ten" and "domination of baseball." When Walker says Bob Feller was the greatest, he can prove it. A former NBA player needed a hand with his team so Walker added "team production" and "spark ability" to his other stats to aid in a 19-7 season.

Now on disability he has time to teach grandkids baseball stats.

ROBERT G. WALKER, born May 18, 1949, in Roanoke, VA. Joined the SABR in 1993 to share his enjoyment of the game with fellow baseball enthusiasts. He is currently a member of the Baltimore/Washington (Bob Davids) Chapter. Baseball expertise: Ballpark architecture - baseball architecture on sports arenas. His interests include the Baltimore Orioles, ballparks, Hall of Fame, Babe Ruth Museum, Negro Leagues and baseball books.

Baseball/SABR Highlights & Memorable Experiences: First SABR convention attended (Arlington, TX); Oriole playoff games in the 70s and 1983 in Memorial Stadium.

He has been married to Jean for 14 years. Employed as project architect in Baltimore.

PATRICK K. WALSH, born Dec. 19, 1948, in Milwaukee. Joined the SABR in 1975 because

he enjoys baseball history and statistics. Baseball interest(s): He attends 15 Brewer games a year and keeps score at every game he's gone to. He has every ticket stub (including the 1975 All-Star and 1982 World Series). Written works include *Baseball All-Time All-Stars* (25 best players from the 26 franchises before 1993).

Baseball/SABR Highlights & Memorable Experiences: He had his picture taken with Robin Yount Nov. 7, 1995, at an "awards" dinner in Milwaukee.

Walsh married Anita Aug. 1, 1981. He has two children, Timothy (15) and Steven (12). He has been a letter clerk at U.S. Postal Service for 26 years. Hobbies and noteworthy accomplishments: He's peddled his bicycle on six cross-country trips through 35 states and 10 provinces before he married. He also owns six bookcases of baseball books, including the complete collection of all the *Baseball Guides* and *Baseball Registers.*

EDWARD H. WALTON, born April 21, 1931, in Easton, PA. Joined the SABR in 1976 because of his interest in baseball research. He is currently a member of the Southern New England Chapter. His mentor is Robert Lindsay. Baseball expertise: Boston Red Sox history - player evaluations. His interests include the Boston Red Sox and the 30s and 40s. He is a member of the Boston Red Sox Hall of Fame Committee. Written works include *This Date in Boston Red Sox History, Red Sox Triumphs and Tragedies, The Rookies* and many articles.

Baseball/SABR Highlights & Memorable Experiences: Having a player from each era since 1901 as a friend.

He is married to Ruth and has two children, William and Susan, and four grandchildren: Stephen, Amy, Greg and Tyler. Employed in management positions in industry and a university. Hobby: Baseball. Accomplishments: Having four books and many articles published.

EDWARD ROBERT WARD, born in Chicago, IL, Nov. 26, 1946, he was "raised" on the Chicago White Sox, although travel through the country for academic reasons caused him to "get into" various Major and Minor League teams over the years. A love of old parks was born over the years. He has been a member of SABR since the early 1990s. Baseball expertise and interests: Poetry and history. He recently has written *Where Memory Gathers: Baseball and Poetry* (San Francisco: Forum, 1998), a collection of baseball poems. One of them, "A Fevered Time," was read at the recent conference at LIU-Brooklyn on the life of Jackie Robinson.

Ward was ordained to the priesthood in the Catholic Church June 9, 1973. He is a member of the Carmelite Order. He lives and works at St. Joseph's Church in Bogota, NJ. Writing about

baseball and social issues continues to be a hobby.

GUY WATERMAN, born in New Haven, CT, May 1, 1932, and educated at George Washington University, Waterman's interest in baseball has

waxed and waned over a career that included playing piano in Washington, D.C. nightclubs, speech writing on Capitol Hill and in the corporate world, and finally 25 years homesteading in the backwoods of Vermont with his dear wife, Laura.

He is one of the founders and first officers of SABR's Larry Gardner Chapter (Vermont) and a frequent contributor to both *The National Pastime* and *Baseball Research Journal.* He also writes for *Baseball Digest* and *NINE.*

Memorable baseball recollections include watching Jim Tobin set the record of three homers by a pitcher in one game (1942), Roger Maris' 60th (1961) and Willie Mays' first game back in the Polo Grounds as a San Francisco Giant (1962). He also treasures meeting and talking with Jackie Robinson in 1961.

JOSEPH M. WAYMAN, born March 22, 1927, in Strasburg, VA. He completed his education graduating from Virginia Tech in 1952. He joined SABR Aug. 8, 1979, but had been receiving its literature before its formal birth, Bob Davids' early *Baseball Briefs.* His mentors are Pete Palmer and especially Frank Williams.

Wayman's first published articles appearing in the *Baseball Bulletin* 1984 led to his self published *Grandstand Baseball Annual.* An annual which is described as "fun stats for grandstand fans"—but it's more than just that. A number of discovered and revised stats in its pages have made their way into *Total Baseball.*

Importantly, recent *Grandstand Baseball Annual* articles have been the recipient of Macmillan-SABR Baseball Research Awards: 1995 "Walter Johnson: The California Comet?" by Hank Thomas and Chuck Carey (Johnson's youth days in California), 1996 "Pitching W-L Records: NL 1890-1899," by Joseph M. Wayman (W-L records compiled as closely as possible to the day's official decisions), and 1997 (two articles) Nate Moreland, "Mystery to Historians," by John McReynolds (little awareness that Moreland is the first recognized black to play in organized baseball west of the Mississippi) and "The History of Major League Tie Games," by Clifford Blau (excellent review).

Wayman is a member and attends his Allan Roth SABR meetings in Los Angeles. He is single and is currently retired. His *Grandstand Baseball Annual* has become a full-time work hobby.

CHARLES (NEWT) WEAVER JR., born April 23, 1952, in Salisbury, MD, but makes his home in Ocean City, MD. He graduated from Mount St. Mary's College in Emmitsburg, MD, with

a degree in history. He joined SABR in 1987 in order to further his studies in baseball's illustrious history.

Since first joining the 19th Century Committee, Weaver's enthusiasm has not waned, as he now retains memberships in the Statistical, Biographical and Baseball Records Committees. He is a member of the Bob Davids Chapter of SABR, as well as a member of the Eastern Shore Baseball Foundation. His mentors include Daniel R. Mumford, esquire and the late publisher, Ralph Horton.

His vast knowledge of the amateur era (1845-65) and the 'semi-professional' period (1866-76), coupled with data on the first 'Minor Leagues' (1877-79), has allowed Weaver to experience interesting exchanges with other authorities sharing similar concerns. He is an expert on the career of Louis Pessano "Buttercup" Dickerson. Some of his published studies include articles on Frank "Home Run" Baker, Jimmie "Double X" Foxx, Yogi Berra, a brief history of the Atlanta Braves, and a concise history of the Eastern Shore Baseball Hall of Fame.

Weaver's most memorable experience was helping to advance the nomination of "Buttercup" Dickerson for induction into the Eastern Shore Baseball Hall of Fame in 1996. He relishes collecting first edition baseball books and guides published in the 19th century.

He is presently contributing work on a games played index and team/roster directory of the amateur era. Weaver is single and is the co-owner/manager of Weaver Bros. Beer & Wine Carry Out in Ocean City.

KENNETH J. WEAVER, born Sept. 29, 1951, in Milford, CT. Joined the SABR in 1996 to learn/research 19th century baseball clothing, equipment and rules of the game. He is currently a member of the Lajoie-Start Chapter (Southern New England). Baseball expertise: 19th century baseball uniforms and equipment. His interest is in 19th century baseball and he is a member of the 19th Century Committee. Written works: Copyrights for *19th Century Base Ball Uniform & Cap Patterns*.

Baseball/SABR Highlights & Memorable Experiences: Member of VBBA (Vintage Base Ball Association).

He is married to Paula. Weaver is a senior production planner, product development engineer. Hobbies: Civil War re-enacting, 19th century baseball, woodworking, player/manager New Haven Elm City's Baseball Club (Connecticut 1874).

PAULA M. WEAVER, born Dec. 11, 1954, in Derby, CT. Joined the SABR in 1996 to learn/research 19th century baseball clothing. Currently a member of the Lajoie-Start Chapter (Southern New England). Baseball expertise: 19th century baseball uniforms. Her interest is in 19th century baseball and she is a member of the 19th Century Committee. Written works: Copyrights for *19th Century Base Ball Uniform & Cap Pattern*.

She is married to Kenneth. Employment: *19th Century Clothier* of men's Civil War era clothing & baseball uniforms. Prior work: Special education teacher, project leader/programmer. Her hobbies are sewing and historical research.

MAX WEDER, a tax litigation lawyer with Ladner Downs in Vancouver, B.C. Prior to this he spent 14 years tilting at windmills in that field with the federal Dept. of Justice. It was then said the definition of a "tax loophole" was the last case he argued. He has taught tax and business law at local colleges. Weder also sells used books on the Internet and is a collector of baseball books, specializing in early boys' fiction. He was born in June 1958 and is married to sports artist and SABR member Jennifer Ettinger. They don't have children, but are fully occupied with Annie, the Australian shepherd. Weder's baseball career ended at 13 when his team won one game all year, despite his .235 average. Basketball and

hockey followed, where he enjoys similar success to this date.

FRANK WEILER, born May 5, 1943, in Utica, NY. Joined the SABR in 1993 because of his love of baseball statistics. His interests include history, statistics and Minor League statistics.

Weiler is single and is an audit manager, Air Force Audit Agency. Hobbies: Bowling—member Professional Bowlers Association (PBA).

DON WEISKOPF, born June 8, 1928, in Libertyville, IL. Following his studies at the University of Illinois and military service in the Korean War, the long-time college professor began a versatile career, including professional baseball, college teaching and coaching, recreation and park administration and authoring books and articles. Weiskopf joined SABR in 1993 to  share baseball interests and research involvement and encourage those in SABR to help protect the best interests of the game. A resident of El Dorado Hills, CA, he is a member of the SABR chapter in Sacramento.

Many of his 14 books and numerous articles have been on baseball, including *The Complete Baseball Handbook*, co-authored with Walter Alston, manager of the Los Angeles Dodgers for 23 years. Since the 1950s Weiskopf has written extensively on how the game is played, including over 100 articles for *Athletic Journal* and how-to books for *The Sporting News*. Since 1993 he has been heavily involved with an evaluative analysis of the major problems, issues and needs of baseball, a project he presented to the 1998 SABR convention. The official report of the 5-year project and his new book, *Baseball Play in America*, will feature a Plan for Baseball to help "Restore the Greatness of Baseball."

Weiskopf has been married to Annegrete for over 35 years. They have two daughters, Christine and Lisa.

LAWRENCE H. WENTZ, born Nov. 26, 1937, in Philadelphia, PA. Joined the SABR in 1986 at suggestion of Paul MacFarlane of *Sporting News*. His mentors are Paul MacFarlane and Edward "Dutch" Doyle (deceased). Baseball expertise: Player in high school, college legion and 28 years coaching boys and girls ages 10-13. His interests are writing and baseball period 1930s to date. He has written two books about Notre Dame.

Wentz created the Dick Littlefield Club in 1979, with cooperation of Mr. Littlefield. They honored 11 retired players, 1984-88. Five have since been enshrined at Cooperstown.

Baseball/SABR Highlights & Memorable Experiences: Made presentation to SABR meeting in Cooperstown in 1987.

Wentz is married to Lou Ann and has 12 children and 10 grandchildren. He is president, Kindt, Kaye and Wentz Insurance Brokers (fulltime). Hobbies: Photography and writing. Honored twice by the Notre Dame Alumni (class of '59).

MARK J. WERNICK, born June 16, 1948, in San Antonio, TX. Joined the SABR in 1997 for access to research. He is currently a member of the Houston Chapter. His mentor, in the Houston Regional Group, is Bill Gilbert. Baseball expertise: Houston Colt .45s, Houston Astros and New York Yankees.

Baseball/SABR Highlights & Memorable Experiences: All of the regional meetings are memorable to him.

He is married to Anne and has a son, Aaron (6). Wernick is a psychologist (PhD) in private practice. Hobbies: Paleo-anthropology, archeology, vintage cars and collecting baseball books and cards.

HERMAN L. WHEELER, born July 13, 1938, in Zanesville, OH. Joined the SABR May 15, 1991. The Hall-Ruggles Chapter of SABR sponsored a luncheon honoring Ernie Harwell May 15, 1991. Although he was not a SABR member at the time, since the luncheon was open to the public, he attended. At that luncheon he was introduced to Howard Green and other members of the chapter who introduced him to SABR. He joined, and  has been a member ever since. His mentor is Howard Green. Baseball expertise: Long-time fan. His interests include old radio broadcasts and interviews. Also, old ballparks. Wheeler is a member of the Oral History Committee.

Baseball/SABR Highlights & Memorable Experiences: SABR highlights include the Ernie Harwell Luncheon in 1991. Also, the SABR conventions he attended in St. Louis, Kansas City and Louisville. The most memorable convention is the one their chapter hosted in 1994. Finally, memorable SABR experiences include the several taped interviews he made with retired players. Outside of SABR, the most memorable baseball game he ever attended was being present for Nolan Ryan's seventh no-hitter.

He is married to Carolyn and has one son, Glenn; one daughter, Sharon; and four grandchildren. Wheeler is a customer service specialist for Internal Revenue Service. Hobbies: Strat-O-Matic Baseball.

RALPH J. WICK, born June 4, 1948, in Oak Park, IL. He joined SABR in 1987 to learn more about the game and share his love of the game with other baseball fans. He is currently a member of the Emil H. Rothe Chapter in Chicago, IL. His expertise is the Chicago White Sox and he has general interest in the statistical and historical aspects of the game. His most memorable experience was having the opportunity to conduct tours of old Comiskey Park in 1990 for Chicago White Sox charities.

Wick is single and is an assistant vice president at the First National Bank of Chicago. His hobby is collecting statistical and historical baseball books.

WARREN N. WILBERT, born Feb. 23, 1927, at Kohler, WI. Joined the SABR in December 1993. Since moving to Fort Wayne in October 1997 he has not been in a group but is a former member of Fred T. Smith Chapter, Detroit, MI. Baseball expertise: White Sox and rookies. His interest is in history, especially '20s and '30s. Written works include *The Chicago Cubs: Seasons at the Summit*, with Bill Hageman ('97); *Yankee Seasons at the Summit*, with Bill Hageman (spring, '99); articles for SABR *Baseball Research Journal*; and rookie book due 2000.

He is married to Virginia (Ginny) nee Kuhlman (St. Louis) and has three daughters and 11 grandchildren. Wilbert is a retired dean of Lifelong Learning Services, Concordia University System at Ann Arbor, MI. Also had coaching career from 1949-63 in football, basketball and baseball.

Accomplishments: Recipient, $10,000 postdoctoral Behnken Memorial Award, Lutheran Church, for studies in residential continuing education at Oxford (England) University.

GEORGE THOMAS WILEY, born in Cleveland, OH, where he saw his first Indians game in 1935. Later, through SABR, he became friends with Roy Hughes, second baseman on that club. Wiley saw service in the Philippines with the Navy during WWII. He graduated from Oberlin College (Ohio). Three of his varsity letters were in baseball. In 1998 he was elected to the Oberlin Athletic Hall of Fame. Wiley's research interests are wide-ranging. His "Computers in Baseball Analysis" received special mention for work published in the first decade of the *Research Journal*. "When the Best Played the Best" analyzed in the *Journal* the head-to-head competition of the Yankees and Athletics, 1927-32. In the 1980s Wiley gave four papers at four successive SABR conventions supporting the claim of the 1936-39 New York Yankees as the greatest teams ever. Wiley's first love, however, is the Cleveland Indians. His compilations of box scores and articles on the 1920, 1936, 1948 and 1954 Indians have been popular with collectors. During the research on the 1948 Indians he became friends with Ken Keltner. Wiley has done work on baseball in coal-mining towns in the 1930s and prepared a slide presentation on *The Baseball Magazine goes to War*. He has given papers at several Popular Culture conventions on sports topics, including his favorite author, Harold M. Sherman, a writer of juvenile sports fiction. Wiley has been a teacher of history for 50 years, the last 33 at Indiana University of Pennsylvania. He lives with his wife, Janet. They are the parents of three children: Kenneth, Andrew and Kathleen; and have one grandchild. Wiley has been a member of SABR since 1972 years.

OTTO EDWARD (ED) WILLIAMS, born Aug. 16, 1917, in Shawnee. Joined the SABR in 1976. As league statistician he hoped to help in accuracy and others research. His mentors are Kachline, Weiss and others. Baseball expertise: Statistician American Association (1971-82); International (1974-78); Texas League (1975-83); and Sooner State League (1954-57). His interests include stats, rules and scoring. Written works are *Sooner State League Record Book* (not published).

He married Wilda in 1946 and has one daughter, Elaina Hunt and two grandsons, Bryan and Jeffrey. Employment: Post Office (38 years). He is a WWII veteran with seven battlefield decorations and was in Patton's 3rd Army.

FRANK JOHN WILLIAMS, born March 26, 1942, in Bridgeport, CT. Graduated from the University of Bridgeport in 1965 with a degree in accounting.

He joined SABR in 1978 because of his interest in baseball and the research committees. He is a member of the New England Regional Group.

He is interested primarily in pitching won-loss practices 1876-1919 and all Boston baseball teams (Red Sox, Braves, Reds and Unions).

His major work was done in the correcting and compiling of all day by day pitching won-loss decisions for all American League pitchers for 1901-19, including relief won-loss, saves, starts, complete games and shutouts.

These corrections to American League pitching won-loss decisions for 1901-19 now appear in *Total Baseball*, the official encyclopedia of Major League baseball, the *Macmillan Baseball Encyclopedia* and *The Sporting News Major League Fact Book*.

His two major discoveries were finding that Walter Johnson had 33 wins in 1912 which meant that he had 417 wins lifetime and discovering an 18 game winning streak by the Boston Beaneaters in 1891. He found out about this 18 game streak back in 1980 and it took him 12 years to get it corrected in all the record books.

In the area of consecutive game hitting streaks, Williams made two major discoveries. The first one was Tris Speaker having a 30 game and two 20 game hitting streaks in 1912 which made him the only Major League player ever to do this. The second one was Cal McVey having a 30 game hitting streak in 1876 which made him the first player in Major League history to have a 20 or more game hitting streak and the first to have a 30 or more game hitting streak.

He also compiled all the statistics for the 1892 National League Championship series which is now shown in *Total Baseball*.

He has also made corrections for pitcher's won-loss for the period 1876-1900 for all Major Leagues and for the National League, 1901-19 which is now shown in the record books previously mentioned.

Williams belongs to the SABR Baseball Records, 19th Century and Minor League Committees. He is also a member of the Boston Braves Historical Association

His written works include a book, *The Battle For Baseball Supremacy In Boston: A Chronicle of the Annual City Championship Series Between the Boston Red Sox and Boston Braves*. This was published in 1998 by the Boston Braves Historical Association

He has also written over 20 published baseball articles including, *Smoky Joe Wood and the 1912 World's Champion Boston Red Sox* and *Waite Hoyt's Deprived Win*. These were published in Joe Wayman's *Grandstand Baseball Annual*.

His most memorable experience in baseball was being friends with Smoky Joe Wood for seven years. The many conversations with him at his house in West Haven, CT, about pre-1920 baseball were an education in themselves.

Meeting Waite Hoyt at the Hall of Fame in Cooperstown and corresponding with Harry Hooper were other memorable experiences.

All three of these baseball players knew Babe Ruth very well and had some great stories about him.

Williams' Minor League interests center on

James O'Rourke and his Bridgeport Orators. O'Rourke, the only Hall of Famer from Bridgeport, was born here and he died here in 1919. Williams has compiled the complete Minor League record of James O'Rourke. He is single and employed as an accountant.

JOSEPH C. (JOE) WILLIAMS, born Jan. 26, 1967, in Poughkeepsie, NY. Joined the SABR in 1990 when a friend alerted him to a book by SABR and he discovered he could become a member. He is currently a member of the Start-Lajoie Chapter (Rhode Island). Baseball expertise: Candidates for the Baseball Hall of Fame. His interests include the Hall of Fame, memorabilia, 19th century, Negro Leagues and history of the game in general. Williams is a member of the 19th Century and Negro Leagues Committees.

Baseball/SABR Highlights & Memorable Experiences: Has attended Hall of Fame inductions since 1987; flew to Oakland to watch Rickey Henderson break stolen base record but instead stole base 937 and was injured shortly after - it was however Chuck Knoblauch's first Major League game; and 1986 New York Mets World Series victory, his biggest thrill, he attended ticker tape parade.

Williams is married to Carol and has two children, Anthony (Tony) and Jacqueline (Jackie). He is employed with Day, Berry & Howard LLP as law library assistant. Hobbies: Collects memorabilia, huge Eddie Murray fan and New York Mets fan.

C. NORMAN WILLIS, born July 5, 1924, in Washington, D.C. Joined the SABR in the early 1980s to aid research for his book. He is currently a member of the Baltimore/Washington Chapter. Baseball expertise: Washington Senators baseball history. His interests include history, records and statistics. He has served as president of the local PTA. Willis is in the process of writing a book on the Washington Senators.

Baseball/SABR Highlights & Memorable Experiences: Witnessed "Schoolboy" Rowe's 16th straight win.

He has been married to Frances L. for 52 years. They have three children: Glenn, Larry and Joel, and six grandchildren: Casey, Amy, Kayla, Kelly, Naomi and Maggie. Willis retired from National Security Agency after 38 years. Hobbies and noteworthy accomplishments: Baseball cards/contributed to success of "Venona."

AMY S. WINNICKI, born Sept. 22, 1963, in Attica, OH. Joined the SABR because of her love of the game and is a member of the Jack Graney Chapter. She grew up in a "baseball family." Her summers were spent watching Little League, listening to Herb Score and the Cleveland Indians, and playing many backyard games! She met her husband, Tim, at BGSU and realized they both loved the game. Their honeymoon included a day at the Hall of Fame in Cooperstown, NY. They are devoted Indians fans and either go, listen to, or watch all of the games. They have also added to the next generation of "baseball lovers" in their children: Sarah (July 29, 1994), Joseph (June 5, 1996) and Anna (June 15, 1998). Although she has not contributed much to SABR as far as research goes, she does enjoy the organization. It is great knowing there is a whole "society of lunatics!" Winnicki is a recreation program supervisor.

ALLAN WOOD, born in Burlington, VT. In 1975, shortly before his 12th birthday, he became a Boston Red Sox fan. He attended his first Major

League game Aug. 22, 1976, at Fenway Park: Oakland 7, Boston 6, in 11 innings. Since then, he has seen games at 12 Major League parks, including a 22-inning shutout in Montreal.

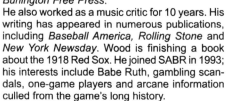

At age 16 he began writing about sports for *The Burlington Free Press*. He also worked as a music critic for 10 years. His writing has appeared in numerous publications, including *Baseball America, Rolling Stone* and *New York Newsday*. Wood is finishing a book about the 1918 Red Sox. He joined SABR in 1993; his interests include Babe Ruth, gambling scandals, one-game players and arcane information culled from the game's long history.

He lives in New York with Laura Kaminker, a Yankee fan, and their two dogs, Gypsy and Clyde.

JOHN M. ZAJC JR., born in March 1965 in Cleveland, OH. A 1987 graduate of Ohio Northern University, he joined SABR in 1990 just prior to being hired to fill a newly-created clerical position. Now manager of membership services for SABR, Zajc does not have any particular research interest, but tries to keep abreast of which SABR members do have an expertise. He expects to learn much more from this book.

Zajc's lasting SABR impression is the camaraderie of SABR members, something that is especially evident at the National Conventions, where friendships that last a lifetime are formed over just a couple of days.

Zajc has been married to fellow member, Catherine Smythe Zajc, since 1995. They enjoy urban living just a mile south of Jacobs Field with their dog, Zoe.

HARRY ZELKIN, born June 8, 1955, in Haifa, Israel. He joined the SABR in November 1995 because of his intense love of the game and New York Yankees. He is currently a member of the Casey Stengel Chapter (New York). Baseball expertise: European baseball. His interests include 19th century ball, Negro Leagues, collecting publications and the Yankees.

Baseball/SABR Highlights & Memorable Experiences: Sharing camaraderie at regional conventions.

Zelkin is a doctor of veterinary medicine. He lived in Italy for 10 years.

JACK R. ZERBY, born May 9, 1943, in Knox, PA. Joined the SABR in October 1993 to associate with others of similar interests and expertise. Baseball expertise: Career of Bill Werber (1933-42) and writings of Red Barber. His interests include the 1939-40 Cincinnati Reds, Florida State League, Moe Berg and abolition of DH rule.

Baseball/SABR Highlights & Memorable Experiences: Trips to Forbes Field and touring present and past Florida State League parks.

He married Diana in 1970. Employed as a paralegal with Cummings & Lockwood, Attorneys. Hobbies: Collecting baseball books, tennis and general reading.

DIAMANTIS ZERVOS, author of *Baseball's Golden Greeks*, was born in Athens, Greece, May 17, 1956. He moved to the U.S. with his family in 1971 at the age of 15. He established himself as a soccer player in high school and college and graduated from the University of Massachusetts with a degree in biology. He is a successful entrepreneur and sports enthusiast. Zervos resides in Canton, MA, with his wife, Evangeline, and their two children, Anastasia

and Michael. He is owner of a dry cleaning business.

Zervos was interested in baseball at an early age. In fact, he had a collection of baseball cards while a young boy in Greece, courtesy of his late uncle, before he even saw a game played or understood what baseball was all about. Subsequently, he fell in love with baseball when he watched the 1975 World Series. He joined the SABR in 1996 for baseball research.

In 1998 he authored *Baseball's Golden Greeks: The First Forty Years*. Following research involving over a three-year period on the careers of the first 20 Greek-Americans in Major League baseball, he showed for the first time ever their contributions to America's national pastime from 1934-74. *Baseball's Golden Greeks* is published by Aegean Books International, Canton, MA.

DAVID ZINK, born Jan. 29, 1948, in Bushton, KS. Joined the SABR in 1988 because he enjoys baseball history and this looked like the ideal organization. Baseball expertise: Minor League history of Great Bend, KS. His interests include Minor Leagues and New York Yankees. He is a member of the Biographical and Minor League Committees.

Baseball/SABR Highlights & Memorable Experiences: Having an article published in *Unions To Royals*, SABR 26 convention publication.

He is married to Sandi and has three children: Sarah, Laurie and Regina. Zink is a certified public accountant. Hobbies: Reading - baseball and WWII.

TOM ZOCCO, born in Hartford, CT. Joined SABR in September 1971. Greatest thrill in SABR was attending first convention in 1974 in Philadelphia. When he first walked in someone was talking about Don Hoak. Zocco joined in that conversation. Someone else was talking about John McGraw. He was trying to listen to two conversations at the same time. Another conversation was going on about the Baltimore Orioles.

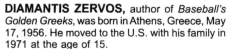

Listening to all this baseball talk he thought he had died and gone to Heaven. He has been to every convention since then. Twenty-five consecutive years. He served as SABR secretary in 1977.

Dislikes the designated hitter rule. An area of expertise is pitchers' batting records. Has a list of every pitcher with two or more hits or three or more RBIs from 1958 to present.

Is on the Records Committee as well as the Collegiate Baseball Committee.

Was on the team that won the national trivia contest four times. Team made the final four eight consecutive years. After winning the title three consecutive years they decided to break up the team.

Lifelong Dodger fan going back to the Brooklyn days.

Zocco collects baseball books as a hobby.

SABR Convention in Columbus, OH in 1977. From left: Cliff Kachline, John Pardon, Tom Hufford, Joe Simenic, Bob Davids, Ray Gonzalez, Bob McConnell and Bill Gustafson.

INDEX

The roster and bio sections are not included in this index since they appear in alphabetical order in their respective sections.

A

Adams, Dallas 22
Adams, Doris 37
Adams, Thomas J. 36
Adcock, Joe 37
Adelman, Melvin 26
Adesman, Marshall 20, 27
Adomites, Paul 19, 21
Ahrens, Art 18
Albany, NY 16, 21, 40
Alexandra, Tasha 39
Allen, Dick 36
Allen, Harry 39
Allen, Lee 9, 19, 24
Allen, Mel 14, 37, 46
Allen, Robert 11
Alvarez, Mark 17, 18, 19, 27, 31
American Giants 45
Anderson, Brady 45
Anderson, Dave 23
Anderson, Sparky 15
Andres, Ernie 16
Andresen, Paul 12, 27
Angels 45
Anson, Cap 42
Appel, Marty 20
Appling, Luke 16, 45
Ardell, Jean 27
Arizona Diamondbacks 42
Arizona Flame 16
Arlington, TX 15, 16
Arlington, VA 15
Aronstein, Mike 47
Arrington, Norman 63
Asinof, Eliot 25
Athletics 45, 46
Atlanta Braves 32, 42, 43
Atlantic City, NJ 17
Auburn (New York) Astros 42
Auker, Elden 22
Auker, Eldon 44
Averill, Earl 19

B

Ballard, Sarah 40
Ballou, Bill 21
Baltimore Orioles 44, 47
Baltimore Stars 46
Bankes, Jim 18
Barber, Red 37, 46
Barney, Rex 15
Bartell, Dick 45
Batista, Miguel 16
Battle Creek 21
Bauer, Carlos 17
Bavasi, Buzzie 16
Bean Eaters 38
Bearden, Gene 35
Becquer, Julio 16
Begley, Evelyn 12, 63
Beirne, Gerry 21
Bell, Cool Papa 15
Benson, Gene 15, 22
Benson, John 26
Benton Harbor 21
Berardino, Johnny 44
Bergen, Phil 17
Berger, Wally 15, 20
Bergman, Dutch 42
Bertoia, Reno 15
Bescher, Bob 42
Bevacqua, Kurt 15, 16, 21, 22
Beverage, Dick 12, 27, 63
Biesel, Dave 31
Bingham, Dennis 23
Bjarkman, Peter 18, 23, 26
Black, Don 35
Black Sox 33
Blass, Steve 21
Blattner, Buddy 15
Blau, Clifford 26
Blengino, Tony 26
Bloomberg, Mort 37, 38
Blue Jays 43
Bluthardt, Bob 18, 22

Boca Raton, FL 13
Bochy, Bruce 16
Borom, Red 22
Borst, Bill 14
Boslett, Frank 21
Boston Braves 35, 37, 38
Boston Red Sox 21, 30, 32, 33, 34, 35, 37, 38, 42, 43 44, 46
Boswell, Thomas 44
Bottomley, Jim 19
Boudreau, Lou 35
Boutlier, Martin 44
Bouton, Jim 31, 32
Bouton, Michael 32
Bowmanville, Ontario 43
Boynton, Bob 27, 32
Bradley, Rick 23
Brady, Jim 42
Bragan, Bobby 16
Brandt, Jackie 21
Bready, James 13
Brennaman, Marty 16
Bressoud, Eddie 16
Brewer, Chet 21
Brewers 33
Bridgewater, MA 15
Bristol, PA 34
Britt, Jim 37, 38
Brodsky, Chuck 36
Broeg, Bob 18, 21, 27
Broglio, Ernie 16
Bronx Bombers 31
Brookfield, CT 38
Brooklyn Dodgers 16, 31, 35, 38, 40
Broomes, Vincent 12
Brosius, Scott 47
Brown, Bobby 16
Brown, Joe L. 15
Brown, Mordecai 19
Browns 45
Bruton, Billy 37
Bucha, Johnny 14
Buckner, Bill 30
Buege, Bob 25, 27
Buhl, Bob 37
Bunning, Jim 15, 16
Burbage, Buddy 15, 22
Burdette, Lew 37
Burgeson, John W. 35
Burgos Jr., Adrian 26
Burk, Bob 26
Burkett, Jesse 21
Burlingame, CA 16, 17
Burlington, VT 30
Burris, Paul 38
Burtt, Dick 12

C

Cain, Bob 21
Campbell, Jeff 24, 27
Campbell, Jim 22
Campbell, Neil 10
Caray, Harry 37
Carey, Chuck 26
Carle, Bill 12, 17, 25, 26, 63
Carlisle, Cecil A. 39
Carlson, Jack 27
Carrasquel, Chico 15
Carroll, Bob 18
Carroll, Patrick 23
Carter, Joe 43
Case, George 19
Cash, Bill 16, 22
Cashman, Terry 16
Cato, Nancy Mudge 16
Cavender, Tony 21
Cepeda, Orlando 16, 17
Chadwick, Henry 19
Chambers, William 27
Chance, Frank 45
Chandler, Happy 22
Chapman, Ben 46
Chapman, Jean 19
Chapman, Ray 20
Chapman, Sam 15

Chase, Hal 45
Chattanooga, TN 21
Chevy Chase, MD 19
Chicago Black Sox 25
Chicago White Stockings 43
Chipman, Bob 38
Chipp, Mil 22
Christopher 35
Cimoli, Gino 16
Cincinnati Reds 35
Clark, Dick 17, 26
Clark, Ellery 13, 47
Clemente, Roberto 34
Cleveland Indians 36
Cleveland, OH 16, 21, 24, 25
Cleveland Sockalexi 42
Clift, Harlond 44
Cobb, Ty 19, 22, 33, 34, 42, 45
Cochrane, Mickey 15, 19, 38
Coffin, Don 22
Cohasset, MA 13
Cohen, Syd 47
Collins 19, 22
Columbus, OH 14
Combs, James 24
Comley, Clem 22
Conkwright, Al 45
Connor, Roger 19
Conrad, Emery 34
Conroy, Bill 46
Conway 35
Cooper, Mort 44
Cooperstown, NY 8, 10, 23, 24, 43
Cope, Ev 22
Coscarart, Pete 16
Coughenour, Dean 18
Counsell, Craig 42
Coupland, Frank 39
Cox, John W. 25, 26
Cram, Jerry 21
Cramer, Dick 12, 14, 18, 22
Crandall, Del 37
Crawford, Sam 33
Criger, Lou 21
Criscola, Tony 16
Crissey, Kit 11, 14
Crosetti, Frank 46
Cubs 45
Cummings, Steve 39
Cunningham, Joe 16
Cunningham, Laura 46

D

Dalton, Harry 22
Daniels, Bert 42
Daniels, Jon 15, 63
Daniels, Marge 12, 13, 27, 63
Darkin, Tony 21
Davids, Bob 8, 9, 10, 11, 12, 13, 14, 17, 18, 19, 23, 25, 26, 47, 63
Davis, George 21
Dean, Dizzy 35
Dean, Jimmy 12
Deane, Bill 18, 24, 26, 27
Del Rossi, Al 23
Delhi, Flame 21
Dellinger, Harold 13
Delsing, Jim 16
Demarest, Jay 15
DeMoll, Merl 38, 39
Detore, George 46
Detroit Tigers 22, 41, 42, 44
Deutsch, Jordan 17
DeValeria, Dennis and Jean 27
Dials, Lou 45
Dickson, Paul 26
Dierker, Larry 21

DiMaggio, Joe 19, 31, 35, 42
Dischley, Dan 10, 14
Dittmar, Joe 26
DiTullio, Ted 18
Dixon, Phil 26
Doby, Larry 35
Doerr, Bobby 32, 46
Dombrowski, Dave 21
Donaldson, Sam 22
Dorinson, Joseph 26
Doubleday, Abner 43
Duffy, Hugh 22
Dugan, Joe 14
Dunne, Bert 42
Durgey, David 27
Durham, NC 20
Dwyer, Joe 22

E

Eagan, John J. 39
Earley, Joe 35
Early, Jake 35
Eckhardt, Oscar "Ox" 31
Eckhouse, Maria 23, 63
Eckhouse, Morris 5, 20, 23, 24, 25, 27, 31
Edwards 35
Eisenhardt, John J. 34
Eisenhardt, Roy 15
Ellis, James C. 41
Ellis, Vanetta 16
English, Woody 45
Epstein, Eddie 22
Ernest Nagy 19
Erskine, Carl 16
Essex County, NJ 42
Eugene 20
Evans, Tom 12
Everett 20

F

Face, Elroy 16
Fanning, Jim 22
Fehr, Steve 16
Feller, Bob 16, 35
Fenway Park 30
Ferrell, Rick 45
FerricR, Tom 22
Fields, Wilmer 16
File, Larry 14
Flannagan, Don 39
Flatow, Scott 27
Fleming, G. H. 18
Fletcher, Art 19
Flinn, F. X. 24
Florida Marlins 21, 42
Fonseca, Lew 14
Ford, Adam 43
Formo, Tony 23
Fort Lauderdale, FL 45
Fowler, Bud 21
Foxx, Jimmie 34
Franco, Chris 21
Frankfurt, NY 21
Freitas, Tony 46
Frick, Ford 42
Fridley, Jim 14
Frierson, Eddie 16
Frisch, Frank 35
Frisz, Paul 10, 12

G

Gabriel, Ron 12, 19
Gaffke, Fabian 15
Gagliano, Phil 21
Gagnon, Cappy 11, 12, 21, 23, 27, 41, 42
Gammons, Peter 47
Garagiola, Joe 18, 22, 42
Garcia, Mike 35
Gardner, Larry 21
Garrett Park, MD 25
Garver, Ned 15, 16
Gehrig, Lou 22, 40, 44, 45

Gerlach, Larry 4, 12, 23, 25, 26, 27
Gershman, Mike 26
Gettel, Al 35
Gettleson, Leonard 9, 13, 22
Giblin, Bob 21
Gietschier, Steve 12, 19
Gilbert, Bill 27
Ginsburg, Dan 10
Gipp, George 42
Gleason, Bill 15
Gold, Eddie 13, 14
Goldstein, Richard 22
Gonzalez, Ray 10, 12, 13, 18
Goodenough, Hal 15
Goodhue, Ann Eagan 39
Gordon, Sid 37
Gorman, Lou 15, 22
Graber, Ralph 19
Graber, Rod 16
Graney, Jack 20, 21
Green, Dan 41
Green, Ernest 17, 27
Green, Jason 44
Greenberg, Hank 22, 44
Greenfield, MA 20
Greensboro, NC 20
Greenwade, Tom 24
Greenwell, Paul 18
Gregorich, Barbara 26
Gregory, Bob 26
Gregory, Jerry 12, 22
Griffith, Calvin 22
Grosshandler, Stan 11, 12, 13, 14, 22
Gustafson, Bill 10, 12
Gutman, Dan 26

H

Haas 13, 22, 34
Haber, Bill 10, 13
Hadley, Bump 38
Haines, Hinkey 14
Hall, Dick 15
Hall, Scott 20
Hanks, Mike 17
Hannan, Jim 42
Hargreaves, Charlie 14
Harkness, Linda 26
Harrigan, Patrick 27
Hartman, J.C. 16
Hartnett, Gabby 18
Harwell, Ernie 15, 41
Haskell, Everett 41
Hathaway, Ted 23
Hauser, Joe 16, 34, 45
Hawes, Roy 21
Heaphy, Leslie 23
Hegan 15, 35
Heilmann, Harry 41
Heitz, Tom 8, 19, 24, 27
Hemond, Roland 22
Henrich, Tommy 16
Hernandez, Keith 31
Hetrick, J. Thomas 34
High, Andy 15
Highlanders 40
Hiller, Frank 22
Hilton, George 26
Himrich, Brenda 20
Hines, Paul 30
Hirshberg, Al 38
Hisler, Steve 31, 32
Hittner, Arthur 25, 27
Hodesh, Stuart 27
Hodiak, Chris 26
Hoff, Chet 45
Hogue, Bobby 38
Hoie, Bob 12, 17, 18, 26
Holaday, Chris 26
Holmes, Tommy 38
Holway, John 12, 17, 18, 19, 25, 26
Honesdale, PA 13
Hooper, Harry 33
Hoover, Dick 14
Horton, Ralph 13, 14

Howard, Frank 34
Howe, Joseph 44
Howell, Colin 44
Hoyt, Waite 22
Hubbell, Carl 33, 35
Hufford, Tom 10, 12, 14
Hughes, Roy 14, 15, 21, 22
Hugo, Bill 12
Humber, Bill 12, 20, 43
Hunter, Billy 15
Hunter, Bob 14
Hunzinger, Walt 14
Husman, John 23

I

Indians 33, 46
Inks, Bert 42
Iowa Cubs 16
Israel, Clarence 22
Ivor-Campbell, Fred 12, 13, 18, 23, 26, 27

J

Jackson, Joe 21, 44
Jacobs, Spook 22
James, Bill 9, 18, 22, 27
Jansen, Larry 16
Jeter, Derek 47
Jethroe, Sam 38
Jimenez, Jose 16
Johnson, Connie 16
Johnson, Dick 38
Johnson, Judy 20
Johnson, Lloyd 12, 13, 18, 23, 24, 25, 26
Johnson, Richard 17
Johnson, Rodney 12, 16
Johnson, Roland 17
Johnson, Walter 19, 22, 45
Jolley, Smead 46
Jordan, David M. 26
Jozwik, Tom 12, 15, 22

K

Kachline, Cliff 9, 10, 11, 12, 14, 17, 18, 22, 24, 25, 26, 47
Kachline, Evelyn 14
Kagan, Charlie 17
Kahn, Roger 44
Kane, Frank "Bud" 44
Kansas City, MO 12, 16
Kanter, Mark 21, 27
Kaplan, Jim 17
Kavanagh, Jack 11, 12, 13, 19, 21, 26, 27
Kearney, Seamus 24
Kelleher, Gary 20
Keller, Earl 16
Kelley, Gene 14
Kelly, George 19
Keltner 35
Keltner, Ken 15, 22
Kemp, David 17
Kennedy, Bob 35
Kennedy, Terry 22
Kermisch, Al 13, 18
Kerr, Johnny 45
Kimbrough, Larry 22
Kiner, Ralph 9, 22, 38
King, J.C. 39
Kingman, Dave 31
Kinlaw, Francis 20
Kinsella, Ray 44
Kinsella, W.P. 44
Klein, Chuck 19
Kleinknecht, Merl 14, 17
Klieman 35
Klippstein, John 15
Koslofski, Kevin 16
Kovach, John 23
Krabbenhoft, Herm 26, 33
Kraich, Norbert 25
Kramden, Ralph 30

111

Kravitz, Danny 14
Kreuz, Jim 24
Kubek, Tony 22
Kuczynski, Bert 22
Kuklick, Bruce 26
Kurth, Sue 41

L

Laabs, Chet 44
Labine, Clem 15
Lajoie, Nap 13, 18, 19, 22
Landes, Stan 15
Landsdowne, PA 21
Lanfranconi, Walter 38
Lang, Jack 27
Langner, E.E. (Gene) 39
Lanigan, Ernie 13, 22, 24
Lannin, Ed 15
Lavelle, Howard 19
Lawler, Joe 23, 47
Layne, Hillis 21
Leachman, Nancy Jo 20
Leeds, Stuart 18
Lehan, Mel 44, 45
Lemon, Bob 35
Lenhardt, Don 16
Leonard, Buck 46
Leonard, Ed 20
Lester, Larry 17
Levin, Len 12, 19, 21, 25, 26, 27
Lewis, Allen 27
Lieb, Fred 13, 14, 18, 27
Liebman, Ron 18
Light, Jonathan Fraser 26
Ligonier, Joe 25
Lindsay, Bob 13
Linthurst, Randy 12
Lipon, Johnny 14
Lipset, Lew 18
Lloyd, John Henry "Pop" 17
Lockett, Lester 15
Logan, Johnny 37, 38
Lombardi, Ernie 19
London, England 21
London Tecumsehs 43
Longert, Scott 19
Los Angeles Dodgers 22, 40
Loughman, Bill 14, 19
Louisville, KY 15, 16, 25, 26
Louisville Redbirds 16
Lowenfish, Lee 14, 31
Lowry, Phil 12, 17, 18, 22
Loyola University Lakeshore 15
Lucadello, Johnny 44
Lucchesi, Frank 16
Ludington 21
Lund, Don 16
Lupien, Tony 14, 15, 22
Luse, Vern 12, 13, 17, 22, 26
Luteran, Ed 16, 27
Lyons, Ted 45

M

Macht, Norman 12, 13, 19, 21, 23, 27
Mack, Connie 12, 34, 35, 46
MacPhail, Andy 16
Madden, Bill 22
Madison, Wisconsin 21
Malarcher, Dave 14, 17
Mansch, Larry 33
Mantle, Mickey 19, 32, 33, 34
Maranville, Rabbit 19
Marchildon, Phil 15
Marion, Marty 16
Markusen, Bruce 27
Marquard, Rube 32, 33
Marquette University 15
Marshall, Clarence 16
Marshall, Ron 21, 27
Marshall, Willard 38
Martin, Babe 16
Martin, Jack 14
Mathews, Eddie 37
Mathewson, Christy 13, 16, 19, 33
Maxcy, Brian 16

Mayer, Henry 16
Mays 19
Mays, Willie 33
Mazeroski, Bill 16
McAfee, Skip 12
McCarver, Tim 22
McConnell, Bob 9, 10, 12, 13, 17, 18, 19, 22, 23, 25, 26, 27
McConnell, Jim 26
McCord, Butch 16
McCormack, John 12
McCormick, Mike 16
McCosky, Barney 44
McCoy Stadium 30
McCue, Andy 23, 26, 27
McDonough, Pat 10, 11, 13, 14
McDowell, Sam 16
McGill, Willie 42
McGillen, Joe 12
McGinn, Dan 42
McGinnity, Joe 19
McGraw, John 19, 33
McGwire, Mark 47
McHale, John 42
McKenna, Jim 27
McKeon, Jack 22
McKinstry, Mark 20
McLain, Jeep 15, 22
McMartin, Pete 44
McNamara, Tim 21, 22
McNeilly, Ian 21
McQuinn, George 19
McReynolds, John 26
Mednick, Barry 16, 27
Meer, Vander 44
Menchine, Ron 11
Merkle, Fred 33
Metkovich, George "Catfish" 22
Metro, Charlie 22
Meyer, Bruce 42
Michalek, Chris 42
Mickelson, Ed 16
Miller, Jim 26
Mills, Rubert 42
Milwaukee Brewers 40
Minnesota Twins 22
Mocek, John 23
Moen, Joe 41
Mohardt, John 42
Mondor, Ben 15
Montana 20, 22
Moore, Terry 21
Morgan, Joe 21
Morley, Patrick 21
Morris, Pete 27
Morris, Steve 21
Morton, Sy 15, 22
Muncrief 35
Munro, Neil 22
Munson, Joe 22
Munzel, Edgar 45
Murdock, Gene 11, 13, 14
Murphy, Jack 21
Murphy, Jim 18
Murphy, Joe 17
Murray, Red 42
Musial, Stan 16
Myers, Chief 33

N

Nadel, Steve 19, 27
Naiman, Joe 16, 32
Neel, Joanne 12
Neft, David 17
Nelson, Don 18
Nemec, David 25, 26, 63
Nemec, Ray 9, 10, 11, 13, 17, 18, 25, 63
New Brunswick, NJ 21
New Feds 42
New York Giants 31
New York Metropolitans 15, 30, 46
New York Mets 31, 35
New York Yankees 30, 31, 35, 40, 46
Newark, NJ 14
Newhouse, Rich 21, 27
Newsom, Buck 44
Nichols, Kid 21
Nicholson, Lois 12
Noren, Irv 16

Notre Dame 42
Nuxhall, Joe 16
Nye, Rich 15

O

Oakland, CA 15
Obojski, Robert 31
O'Connell, Dick 16
O'Doul, Frank "Lefty" 20, 31
O'Grady, Michael 26
Okkonen, Marc 18, 21, 26, 40
Olbermann, Keith 47
Olsen, Al 16, 32
Omaha, NE 21
O'Malley, Peter 22
O'Neil, Buck 16
Oregon 20
Orengo, Joe 22
Orioles 45
Orodenker, Richard 26
O'Rourke, Orator 31
Otis, Paul 45
O'Toole, Andrew 26
Otto, Phyllis 23
Overfield, Joe 13
Owens, Dale 16

P

Pafko, Andy 15, 22, 37
Page, Ted 14
Paige, Satchel 35
Palmer, Pete 18, 22, 26, 47
Pappas, Doug 24, 63
Pappas, Milt 16
Paramus, NJ 14
Pardon, John 10, 11, 12, 13, 14, 17, 20, 23, 25, 26
Parkes, Andy 21
Parnell, Mel 16
Pastier, John 27
Patterson, Walt 21
Paulin, Roland L. 39
Pawtucket Red Sox 15
Pechette, Bill 20
Perini, Lou 37
Perry, Claudia 12, 21
Peterjohn, Al 19
Pfenninger, Allen 20
Phelps, Frank 12, 13, 23, 26, 27
Philadelphia A's 34
Philadelphia Phillies 31
Phoenix, Arizona 21
Pietrusza, David 12, 27
Pipp, Wally 21
Pitoniak, Andrew 47
Pitoniak, Scott 46
Pitts, Gaylen 16
Pittsburgh Pirates 34, 45
Poholsky, Tom 16
Port Jefferson AC 35
Portland, OR 20
Potter, Nelson 15
Presnell, Tot 16
Price, Jim 26
Pride, Charlie 16
Prince, Bob 37
Providence Grays 15, 30, 46
Providence, RI 15, 30
Puff, Richard 12, 16, 19

R

Radcliffe, Ted 15
Raimondi, Bill 15
Raritan, NJ 14
Reading, PA 20
Reed, Ron 42
Reese, Jimmie 45
Reese, Pee Wee 16
Reichler, Joe 27
Reinholz, Betty 41
Repp, Dennis 27
Restelli, Dino 16
Reulbach, Ed 42
Richardson, Bob 23
Richman, Arthur 22
Richman, Milton 27
Rickey III, Branch 16

Rigney, Bill 16, 17
Riley, James A. 4
Riley, Jim 12, 17, 21, 26, 27
Ripken, Cal 44, 45
Ritter, Larry 18
Ritter, Lawrence 32, 33
Rizzuto, Phil 16, 37
Roarke, Mike 21
Roberts, Robin 15, 16
Robinson, Brooks 19, 22
Robinson, Earl 15
Robinson, Jackie 26
Robinson, Wilbert 19
Roepke, Sharon 23
Roettger, Oscar 22
Rome, NY 47
Rosen, Goody 15
Ross, Mike 21
Rossi, John 26
Rotblatt, Marv 15
Roth, Allan 19
Rothe, Emil 12, 13, 14, 19
Rothgerber, Harry 16
Royals 33
Rubeling, Al 15
Ruck, Rob 26
Rucker, Mark 12, 18, 19, 23, 26
Rue, Joe 15
Ruhle, Vern 21
Ruland, Bob 12, 25
Runge, Ed 16
Rusie, Amos 19
Ruth, Babe 22, 30, 33, 34, 35, 38, 43, 44, 45, 47
Ryan, Nolan 33
Ryczek, Bill 26

S

Salamon, Rick 12
Salisbury, Luke 12, 25
Salsberg, Bob 38
San Diego Padres 16, 22, 32
San Francisco Seals 31
Sanders, David 18
Sauer, Hank 16
Sauget, Rich 42
Savage, Ted 16
Sayles, Bill 22
Schalk, Ray 19
Scheffing, Bob 22
Schenectady, NY 33
Schiller, Elten 22
Schmitt, Thomas 20
Schoendienst, Red 16
Schott, Art 12, 13, 63
Schramka, Paul 22
Schroeder, Bill 13
Schuld, Fred 20
Schultz, Howie 16
Schuster, Bill 20
Schwartz 19, 31, 32
Scottsdale, AZ 16, 17
Scully, Vin 37
Seattle 20
Seaver, Tom 42
Seerey, Pat 35
Selig, Bud 22
Selko, Jamie 17
Selzer, Jack 18
Seminick, Andy 22
Senators 46
Seymour, Harold 18, 22, 26, 27
Shannon, Mike 14
Shantz 19
Shaughnessy, Frank 42
Shea, Tom 10, 11, 13, 27
Sheed, Wilfred 46
Sheffield, Gary 32
Shepard, Bert 15
Shibe Park, PA 34
Shieber, Tom 5, 12, 24, 27
Shlensky, Bill 12
Siegle, Tony 22
Sievers, Roy 22
Silver, Ralph R. 39
Simenic, Joe 10, 11, 12, 14, 17, 25, 26, 63
Simmons, Harry 13

Simon, Tom 21
Simonsen, Eric 12, 14, 15
Sisler, George, Jr. 14, 19
Sisti, Sibby 38
Skoog, Gary 13, 23
Smalley, Roy 15
Smith, Ballard 22
Smith, Carl 63
Smith, Fred T. 20
Smith, Gary 26
Smith, Jim 20, 26, 30, 45, 46, 47
Smith, Les 38
Smith, Red 42
Smith, Tal 12, 21
Smythe Zajc, Catherine 63
Snodgrass, Fred 33
So You Think You Know Baseball 36
Soderman, Robert 12, 14
Soolman, Arnold and Harvey 20
South Bend, IN 21
South Carolina 22
South Dakota 22
Spahn, Warren 37
Spalding, Albert 19, 43
Sparrow, Mike 19, 20
Spatz, Lyle 19, 22, 23, 27
Speaker, Tris 19, 22
Spelius, George 41
Spencer, George 14
Spink, J.G. Taylor 9, 27
Spokane 20
St. Louis Browns 16, 40
St. Louis Cardinals 16, 35
St. Petersburg, FL 13
Stagno, Michael 23
Staley, Gerry 20
Stang, Mark 26
Stanka, Joe 22
Starr, Bill 22, 46
Statz, Jigger 15
Steadman, John 15
Stein, Fred 18
Steinbrenner, George 32
Steinecke, Bill 22
Stengel, Casey 20
Stenhouse, Dave 15
Stevens, Chuck 16, 22
Stevens, Dave 31
Stevens, Ed 16
Suehsdorf, A.D. 19, 26
Sullivan, Brad 19
Sullivan Jr., Billy 42
Sunnen, Gene 11, 19, 20, 25
Surrett, Slick 16
Sutton, Keith 9, 10, 11, 13
Swartz, John 22
Symmes, W. Kirkland 30

T

Tacoma 20
Tanner, Chuck 16
Tardani, Mart 40
Tattersall, John 9, 13, 18
Taylor, Ron 43
Templeton, Garry 16
Tholkes, Bob 16, 20
Thomas, Frank 16
Thomas, Hank 26
Thompson, Dick 9
Thompson, Richard 5
Thompson, S. C. 17
Thompson, Sam 19
Thompson, 'Shag' 45
Thomson At The Bat 37
Thomson, Bobby 21, 33
Thorn, John 18, 19, 22, 23, 27
Thornley, Stew 20, 27
Tiemann, Bob 18, 23, 26
Tingley, Gillian 13
Tomlinson, Gerald 18
Topp, Barbara 15
Topp, Rich 11, 17, 23, 25, 26, 27
Torgeson, Earl 38
Toronto, Ontario 15, 20
Torre, Joe 47
Tourangeau, Rich 30, 47
Traven, Neal 22, 27

Traynor, Pie 45
Trouppe, Quincy 15
Tubbs, Gregg 12
Turiansky, Wayne 21
Turkin, Hy 17
Turner, Thomas 16
Turocy, Ted 24

U

Ueberroth, Peter 22
Usher, Bob 16

V

Valero, Eduardo 23
Valley Forge, PA 39
Van Atta, Russ 14
Vander Meer, Johnny 35
Vann, J.T. 39
Varner, Buck 21
Vaughan, Arky 19
Vecchio, Anna 35
Veeck, Bill 35
Vellano, Joe 27
Vincent, David 12, 13, 19, 26
Voigt, David 11, 13, 18, 31
Von Borries, Philip 5

W

Wagner 19
Walczak, Ed 22
Walsh Jr., Ed 42
Ward, Arch 42
Ward, John Montgomery 31
Warmund, Joram 26
Warren, Buell B. 39
Washington 20
Washington, D.C. 14, 40
Washington Senators 34
Watkins, Bud 16
Waugh, Jim 14
Wayman, Joe 13, 26
Webb, Tweed 13, 17
Weber, Ralph Lin 13
Weiser, Ben 14, 18
Weiss, Bill 13
Welch, Mickey 19
West, Joe 21
West, Max 20
West Palm Beach 32
White, Deacon 31
White, Sol 40
Wicklund, Barbara 14
Wight, Bill 35
Wiles, Tim 36
Williams, Cy 42
Williams, Dick 15, 16, 31, 32
Williams, Frank 13, 18
Williams, Ted 16, 21, 22, 30, 32, 34, 46
Wilson, Hack 19
Wise, Rick 20
Wisnia, Saul 38
Wolff, Miles 26
Wood, Allan 30
Wood, Bob 47
Wood, Joe 45
Wood, Rob 22
Wood, Smoky Joe 33
Woodstock, Ontario 43
Worcester, MA 21
Wright, Bob 45
Wright, Craig 22
Wright, Marshall D. 26
Wyoming, MI 21, 22

Y

Yakima 20
Yankees 40, 46
Yastrzemski, Carl 42
York, Rudy 44
Young, Cy 22, 45

Z

Zajc, John 5, 17, 26, 27, 31
Zang, David 27
Zocco, Tom 12, 20, 27
Zoldak 35

112

er, to

ity, of
ck.

having
54 and

s best
trial—

s best
runs

he lo-
watch
empted

out, it
ported
e was

Pastorius.

READING AT WILLIA
ly batting gave William
victory, Reading being de

William't.	AB.	R.	B.	P.	A.	E
O'Hara, lf.	4	1	2	1	1	1
Marhe'a, ss	3	0	1	4	5	1
Cannell, cf	4	0	1	2	0	0
Conn, 2b..	4	1	1	5	2	1
Cough'n, 3b	4	0	1	1	0	0
Lister, 1b.	3	0	1	6	0	0
White, rf..	4	0	0	2	0	0
Therre, c.	3	0	0	6	4	0
Stroud, p.	2	2	1	0	0	0
Totals..	31	4	8	27	12	3

Reading 0
Williamsport 0

Two-base hit—Coughli
Conn. Left on bases—W
Struck out—By Stroud 5,
Off Stroud 4, Odell 2. E
Umpire—Gochnauer. Tim

YORK AT JOHNSTOW
loose game Johnstown

MSPORT JUNE 7.—Time-
port its sixth consecutive
eated. Score:

Reading.	AB.	R.	B.	P.	A.	E
Rath, 3b..	3	0	1	1	2	0
Lynch, ss.	4	0	0	3	0	0
Lelivelt, cf.	4	0	1	2	0	0
Foster, lf..	3	0	0	0	0	0
Clay, rf...	2	2	1	5	0	0
Crooks, 1b	4	0	3	7	0	0
Barton, 2b.	4	0	1	1	1	1
Millman, c	4	0	0	5	2	0
Odell, p..	3	0	0	0	3	0
Totals..	31	2	7	24	8	1

1 0 1 0 0 0 0 0—2
0 0 1 2 0 1 0 x—4
    Stolen bases—O'Hara,
lliamsport 6, Reading 6.
Odell 4. First on balls—
t by pitcher—By Odell 1.
—2.05.

N JUNE 7.—In a rather
eated York. The game

Printed in the USA
CPSIA information can be obtained
at www.ICGtesting.com
JSHW060055150824
68134JS00032B/2742